REFORMING POLITICAL INSTITUTIONS
Ireland in Comparative Perspective

REFORMING POLITICAL INSTITUTIONS

Ireland in Comparative Perspective

JOHN COAKLEY

IPA
INSTITUTE OF PUBLIC
ADMINISTRATION

First published in 2013
by the
Institute of Public Administration
57–61 Lansdowne Road
Dublin 4
Ireland

www.ipa.ie

British Library cataloguing-in-publication data
A catalogue record for this book is available
from the British Library

ISBN: 978-1-904541-33-2

Cover design by Slick Fish Design, Bray, Co. Wicklow
Typeset by Carole Lynch, Sligo
Printed in Ireland by Colour World Print Ltd, Kilkenny

CONTENTS

LIST OF TABLES

APPENDIX TABLES

LIST OF FIGURES

PREFACE

The question of political reform is one whose topicality waxes and wanes over the decades. A recent wave of debate reached a climax at the end of the first decade of the twenty-first century, as Ireland's political institutions were blamed for the crisis that had befallen the country. Economic collapse, political turmoil and external intervention in the management of the state seemed to point to an institutional failure that had cost Ireland dear, and, perhaps not surprisingly, they were followed by demands for a constitutional overhaul.

This book is not an attempt to jump on the reformist bandwagon. In fact, it questions the value of constitutional or institutional reform that is not matched by a shift in the political-cultural perspectives of Ireland's policy sector, broadly defined. This is not to argue that reform of under-performing institutions is pointless. The several detailed examinations of major aspects of Ireland's constitution that have taken place since the mid-1990s have made a balanced case for change, and it seems sensible to follow this up; but even perfectly designed institutions are no protection against systematic human failure. Flawed political decisions and defective advice from professional public servants cannot be blamed purely on deficiencies in Irish political institutions, and inappropriate intervention in the policy process by private vested interests cannot simply be laid at the door of the constitution.

The debate on institutional reform, in other words, should not distract us from the role played by the pattern of values and attitudes that are characteristic of the Irish political establishment (again, using the term widely, to incorporate also business elites), and, perhaps, of broader Irish society. These were displayed at their most crass in the notorious taped exchanges between senior officials at Anglo-Irish Bank, poster-boy of the Celtic Tiger boom, dating from 2008 but made available by the *Irish Independent* from 24 June 2013 onwards. These bankers formed, however, part of a wider circle of privileged decision makers—products of a society and an educational system whose institutions (including churches, schools and universities) must surely bear some responsibility for the value system whose consequences proved so disastrous.

Notwithstanding the importance of the cultural dimension, though, this book leaves aside that huge topic. It also ignores another major question: the role that administrative reform, procedural overhaul or legal initiative might play in enhancing the quality of the state's decision-making mechanisms. Instead, the book's focus is on political structures. Its aim is to explore the role of a set of very specific institutions in Irish political life—to set these in comparative and historical context, and to review the extent to which they appear to serve their purpose usefully. These include two important and well-known institutions, the President and the Seanad. The most obvious topics to accompany these might well be the Dáil, the Government and the Taoiseach. Instead, however, in the interest of manageability, the focus is narrowed to three more precise sub-topics: the much-debated issue of the Dáil electoral system, and two largely ignored matters—the system of Dáil constituency boundary delimitation, and the route to ministerial office in the Government.

Several of the chapters that follow are based on work published earlier in journal or other format. I am grateful to the editors and publishers of *Polis* and *Politologická revue*, in which earlier versions of the comparative sections of two chapters appeared; to the Institute of Public Administration and Tony McNamara, editor of *Administration*, in which earlier versions of two chapters appeared; and to Palgrave Macmillan and the editors of *How Ireland voted 2011*, in which part of one chapter appeared.

Researching topics of the kind covered here has been greatly facilitated by the existence of rich and accessible official data provision services, whose contribution I would like to acknowledge: the Irish Central Statistics Office (cso.ie), the United Nations Economic Commission for Europe (unece.org), and the EU's statistical service (epp.eurostat.ec.europa.eu) and its public opinion monitoring programme (ec.europa.eu/public_opinion). I am grateful to a number of data archives for supplying original data in SPSS format for re-analysis: the Irish Social Science Data Archive at University College Dublin (for Irish opinion poll data), the Norwegian Social Science Data Services at the University of Bergen (for the European Social Survey), and GESIS–Leibniz Institute for the Social Sciences in Germany (for the Eurobarometer series). I am indebted to Michael Marsh (Trinity College Dublin) for supplying a copy of the Irish National Election Study, 2011, in SPSS format, and for making available an invaluable collection of opinion poll data (www.tcd.ie/Political_Science/IOPA), and to Mark Walsh (Ipsos-MRBI) for supplying further opinion poll tabulations. I have also relied heavily on the major data collections made available by the Inter-Parliamentary Union (ipu.org), the International Institute for Democracy and Electoral Assistance (idea.int), the Comparative Constitutions Project maintained by Zachary Elkins and Tom Ginsburg (comparativeconstitutionsproject.org) and the Electoral Systems site maintained by Michael Gallagher (www.tcd.ie/Political_Science/staff/ michael_gallagher/ElSystems).

Warm thanks are due to friends and colleagues who commented on one or more chapters of the book (in either recent or earlier form), or who assisted in other ways: Michael Anderson, John Baker, Stephen Collins, Joe Durkan, Bryan Fanning, David Farrell, Christopher Farrington, Michael Gallagher, Paul Gillespie, Yvonne Galligan, Tom Garvin, Claire Gormley, Katy Hayward, Iseult Honohan, Michael Laver, Maurice Manning, Michael Marsh, John O'Dowd, Diarmuid Ó Sé, Richard Sinnott, Andy Storey and Ben Tonra. I am indebted to the staff of Áras an Uachtaráin and of the Houses of the Oireachtas (and especially of Seanad Éireann) for the many enquiries with which they have dealt so helpfully.

Finally, I am grateful to the staff in or associated with the Institute of Public Administration's publication section for their commitment, professionalism and patience in piloting this book through to publication: Richard Boyle, Carolyn Gormley, Carole Lynch, Brendan O'Brien, Hannah Ryan and Slick Fish Design.

John Coakley
July 2013

1
INTRODUCTION: STABILITY AND CHANGE IN IRISH POLITICS

At the opening of the Convention on the Constitution in Dublin Castle in December 2012, a High Court judge and leading authority on the constitution offered an eloquent, balanced defence of the 1937 document. Noting the volume of criticism that had been directed against it, he observed that 'what I find intriguing is the extent to which the Constitution's obvious strengths and considerable achievements are almost never mentioned in this public discourse' (Hogan, 2012a: 4). This implicit warning shot about the perils of ill-considered constitutional amendment was not, of course, an argument against change; but it acts as an important counterweight to the reflex calls for revision that have become so prominent since the crisis of 2010. Of course, the centrality of political institutions in managing social processes and in coping with social and political change cannot be doubted (Marsh and Olsen, 2006: 7–10). It is not surprising, then, that the economic turmoil that has placed huge pressure on the state's institutions since 2010 has resulted in vociferous calls for constitutional overhaul. The economic crisis that was associated with the collapse of 14 years of Fianna Fáil-led rule in 2011 was thus accompanied by strong demands for political reform. As the then main opposition party put it,

> Changing the politicians around the cabinet table is necessary to restore confidence in Ireland's government, but that alone will not be enough to put the country back on track. What are also needed are fundamental changes in the structures and systems of the State itself to improve the quality of governance experienced by the country. (Fine Gael, 2011: 2)

1

Not surprisingly, then, the Fine Gael–Labour coalition that took office in March 2011 placed political reform at the centre of its programme for government. The two parties justified the impetus behind the drive for political reform by reference to the 'democratic revolution' that had taken place in the 2011 election, as 'old beliefs, traditions and expectations were blown away' in a 'political whirlwind' that demanded change (Department of the Taoiseach, 2011).

But to what extent is institutional and constitutional reform likely to serve as an effective antidote to Ireland's current ills? That is the question that is addressed in this book. This introductory chapter begins by examining the debate on Ireland's recent economic crisis, in respect of which there is by now substantial consensus. It continues by looking at the implications of the economic crisis for the policy sector (including the political world). The following section looks at the debate about constitutional and institutional reform that had been kick-started long before the Celtic tiger was even born, but was given added impetus by economic collapse. A short concluding section brings these discussions together by looking at the extent to which they have overlapped in their focus on particular political institutions, indicates why these institutions have been selected for further analysis, and outlines the manner in which each of these topics will be addressed in the book.

TRACKING ECONOMIC DECLINE

We do not need to look far for immediate explanations of Ireland's 2010 crisis. As is well known, a sharp global economic downturn had a big impact on a relatively open Irish economy, which itself was collapsing under the weight of excessive investment in construction, funded by banks that suddenly found themselves hopelessly over-exposed. This led in November 2010 to far-reaching intervention led by a 'troika' comprising the EU, the European Central Bank and the International Monetary Fund that compromised Irish economic sovereignty.

Early analyses pointed to general factors behind the crisis. Thus, Kieran Allen (2009: 90–97) attributed the emerging collapse to the inherent instability of capitalism. For Peadar Kirby (2010: 5–9), the issue was one of sustainability: the rapid pace of economic growth had been excessively dependent on foreign direct investment and construction rather than promoting balanced development, and the state had spurred on a housing boom while failing to regulate the banking sector. For many commentators, bankers shared responsibility with politicians—between them, they had allowed the property bubble to become dangerously inflated, with the abandonment of traditionally cautious lending norms, aggravated by lax regulation and excessively generous tax breaks (Murphy and Devlin, 2009). As one economist vividly put it, the housing and property bubble was 'a classic mania'; there was 'enough economic history to tell policymakers that it would end badly but the euphoria led them to believe that this time it really was different' (Durkan, 2012).

The crisis indeed needs to be seen in the context of longer-term trends in the Irish economy; it was rooted in the very circumstances that had facilitated rapid economic growth in the first place (for overviews, see O'Hearn, 1998; Barry, 1999; Nolan, O'Connell and Whelan, 2000; Clinch, Convery and Walsh, 2002; Sweeney, 2008; Mulreany, 2009). For some analysts, signs of the weaknesses whose effects were so deadly were to be detected already during the boom period (Whelan, 2009, 2010). A tiny number of commentators broke ranks with the complacent majority and predicted the disaster that was to follow. Among journalists, they included David McWilliams, who drew an analogy between the early stages of the Irish property price crash (and associated vulnerability of the banking system) and the 'South Sea bubble' of 1720, in which a frenzy of speculative investment led to economic ruin for many of those involved (McWilliams, 2007b). Accusing political leaders of being 'in denial', he argued that 'the Irish economy left the miracle phase a few years ago and is now being sustained by hot air and cheap credit, largely driven by ludicrous valuations in the housing market' (McWilliams, 2007a). Among academic economists, Morgan Kelly stood out, with a bleak warning that won him no friends among the country's leaders. Basing his findings on analysis of all boom–bust cycles in OECD economies since 1970, he concluded that

> there is a close relationship historically across very different economies and housing markets between the size of increases in real house prices, and subsequent declines. If this relationship were to hold for Ireland, the expected fall in average real house prices is in the range 40 to 60 per cent, over a period of around 8 years ... Given the unusual reliance of the Irish economy on building houses, the effects of any such fall on national income may be somewhat larger than that experienced at the end of other housing bubbles. Policy implications are straightforward. Booms and busts are a normal part of property markets. The government did not cause the current

boom, and is powerless to do anything about a subsequent bust.
(Kelly, 2007: 53)

Subsequent events were to show that, for all of the vilification that his
projection attracted, Kelly had erred on the side of optimism: a 50% drop in
residential property prices (as measured by mortgage draw-downs) had
occurred already before the end of 2012, well before the end of the eight-
year term he had predicted (Central Statistics Office, 2012: 1).

In hindsight, it was easier to see what had gone wrong, although the most
sustained and extensive analyses focused on a much more specific matter—
the factors behind the banking crisis. Three early officially sponsored
inquiries of this kind were necessarily general, and served as no more than
introductory notes to the kind of penetrating inquiry that is required, but
that has been notably slow in the making. The reports have in common the
fact that, while they acknowledge the great importance of the international
environment, they see the crisis as rooted in domestic policy making.

In a report commissioned by the Minister for Finance, two former IMF
officials, Klaus Regling and Max Watson (2010: 6), concluded that, while
Ireland's banking crisis bore the imprint of external factors, it was in an
important sense a domestic one, in that 'official policies and bank governance
failings seriously exacerbated Ireland's credit and property boom'. The new
Central Bank Governor, Patrick Honohan (2010: 15–18), similarly, came to
the conclusion that the crisis was due to a 'a comprehensive failure' of bank
management to maintain sound banking practices, but also blamed the nature
of the state's macroeconomic and budgetary policies, and insufficiently
effective regulation on the part of the Central Bank and the Financial
Regulator. The third report, also commissioned by the government, was more
explicit: in exploring the background to the crisis over the years 2003–09, a
distinguished Finnish economist, Peter Nyberg (2011: i–x), found frequent
evidence of 'behaviour exhibiting bandwagon effects both between institutions
("herding") and within them ("groupthink"), reinforced by a widespread
international belief in the efficiency of financial markets', with external auditors
functioning passively as 'silent observers', a complacent Central Bank and
Financial Regulator, a government actively supporting a 'national speculative
mania' in the housing market, and the Department of Finance offering only
weak opposition to what would turn out to be disastrous policies.

Quite apart from the direct and obvious consequences of collapse, economic development was also accompanied by a range of other changes to
which a resolution was not necessarily easily available. One of the most

obvious of these was the extent to which growing socio-economic disparities opened up between different groups, with some gaining immensely from the pace of growth and others being left behind (Nolan et al., 2000; Allen, 2009; Kirby, 2010). It has been argued that such inequalities need not be seen merely as an accidental side-effect of neoliberalism; they formed part of a 'determined political project' to reconstitute elite power (Kirby, 2009: 203). Alongside these inequalities was a growing problem of relative poverty and even homelessness in an otherwise prosperous Ireland (Healy, Reynolds and Collins, 2011). In addition, economic development and EU expansion to the east resulted in the appearance of a large immigrant population, a challenge to which Irish governments were relatively slow to respond, with an absence of policy that represented not just 'benign tolerance' but also 'benign indifference' (Fanning, 2011: 178).

Economic and social change in late twentieth- and early twenty-first-century Ireland, not surprisingly, placed very considerable strains on the country's political leadership and institutional structures—strains to which, critics argued, the system has responded poorly. The spotlight, therefore, began to fall increasingly on political decision makers and on the policy-making process more generally, in view of the extent to which new problems owed their origins to alleged deficiencies in policy and failures in administration. This is the issue to which we now turn.

ASSESSING POLITICAL CRISIS

The immediate political consequences of the economic crisis were highly visible, as the ruling Fianna Fáil–Green coalition government broke apart and recorded a catastrophic general election performance in February 2011. Not only were the Greens left entirely without Dáil representation following the election, but Fianna Fáil suffered a crushing defeat, dropping from 77 seats after the 2007 election to 20 in 2011 (see Gallagher and Marsh, 2011; Hutcheson, 2011; Little, 2011). Following an overview of the political crisis, this section reviews the main lines of criticism of Ireland's political institutions and of those who operated them, draws attention to the arguments of defenders of the present system, and highlights a major difficulty that has been largely ignored—the issue of political culture.

The demise of Fianna Fáil, which had traditionally sought to project itself as a 'national movement' rather than a mere political party, represented a profound reversal of Ireland's long-standing political order. Deep factionalism within the party since the 1970s was accompanied by a growing association of the party leadership with the pursuit of personal profit, especially in the area of building development (Foster, 2007: 67–9). The seismic consequences of this shift were matched by public loss of confidence in other traditional pillars of probity, such as the banking system and the Catholic church.

Even in its worst earlier election, its very first in 1927, Fianna Fáil had won 44 seats. As the most recent historian of the party asked, 'how could a party that had risen so high so quickly, and had stayed up for so long, fall so low, and so suddenly?' (Whelan, 2011: 3). The answer appeared to lie in perceptions that the party had adopted policies of 'economic recklessness', and had engaged in prodigal behaviour: 'like some errant heir, the present leaders had gambled away the family treasures, pillaged the family finances, allowed the party organisation to rot and neglected the gardens, where the grass roots were once so carefully tended' (Whelan, 2011: 2). Alongside accusations of defective political leadership, prominent party members faced a string of corruption allegations that were investigated by expensive, long-running tribunals. This led Elaine Byrne to draw attention to the extent of change since the parsimonious early years of state: in 1922, ministers were expected to absorb personally even costs arising directly from their work, but by the end of the century expectations of largesse from the public purse had increased so much that it was possible to describe politicians' costs as 'the systematic exploitation of the taxpayer' (Byrne, 2012: 209).

A recurring theme in analysis of the shortcomings of Irish public life in the early twenty-first century was criticism of the focus on incremental problem-solving rather than on values-based, long-term planning. This was blamed for failure to address not just longer-term developmental issues, but also such quality-of-life issues as income inequality (Murphy, 2009: 188). Perceptions of such inequality resulted in widespread public cynicism, and a view that 'a small elite was closely connected and designed policies to serve itself rather than its people' (O'Malley, 2011: 205). The problem has been ascribed to a failure to engage in original thinking, with politicians obsessed with re-election, and risk-averse bureaucrats 'who despite independence still looked to Britain for guidance whenever new issues arose':

> The state lacked the ability to engage in strategic thinking. Even the National Development Plans had the appearance of a shopping list of electoral goodies rather than a serious attempt to plan for the country's future. There was no attempt to design the physical layout of the country and the legacy of the Celtic Tiger is an urban sprawl of nondescript housing estates and retail parks. The policy of

decentralisation of the bureaucratic system outside Dublin foundered because of the attempts to gain local electoral benefits. (O'Malley, 2011: 204)

Indeed, new and more compelling pressures began to be felt towards the end of the first decade of the twenty-first century. As discussed above, the economic collapse that began to become obvious in 2008 was in part a consequence of international factors over which the state had no control; but there also emerged a near-consensus that flawed political decision making had played a much bigger part. The effort to take corrective action thus drew attention to decision-making processes and to the institutional and constitutional framework within which they operated. As the position has been summarised:

> Three clusters of issues frequently attract attention in debates about the defects in the Irish political system. The first concerns the quality of political representation, that is, the kind of people attracted into public life, and the scope for them to engage in national-level policy deliberation as opposed to committing time to constituency-level service activities. Allied with this is the sense that the mechanisms are weak for ensuring appropriate levels of political accountability for poor-quality policy decisions, and of administrative account-ability for poor policy implementation or poor stewardship of public resources. The second issue has to do with the quality of public administration and of the policy advice flowing into political decision-making. The third concern is about the way in which fiscal policy is made; the European Union has flagged this as an area in which increased levels of European surveillance can be expected into the future. (Hardiman, 2010: 55)

This analysis by no means suggests that any kind of 'quick fix' might be available for such deeply entrenched obstacles to responsible and accountable political decision making. Indeed, even a perfectly designed Irish political system would have encountered certain challenges from its participation in the eurozone, with its 'perverse incentives for fiscal expansion' (Dellepiane Avellaneda and Hardiman, 2010). Nevertheless, the pursuit of constitutional and institutional cures to Ireland's political decision-making ills has con-tinued. The commitment to institutional reform that became a formal part of the programme of the Fine Gael–Labour coalition in March 2011 had not emerged from nowhere. Each party was already committed to substantial institutional reform, and in this they were matched, in varying degrees, by Fianna Fáil and Sinn Féin.

If we are to attribute economic and political failure to an absence of strategic thinking and long-term planning, we are still left with the challenge of explaining how and why this approach to policy making came to emerge. One perceptive analysis identified three potential culprits—politicians, bureaucrats, and 'the system':

> Some commentators point to our elected representatives, claiming ineptitude and even dishonesty. Others castigate 'the system', alleging that the political system rewards those who think in the short term, who look after vested interests and concentrate almost exclusively on local rather than national concerns. The bureaucratic system in turn stands accused of being too deferential to political and business interests and failing to protect the long-term interests of the state. (O'Malley and MacCarthaigh, 2012: 1)

The country's political leaders were, then, an obvious target. According to Lynch (2010: 211), their policies were irresponsible, with an over-reliance on the market and insufficient political will to shape developments and to provide competent regulation. As Sweeney (2009: 208) bluntly put it, 'our politicians have created the perfect economic storm due to their incompetence'. In the view of one of Europe's most distinguished political scientists, the late Peter Mair, the core feature of the problem was a long-term failure of the political class to accept responsibility for leadership. Instead, it had allowed the civil service to take over most policy making and design, with the Catholic church retaining a major role in the areas of education and health policy, and the banks and big business lobbies controlling the financial sector (Mair, 2010). In all of this, Fianna Fáil came in for particular criticism, as we have seen—it had, after all, been in office continuously since 1997.

The process of government is not, however, confined to elected politicians, and the 2010 crisis resulted in the spotlight also falling on professional state employees. Those in the Central Bank and the Financial Services Regulator were obvious early targets, but so too was the civil service more generally. The civil service 'decentralisation' project launched in 2003—expensive, incoherent and calculated to produce fragmentation rather than integrated policy implementation—has been described as 'perhaps the most telling symbol of the recklessness towards good governance and quality public institutions' on the part of Ireland's political leadership (Laffan, 2010: 2). But this episode appeared also to give the lie to the classic relationship between ministers and their civil servants satirised in the popular television series *Yes, Minister*, with wily senior officials neutralising projects dreamt up by politicians in pursuit of short-term popularity. In Ireland at this time, the problem was not one of the Permanent Secretary, Sir Humphrey Appleby, stonewalling his minister; Sir Humphrey appeared to have left the stage. To the extent that he was still there, it has been suggested, his independence and that of his colleagues had been fatally compromised by corrosive political influence at senior levels in the civil service, undermining the capacity of civil servants to offer detached advice in the interest of the public good (Barry, 2013). Boyle and MacCarthaigh (2011) cite a prominent commentator's colourful but unflattering comparison of contemporary policy problems with a notorious episode in agricultural policy implementation:

> Ken Whitaker once described the Bovine TB Eradication Scheme, still trundling along after 50 consecutive years of failure, as the greatest scandal in the history of the State. This judgment must now be revised. The Irish public administration has produced an even more spectacular failure in the shape of the collapsed banking system. (McCarthy, 2011)

Perhaps not surprisingly, explanations of political incompetence also fastened on a predictable bogeyman, the electoral system. For Kirby (2010: 193–4), the single transferable vote system reinforces populist tendencies: it promotes the pursuit of a broad consensus rather than encouraging politicians to make hard choices, it assists clientelist practices, and it facilitates the politics of the 'trickster'. Coleman (2009: 140–5) criticised the system from a different perspective, arguing that it prevented the formation of strong, single-party governments, instead encouraging parties to pander to their rivals for lower preferences and turning political competition into a 'Dutch auction'.

Yet not all observers attributed the blame to the trio of politicians, civil servants and 'the system'. As recently as 2008 an important OECD report gave the Irish civil service a relatively clean bill of health (Boyle and MacCarthaigh, 2011: 9). Ireland's political leadership was also reasonably favourably rated, with Ireland performing well on international comparative indices of government effectiveness (O'Malley and MacCarthaigh, 2012: 1). The electoral system has also been vigorously defended against the faults attributed to it (Gallagher, 2009; Gallagher and Komito, 2010; Farrell, 2010).

So, too, has the constitution more generally. The year 2012 was the 75th anniversary of the 1937 constitution itself. Much of the mood was celebratory, if in a balanced and critical way. Tribute was paid to 'the vibrancy and potency of the Constitution' and to its 'fundamental and unquestioned importance' (O'Connor, 2012: vii). Its capacity to withstand the test of time, in spite of certain dated rhetorical flourishes, was noted, and it was lauded as 'an impressive basic law for the twenty-first century' (Kavanagh, 2012: 99–100). It was described as 'a model of a successful liberal constitution', one which is now 'deeply-rooted, relatively stable and manages to strike a workable balance between protecting rights and facilitating the free-flow of politics' (Ó Cinnéide, 2012: 249). The anniversary was marked by the publication of a collection of documents and commentaries on the drafting of the constitution in the 1930s (Hogan, 2012b), a collection seen as illustrating 'the richness and potential of the text as it exists' and as a warning to would-be reformers of 'the complexity of drafting a state constitution' (O'Malley, 2012). This view—that the constitution had served its purpose well, even if a case for tweaking it in various respects could be made—echoed that on its 50th anniversary in 1987 (Farrell, 1988; Litton, 1988). This more conservative position was in line with a long tradition of official investigations into different aspects of the constitution, a literature that had been growing since 1996. The reports resulting from these, when they recommended change at all, tended to favour minor amendments.

Whatever about structural or institutional defects, Irish public life has been beset by another problem. For some time, observers have identified the character of elite and mass political culture as a key obstacle to effective government (Farrell, 2010; Leahy, 2010, 2011). This perspective is reflected also in Fintan O'Toole's perceptive explanation as to why a 'hyper-charged globalised economy' had failed. He argued that the underlying system of political governance and public morality was insufficiently developed to sustain it:

> Large chunks of classic democracy were missing—the shift from religious authority to public and civic morality; the idea that the state should operate objectively and impersonally rather than as a private network of mutual obligations; the notion of the law as a universal and neutral check on everyone's behaviour, whatever their status; the belief in an independent parliament that exists to legislate rather than to service clients and to make government accountable rather than to keep it in place at all costs. (O'Toole, 2010: 213–14)

Bearing in mind the significance of cultural rather than structural factors, then, and noting the likelihood that reform of constitutional arrangements is likely to have limited impact, it is worth reviewing current proposals for institutional change. The next section considers the debate on political reform as it emerged from an older tradition of constitutional investigation, modified by its new perceived relevance as a response to the problems discussed above.

DEBATING INSTITUTIONAL REFORM

Reviews of the performance and adequacy of Ireland's political institutions were nothing new in the late twentieth century. Aside from specific inquiries into particular institutions such as the Seanad, several systematic reviews were undertaken. The first was the Constitution Committee, an informal inter-party group of TDs and senators that examined the constitution article by article and reported in 1967, the constitution's thirtieth anniversary. The committee suggested that the constitution was broadly effective as a political framework, but made some recommendations for changes in certain articles (Committee on the Constitution, 1967). In general, though, the Constitution Committee was silent on the desirability of change, confining itself to a rehearsal of the arguments for and against retention of existing arrangements.

Second, a Constitution Review Group, made up of non-political experts appointed by the government, reported in 1996 (Constitution Review Group, 1996). The sheer size of this report makes it difficult to summarise its recommendations, which were concerned mainly with a tidying up and modernisation of the text. One overview of its coverage described it as exploring the role of the President, provisions for Dáil elections, the constitutionality of bills and laws, international relations, the role of the Attorney General, the Council of State, the Comptroller and Auditor General, and the process of constitutional amendment and the referendum; and it made further proposals relating to the office of ombudsman, local government and protection of the environment (Morison, 1997: 57). It largely avoided the thorny issue of the Seanad; it took the view that it 'does not appear to satisfy the criteria for a relevant, effective and representative second house', but recommended that because of the scale of the issue this be considered in detail in a separate report (Constitution Review Group, 1996: 71).

Third, it was the turn of parliamentarians to consider the recommendations of the Constitution Review Group. An All-Party Oireachtas Committee on the Constitution was established in 1996 and renewed after the 1997 and 2002 general elections. By 2006 it had produced a total of 10 reports, covering selected areas of the constitution, as follows:

1. General and miscellaneous matters (1997)
2. Seanad Éireann (1997)
3. The President (1998)
4. The courts and the judiciary (1998)
5. Abortion (2000)
6. The referendum (2001)
7. Parliament (2002)
8. Government (2003)
9. Private property (2004)
10. The family (2006).

The same format was followed after the 2007 general election, but the committee was now labelled the Joint Oireachtas Committee on the Constitution. By the time its work had come to an end in early 2011 it had produced a further five reports:

1. Freedom of expression (2008)
2. Amendment of the constitution and referendum (2009)
3. Survey of Oireachtas members: the electoral system and representation (2010)
4. The Dáil electoral system (2010)
5. Parliamentary power of inquiry (2011).

The debate on constitutional and institutional reform was strongly influenced by the changed circumstances of Ireland since the 1990s. The very first report of the Oireachtas committee identified the demand for amendment as being driven by Northern Ireland, the European Union, international human rights developments, socio-economic change (and especially the transition from a predominantly rural to an urban society), working experience (in such areas as dissolution of the Dáil, composition of the Seanad and other areas where perceived gaps had been identified), the outdated nature of certain provisions, and simple inaccuracies (All-Party Oireachtas Committee, 1997a: 4–7).

While the various reviews of the constitution were carefully balanced and modest in their proposals for change, they did sometimes feed directly into the process of constitutional amendment. Thus, two referenda in 1968, on replacement of proportional representation by the plurality system in Dáil elections and on 'tolerance' of a wider measure of discrepancy in the deputy–population ratio from constituency to constituency, each defeated, flowed directly from the report of the Committee on the Constitution (1967)—though that body had not actually recommended these changes, just weighed up the arguments. Two other successful amendments fell into the same category: lowering the voting age to 18 (1972) and permitting the system of university representation in the Seanad to be altered by law (1979). One unanimous recommendation of the 1967 committee was also successfully incorporated: reference to the 'special position' of the Catholic church as the church of the majority was dropped (1972).

Most reforms, however, were driven by immediate political pressures, whether a result of European treaties, developments in Northern Ireland, or other considerations, such as adverse court decisions. Sometimes this pressure was filtered through the Oireachtas committee. For example, following a Supreme Court ruling in 2002 to the effect that parliamentary committees do not have a clear-cut right to conduct inquiries that might damage the reputation of individuals, the Joint Oireachtas Committee on the Constitution placed this issue on its agenda (the specific case concerned an investigation into the circumstances surrounding the killing of John McCarthy by Gardaí in Abbeylara, Co. Longford, in 2000). It reported in 2011, recommending that the constitution be changed to allow such inquiries to take place; but the proposal was defeated at a referendum in October 2011.

Other initiatives emerged from outside the political arena. The public debate was stimulated initially by the work of an active think-tank, TASC (Think-tank for Action on Social Change), which focused on improving the quality of Irish democracy and predated the economic collapse.[1] A group of political scientists, taking the view that the resources of the discipline should not be confined to the academic world but rather shared with policy makers, established a 'Political Reform' forum in 2009; it created a web page and thematically organised discussion groups (see politicalreform.ie and irishpoliticalreform.wordpress.com). Parallel to this, an important initiative in grassroots democracy, 'We the Citizens', deriving much of its inspiration from Canadian models, kicked off a debate that covers political reform, among other areas. Its online polling and discussion forums offer an important insight into the reform priorities of users of the site—ones that are not necessarily representative of the broader population, but that at least represent the thoughts of a particular politically engaged community (see wethecitizens.ie).

In reality, though, it is governments that have the initiative in promoting institutional change, and the new Fine Gael–Labour coalition government was committed not just to an ambitious reform programme extending over economic and social issues, but also to a major institutional overhaul. The centrepieces of this programme included abolition of the Seanad, a strengthening of parliamentary oversight, and a broad constitutional review that would cover the Dáil electoral system, the term of office of the President, the minimum age for voting, and other matters (Department of the Taoiseach, 2011). For a range of reasons, the first item on the reform agenda, abolition of the Seanad, was leapfrogged by one that had been scheduled for later: the creation of a new Convention on the Constitution. This met for the first time in Dublin Castle on 1 December 2012, with terms of reference that required it to make recommendations in the following areas:

  (i) reducing the Presidential term of office to five years and aligning it with the local and European elections
 (ii) reducing the voting age to 17
(iii) review of the Dáil electoral system
(iv) giving citizens resident outside the State the right to vote in Presidential elections at Irish embassies, or otherwise
 (v) provision for same-sex marriage
(vi) amending the clause on the role of women in the home and encouraging greater participation of women in public life
(vii) increasing the participation of women in politics
(viii) removal of the offence of blasphemy from the Constitution
 (ix) following completion of the above reports, such other relevant constitutional amendments that may be recommended by it (Convention on the Constitution, 2013a).

The Convention was set up with a chair (Tom Arnold, chief executive of the charity Concern) and 99 members: 66 members selected randomly from the population, 22 Dáil deputies, seven senators and four members of the Northern Ireland Assembly. It was required to report to a staggered timetable within one year of its first public meeting.

When the reflections of committees studying the constitution, the proposals of the political parties and the suggestions of other observers and online communities are combined, we get a formidable list of potential reform areas. Some of these recur again and again; but not all strike a chord with the public. We may, however, assess public reaction to some of these by considering two sets of survey data. The results of the first, the most recent Irish national election survey, conducted at the time of the 2011 Dáil election, are summarised in Figure 1.1. This probed respondents' views on selected areas where institutional reform had been discussed. The survey shows very strong support for a reduction in Dáil size and for the appointment of non-political ministers from outside the Dáil, substantial support for the view that Dáil deputies should resign their seats on becoming ministers, for the granting of more power to local government and for abolition of the Seanad, and modest support for an increase in the number of women candidates at elections. But it shows little support for one of the favourite demands of many reformers, abolition of the current electoral system; in fact, more respondents were opposed to this than were in its favour.

Figure 1.1: Attitudes to selected areas of reform, Ireland, 2011

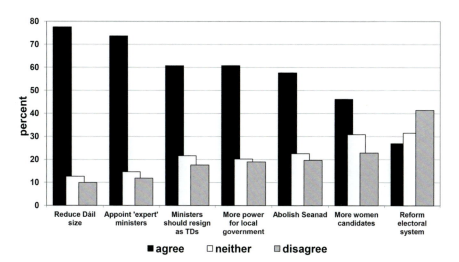

Note: The question was: 'During the election campaign, there were a lot of discussions by various parties about the political reforms that would be made. Considering each one of these, how much do you agree or disagree with each?', with respondents invited to agree strongly, agree, agree slightly, neither agree nor disagree, disagree slightly, disagree, or disagree strongly with the following propositions, whose order was rotated: 'the Seanad should be abolished', 'cabinet ministers should step down as TDs to concentrate on running their ministries and be replaced by someone else from the same party', 'some experts who are not TDs should be brought into the cabinet', 'the number of TDs should be significantly reduced', 'local government should be given power to raise and to manage their own finances', 'our PR-STV (single transferable vote) electoral system should be replaced', 'parties should be forced to nominate more women as candidates'; $N = 1,853$ adults aged 18 or more; fieldwork conducted March–April 2011.

Source: Computed from Irish National Election Study 2011. I am grateful to Michael Marsh for supplying the data file.

Responses to a second survey, conducted in late 2012, are reported in Figure 1.2. These focus more tightly on items on the agenda of the Convention on the Constitution, though including three additional items (Seanad abolition, requiring the Taoiseach to appoint two ministers from outside the Dáil, and giving citizens the right to trigger a referendum in certain circumstances), and not covering two items on the convention's agenda (review of the Dáil electoral system, and increasing the participation of women in politics). In all but one area, supporters of change outnumbered opponents. The exception was the reduction of the voting age from 18 to 17, supported by only 30% of respondents, with 56% opposed. Since, however, these issues have barely broken the surface in public debate, it is too early to predict how they might fare in the context of a referendum campaign.

Figure 1.2: Support for selected areas of reform, Ireland, 2012

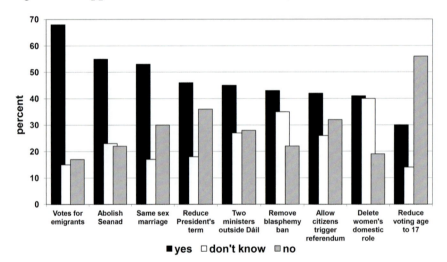

Note: The question was: 'for each of the proposed changes, would you vote yes or no?', with the following propositions: 'to reduce the term of the President from 7 to 5 years', 'to give Irish citizens living abroad the right to vote in presidential elections', 'to allow same sex marriage', 'to remove reference to women's life within the home from the constitution', 'to remove the offence of blasphemy from the constitution', 'to reduce the voting age to 17', 'to abolish the Seanad', 'to require the Taoiseach to appoint two ministers from outside the Dáil', 'to give citizens a right to petition for a referendum to change the constitution if they can collect 10,000 signatures'; $N =$ 1,000 adults aged 18 or more; fieldwork conducted October–November 2012.
Source: Ipsos–MRBI poll, 'Ireland 2012: our changing attitudes and values'. I am indebted to Mark Walsh for supplying tabular summaries of the data.

An Ipsos-MRBI poll in June 2013 offered a further straw in the wind as regards the prospects for the reform agenda. Ranking the issues in order of the size of the majority in favour of change, the matter enjoying most support was allowing the Irish abroad to vote in presidential elections (72% in favour, 22% against), followed by permitting same-sex marriage (69%–22%), abolishing the Seanad (55%–21%), removing from the constitution the references to the woman's life as being in the home (49%–17%) and to blasphemy (50%–20%), and reducing the presidential term to five years (52%–41%). Reduction in the voting age to 17 was not popular, with 34% in favour and 62% against (*Irish Times*, 15 June 2013).

CONCLUSION

The discussion so far has sought to do two things. First, it has identified a particular dilemma: a political system that is in distress, with its lack of capacity to manage economic development as eloquent evidence of this. It has suggested that, while institutional reform may have a contribution to make, the big challenges lie in the political cultural domain: it is much harder to engineer cultural transformation than to tinker with political institutions. Second, to the extent that institutional reform is appropriate, it has sought to identify the areas within which this has been advocated. This generates a formidable list, and seeking to tackle all items on it in appropriate depth in this book would be virtually impossible, and in any case pointless.

Furthermore, to the extent that the case for reform is designed to cure a 'problem', it is important to identify this problem accurately. For this reason, Chapter 2 considers certain patterns of change in Irish society in recent years. The country's economic downfall, and the economic boom that preceded this, may be the most obvious problem. But there are others, and in considering institutional reform they, too, need to be borne in mind. Chapter 2 consequently examines, in comparative perspective, a set of areas that have implications not just for constitutional design but also for Irish political culture. As well as economic change, these include demographic transform-ation, cultural diversity in the wake of large-scale immigration, language shift, changing patterns of national identity (with a steady shift in attitudes to Northern Ireland, Britain and Europe), decline in religious practice and values, and shrinking levels of trust in public institutions.

Having set the scene in Chapter 2, the rest of this book assesses the potential for institutional reform. One important study has suggested that the effectiveness and legitimacy of the Irish state require institutional reform in four areas: mechanisms for ensuring executive accountability, pathways of recruitment to government, systems of delegated governance, and improved public sector structures (Hardiman, 2012: 217–24). In this book, the focus is narrower: five rather more specific areas are discussed. The basis of selection of these areas is not that the particular area is crying out for reform; rather, it is selected as being representative and important, and as offering significant evidence about the desirability of change, even where no change is being advocated here. The discussion, then, is not intended to be comprehensive; it is selective. Furthermore, with a view to making this project more manageable, the focus in general is on the make-up of the institutions being discussed rather than on their functional adequacy. This is no reflection on the importance of the latter perspective; considerations of feasibility preclude their detailed examination in this book. The first two areas correspond to major state institutions whose performance has been questioned over the years. The three remaining areas are narrower and more technical, but still of potentially great political consequence.

- **The office of President**. Practically all states have a formal head of state, and some combine direct election with an almost entirely ceremonial role, as in Ireland. The tension between these two features is explored, as is the issue of potential reform of the office.
- **The composition of the Seanad**. Second chambers in unitary states are more the exception than the norm, and no compelling case for retaining the Irish senate has been made. However, in circumstances where its continued existence is in doubt, it is worth reviewing its function in the Irish political system, and setting this in comparative context.
- **The Dáil electoral system**. Vigorous arguments have been advanced for alternatives to the single transferable vote system of proportional representation on the grounds of its alleged tendency to promote clientelist politics; this conflicts with a near-consensus among Irish political scientists to the effect that the TD's role in Ireland reflects Irish political culture rather than being merely a consequence of the electoral system. It is argued that alternative electoral systems all have political consequences that are sometimes ignored.
- **Constituency boundaries for Dáil elections**. Ireland is unique among countries using proportional representation in the frequency with which constituency boundaries are changed in response to shifting demographic patterns. It is argued that the Irish system

should be brought into line with international practice in respect of multi-member constituencies by having fixed boundaries and adjusting the allocation of deputies to these after each census to maintain the principle of suffrage equality.

- **The selection of government ministers.** Ireland is unique in drawing practically all of its ministers (with only two exceptions since 1937) from its lower house, and in accepting, in effect, a dual minister–deputy mandate. It is argued that the quality of government ministers and the capacity of the Dáil to play a strong role in monitoring government would be greatly enhanced by bringing Ireland in line with international practice and abolishing this dual mandate.

In each of these areas, discussed respectively in Chapters 3 to 7, a common framework is followed. First, the debate about change is introduced, as this has featured in earlier analysis of the constitution or in more recent political debate. Second, the comparative position is reviewed—a perspective that sometimes shines a glaring light on the exceptional character of the Irish experience. Third, the manner in which the institution in question has functioned in the course of Irish political development is described. Finally, the options for change are considered, and the case for and against retention of the current system is presented.

The general conclusion to which these considerations are leading (discussed at greater length in Chapter 8) should be clear from the thrust of the arguments made above. Institutional change, given effect through constitutional amendment or otherwise, clearly has a role to play in enhancing the quality of Irish democracy. But underlying patterns of values and expectations tend to be highly resistant to institutional stimuli, and many of the problems that have beset Ireland in recent years are in large measure a function precisely of these values. This book, then, aims not to celebrate the merits of institutional reform, but rather to highlight its limitations. The challenge of the future is not so much to refine the representative system of the state as to reshape the value system of its people and their leaders.

NOTES

1. See Hughes et al., 2007, and www.tascnet.ie; for the report of the Democracy Commission, see Harris, 2005, also available at www.tascnet. ie/upload/ Democratic Renewal final.pdf [accessed 2 May 2013].

2

A SOCIETY TRANSFORMED: ECONOMIC CHANGE AND CULTURAL CHALLENGE

Before considering what kinds of institutional reform might be desirable in responding to Ireland's problems, it is important to examine the nature of these problems in the first place. In one sense, identifying the problem is easy: the devastating economic crisis that resulted in the agreement between the Irish government and the 'troika' made up of the EU, the European Central Bank (ECB) and the International Monetary Fund (IMF) on a loan package in November 2010. Its central feature was not just the public sector deficit. The abrupt end to the country's housing boom resulted in a shortfall in government revenue against a background of escalating expenditure, but also in rapidly growing unemployment and continuing problems of poverty and inequality.

Alongside economic change, another set of radical shifts in Irish society was also rapidly taking place. A country whose self-image was rooted in the notion that its people were available for export, and would have to emigrate in times of economic difficulty, was forced to see itself not as a supplier of labour to other countries but as a host to large-scale immigration from Europe and elsewhere. The resulting multicultural character of Irish society brought Ireland into alignment with other developed west European societies, but also offered an unfamiliar challenge: how to accommodate new ethnically and culturally distinct groups that now comprise more than 11% of the population of the Republic of Ireland. This process had implications, too, for Ireland's own long-standing cultural distinctiveness, including the survival of the Irish language and the traditional position of religious minorities: Irish has been overtaken as a spoken language by the languages of new immigrants, and immigration has resulted in a significant increase in the size of religious minorities in the Republic. These changes coincided with a profound shift in Irish religious culture, with traditionally extremely high levels of religious practice and belief suddenly plummeting—a development no doubt influenced by a series of disturbing child sex abuse scandals involving Catholic clergy, but likely to be mainly a consequence of the rapid pace of socio-economic change and the new world views associated with this.

Finally, of course, quite apart from measurable changes in Irish economic, social and cultural life of a quasi-'objective' character, it is clear that Irish values and attitudes have been profoundly transformed. Cultural change has implications for patterns of national identity, and Ireland's 40-year-long engagement with the European Union is likely also to have left its mark. This package of attitudinal changes extended not just to a rejection of the traditionally dominant political party, Fianna Fáil, but also to growing levels of mistrust of traditional institutions such as parliament, the civil service, the banking sector and the Catholic church.

The present chapter looks at the background to institutional reform by considering the three areas just mentioned. It seeks to provide an overview of the nature of the economic crisis, the pace of demographic and cultural transformation, and the pattern of value change. In each case, an effort is made to set recent developments in longer-term historical perspective, but also to explore them in comparative context. It is sometimes possible to do this by looking at European averages. Often, however, such averages make no sense, or cannot be computed. With a view to maintaining a comparative perspective, other comparator countries have been selected for illustrative purposes. While a large range of countries is available from which to choose, the focus here is generally on three others. The first obvious one is Ireland's nearest neighbour, the United Kingdom, notwithstanding the difference in scale between the two countries. The other two are smaller west European countries, comparable in size with Ireland: Denmark (a small country traditionally marked by a relatively high level of socio-economic development, and a socio-political tradition influenced by Protestant values) and Portugal (also small, but traditionally facing stronger socio-economic challenges, and marked by traditional Catholic values).

ECONOMIC DISTRESS

As is well known, the impact of Ireland's economic recession has been profound, with implications not just for people's material living standards but also for wider social and political priorities. Although the character of economic development is not the focus of this book, it is important to set the Irish economic crisis in context, since much of it was substantially influenced by the state's decision-making processes. This entails looking at some general indicators of the health of the economy. The performance of Ireland's gross domestic product (GDP) is one of the most obvious; but to this may be added the profound crisis in the balance of public sector revenue and expenditure, and the pattern of growing unemployment associated with the economic recession. Having considered these issues, certain legacies of the years of the 'Celtic tiger' (a period extending from the mid-1990s to 2008) will be explored: continuing problems of material inequality, and the challenge posed by an apparently unregulated building boom.

Economic recession

As is well known, using GDP as a measure of economic growth is hazardous in the Irish case, where GDP levels are inflated by inclusion of the profits of Irish-based multinationals, many of which have a limited impact on the day-to-day functioning of the Irish economy. Nevertheless, if used with caution GDP can be a useful indicator of comparative change; indeed, the fact that it is so widely reported, and that comparative data are readily available, leaves little alternative to its use. Figure 2.1 thus presents this very general summary of economic development: GDP per capita, controlling for purchasing price parity, over the period 1990–2011. It is clear that the Irish economy enjoyed a sustained period of remarkable growth before succumbing to recession in 2008. In 1990, Ireland was only just above Portugal, lagging well behind the UK and Denmark. By 1998, however, the Irish level had surpassed that of the UK, and it overtook Denmark two years later. With near-full employment, traditional patterns of emigration were halted and even reversed, and the state recorded substantial balance of payments surpluses. Economic development was further fuelled by the availability of cheap credit after Ireland adopted the euro as its currency in 2002.

The bursting of the credit bubble lay at the centre of a wider, sharp economic downturn. This is reflected in Figure 2.1 in the sharp drops in 2008 and 2009 in GDP per capita, once again narrowing the gap with the comparator countries, but still apparently leaving the Irish relatively well off. But this setback was more profound. The bursting of the bubble brought in its wake enormous difficulties for the banks that had gone along so enthusi-astically with the euphoric growth predictions that in fact were attributable to the abundant supply of credit, and also resulted in a collapse in state

Figure 2.1: GDP per capita, Ireland and selected European countries, 1990–2011

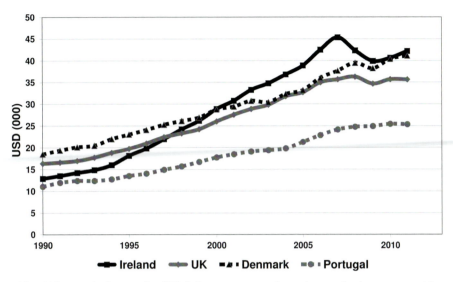

Note: Values are in thousands of US dollars at current prices using purchasing power parities.
Source: Computed from United Nations Economic Commission for Europe statistical database, available www.unece.org

revenue. It was this collapse, set against a background of high and increasing public expenditure, that ultimately provoked the crisis that brought about intervention by the EU–ECB–IMF 'troika'.

Figure 2.2 reports the general government surpluses or deficits from 1995 to 2012. For almost all of this period, Ireland performed extremely well relative to the comparator countries, surpassing even Denmark in the earlier years, with a sizeable excess of revenue over expenditure. This made the drop in 2008 and 2009 even more dramatic. But this decline was placed in the shade by the huge excess of expenditure over revenue in 2010, the development that sparked the 'bail-out'. The enormous 2010 deficit, 31% of Ireland's GDP, was, however, a consequence not just of a normal excess of expenditure over revenue in general government spending but of the costs of the huge sums that had to be transferred to banks, and in particular to Anglo-Irish Bank, during that year. This was not repeated in the following year, but it still leaves the state with huge liability for repayment of capital and interest on the loans necessary to bridge the spending gap. By 2011, the deficit was still as problematic as it had been in 2009. Since then the position has improved, with the deficit dropping to 7.9% of GDP in 2012, and estimated

Figure 2.2: General government surplus/deficit, Ireland and selected European countries, 1995–2012

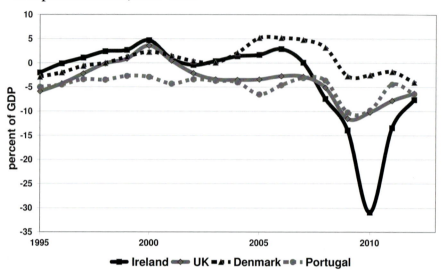

Note: Values refer to excess of revenue over expenditure of the general government sector as percentage of GDP.

Source: Computed from Eurostat Statistics Database, available epp.eurostat. ec.europa.eu

deficits of 7.5% and 5.1% for 2013 and 2014 respectively, projections not reflected in Figure 2.2 (Economic and Social Research Institute, 2012: 15).

One of the more visible features of economic decline has been lengthening dole queues. The rapid reversal in Ireland's fortunes in this respect is illustrated in Figure 2.3, which summarises the unemployment rate from 1990 to 2012. The picture in Ireland had been even grimmer before this: a catastrophic economic reversal saw the unemployment rate rising from 7% in 1979 to 17% in 1986, leading to large-scale emigration and population decline (Walsh, 2006: 187). Figure 2.3 captures the tail-end of this: the 1990s indeed began with all-too familiar levels of high unemployment that for a time exceeded the 15% level. From 1994 onwards, however, as the economy grew, unemployment fell, bottoming out at 4–5% from 2000 to 2007, before once again embarking on a steep rise, reaching 14% in 2010 and almost 15% in the two following years. This contrasted with less extreme patterns in Denmark and the UK, where unemployment levels followed the same broad pattern but at a lower level, typically staying below 10%. Portuguese unemployment levels fluctuated around 4–8% until the end of the period, when they climbed upwards to match the Irish level, and to exceed it in 2012.

Figure 2.3: Unemployment rate, Ireland and selected European countries, 1990–2012

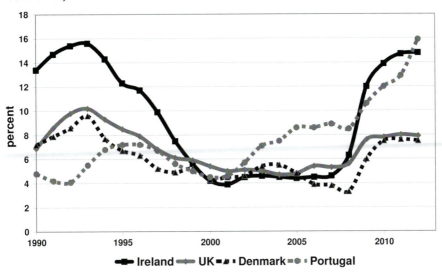

Note: Values refer to percentage of unemployed in the labour force.
Source: Computed from United Nations Economic Commission for Europe statistical database, available www.unece.org

It should, however, be borne in mind in respect of the Irish data that unemployment levels would have been much higher but for the reappearance of an older practice: many workers faced with unemployment, and new labour market entrants, reverted to the traditional Irish solution to problems of unemployment by simply emigrating. Annual emigration levels from Ireland rose from 36,000 in 2006 to 87,000 in 2012, though it should be noted that Irish nationals accounted for only 53% of this level in the latter year, with the rest accounted for by various forms of return migration (Gilmartin, 2012: 10). In addition, labour market participation levels have fallen, with evidence that a significant portion of younger people have left the labour force to return to education (Conefrey, 2011).

The falling GDP and public accounts graphs and the rising unemployment rate tell much of the sad story of the Irish recession, but they by no means tell the full story. Enormous levels of personal debt were built up as a consequence of irresponsible borrowing by individuals, reckless bank lending policies, and the failure of the state to regulate these. Since much personal debt will have to be written off, the prospect arises of further burdens on banks and taxpayers. The huge property portfolio of the National Assets

Management Agency (NAMA) is based on a gamble that property values will ultimately rise to a level that will allow the agency to break even through selling off its portfolio. This is in addition to the gigantic debt that the state continues to owe to cover losses in the banking sector. The full impact of these liabilities cannot be predicted at present, but will pose a big challenge for the future—a challenge of unknown dimensions.

Economy and society

The consequences of the recession seem to have been quite unevenly distributed. While many of the super-rich whose flawed decisions led to ruin have lost their empires, they have reverted to lifestyles that could still be described as luxurious; others have survived with their fortunes substantially intact. But the ordinary citizens, most of whom had limited capacity to take advantage of the expansionary bandwagon, have suffered significant deterioration in their lifestyles, with living standards for some dropping from modest to marginal, and for others from marginal to bare survival. The impact of the recession was uneven across the major sectors of Irish society—but so too had been the impact of the boom. The Gini index of income inequality may be used to assess this; it ranges theoretically from zero (complete equality) to 100 (complete inequality). We may use this to compare Ireland with the 15 oldest EU member states (EU15), which correspond largely to a set of long-established liberal democracies with shared social and political traditions, and exclude the new post-communist and other member states that joined in the early twenty-first century.[1] The Gini index of disposable income for this group remained relatively stable from 2003 to 2009, at about 30. From 2003 to 2006 the Irish index rose from 30 to 32, suggesting that inequality levels were similar to those for the EU15, but rising. Since then, however, the Irish level has been dipping, and had fallen below the EU15 level, to 29, by 2009. At this time, the index for Denmark was 27, for the UK 32, and for Portugal 35 (Eurostat, 2012a).

The years of the boom in Ireland also failed to tackle serious problems of poverty. During the years 2005–09, spanning the last years of the boom and the first years of the recession, it was estimated that in the 15 oldest EU states a steady 22% of the population was living at risk of poverty or social exclusion (a complex index taking account of income, capacity to avail of mainstream household facilities, and household unemployment levels). The Irish level was consistently significantly higher than this, and had reached 26% by 2009. At that time, the corresponding 'at risk' levels were lower in the three comparator countries, at 18% for Denmark, 22% for the UK and 25% for Portugal (Eurostat, 2012c). Of course, it needs to be borne in mind that poverty measures used within the EU are usually relative, not absolute: they quantify *relative* access to necessary life resources by comparing population strata within a society, rather than by setting an objective benchmark. As the parent of the objective measure in the USA, Mollie Orshansky (1969: 37), put it, 'for deciding who is poor, prayers are more relevant than calculation because poverty, like beauty, lies in the eye of the beholder'. When we move from the relative EU measure to the Orshansky one, Ireland's relative standing changes. While the former showed the proportion of persons in poverty increasing in Ireland from 19.1% to 21.4% between 1996 and 2000, the Orshansky index showed a sharp decline, from 20.1% to 10.6% over the same period. In fact, the Orshansky measure for 2000 showed a quite different ranking from that described above, with only 3.4% falling below the poverty line in Denmark, and 9.3% in the United Kingdom, but with 32.2% in poverty in Portugal (Notten and de Neubourg, 2007: 10).

Given the extent to which Ireland's boom was driven by the construction sector, it is not surprising that the provision of abundant housing was a central feature of the years of the 'Celtic tiger'. Thus, at a time when the proportion of the population living in overcrowded housing conditions was about 10% for the older EU states (2005–09), the level in Ireland was half this, and it had declined to 4% by 2009 (at that point, the level in Denmark was 8%, the UK 7% and Portugal 14%; Eurostat, 2012b). But it was, of course, the collapse of the property bubble that drove the recession, resulting ultimately in a sharp decline of employment in the construction sector, a collapse of revenue from tax and stamp duty on house sales, and a massive overhang in unsold properties. While this was of critical importance in driving the banking collapse and the financial crisis, it also left a legacy of unfinished houses and housing estates, unoccupied dwellings and unsold buildings. Since all building construction requires permission from the local authority (whose responsibilities are ultimately controlled by the central government through the Department of the Environment), it seems clear that responsibility for this rests with the state's decision-making structures. As it has been put by one set of experts,

> As well as a catastrophic failure in Ireland's banking and financial regulatory system, there has been a catastrophic failure of the planning system at all scales. Planning should have acted as the counter-balance to the excessive pressures for development, working

for the common good to produce sustainable patterns of residential
and commercial property. Instead, both fiscal and planning policy
formation, implementation and regulation were overtly shaped by
the neoliberal policies adopted by the state, particularly in the period
from 1997 onwards. (Kitchin et al., 2010: 55)

Instead of political leadership, these authors argue, the state incentivised
construction, failed to regulate the financial sector, reduced the tax burden
on developers, speculators and banks, allowed buyers to over-extend themselves and failed to control development—and, once again, much of the blame
has been attributed to a culture of 'localism, clientelism, and cronyism'
(Kitchin et al., 2010: 55). This was responsible not just for unplanned and un-
needed construction projects, but also for a failure to implement appropriate
building regulations, resulting not just in over-supply but also in defective
standards, with notorious instances of housing in flood plains and use of
substandard building materials. The full scale of these abuses has never been
assessed, nor has its long-term social and economic cost been calculated.

This experience also promoted cynicism about the concept of planning.
The government's 'national spatial strategy' announced in 2002 envisaged
18 cities or towns acting as 'gateways' or 'hubs' in the promotion of economic
development, but was quickly undermined by the government's own
'decentralisation' plan for the civil service, which envisaged the transfer of
more than 10,000 civil servants from Dublin to 53 towns spread over 25
counties, opening up opportunities for competition by local vested interests.
The outcome was 'an enormously costly' failure, with increasingly diffuse
settlement patterns 'consolidating a trend towards increasing numbers of
unsustainable commutes within extended local labour market areas'
(Meredith and van Egeraat, 2013: 5).

Before even going beyond the economic domain, then, critical shortcomings in political decision making are obvious. Furthermore, even a
sudden change to a system informed by the wisdom of Solomon would leave
a formidable legacy of problems. These include bridging the enormous gap
between revenue and expenditure in Ireland's public finances, coping with
the economic and political consequences of unprecedented levels of personal
debt, maintaining social cohesion in a context of declining living standards
and growing inequality, managing an unstable housing market, and responding to the physical, social and environmental legacy of an insufficiently
regulated splurge in construction.

CULTURAL TRANSFORMATION

It was always inevitable that rapid economic change would bring far-reaching social transformation in its wake. This appears to have had an impact on Irish society in two ways. First, Irish population structure has been significantly changed by a sudden wave of immigration from other parts of Europe and the world. Second, the newly wealthy segments of Irish society appear to have adjusted, as in other societies, to more materialistic lifestyles that attached lower priority to traditional cultural values. This placed pressure not only on the Irish language, already struggling for survival, but also on belief in orthodox religious values and practice of religious faith, particularly noticeable among Catholics. The significance of these changes is difficult to quantify, but should not be underestimated. The residual link between the Irish language and national identity is likely to diminish with the steady decline of the Gaeltacht as a bailiwick of Irish culture; and the erosion of traditional religious belief, which formed an important if complex component in public morality, creates the risk of moral recession in a context where secular morality has not had the time or opportunity to develop.

The emergence of a multicultural society

The casual, unplanned manner in which immigration-fuelled economic development was facilitated and, indeed, reinforced by political decisions was striking to observers. It has been argued that the opening of the Irish labour market in 2004 to the populations of the new EU member states of central and eastern Europe was perhaps 'the largest act of social engineering since the [seventeenth century] Plantations' of English and Scottish settlers in Ireland:

> And so everything changed just like that! A society with a long aptitude for squeezing out surplus family members and, it seemed during the 1950s and 1980s, entire generations threw open its doors unequivocally to four hundred million fellow Europeans and conditionally to cherry-picked migrants from elsewhere. No Statue of Liberty or Ellis Island was needed. No grand proclamations of an Irish Dream were issued. A commitment to immigration-fuelled economic growth was blandly inserted into a national development plan. (Fanning, 2009: 7)

Figure 2.4: Non-nationals as proportion of total population, Ireland and selected European countries, 1985–2012

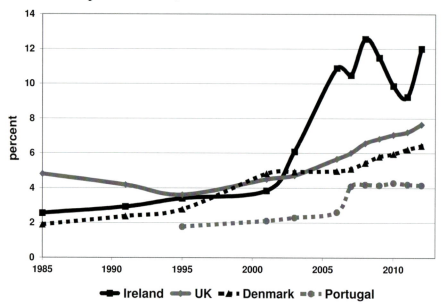

Source: Computed from Eurostat Statistics Database, available at epp.eurostat.ec. europa.eu

The intense and immediate impact of this policy shift is summarised in Figure 2.4, which shows the proportion of the active population accounted for by those who were not citizens of the Republic of Ireland. Up to the end of the twentieth century this remained modest, with Ireland shadowing countries with similar economic profiles, such as Denmark, and lagging behind the United Kingdom. In 2002, however, the Irish level began a steep climb, reaching 12.6% by 2008—approximately double that of the UK and Denmark—and, after a sharp drop, climbing back to 12.0% in 2012. This expansion drew on different sources from those that had traditionally accounted for people born outside the territory of the Republic. As Figure 2.5 shows, these had for long comprised mainly people born in Great Britain, with the USA and Northern Ireland as the main additional contributing jurisdictions. In 1996, Germany and France were the two other most important countries. By 2011, however, 'other countries', which now accounted for a big majority of those born outside the state, included people from across the world. The list of countries that contributed more than 15,000 people in respect of the usually resident population was still headed by Great Britain (230,000), with a further 58,000 from Northern Ireland; Poland followed with 115,000, while Lithuania (35,000), the USA (28,000), Latvia and Nigeria (20,000 each), and Romania and India (18,000 each)

Figure 2.5: Birthplaces of population born outside Republic of Ireland, 1986–2011

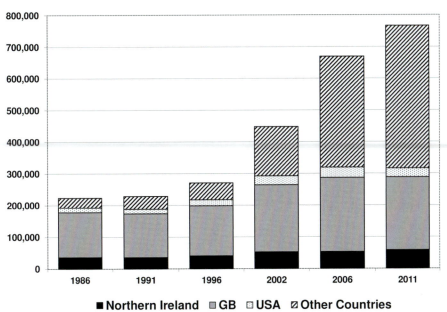

■ **Northern Ireland** ▨ **GB** ▨ **USA** ▨ **Other Countries**

Note: Data refer to total population present on census night.
Source: Computed from Census of Ireland, 1986–2011, www.cso.ie

made up the rest (Ireland, 2012b: 84). Using nationality rather than place of birth as a criterion shows a similar profile, with one big exception: the number identifying as 'British' (112,000) is much lower (Ireland, 2012b: 89). This suggests that many people born in the United Kingdom regarded themselves as Irish.

The state has responded unevenly to the challenge posed by this sudden immigrant influx. Since the right to vote in local elections is governed by a residency requirement (it is not necessary to be an Irish citizen), political parties and public authorities responded positively in 2009 to initiatives by NGOs to encourage voter registration, with parties including immigrants as party members and candidates (Fanning and O'Boyle, 2010: 418; Fanning, 2011: 157). The Department of the Environment published its guide to procedure at local elections, *How members of local authorities are elected*, in seven languages as well as English: Latvian, Lithuanian, Mandarin Chinese, Polish, Romanian, Russian and Slovak.[2] The Department of Social Protection, similarly, publishes such documents as its booklet on *Your social security rights in Ireland—a guide for EU citizens* not just in English and Irish, but also in

French, German, Latvian, Lithuanian, Polish and Spanish.[3] On the other hand, the Department of Education has struggled to cope with the much more demanding but also more important challenge of providing English-language instruction to schoolchildren whose first language is not English.

The challenge to traditional culture

Given the traditional stress on the Irish language as a core component in Irish culture, as reflected in the stated commitment of post-independence govern-ments to 'revive' it, its constitutional status as 'first official language', and its attainment of official status in the EU in 2007, there is a good deal of evidence that it has suffered further reverses—a development of limited visible significance for the practicalities of everyday life, since native speakers form so tiny a proportion of the population, but of potentially profound importance for the Irish self-image. The 'official' story, as reflected in census data, is one of unrelenting rise since independence. Graphs show a characteristic U-curve in knowledge of Irish since the first census at which this was measured (1851): in the present territory of the Republic, those with a knowledge of Irish dropped from 1.5 million in 1851 to just half a million in 1911, but then increased steadily to 1.8 million by 2011. But the impression of reversal of decline is misleading for two reasons. First, it is to be assumed that in the nineteenth century most Irish speakers had acquired the language colloquially (they had few opportunities to do so at school), and that 'knowledge' implied a reasonable degree of oral fluency. Since 'knowledge' is, however, self-defined, and the state's vigorous commitment to teaching Irish left few unaffected, it appears that most of those reported as Irish speakers by the early twenty-first century had learned the language in school. Indeed, by 2011 only 77,000 people stated that they spoke the language on a daily basis (outside the educational system, that is). Second, the Irish-speaking (Gaeltacht) districts have continued to retract. In 1926, Irish speakers in the Gaeltacht (then more broadly defined than today) numbered 247,000 (52% of the population), and the great majority had presumably learned the language colloquially rather than in school; by 2011, the number of people in the Gaeltacht who reported using Irish on a daily basis was less than one tenth of this: 23,000 (24% of the Gaeltacht population; Ireland, 2012b: 40–1).

Yet another cultural feature that had been associated with Irish identity in the eyes of many also came under pressure: religious belief. It is true that the census shows a rather slow pattern of change in respect of religious affili-ation, with the proportion of Catholics dropping steadily from a peak of 95% in 1961 to 84% 50 years later—still a position of massive demographic

Figure 2.6: Weekly church attendance, Ireland and selected European countries, 1973–2011

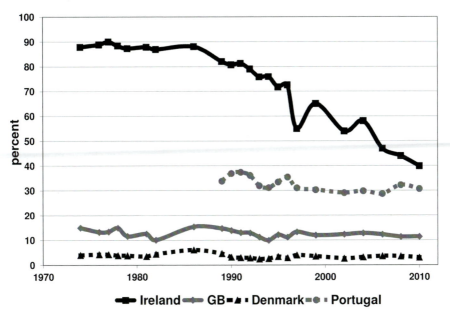

Note: Data refer to those attending church once weekly, or more frequently, as a percentage of the total sample. Due to a technical anomaly, the Irish data for 1996 probably understate the actual attendance level. Fieldwork for the last four data points in the Irish case and for the last three in the Portuguese case was carried out a year later than recorded here (2003–2011 and 2005–2011 respectively, rather than 2002–2010).
Source: Computed from Eurobarometer Trend File 1970–2002 (up to 1998) and European Social Survey, pooled data, 2002–08, and round 5, 2010

dominance. But undoubtedly a qualitative change has taken place. If we consider religious practice, the shift has been sharp. Figure 2.6 compares the pattern in Ireland with that in three other west European countries over the period 1973–2010/11. The remarkable feature of the Irish pattern is not so much the decline as the very high level of weekly church attendance up to the mid-1980s; there are no parallels for this elsewhere in Europe. Given the centrality of weekly church attendance in the Catholic tradition, Portugal is probably the most useful basis of comparison; but there weekly attendance has remained stable at about 30%, while in Ireland it dropped from close to 90% in the 1980s to 44% in 2011. It should be noted that other traditionally Catholic societies, such as Spain, Italy and Belgium, resembled the Portuguese pattern, but with France recording much lower levels of church attendance. Comparison with Denmark (where church attendance resembled that in other Scandinavian societies) is less appropriate in this case, since in Protestant societies there is no theological or ecclesiastical requirement of weekly attendance at church comparable with that in the Catholic tradition. The difference between the two traditions is illustrated by the case of Great Britain, where Catholic church attendance rates in the 1980s and 1990s were close to 50%, with Protestant levels typically falling well below 20%. The British church attendance rates reported in Figure 2.6 reflect the overall outcome of the pull from these two different directions.

Importantly, this change in Ireland seems set to continue. This is illustrated by the substantial variations in church attendance by different age groups in 2011, as illustrated in Figure 2.7. This shows a big slump in weekly church attendance as one moves from older to younger age cohorts: the level is 80% for those aged 70 or more, but only 22% for the under-30s. Such changes in religious practice are likely to be accompanied by shifts in belief. In 1999, for example, when the moral authority of the church was already suffering from its handling of the child abuse issue, majorities of those aged 70 or more were still prepared to see it as having an important role in providing answers to problems in specific areas, but among the under-30s the role of the church was rejected by big majorities. Thus, 58% of the older group, but only 16% of the younger group, accepted a church role in relation to moral issues; for family life problems the respective proportions were 53% and 20%; and for social problems they were similar, at 52% and 19%. Only in the area of catering for spiritual needs was the role of the church still widely accepted (by 80% of the over-70s and 60% of the under-30s).[4]

The changes in key aspects of Irish society described above are easily measurable. The sudden and dramatic appearance of a large immigrant population challenged the foundations of a society more accustomed to emigration. A bicultural system where the main challenge to Anglophone culture was a decaying Irish language was replaced by one where new languages from other parts of the world became much more prominent. While a new influx of practising Catholics, notably from Poland and Lithuania, added to the Catholic segment of the population, the long-standing hegemony of the church was undermined not just from without by the new vigour of such religions as evangelical Protestantism and Islam but from within by declining levels of belief and practice. It is still too early to determine the impact that the new immigrant population will have on the current party system. While indications to date are that this may not be very great, most immigrants are still precluded from voting in Dáil elections and levels of integration in the political community are relatively low.[5]

Figure 2.7: Church attendance by age group, Ireland, 2011

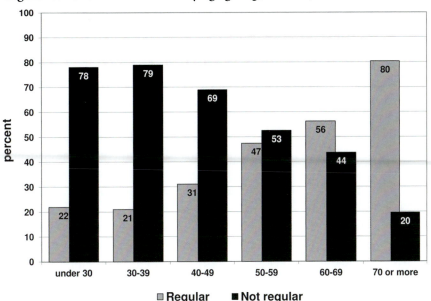

Note: Regular churchgoers are defined as those attending at least weekly. All others (including non-religious) are classified as not regular.
Source: Computed from European Social Survey, wave 5, 2011.

ATTITUDINAL SHIFT

The social and cultural changes already discussed have big implications for value shift in Ireland—a transformation likely to define or redefine the population's relationship with its political rulers. Some shifts signify acceptance of the consequences of long-standing, incremental changes that have a bearing on key components of Irish identity (such as attitudes to Northern Ireland, Great Britain and the EU, and perspectives on the Irish language). Others have direct consequences for the relationship between rulers and ruled (such as levels of trust in different components of the political world).

Irish identity

As is well known, the new state that appeared in southern Ireland in 1922 was located in a divided and embittered society, its birth marked by a civil war that was more violent than the war of independence that preceded it (while the precise numbers of casualties are not known, one estimate placed those in the war of independence at 2,000 and in the civil war at 5,000; Curran, 1980: 62, 376). The civil war not only had devastating consequences for the political leadership on both sides; it bequeathed a legacy of unresolved issues to the succeeding generations of politicians and 'left a permanent scar on the national psyche' (Hopkinson, 1988: 273–4). There was no mutual forgiveness pact, truth commission or tribunal of inquiry to help to bridge the gap between the two sides and heal the wounds of conflict. Memories of the excesses of the period 1922–23 were suppressed, apart from occasional outbursts in the Dáil and at election time; it took the passage of at least two generations for the intensity of the bitterness to ebb.

The pro- and anti-treaty positions coincided with long-term, profoundly felt differences between Fine Gael and Fianna Fáil, but there is some evidence that these had eroded by the early years of the twenty-first century, with a steady move towards consensus on less nationalist positions than in the past. In 1969, for example, differences between the two parties on sensitive indicators touching on national identity were still clear. In a survey in that year, 37% of Fianna Fáil supporters said that they considered the revival of the Irish language as a 'good idea', but only 20% of Fine Gael supporters took this perspective. On attitudes to Northern Ireland, 21% of Fianna Fáil supporters but only 15% of Fine Gael supporters felt that the government should make a greater effort to influence developments there.[6]

With the further decline of the Irish language as a living speech form, official policy is likely to come under pressure, and there continue to be noticeable differences in emphasis between the leadership of the two parties; but the issue is one of very low salience. Differences between the two parties have also persisted in relation to Northern Ireland, with Fianna Fáil supporters likely to be more strongly in favour of Irish unity than Fine Gael supporters. By 2002, for instance, 78% of Fianna Fáil supporters, and a slightly lower 72% of Fine Gael supporters, agreed that Irish unity should be a long-term policy. A different question in a 2011 survey showed a clear difference between Fianna Fáil and Sinn Féin, on one side (where slim majorities still supported Irish unity), and Fine Gael and Labour on the other (where only about a third of respondents did so).[7] The salience of the Northern Ireland issue is, however, very low. Even in 1997, while interest in Northern Ireland was at a high point, with Irish politicians engaged intensively in the process that led to the Good Friday agreement of 1998, Irish survey respondents ranked the Northern Ireland issue eighth in importance (far below unemployment, crime, taxation and other material issues); supporters of Fianna Fáil and Fine Gael ranked it sixth and eleventh, respectively.[8] In a major election survey in 2011, it was not included at all in a long list of issues that potentially influenced voters.

One of the most remarkable changes in Irish society, shared in varying degrees with other European countries, has been the evolving relationship with the EU—an issue with big implications for national identity. Much of the debate on the significance of this relationship, in Ireland as elsewhere, has focused on the growth of hostile attitudes to the EU, often dismissed as 'euroscepticism'. Efforts to explain the growth of negative perceptions of European institutions and of resistance to the process of European integration, however, risk missing a central point. From the perspective of the comparative study of nationalism, what is remarkable about recent attitudinal change is not the mobilisation of negative attitudes to European economic and political integration, but the willingness of elites and of many voters to tolerate a level of political union that increasingly challenges the survival of their own countries as independent states (see Chapter 8).

The European unification project, then, may be seen as a remarkable effort to create a federal or federal-type state in circumstances where the population of the federation will have been socialised into a powerful sense of sub-federal identity, as Germans, French, British or Irish, for example (Coakley, 2012c: 249). This points to a significant gulf between union-building elites and the mass population, in circumstances where those pursuing the integration agenda need at least a 'permissive consensus' on the part of voters—not necessarily warm endorsement of the project, but at least the absence of wide-scale, determined opposition. The extent to which it will be possible in the longer term to resolve the tension between European integrationist ideology and traditional nationalist values, in Ireland as elsewhere, remains to be seen.

Political trust

If the bitterness of earlier generations has waned among contemporary supporters of the 'civil war parties', with a sea-change marked by an invitation in 2010 to Fianna Fáil finance minister Brian Lenihan to address the annual meeting in Béal na mBláth, Co. Cork, commemorating the death of Michael Collins, other problems remain at the level of the political elite. There appears now to be widespread dissatisfaction with and little trust in politicians, and in the political process more generally. Figure 2.8 reports responses to a series of questions about trust in public institutions, where respondents were invited to place themselves on an 11-point scale ranging from 0 (no trust at all) to 10 (complete trust). Thus, responses below the mid-point, 5, would indicate relative mistrust, and responses above this relative trust. It is striking that, of the four countries considered, the borders were marked by Denmark (where levels of trust in public institutions were usually much higher than in the other three cases) and Portugal (generally recording the lowest levels of trust). Ireland and Great Britain are in the middle, with very similar profiles. Of the four institutions considered, the most central, parliament, does not fare particularly well except in Denmark, with declining levels of trust in the late 2000s. But trust in parliament's occupants, politicians, was lower still, with sharply declining levels of trust in Ireland and elsewhere from 2007 on. The legal system, by contrast, attracted moderate levels of trust, with respondents clustered around the middle of the scale; and in the case of the police levels of trust were highest of all.

Figure 2.8: Trust in public institutions, Ireland and selected European countries, 2002–11

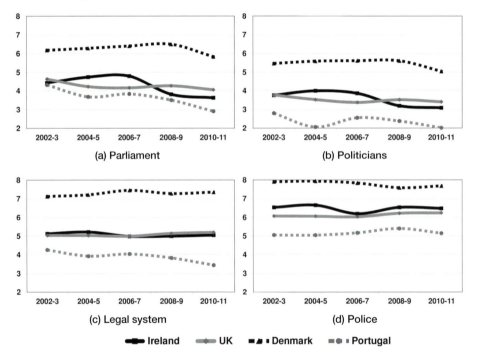

Note: Lines refer to the mean level of trust on an 11-point scale (0–10). The question was: 'Using this card, please tell me on a score of 0–10 how much you personally trust each of the institutions I read out. 0 means you do not trust an institution at all, and 10 means you have complete trust.' The questions referred to the country's parliament, politicians, the legal system and the police.

Source: Computed from European Social Survey, cumulative datafile rounds 1–4, and round 5.

Figure 2.9: Satisfaction with institutions or policies, Ireland and selected European countries, 2002–11

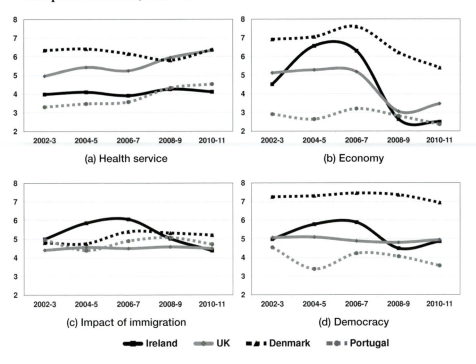

(a) Health service   (b) Economy

(c) Impact of immigration   (d) Democracy

Ireland   UK   Denmark   Portugal

Note: Lines refer to the mean level of satisfaction on an 11-point scale (0–10). The questions were: 'Please say what you think overall about the state of health services in Ireland [etc.] nowadays?', 'On the whole, how satisfied are you with the present state of the economy in Ireland?', 'Would you say it is generally bad or good for Ireland's economy that people come to live here from other countries?', and 'On the whole, how satisfied are you with the way democracy works in Ireland?'. In each case, respondents were asked to use a card showing an 11-point scale (0–10), ranging from 'extremely dissatisfied' to 'extremely satisfied' for two questions, 'extremely bad' to 'extremely good' for the question on health services, and 'bad for the economy' to 'good for the economy' for the question on immigration.
Source: Computed from European Social Survey, cumulative datafile rounds 1–4, and round 5.

The reaction of citizens to changed economic circumstances is of particular interest. No doubt, declining levels of trust in parliament and politicians reflected a perception that they had mishandled the economic crisis; but we have more direct evidence of the manner in which people responded to this crisis. Figure 2.9 reports average levels of satisfaction with the state of the economy and of the health service, as well as general satisfaction with the operation of democracy and opinion as to whether immigration was good or bad for the economy. Perhaps surprisingly, Great Britain and Portugal registered increasingly favourable assessments of the health service and, notwithstanding the impact of the recession, levels of dissatisfaction with the Irish health service remained modest, and stable. But when it came to assessing the impact of immigration, there was a significant change in Irish attitudes. Here, assessments of the positive impact of immigration on the economy increased up to 2007, but then began to fall steeply. This difference between Ireland and the other three cases is more marked when it comes to the state of the economy (with Ireland recording the sharpest drop of all, not surprisingly, between 2007 and 2009), and is reflected also in declining levels of satisfaction with the operation of democracy (with levels in Ireland falling back sharply in the same period).

CONCLUSION

The purpose of this chapter was not to offer an analysis of changing perspectives and practices in Ireland *per se*, but rather to indicate how change in this area has offered new challenges to political leaders. Broadly speaking, we may see change as registering in three areas. The first is the set of traditional values around which Irish politics (and, more specifically, party politics) crystallised in the 1920s. Much of the life of the early decades of independent Ireland was marked by a struggle to consummate the partial independence that had been won in 1922—an independence that was seen as incomplete not only because of the continuing British presence for which the 1921 treaty made provision, but also because it partitioned Ireland. By 1949, however, any remaining formal links to the United Kingdom had been broken, and by 1998 the reality of the partition settlement appeared to have been widely accepted, as indicated by massive support for the Good Friday agreement in a constitutional referendum in that year. Some 90 years after it was adopted, the programme of attempting to transform an English-speaking population into fluent Irish speakers appeared to have entirely failed, and, in part because of policy neglect, the small but still vibrant Irish-speaking communities of the 1920s had been transformed into predomin-antly English-speaking ones.

Such changes—complete success in establishing political independence of the United Kingdom and substantial failure (as yet, imperfectly registered in the popular consciousness) in securing Irish unity and revival (or even survival) of the Irish language—may well have effectively depoliticised these issues. The relationship between the Republic of Ireland and the United Kingdom appears now almost to resemble that between two neighbouring sovereign states, and future problems relating to Irish sovereignty are likely to focus on the Dublin–Brussels rather than the Dublin–London relationship. In particular, the deepening process of European integration may well challenge Irish popular expectations in such areas as military neutrality, foreign policy and economic planning, developments for which political leaders have done little to prepare their voters.

A second challenge began to emerge already in the 1970s, as the first flickers of political secularism began to find expression. The initial flashpoints had to do with the legal position in such areas as the sale of contraceptives, but were quickly followed by the more contentious issues of divorce, abortion and gay rights. Polarised positions on these issues offered a challenge to political leaders, a challenge that has continued well into the twenty-first century. Growing multiculturalism, a consequence both of value change within the traditional Catholic community and large-scale immigration, is likely to pose further challenges. Aside from specific public policy issues such as those mentioned above, control and management of the educational system is likely to be a key battleground. In this, the task of political leaders is likely to be facilitated by the declining moral authority and reduced resource base of the Catholic church; and the very retreat of Catholic religious from involvement in education will leave a gap that the state will be constrained to fill.

Ireland's crisis of the twenty-first century, however, arose neither from nationalist-type conflict nor from the battle over moral values. Its roots lay in the more material issue of economic mismanagement, with the combination of a massive state budgetary deficit and a decision to underwrite unlimited bank debt resulting in the loss of economic sovereignty, and associated costs (in such areas as welfare provision and environmental degradation). This raised fundamental questions about the capacity of Ireland's political leadership to govern an independent state. Political managerial incompetence led to the resurrection of the debate of the early twentieth century—largely driven by quasi-racist prejudice—about the fitness of the Irish for self-government. For several commentators, intervention by the EU–ECB–IMF 'troika' meant that 'the adults are now in charge', with Irish politicians sidelined by competent officials from outside who not only saw what needed to be done but were prepared to insist on action. From this perspective, there were corresponding dangers once this external pressure was removed. As one influential commentator put it:

> For anyone with a patriotic bone in their body, the arrival of the troika in November 2010 was a personally felt humiliation. But the

technocrats have been a much-needed antidote to the State's chronic implementation deficit disorder. As such, their departure at the end of the year is cause for concern. Without external pressure, what is the likelihood that the Coalition will revert to the default position of the political system – to implement as little reform as possible and do it as late as possible? (O'Brien, 2013)

Thus, the Irish government was forced to confront the pharmaceutical sector to secure a less inequitable level of payments for necessary drugs, to take on the medical and legal establishments to secure better value for money, to intervene in the banking sector in an effort to revive it, and even to bring Ireland into conformity with other advanced industrial societies by reintroducing a property tax and bringing in household water charges. But if changes in these areas are indeed necessary, there are many who would argue that it is a terrible indictment of Irish political leaders that they were too timid or too reluctant to tackle these issues until forced to do so by external forces. The fact that Irish political leaders were apparently prepared to make necessary changes in policy and its implementation only under duress raises disturbing questions about their fitness for government; and their willingness to see through the changes that were imposed by the 'troika' will be an important test of the extent to which lessons have been learned.

NOTES

1. The EU15 group includes the following countries: Austria, Belgium, Denmark, Finland, France, Germany, Greece, Ireland, Italy, Luxembourg, Netherlands, Portugal, Spain, Sweden, United Kingdom.
2. See www.environ.ie/en/LocalGovernment/Voting/LocalElections [accessed 2 May 2013].
3. www.integration.ie/website/omi/omiwebv6.nsf/page/infoformigrants-socialwelfare-en [accessed 2 May 2013].
4. Computed from European Value Survey, 1999. I am indebted to GESIS – Leibniz Institute for the Social Sciences for making this dataset available (ZA3811).
5. In 2011–12, a large survey included 406 respondents born outside the country. Of these, only 24% reported having voted at the most recent election, by contrast to 74% of Irish-born respondents, presumably reflecting different levels of enfranchisement. The party support profile of the two groups was similar, though with some tendency for non-Irish born to support Labour and Sinn Féin more strongly (chi-square significant at 5% level; derived from European

Social Survey, round 5). I am indebted to the Norwegian Social Science Data Services, Bergen, for making this dataset available.

6. Derived from Gallup poll, 1969, available at www.tcd.ie/Political_Science/ elections/elections.html; $N = 2,134$, with 879 Fianna Fáil and 506 Fine Gael respondents. I am grateful to Michael Marsh for making this dataset available.

7. Derived from Irish national election study, 2002, and Irish national election study, 2011. I am grateful to Michael Marsh for making this dataset available.

8. Based on the number of respondents mentioning the respective issues first as influencing their voting intention; derived from Lansdowne/RTE exit poll, 1997, available www.tcd.ie/Political_Science/elections/elections. html. I am grateful to Michael Marsh for making this dataset available.

3

THE PRESIDENT: LEADER
OR FIGUREHEAD?

Europe's largely ceremonial heads of state rarely make it into the news. They are usually entirely overshadowed by their prime ministers. It was thus something of a surprise when, in a move that was widely criticised, Czech President Vaclav Klaus announced an amnesty for over 6,000 prisoners in January 2013. Many observers were surprised at the strong words of Italian President Giorgio Napolitano in rebuking members of Silvio Berlusconi's People of Freedom party for demonstrating against the judiciary in Milan in March 2013. Even otherwise retiring figurehead monarchs sometimes attract controversy, as when the King of the Belgians refused to sign a bill liberalising the law on abortion in 1990.

The President of Ireland has attracted no controversy at this level, notwithstanding some moments during the presidency of Mary Robinson when old moulds were broken, and frank public comments by Michael D. Higgins in 2013. The office of President is one about which political debate is now rather muted. The constitutional convention launched in December 2012 was invited to consider only one aspect of the office: whether the President's term should be shortened from seven to five years. But the absence of debate on the office of President comparable with, say, that on the Seanad is a new development, and presumably reflects the very favourable ratings that recent presidents have enjoyed in opinion polls.

This chapter examines the role of the President in Irish political life, assessing its effectiveness in filling the position defined in the constitution and asking how appropriate the constitutional definition of the role is. In doing this, it is important to begin with the comparative perspective, and to explore why a peculiar bifurcation of state functions—unknown in the presidential systems of the western hemisphere, where they are concentrated in a single individual—has survived at least in a formal sense in Europe. It is difficult to approach this question without examining the issue of the position of head of state more generally. Does this correspond to something more than a straightforward desire to secure effective government? Are there other societal needs whose satisfaction requires not merely an efficient chief executive but also a ceremonial national figurehead? Following this comparative overview, the manner in which the Irish presidency is defined in the constitution is explored. The next section looks at the manner in which incumbents to date have shaped the office. The last main section assesses the case for change.

PRESIDENTS: A COMPARATIVE PERSPECTIVE

In setting the Irish President in comparative context, three broad areas need to be explored. The first has to do with the origins of the office—not just that of President of Ireland, but of state presidents in general, office holders who have emerged from the ruins of post-medieval monarchy. Second, it is worth examining the various formulas that are used globally for selection of the head of state. Finally, we need to consider the functions of the head of state—those which are primarily political ones, and those which are essentially ceremonial, but whose significance should still not be underestimated.[1]

Origins of the office

The origins of the modern office of head of state are to be found in the role of the king in traditional society (the role was normally a male one, notwithstanding the historical prominence of certain queens). While the nature of traditional kingship has varied, one of its outstanding features has been the extent to which it brought together an extraordinarily broad range of functions, including religious as well as secular ones. In the Christian tradition, this eventually took the form of kings claiming to reign 'by the grace of God', a form of divine approval that legitimised the rule of the royal family (Dabbs, 1971: 9–12). In many traditional societies, the king's role was to defend his people not only by wise rule but also by religious ceremonial and magical intervention. The king, in other words, not only maintained order and defended his people against external attack; he also propitiated the spirit world and sought its support for temporal objectives. This role was illustrated into modern times by the myth of the 'royal touch'—the belief that the king could cure certain diseases such as tuberculosis by his touch.

This power was associated with French kings until the revolution, and in Ireland as late as the beginning of the twentieth century there were people who believed that it was vested in the exiled Stuart pretenders to the throne (Bloch, 1973: 221–3). In certain other societies, the king was endowed with divine or quasi-divine qualities. It was only after the Second World War, for instance, that the Japanese emperor renounced his divinity.

It was, however, secular rather than religious affairs with which the typical king was primarily concerned, though the actual domains of royal authority varied from society to society. At their maximum, the king's powers extended to leading his army to maintain domestic order or to defend the frontiers of the realm, representing the kingdom in its relations with other states, convening assemblies to deliberate on laws or ordinances or himself issuing such ordinances, supervising the enforcement of these laws and the collection of taxes, and acting as supreme judge. One of the principal features of the growth and modernisation of the state was the differentiation of these functions and their partial democratisation. In some cases religious and secular functions were differentiated from a very early stage, or had never been integrated; in others, the process was long and painful, associated with church–state battles. Except in a small number of unusual cases, though, the outcome was the same: the monarch's real powers became confined to the secular domain, though some symbolic religious functions might well have remained.

In the secular arena, the concentration of power in a hereditary monarch was entirely incompatible with the emerging ideology of democracy. Broadly speaking, there were two paths towards resolving this tension. The first rested on a process of institutional differentiation: effective power in the legislative, executive and judicial domains passed to the parliament, the government and the courts system, leaving the monarch as a figurehead shorn of real power. The key feature in the second path was political democratisation: the position of head of state was made subject to some form of popular election. An effort is made in Table 3.1 to show the relationship between the two approaches. In the interest of clarity of presentation, democratisation is presented as a dichotomy: the office either has been 'democratised' or it has not (this table sidesteps other pathways, as when absolute monarchs are replaced by autocratic or authoritarian rulers). The power of the head of state might be similarly reduced to a dichotomy. The long-standing distinction between parliamentary and presidential systems by implication does precisely this (see Lane and Ersson, 1994: 160–2), and even more elaborate, multi-dimensional classifications (such as Lijphart, 1992: 5–10) may be simplified to produce two similar clusters. In practice, though, so many political systems lie somewhere in the middle of the presidential–parliamentary continuum that it makes sense to identify a third intermediate category, semi-presidential government, where the head of state has modest powers (Duverger, 1978, 1980, 1986; Gallagher, Laver and Mair, 2011: 27–8; Hague and Harrop, 2008: 334–7; Needham, 2009: 135–6).[2]

In principle, modernising states that functioned initially as traditional monarchies may, then, move in two directions: by reference to Table 3.1, either vertically or horizontally from their initial position in the top left-hand cell. The classical European route was to move downwards: traditional monarchies were increasingly challenged by power-hungry assemblies, with which they were eventually compelled to compromise; the king was forced to share power with parliament in the appointment of ministers and in the conduct of government, a reform that took place in much of Europe in the nineteenth century. The ultimate stage consisted of a shift to the bottom left-hand cell: the monarch's powers were reduced to symbolic ones, as the royal veto on legislation was eliminated, ministers became answerable in practice to parliament only, and the courts became entirely independent of the monarchy. This is the position in the major west European monarchies of today. This process, incidentally, coincided with the democratisation of parliament: institutionalisation of the principle that elections must be by direct, universal suffrage where all votes are equal, and balloting is secret.

The second characteristic route out of traditional monarchy is represented by a horizontal direction in Table 3.1. This was the classic route of the western hemisphere. Instead of divesting the monarchical office of power, the office itself was democratised. In the place of a king ruling by virtue of the principle of heredity, a president elected normally by mass suffrage appeared. Typically, this president inherited the powers of the traditional monarch: to introduce and veto legislation, to appoint ministers and conduct the business of government, and to pardon offenders, as we may see from the example of the President of the United States. As in the case of parliamentary democracies, the institution of parliament was also gradually democratised.

Table 3.1: A typology of heads of state

Extent of power	Level of democratisation of office	
	Low	High
High	Traditional monarchy	Presidential republic
Medium	Limited monarchy	Semipresidential republic
Low	Parliamentary monarchy	Parliamentary republic

In some cases, movement took place in both directions. Especially where the monarchy resisted the drive towards reform, efforts to democratise it and to reduce its powers were both successful: the monarch was replaced by an elected president whose powers were symbolic only. This was the typical outcome in those European countries where anti-monarchical sentiment was strong (such as Austria and Ireland) or where there was a reaction to an earlier, all-powerful head of state (such as Germany and Italy). There are also circumstances where countries will not fit comfortably into the cells in Table 3.1 (for example, 'revolutionary' dictatorships and military regimes), or the post of head of state may be dispensed with (its functions may be discharged by the president of parliament, as in many communist-run countries in the past, or by the head of government, as in Switzerland and interwar Estonia). Of course, movement within Table 3.1 need not be unidirectional. Spain has reintroduced its monarchy, and the history of such countries as Greece illustrates alternations between monarchy and republicanism, to quote just two examples.

Table 3.2: Types of state by constitutional status of head of state, 1910 and 2010

Head of state	1910	2010
Monarch	31	26
Monarch through Governor-General	–	13
President (executive)	20	51
President (limited power)	3	91
Other	1	3
Total	55	184

Note: 'Other' refers to Switzerland (1910, 2010) and to Andorra and Iran (2010). *Sources:* For 1910, calculated from *Statesman's Yearbook* 1910, *Encyclopaedia Britannica*, 11th ed., 1910–11 and other sources; for 2010, derived from Comparative Constitutions Project database (www.comparativeconstitutionsproject.org).

The broad profile of contemporary regime types is reported in Table 3.2, which contrasts the position in 2010 with that a century earlier.[3] The survival of monarchical government is striking, though in most cases the monarch has been shorn of all substantial power. The resilience of royalty is illustrated by the number of Commonwealth countries that continue to recognise the British Queen as their head of state, though her functions are exercised by a local governor-general. An enormous expansion has, however, taken place in the number of states that are headed by a president, whether that office is associated with significant powers on the American model (51 cases), or is largely ceremonial (a category that has registered a huge increase, from three to 91).

Selecting heads of state

As societies have modernised, then, royal birth has increasingly been replaced by the endorsement of universal suffrage as a medium for the consecration of new heads of state (see Bendix, 1978). Table 3.3 classifies heads of state according to the manner in which they are selected. The first category, the principle of heredity, is superficially simple, but may nevertheless raise difficult issues of succession law. The debate in 2013 on the UK Succession to the Crown Bill illustrates the possibility of lingering controversy; while the principle of gender equality appears now to be accepted, the notion of a Catholic succeeding to the throne remains excluded. Although monarchical succession in the modern period is usually based on an uncontroversial rule of primogeniture, royal legitimacy in the premodern period was potentially based on a range of other principles, including qualified election (Le Goff, 1993: 8), and there are cases where this notion has survived.[4] A related procedure applies in those Commonwealth states that continue to recognise the British Queen as their head. In such realms as Australia and Canada, the Queen (on the advice of the realm government) formally appoints a deputy, or governor-general, who fills the conventional functions of the head of state.

Certain forms of 'indirect election' are also common. By indirect election is meant a process by which the ultimate selection is made by an intermediate body between the larger electorate and the office holder (Steed, 1987). Three mechanisms may be distinguished. In the first (very common) pattern, the president is simply elected by parliament, as in Greece and South Africa. In a second pattern, the president is elected by an electoral college comprising parliamentarians supplemented by certain others, such as a small number of regional representatives (as in Germany and Italy), or a large number of regional councillors (as in India and Pakistan). In the third pattern, the general electorate is involved: it elects a special electoral college which has a single duty, to select the president. This mechanism is declining in importance, with the United States as the outstanding surviving example. At the beginning of the twentieth century a handful of other countries also used this system. They were joined after its independence in 1918 by Finland, which, however, moved in 1987 to direct election.[5]

Table 3.3: Heads of state by selection method, 1910 and 2010

Type	1910	2010
Heredity	31	26
Appointment	–	13
Selection by parliament	6	33
Electoral college: parliamentarians and others	1	5
Electoral college: popularly elected	6	1
Direct popular election	11	101
Other	–	5
Total	55	184

Sources: As for Table 3.2.

But by far the most important mechanism is direct election. This also tends to take a rather characteristic form: the two-ballot system is the norm, though several variants of this system are in use. Of the 101 countries that used direct election in 2010, 81 used the two-ballot system. The fundamental principle is the requirement that a candidate must win an absolute majority of votes cast in order to be elected. If no candidate wins this in the first round of voting, a run-off ballot takes place some time later, normally between the two candidates who led on the first round. In 18 further cases, mainly in Latin America, the system is a plurality one: the leading candidate wins even if he or she does not have a majority. Among presidential electoral systems, Ireland's single transferable vote and Sri Lanka's supplementary vote systems are unique.[6]

Three final points about the selection of heads of state need to be considered: term of office, qualifying age, and candidate filtering procedures. The pattern in respect of term of office is reported in Table 3.4. In some cases, the term of office is not specified (for example, governors-general serve 'at the pleasure' of the Queen, but in practice typically have a five-year term). Monarchs normally serve for life, but in a few cases (such as Malaysia and the United Arab Emirates) the position circulates between traditional rulers at five-year intervals. Among presidents, the extremes are represented by Switzerland (a one-year term) and Botswana (10 years), but the great majority of presidents serve for a five-year term, with much smaller numbers serving for four, six or seven years.

Table 3.4: Terms of office of heads of state, 2010

Term	Number
1 year	1
3 years	1
4 years	24
5 years	92
6 years	14
7 years	12
10 years	1
Life	25
Not specified, not applicable	14
Total	184

Source: Derived from Comparative Constitutions Project database (www.comparative constitutionsproject.org).

Table 3.5: Minimum age requirements for position of head of state, 2010

Minimum age	Monarchies	Republics	Total
16	1	–	1
17	–	1	1
18	11	4	15
20	–	1	1
21	4	4	8
25	–	2	2
30	1	13	14
34	–	1	1
35	–	51	51
40	–	43	43
45	–	4	4
50	–	1	1
55	1	–	1
Not specified	21	20	41
Total	39	145	184

Source: As for Table 3.4.

In most cases, there is a significant age restriction for heads of state, but with important differences between monarchs and presidents (see Table 3.5). In most cases too, a minimum age of 35 is specified (by contrast, for monarchs the age of majority is normally 18, and succession can sometimes take place before this age is attained). Several of England's medieval kings were much younger than 18 on their accession. For the more recent period, the memoirs of the last Emperor of China record a telling incident on the day of his enthronement ceremony in 1908: the new Emperor was not yet three years old, and tearfully wanted to go home while receiving the obeisance of various military and civilian officials in the Forbidden City (Aisin-Gioro, 1989: 31–32).

Finally, however open the electoral procedure itself, there is commonly a filtering mechanism that greatly narrows the choice offered to voters. This is at its most restrictive, of course, in the case of monarchs, where rank in the ruling dynasty is crucial, but it applies also in the case of direct election. Candidate qualification requirements are commonly not specified in the constitution, but Elgie (2012: 514–7) has established the position in respect of 28 popularly elected presidents in democratic states, excluding those in 'presidential' systems. The main nomination systems are as follows.

- Nomination by a specified minimum number or proportion of voters (20 cases), with the number of signatures required ranging from 1,000 in Cape Verde to 500,000 in Ukraine, though most countries lie in the 5,000–20,000 range. Expressed as a proportion of the population, the minimum number ranges from Austria and Portugal (0.07%) to Georgia (1.1%). There is sometimes a require-ment that nominating signatures show a minimum level of support across regions. Some countries specify the number of signatures as a percentage of the electorate, as in Taiwan and Montenegro (each of which specify 1.5%).
- Nomination by a registered party (nine cases), though in most cases evidence is required that the party has significant electoral support (for example, in Slovenia the party nomination must be supported also by at least three members of parliament or at least 3,000 voters).
- Nomination by parliamentarians (six cases), as in Ireland. The Irish ratio of nominees to parliamentarians (20 out of 226, or 9%) is comparable to the level in Slovakia (10%) and Slovenia (11%); the least demanding case is Turkey (20 parliamentarians out of 550, or 4%) and the most demanding is Macedonia (30 out of 123, or 24%).

- Other routes: in a small number of cases, local councillors may nominate presidential candidates, as in Mali; four local councils collectively (but not individual councillors) may do so in Ireland; and combinations of local councillors and parliamentarians may nominate presidential candidates in France. Self-nomination by outgoing or former presidents is unique to Ireland among these cases.

It will be noted that the routes reported above are not mutually exclusive; in five cases, for example, presidential candidates may be nominated either by parties or by voters, and in Ireland three routes are recognised.

Functions of heads of state

If we leave aside for the moment the question of the exercise of political functions in practice, and concentrate instead on bald statements in the constitution, we can detect a remarkable consistency in language in descriptions of the powers of the head of state. This uniformity across constitutions draws attention to the most public activities of the head of state. These extend over the three traditional branches of government recognised in classical separation of powers theory—legislative, executive and judicial functions. In a very special way, furthermore, the head of state exercises functions in the area of international politics, where two rather distinct domains may be identified: those of foreign policy and diplomatic representation, and of military affairs and national defence. Heads of state are also often given special functions at times of crisis (such as declaring a state of emergency and issuing emergency decrees).

A superficial examination of the constitutional definition of the functions of the head of state produces an impressive list. Examples of some characteristic features are listed in Table 3.6: the functions associated with the areas of government just mentioned, and the privileged status of the head of state in enjoying immunity before the law. The identification of the proportion of monarchs and presidents associated with the powers listed in the table is rather mechanical: it is based on the written text of the constitution (discounting unwritten conventions, which may have a big impact on the meaning of the text), and also ignores other articles (some of which may have the effect of entirely redefining the context within which the head of state operates, as will be seen below).

Table 3.6: Formal functions of head of state, 2010

Area	Monarchies	Republics	All
Dissolve the legislature	85	56	62
Approve or reject legislation	82	80	80
Dismiss the cabinet or ministers	79	70	72
Pardon offenders	79	91	89
Act as commander in chief of the armed forces	44	81	73
Represent the state in foreign affairs	36	77	68
Initiate treaties	28	61	54
Issue decrees	38	53	50
Declare a state of emergency	62	68	66
Enjoy full or partial immunity from prosecution	54	59	58
Number of cases	39	145	184

Note: Numbers refer to percentages of heads of state given constitutional functions in the respective areas, except for the bottom row, which indicates the number of cases. *Source:* as for Table 3.4.

The very high percentages reported in each of the 10 areas listed in Table 3.6 suggest that heads of state discharge important duties in the major arenas of government: legislative (determining when general elections will be called, and considering legislation), executive (dismissing ministers), and judicial (pardoning offenders). They are also charged to act in the areas of foreign affairs and defence, and have an important role when there is a national emergency. The special status of the head of state is marked in particular by the standing of the office in the legal system. The quasi-divine role of monarchs may have disappeared, but religious functions commonly survive, as in the UK and Norway; and even when the office has been entirely secularised, the 'inviolable' or quasi-sacred status of the monarch is commonly stressed. This helps to explain why so many heads of state—including presidents—enjoy full or partial immunity from prosecution during their terms of office, though considerations relating to the separation of powers also play a role.

Behind this impressive package of apparent powers, though, lies a more complex reality, within which we may detect three patterns. The first is that of the powerless—or virtually powerless—head of state. How can an office of this kind be reconciled with the impressive list of powers discussed in the paragraphs above? The answer is devastatingly simple: in addition to a range of minor qualifications of the role of the head of state, most constitutions in this category have an important article that comes close to eliminating the discretion of the head of state altogether. This may apply in the case of directly elected presidents ('all official acts of the Federal President shall be based on recommendation by the Federal Government or the Federal Minister authorized by it'; Austria, art. 67.1), indirectly elected ones ('Orders and directions of the Federal President shall require for their validity the countersignature of the Federal Chancellor or of the competent Federal Minister'; Germany, art. 58), or constitutional monarchs ('No actions of the King may take effect without the countersignature of a minister, who, in doing so, takes responsibility upon himself'; Belgium, art. 106). Even if the constitution contains no such provision, as in several older monarchical constitutions, custom and usage may have confirmed the convention that the monarchy exercises discretionary powers only in the rarest of cases, and these are clearly understood.

In the second category is the head of state who exercises modest powers, of the kind that we find in France and several post-communist societies with semi-presidential systems. The impressive powers listed above may be utilised by the head of state, but his or her discretion is not unlimited. Normally, a prime minister acts as an alternative focus of power, and, depending on matters of personality and political context, the balance of power may shift from one office holder to another. Typically, if the political composition of parliament is compatible with the political views of the president, his or her powers are relatively extensive; they may, indeed, be reinforced by the capacity to appoint a prime minister and government of the president's own choosing. If, however, the president and parliament are drawn from opposite sides of the political spectrum, as in France during various periods of *cohabitation*, the president's discretion is severely limited (see especially Duverger, 1986: 101–279).

While problems analogous to those of *cohabitation* may occur also in the third category, the presidential model as it is known in the western hemisphere, they inhibit the freedom of action of the head of state to a much lesser extent. Many American presidents have directed very successful administrations even when Congress was of an unsympathetic political colour. In presidential systems the extent of the constitutional power given to the president is so great that his or her freedom of action is scarcely restricted at all in the executive domain, though a recalcitrant legislature may delay or block segments of the president's legislative programme (see, for example, DiClerico, 1995).

The threefold division of powers of heads of state just discussed may offer an appealing classification system, and is a little more refined than the long-standing presidential–parliamentary classification of democratic polities. But recent investigation of presidential functions has shown that the picture is a good deal more complex than this. Painstaking research into presidential powers shows that these lie on a continuum that does not easily lend itself to simpler systems of classification. Figure 3.1 looks at the distribution of states headed by a president along two dimensions. The first is an index of presidential power developed by Robert Elgie (2012: 506–11), which seeks to combine and normalise scores on three earlier indices and runs potentially from 1 (most powerful) to 0 (least powerful). Elgie has computed this for political systems where presidents share power with prime ministers, whether the former are popularly elected or enter office by some other mechanism; to this have been added in Figure 3.1 comparable figures for presidential systems (based on Siaroff, 2003). The second dimension is population, here presented as the log of the population in thousands, to correct for extreme variation in size. The distribution of course demonstrates the absence of any significant association between presidential power and population size (there are no theoretical reasons for expecting such an association), but it also shows the difficulty of categorising presidents in respect of their power. It is worth noting that there is also considerable overlap between directly and indirectly elected presidents in respect of their location on the Elgie index.

Quite apart from formal and actual power, heads of state appear to respond to significant social psychological needs. This obviously applies to monarchs, and helps to explain their survival in a democratic era. But the representative character of the president, and his or her status as a national symbol above politics, appears also to be a universal phenomenon (see Saunders, 1993: 4–5). The president is frequently defined as president of the 'nation' rather than merely of the state. He or she may be given a role as guarantor of the sovereignty and integrity of the state. Thus, 'the President of the Republic represents the Portuguese Republic, guarantees national independence, the unity of the State, and the regular functioning of the democratic institutions' (Portugal, art. 123). In many cases these responsibilities, which are not necessarily merely symbolic, extend also to defending the constitution. The French constitution, for example, does not stint in committing the President to the preservation of constitutional propriety and national sovereignty: 'the President of the Republic shall see that the Constitution is observed. He shall ensure, by his arbitration, the proper functioning of the public authorities and the continuity of the State. He shall be the guarantor of national independence, territorial integrity and observance of treaties' (France, art. 5).

Figure 3.1: Selected presidents by relative power and national population, *c.* 2010

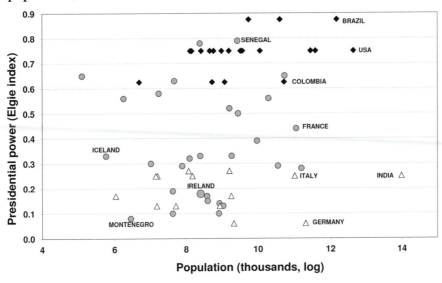

Note: Black diamonds refer to classic 'presidential' systems, grey circles to other directly elected presidencies and triangles to indirectly elected presidencies. Selected countries only are identified. Ireland is indicated by a larger circle.

Source: Derived from Elgie (2012), Siaroff (2003) and United Nations (2012).

THE OFFICE OF PRESIDENT OF IRELAND

The office of President of Ireland shares many of the features of heads of state elsewhere, as discussed from a comparative perspective in the last section. To start with, its origins, too, lay in monarchy, but in Ireland the monarchical context left a uniquely complex legacy (Chubb, 1991: 9–17; Duffy, 1993: 118; Coakley, 2012b). In addition, the constitutional status of the Irish President is characterised by most of the impressive flourishes that are associated with heads of state elsewhere. Finally, the Irish President operates within a specific institutional framework that sets the context for his or her actions. These three aspects of the presidency are discussed in turn in this section.

The creation of the office

The term 'president' was relatively familiar to observers of Irish politics even before 1937. The pre-independence Dáil constitution (1919) provided for a

President, to be elected by the Dáil, who would head the government. This terminology was continued in the Constitution of the Irish Free State (1922), under which the President of the Executive Council (colloquially known simply as 'President') exercised a prime-ministerial role. But while the first two holders of the office, President Cosgrave (1922–32) and President de Valera (1932–37), held effective political power, they did so alongside a figure who symbolised continuing links to the United Kingdom: the Governor-General, representative of the King.

The Governor-General's office was a continuation of that of Lord Lieutenant of Ireland, a post that dated from the medieval period. By the last decades of British rule, the Lord Lieutenant had substantially surrendered effective power in the Irish administration to the Chief Secretary, a figure who was normally of cabinet rank. The relationship between these two figures mirrored that between King and Prime Minister in Great Britain, with the Lord Lieutenant's effective power declining in parallel with (though rather more slowly than) that of the King. Outside times of crisis, the Lord Lieutenant's most visible functions were social rather than political, including the hosting of dinners, balls and levees in Dublin Castle and in the Viceregal Lodge in the Phoenix Park (Johnston, 1963: 16–34; McDowell, 1964: 52–6; Coakley, 2012b: 543–6; Gray and Purdue, 2012).

The compromise between Sinn Féin and the British government that was expressed in the Anglo-Irish treaty of 1921 spelled the end of the position of Lord Lieutenant. In the new configuration of government, the Lord Lieutenant would be replaced in the Irish Free State by a Governor-General, who would represent the King as formal head of the executive, convey the royal assent to legislation and discharge certain other functions that had earlier been the responsibility of the Lord Lieutenant. In Northern Ireland, the Lord Lieutenant's functions would pass to a new Governor of Northern Ireland.

The history of the Governor-Generalship in many ways summarises the history of the British–Irish relationship during the first 15 years of independence (see Sexton, 1989). Notwithstanding the Governor-General's formally elevated status, his real discretion was limited: he was required by the constitution to adhere to the (unspecified, but clear) practice in the Dominion of Canada. But the new Irish government had an even narrower vision of an office which they believed had been forced on them by the British. Ignoring the convention by which governors-general of dominions were British noblemen appointed on the advice of the British government following consultation with the dominion government, the Irish government insisted on the appointment in 1922 of an Irish commoner (former independent nationalist MP Timothy Healy). Healy was replaced in 1928 by an Irish diplomat, James McNeill, with the Irish government this time bypassing the British government. President Cosgrave made it clear that he expected the Governor-General to adhere strictly to the government's wishes, including speedy signature of all bills, eliminating the Governor-General's veto power in practice.

Following Fianna Fáil's electoral victory in 1932, the profile of the Governor-General was further reduced. Shortly after entering into office, de Valera secured the resignation of James McNeill in controversial circumstances, replacing him by a Fianna Fáil backbencher who moved to a suburban residence rather than living in the Viceregal Lodge. The new Governor-General, Domhnall Ua Buachalla, opted out of all public engagements and confined himself to the minimum, purely formal duties of his office. In any case, his few remaining powers were further reduced in 1933. When the office itself was abolished in 1936, most of its remaining formal functions were transferred to the chairman of the Dáil, the Ceann Comhairle (Coakley, 2012a: 44; Sexton, 1989: 164–5).

The removal of the Governor-General from the constitution in 1936, like the abolition of the Seanad in the same year, left de Valera with a relatively clean slate in devising the new constitution. The Seanad came back in new form (see Chapter 4); so, too, it could be argued, did the Governor-General. A new office of President was created to assume many of the functions of the Governor-General, and the post of President of the Executive Council was redesignated Taoiseach, and given marginally greater powers.[7] There were major differences, however, between the President and his predecessor. First, though lacking the extensive powers formally given the Governor-General in the 1922 constitution (powers which, on the Canadian model, he was expected not to exercise), the new President was given a couple of important functions in the areas of government formation and approval of legislation, as will be seen later; these were considerably more significant than the feeble functions remaining in the hands of the Governor-General by 1936. Second, although the 1937 constitution envisaged the President coexisting with the King, as the Governor-General had previously, the new office holder was no longer formally a representative of the King. The functions of the two offices were clearly differentiated, with the King's role restricted to the external domain and the President's to the internal one. Reflecting the very different status of the new office, the President was to be directly elected by the people, removing any hint of subservience to the King. Indeed, the constitution declared that the President would 'take precedence over all other persons in the state', though the British did not accept that this would necessarily apply if the King were to visit Dublin.

The creation of the office of President in 1937, then, brought Ireland into apparent alignment with other democratic states, and gave the country a republican appearance. The method used for selecting the President, popular election, was unusual at that time among parliamentary democracies; in Europe, only Germany, Austria and Portugal followed this model, at least in theory, while Finland used a variant (Elgie, 2012: 503–4). This relatively radical gesture was, however, undermined by the fact that the new President lacked any functions in the area of international relations, which continued to be the formal responsibility of the King. Neither was it helped by the relatively restrictive process by which candidates could present themselves to voters (nomination by 20 members of the houses of the Oireachtas, or by four county or county borough councils). In effect, it was expected that they would have to be endorsed by a major party, given the Dáil arithmetic of the early years of the state, and the highly politicised character of county councils since the 1934 local elections.[8] On the other hand, the unique electoral system (bizarrely labelled 'proportional representation by means of the single transferable vote') opened up the actual mechanics of the voting process in a way that arguably weakened the role of parties, which would have been enhanced by the more normal two-ballot system (see Murphy and Reidy, 2012).

The President's constitutional role

The list of functions given to the President in the constitution is an impressive one, comparable with that of other heads of state, and has remained unchanged since 1937.[9] As in many other parliamentary democracies, there is an important article that reduces almost all of these powers to the symbolic level:

> The powers and functions conferred on the President by this Constitution shall be exercisable by him only on the advice of the Government, save where it is provided by this Constitution that he shall act at his absolute discretion or after consultation with or in relation to the Council of State, or on the advice or nomination of, or on receipt of any other communication from, any other person or body. (art. 13.9)

There is a similar provision in respect of functions conferred on the President by law. The symbolically important functions which have been reduced to mere ceremonial status by this disabling provision may be placed in three categories. The first category comprises the right to appoint and dismiss senior office holders; the President has no discretion whatsoever, but merely acts on the 'advice' (which, in the circumstances, amounts to *direction*) of another organ of state:

- to appoint the Taoiseach on the nomination of the Dáil (art. 13.1.1º) and to accept the resignation of the Taoiseach (art. 28.9.1º)
- to appoint other members of the government on the nomination of the Taoiseach (art. 13.1.2º), to accept their resignation on the advice of the Taoiseach (art. 13.1.3º; 28.9.3º), and to terminate their appointment on the advice of the Taoiseach (art. 13.1.3º; 28.9.4º)
- to appoint the Attorney General on the nomination of the Taoiseach (art. 30.2), to accept his or her resignation (art. 30.5.1º), and to terminate his or her appointment on the advice of the Taoiseach (art. 30.5.3º)
- to appoint the Comptroller and Auditor General on the nomination of the Dáil (art. 33.2) and to remove him or her from office on the basis of resolutions from the Dáil and Seanad forwarded by the Taoiseach (art. 33.5)
- to appoint judges (35.1), to remove judges of the Supreme Court and the High Court on the basis of resolutions from the Dáil and Seanad forwarded by the Taoiseach (35.4), to be present at the swearing in of the Chief Justice (art. 34.5.2º), and to determine the date by which judges must make their declaration on taking office (art. 34.5.3º)
- to commission officers of the defence forces (art. 13.5.2º).

A certain absence of symmetry may be noticed here. In some cases, the President may appoint, accept the resignation of or dismiss an office holder (government ministers and the Attorney General); in one he may appoint or accept a resignation only (the Taoiseach); in yet another, he may appoint or dismiss (the Comptroller and Auditor General); in the case of the swearing in of the Chief Justice, he is merely present.

Another set of presidential functions falls, unsurprisingly, into the legislative domain. These are as follows:

- to summon and dissolve the Dáil, on the advice of the Taoiseach (art. 13.2.1º)
- to fix a date for the first meeting of the Seanad after a general election, on the advice of the Taoiseach (art. 18.8)

- to sign bills passed by the Oireachtas (art. 13.3.1º, 25.1, 2) and to promulgate them as laws (art. 13.3.2º, 25.4.2º)
- to sign amended copies of the Constitution (art. 25.5.2º)
- to sign a bill early on the request of the Government with the concurrence of Seanad Éireann (art. 25.2.2º)
- to sign and promulgate any bill containing a proposal to amend the Constitution on being satisfied that provisions for its legislative passage have been complied with and it has been approved by referendum (art. 46.5).

The first of these functions must automatically be discharged only in circumstances where the Taoiseach retains the confidence of the Dáil, as discussed later. The third obviously assumes that the President has not referred the bill in question to the Supreme Court, as also discussed later. The last two functions allow some presidential discretion, though their full constitutional significance remains unexplored. In particular, the potential importance of the President's role in agreeing to sign a bill early (rather than between five and seven days after its presentation to him, the interval the constitution specifies as the norm) gives an important role to all presidents, and a significant bargaining chip to a politically ruthless one.[10]

Finally, some miscellaneous functions are conferred on the President:

- to exercise supreme command of the defence forces (art. 13.4)
- to pardon or to commute or remit punishment imposed by any criminal court (art. 13.6)
- to carry out any additional powers or functions conferred by law, on the advice of the Government (art. 13.10, 13.11).

Additional functions conferred on the President by law have included the making of a range of appointments, all on the advice of the government: council members and senior professors of the Dublin Institute for Advanced Studies (1940); the Governor of the Central Bank (1942); the chairman of the Agricultural Institute (1958); the Ombudsman (1980); and the Information Commissioner (1997). Other formal functions include the honorary presidency of the Irish Red Cross Society (1944), certain military roles (1954), and the right to grant honorary citizenship (1956) (Kelly, Hogan and Whyte, 2003: 223–4). By far the most visible additional function, however, was the right to represent the state in international relations, which passed from the King to the President under the Republic of Ireland Act, 1948.

In a number of cases, the President may act when certain circumstances arise provided he or she first consults with the Council of State. Having listened to the advice of members of the Council, the President personally decides how to act. Most of these circumstances are connected with the legislative process; six are listed below in diminishing order of importance.

- to refer any bill to the Supreme Court for a decision as to whether any of its provisions are repugnant to the Constitution (art. 26.1.1º)
- to refer to the people any bill that is the subject of a petition to that effect from a majority of the members of the Seanad and one third of the members of the Dáil (art. 27)
- to concur in the abridgement of the time available to the Seanad for the consideration of emergency legislation (art. 24.1)
- to appoint a Committee of Privileges to determine whether a bill is a money bill following a request to this effect from the Seanad (art. 22.2)
- to convene a meeting of either or both Houses of the Oireachtas at any time (art. 13.2.3º)
- to communicate with the Houses of the Oireachtas by message or address, or to address the nation, on any matter of national or public importance, such message or address to have the approval of the Government (art. 13.7).

The first of these is clearly of greatest significance, since the President can in principle refer any bill to the Supreme Court. This is as close as the Irish constitution comes to giving the President a legislative veto, but of course the President's role is confined to deciding whether or not to refer a bill for further adjudication. The President has no further discretion, and is required either to sign or not to sign, depending on the Supreme Court's finding. The second power, to refer a bill to the people, becomes operative only if triggered by a clear majority in the Seanad, supported by a sizeable minority in the Dáil. This implies, in effect, substantial disagreement between the two houses of a kind that is likely to arise rarely, so it is not surprising that the President has never been asked to consider using this power. Neither has the President ever been asked to curtail the Seanad's time to consider emergency legislation, or to set machinery in motion to determine whether or not a bill is a money bill. The President has addressed a combined meeting of the Houses of the Oireachtas on four occasions (in 1969, 1992, 1995 and 1999), but has never formally addressed the nation under the provisions of article 13.7.

Finally, there is one type of circumstance in which the President may act entirely on his or her own discretion: the right to refuse to dissolve the Dáil on the advice of a Taoiseach who has ceased to retain the support of a majority there (art. 13.2.2°), a point discussed further in the next section (in the context of this provision, the President's power to convene a meeting of either house of the Oireachtas may have a particular significance). The President's right to appoint up to seven members of the Council of State (art. 31.3), to accept their resignation (art. 31.6) or to terminate the appointment of such members (art. 31.7), and to convene meetings of the Council of State 'at such times and places as he shall determine' (art. 31.8), is also unrestricted, though not in itself of great importance.

Like other heads of state, the President of Ireland enjoys special status before the law. Early drafts of the constitution offered comprehensive protection to the President in this respect: he was not to be answerable to either house of the Oireachtas for his performance of his public duties, and he could not be prosecuted in court for any matter, public or private. As finally enacted, this clause of the constitution dropped any reference to a possible prosecution of the President in respect of his private affairs, but strengthened his independence in respect of his public role: 'The President shall not be answerable to either House of the Oireachtas or to any court for the exercise and performance of the powers and functions of his office or for any act done or purporting to be done by him in the exercise and perform-ance of these powers or functions' (art. 13.8.1°), a potentially far-reaching provision. Of course, as in the case of other constitutions, in exceptional circumstances the President may face removal from office through impeachment, though certain short-term remedies are also available; this scenario would be most likely to arise if, for instance, the President were to 'go rogue', and overtly flout the constitution's provisions (Gallagher, 2012: 534–6).

But privileged legal position brings certain costs. The most obvious restriction on the President has to do with freedom of speech. The content of any address to the Houses of the Oireachtas or to the nation must be approved by the government, as we have seen, and similar restrictions on the political freedom of the head of state are in force elsewhere. During the Belgian abortion crisis of 1990, for instance, King Baudouin, a committed opponent of abortion, bemoaned the fact that he, alone among Belgians, had no choice: constitutional tradition required him to sign into law a bill permitting abortion. As the King put it in a letter to the prime minister, 'Is it right that I am the only Belgian citizen to be forced to act against his conscience in such a crucial area? Is freedom of conscience sacred for everyone except for the king?' (cited in Conley, 2004: 117). The answer, ironically, would have to be 'yes'.[11] The extent to which the Irish President may accept a more permissive interpretation of this is discussed below.

But there is a more formidable and unusual restriction on the Irish President's freedom: he or she may not leave the state without the government's consent (art. 12.9). In early drafts of the constitution, and, indeed, in the draft introduced in the Dáil, this read 'The President may not leave Eire during his term of office save with the consent of the Government'. In the course of the debate on the constitution, de Valera made it clear that this would prevent the President from going to, say, Belfast without the government's permission.[12] He offered no explanation for this article, but it continued an older tradition in respect of royal representatives. Before 1922, the Lord Lieutenant was required to apply for a licence from the King if he wished to leave Ireland (Wood, 1935: 3). The letters patent (in effect, royal proclamations) establishing the post of Governor-General in British dominions made similar provisions, presumably to prevent the practice—widespread before 1782—of the Governor-General continuing to reside in Great Britain but farming out responsibility to a deputy, often for a profit (Roberts-Wray, 1966: 314).[13] In the Irish Free State the same formulation was followed: 'Our said Governor-General shall not, upon any pretence whatever, quit the said state without first having obtained leave from Us for so doing' (since the King acted on the advice of the Irish government, this gave the government a veto on the Governor-General's right to travel abroad).[14]

Supporting the presidency

Like other heads of state, the President is embedded in a complex institutional structure. In the first place, provision has to be made to deputise for him in his absence. Here, it is possible to see some continuity with past practice. 'Lords Justices' had normally deputised for the Lord Lieutenant. Until the Act of Union (1800), these were usually the principal figures in the religious, political and judicial establishments: the Lord Primate (the Protestant Archbishop of Armagh), the Speaker of the House of Commons, and the Lord Chancellor (who, as well as being head of the legal system, was chairman of the Irish House of Lords). With the disappearance of the Irish House of Commons in 1800, the Speaker was usually replaced by the Commander-in-chief of the army (Wood, 1935: 5). In the closing years of the Union, the Lord Lieutenant usually selected between four and six members of the Irish Privy Council to form a rota for this purpose.[15] The letters patent creating the office of Governor-General of the Irish Free State stated, as in other dominions, that unless otherwise provided the Chief Justice would deputise in the event of a lengthy absence of the Governor-General. When the occasion arose in 1932 following the enforced resignation of the Governor-General, however, the Chief Justice refused to take the oath of allegiance, thus ruling himself out. Consideration was then given to the appointment of an old-style three-person commission resembling that of the eighteenth century, comprising de Valera himself as President of the Executive Council, the Ceann Comhairle and the Cathaoirleach of the Seanad, but this formula was ruled out by the King. The issue was circumvented by the speedy appointment of a new Governor-General, but de Valera returned to the issue in drafting the new constitution. This provides for a Presidential Commission which acts in place of the President when he or she is unavailable; it comprises the Ceann Comhairle, the Cathaoirleach and the Chief Justice.

The body that formally advised the crown before 1922, the Irish Privy Council, was replaced by a much smaller Executive Council in the 1922 constitution. As in other dominions, this was required 'to aid and advise in the government of the Irish Free State', but the theoretical distinction between this body and the cabinet turned out to be less clear than in other dominions. In any case, the Executive Council was replaced in 1937 by a new body, the 'government', which, in a break with British constitutional practice, was declared unambiguously to be the holder of executive power. A new advisory body was created in 1937: the Council of State. The Council includes three categories of members. First, two senior representatives of each of the three classical branches of government are included, together with the Attorney General: the Taoiseach and the Tánaiste (executive), the Ceann Comhairle and the Cathaoirleach of the Seanad (legislature), and the Chief Justice and the President of the High Court (judiciary). Second, all former incumbents of certain high offices are entitled to be members, if willing and able: former Presidents, Taoisigh and Chief Justices. Third, the President may appoint up to seven additional members at his or her own discretion. Presidents often use this right to make symbolic gestures by appointing members of various excluded groups (Duffy, 1993: 134). The Council is required to advise the President in a number of contexts mentioned above, though the President is not required to follow its advice. The Council has only one real power, a residual one: to make provision for the exercise of the President's functions in any area not covered by the constitution.

Table 3.7: Office of the Lord Lieutenant of Ireland, Governor-General of the Irish Free State and President of Ireland, selected years, 1795–2013

Post	Lord Lieutenant			Gov.-Gen.		President		
	1795	1880	1922	1925	1935	1940	1995	2013
Comptroller/Secretary	1	1	1	1	–	1	1	1
Chamberlain/Vice-Chamberlain	2	1	–	–	–	–	–	–
Private/personal secretary	1	1	1	1	1	–	1	1
State steward	1	1	1	–	–	–	–	–
Administrative/secretarial staff	–	1	2	4	–	7	12	19
Gentleman Usher/Assistant	2	1	1	–	–	–	–	–
Master of the horse	1	1	1	–	–	–	–	–
Gentlemen of the bedchamber	2	1	–	–	–	–	–	–
Gentlemen at large	4	2	–	–	–	–	–	–
Pages	2	2	–	–	–	–	–	–
Aides-de-camp	6	11	3	3	–	2	4	4
Medical staff	4	4	9	1	–	–	–	–
Advisory staff	–	–	–	–	–	–	1	4
Others	2	4	–	–	1	–	–	–
Total	28	31	19	10	2	10	19	29

Note: Criteria for inclusion vary over time. 'Others' include the Master of the Riding House and the Gentleman Usher of the Black Rod (1795); Ranger of the Curragh of Kildare, Deputy Ranger of the Curragh of Kildare, Queen's Printer and State Porter (1880); chauffeur-bodyguard (1935). Advisory staff are personal contract appointees of the President (3.5 full-time equivalent posts in 2013, when the administrative/secretarial component was 18.5). In addition, there existed a large number of (honorary) chaplains. In the case of aides-de-camp and medical staff, 'ordinary' and 'extraordinary' categories are grouped; medical staff included physicians, surgeons, surgeon-dentists and a surgeon-oculist. Other military personnel, police and household staff (12 full-time plus eight casual and part-time in 2013) are not included, nor are routine clerical grades in the early years. Two other categories listed in 1795 but phased out in the 1830s are omitted: the Battle-Axe Guards (a colonel, captain, two lieutenants, two serjeants and 50 yeomen armed with ceremonial battle-axes), and (2) the State Music (the Master of the Revels, Master and Composer of State Musick, Deputy Master and Director, Attendant at Balls and 25 musicians—a kettle drummer, six trumpeters, seven violins, four bass viols, two each of tenors, oboes and French horns, and one dulcimer). The Office of Arms (the Ulster King of Arms, three Serjeants at Arms, four pursuivants and two heralds), normally grouped with the Lord Lieutenant's staff until 1922, is also excluded. *Source:* Civil list, 1795, in Johnston, 1963: 302–19; *Watson's almanack*, 1794–98; *Thom's directory*, 1880, 1922, 1937; Sexton, 1989: 108–9, 157; information from Áras an Uachtaráin; and other sources.

The President's secretariat also shows some continuity with that of his predecessors in what is now Áras an Uachtaráin, as may be seen in Table 3.7, which looks at the position at eight representative points in time. When the Lord Lieutenant was at his most powerful, his entourage indeed reflected the elevated standing of his office. In 1795, for example, while it is difficult to define precisely where the boundary lay between the Lord Lieutenant's staff and that of other offices in Dublin Castle and elsewhere in the state structure, total expenditure on the Lord Lieutenant's office (narrowly defined) amounted to over £28,000, or 20% of the total civil list (at that time, this referred to all state expenditure excluding that on the military). Of this, by far the biggest portion was the Lord Lieutenant's allowance of £20,000. The rest was spent on four other components: what might be described as the 'core' secretariat (with 28 people in 1795), the Office of Arms (12 people), the Battle-Axe Guards (55 in number), and the State Music and related posts (29 in all). The last two of these components were phased out in the 1830s (Brynn, 1978: 72–3; Robins, 2001: 118). The Office of Arms, with responsibility for matters of heraldry, genealogy and state ceremonial, became freestanding with the disappearance of the Lord Lieutenant in 1922. Strangely, it survived even after 1937, but following the death in 1940 of the last head of the office, the Ulster King of Arms, its days were numbered. In 1943 it was nominally merged with its English counterpart, with the new post of Chief Herald of Ireland then taking responsibility for heraldry and genealogical research in Ireland (Hood, 2002: 160–4).

It is the set of 'core' members of the Lord Lieutenant's staff that most closely resembles the contemporary President's office. Some of its more ornamental officers had disappeared already before 1922: the chamberlain, gentlemen of the bed chamber, gentlemen at large and pages. What remained was the secretariat itself, headed by the Comptroller up to 1932, and from 1938 by the Secretary to the President. The office of State steward did not survive the change of regime in 1922. Other posts—those of aide-de-camp, chaplain, physician and other medical positions—continued, in some cases on an honorary basis.

The President's staff, which includes the household staff responsible for the upkeep of Áras an Uachtaráin as well as the administrative staff, is modest in size by international standards. It is dwarfed by the Queen's household in the United Kingdom, which numbers about 1,200 in all (including 450 funded directly by the exchequer); other royal households are also large, with that of Netherlands amounting to almost 300 people, and that of Denmark to about 130.[16] Of European presidencies in countries comparable in size with Ireland, it is worth noting that the Austrian President's office has at least 80 administrative and advisory staff, that of Estonia at least 42, and that of Croatia at least 29.[17] The office most comparable in size with that of the President of Ireland is perhaps that of the Governor-General of New Zealand, comprising about 25 full-time staff.[18]

Calculating the financial resources available to the President's office is less than straightforward. Expenditure on the office is reported under a number of headings in the state appropriation accounts: the President's salary and emoluments are drawn on the central fund, annual budgetary provision for the President's secretariat is made under its own heading, and other items of expenditure arise under other government departments. These are regrouped in Table 3.8 to give an impression of the overall pattern.

The Lord Lieutenant's allowance was fixed in 1784 at £20,000—an enormous sum at the time—and it was still at this level in 1921, notwithstanding occasional upward and downward adjustments.[19] This figure was halved for the new Governor-General, whose salary was fixed at £10,000; not surprisingly, following de Valera's accession to power and the redefinition of the character of the Governor-General's office the figure was further reduced in 1933: although the statutory sum of £10,000 remained, the Governor-General would accept only £2,000 of this.[20] The Presidential Establishment Act, 1938, fixed the 'emoluments and allowances' payable to the President at £10,000. But only half of this (£5,000) was designated as the 'personal remuneration' of the President, and when the overall figure was increased in 1947 to £11,500, the President's salary remained fixed at £5,000. In 1973 this was linked to the salary of the Chief Justice; it was defined as 10% above this.[21] The President's salary eventually reached €317,869 in 2008, but President McAleese took voluntary reductions in 2009 and 2010, as did President Higgins; ultimately, the salary was reduced to £249,688 in practice in 2012. To this needs to be added the second row in Table 3.8, which covers pensions to former Presidents (including the former Governor-General in 1940) and to their widows.

The third row in Table 3.8 refers to expenses incurred directly by the President and his predecessors. Before 1922 the very substantial sum paid to the Lord Lieutenant was spent mainly on domestic, entertainment and other costs arising directly from the Lord Lieutenant's office. Indeed, only wealthy noblemen could consider accepting appointment to this post, since the expenses of the Lord Lieutenant frequently exceeded his allowance of £20,000; in other words, Lords Lieutenant themselves personally subsidised the office. Although the Governor-General's salary was only half that of the

Lord Lieutenant, he was allocated an extra £3,000 to cover payments to domestic staff and other household costs (this allowance was reduced to £1,200 in 1934). In 1938, a fixed proportion of the President's allowance (50%, or £5,000) was reserved for expenses of this kind, including salaries of household staff. This sum was increased to £6,500 in 1947, and to £15,000 in 1973. This was pitifully inadequate for the large household staff (about 10 in all), who were very badly paid. Shortly after taking office, President Hillery doubled their salaries by himself subsidising them, and in 1977 responsibility for their salaries was transferred to the Office of Public Works. Though relieved of this burden, the President's expense allowance remained at £15,000 until 1991, when it was increased to £100,000, with provision for increase in this sum on the basis of government orders (it was increased to £120,000 in 1997 and to £250,000 in 1998).

Table 3.8: Approximate costs of office of Governor-General of the Irish Free State and President of Ireland, selected years, 1925–2010

Category	Governor-General		President		
	1925–26	1935–36	1940–41	1990	2010
	(£)	(£)	(£)	(£)	(€)
Salary	10,000	2,000	5,000	76,743	260,000
Pensions (related)	0	0	500	61,372	488,000
Expenses (inc. household)	3,000	1,200	5,000	15,000	320,000
Administrative salaries	2,834	372	4,166	270,643	2,003,000
Administrative expenses	1,177	414	662	80,095	351,000
Buildings and maintenance	10,615	0	4,650	178,000	1,908,000
Other	0	190	0	12,750	1,967,000
Total	27,626	4,176	19,978	694,603	7,297,000
% of public service appropriations	0.118	0.016	0.061	0.011	0.016

Note: 'Pensions' refer to former Presidents and widows of former Presidents; 'Expenses' includes the salaries of household staff in Áras an Uachtaráin in the first three columns; 'Administrative salaries' includes staff salaries and pay and allowances of aides-de-camp; 'Buildings and maintenance' refers to the Office of Public Works, and includes salaries of household staff in the last two columns; 'Other' includes the centenarians' bounty (a payment to people born in Ireland who reach the age of 100 years) and expenditure under the headings of the Garda Síochána and Foreign Affairs. *Source:* Appropriation accounts, relevant years; relevant statutes and statutory instruments; information from Áras an Uachtaráin.

The remaining rows in Table 3.8 refer to the expenses of the presidential office itself, including salaries and wages, travel and incidental expenses, and normal office costs. Maintenance of Áras an Uachtaráin (and, since 1977, payment of household staff) is carried out by the Office of Public Works. The house is not large by the standard of other presidential or royal palaces in Europe, resulting in modest expenditure for its upkeep and for the hosting of state events.

Overall, the cost of the President's establishment is modest. The bottom row of Table 3.8 expresses total expenditure on the office as a percentage of overall public expenditure. In 1795, as mentioned above, the Lord Lieutenant's establishment accounted for 20% of all non-military expenditure. This proportion declined steadily as other areas of public expenditure expanded. By 1925, the Governor-General's establishment accounted for 0.118% of all public expenditure. In 1940, the President's establishment accounted for half of this proportionally; by 2010, notwithstanding a big expansion in the role and cost of the office in the 1990s, it was only 0.016% of the total. The €7.5m that the office cost in that year compares with a reported £38m cost for the British monarchy in 2010 (though other estimates place the true cost of the monarchy at £202m[22]). Overall, it is lower than the cost of the presidency in Germany (€31m) and of the monarchy in such relatively small countries as the Netherlands (€35m), Norway (€25m), Belgium and Sweden (€14m each), Denmark (€13m) and Luxembourg (€9m), though the data for some of these countries are far from transparent (Matthijs, 2012). It is rather higher than the cost of the office of Governor-General of New Zealand (in 2011, NZD5.2m, or €3.3m), though strict comparison is almost impossible.[23]

THE EXERCISE OF PRESIDENTIAL FUNCTIONS

The manner in which the office of President of Ireland has functioned in practice has been in large measure determined by the personalities of the incumbents, and by the political context within which they operated. Of course, the provisions of the constitution provided a framework for this; but the manner in which this was interpreted varied over time, and from President to President. The current section looks first at the occupants of Áras an Uachtaráin, and then summarises the manner in which these individuals have left their imprint on the various presidential functions.

Nine presidents

Many observers have been struck by a sharp change in the role of the President of Ireland that took place in 1990. Prior to that date, it has been argued, the President had been a relatively aloof figure, seeking to remain entirely outside political controversy and confined to largely ceremonial functions. This was outstandingly true of the first three presidents, Douglas Hyde (1938–45), Sean T. O'Kelly (1945–59) and Eamon de Valera (1959–73). President Hyde entered office as an agreed candidate, without election, and his reputation was that of a scholar rather than a politician (Dunleavy and Dunleavy, 1991). As a Protestant with a passionate interest in the Irish language, he filled an important bridge-building role. President O'Kelly, though elected in a hard-fought three-cornered contest in 1945, and, notwithstanding his own Fianna Fáil background, consciously sought to build bridges between the two main parties that had been generated by the civil war, and successfully avoided political controversy (Meehan, 2012: 567–8). President de Valera, a pre-eminent symbol of the anti-treaty side, fought a tough battle with Fine Gael to win election in 1959 and re-election in 1966. He was a potentially more divisive figure, but made a sharp transition from the powerful office of Taoiseach to the more unobtrusive one of President, an office for whose restricted powers he was himself responsible (Meehan, 2012: 572–3).

The election of Erskine Childers in 1973 as Ireland's fourth President (again, after a hard-fought battle with Fine Gael) brought with it a promise of activism and of efforts to expand the boundaries of the office. But despite an energetic social programme, the new President found it difficult to shape the office in the manner he wished, and impossible to realise his campaign promise to create a 'think tank' that would consider issues of broad national significance (Young, 1985). This was blocked by Liam Cosgrave's Fine Gael–Labour coalition; President Childers came close to resigning over the matter, but was dissuaded by Garret FitzGerald (FitzGerald, 1992: 254). Cosgrave's attitude to the office was demonstrated more explicitly during the presidency of Cearbhall Ó Dálaigh, an agreed candidate with a Fianna Fáil background who succeeded Childers following his sudden death in 1974. After an incident during which the Minister for Defence publicly and crudely rebuked the President for having earlier referred the Emergency Powers Bill, 1976, to the Supreme Court, Cosgrave refused to accept the Minister's resignation. This apparent failure by the head of government to appreciate the seriousness of an insult of this kind to the President by a member of his cabinet caused the President to resign instead (Gallagher, 1977), but it is worth noting that the President had earlier considered resignation in protest against the Supreme

Court's finding that the same bill was constitutional (Gallagher, 2012: 532). The new President, Patrick Hillery (1976–1990), though himself a former Fianna Fáil minister, entered office following cross-party agreement, and sought to conduct the presidency in a firmly nonpartisan and, indeed, non-political way (Rafter, 2012: 590–3; Walsh, 2008: 427–518).

After the relatively quiet years of the Hillery presidency, the office of President became much more prominent under Mary Robinson (1990–97), whose vision of the office extended well outside that of most of her predecessors. As she put it shortly before her election:

> The only restrictions on the office of presidency are when the President is carrying out official powers and functions … However—and it's a big however—there is no constitutional restraint on what I do outside of those official functions. As a President directly elected by the people of Ireland, I will have the most democratic job in the country. I'll be able to look Charlie Haughey in the eye and tell him to back off if necessary because I have been directly elected by the people as a whole and he hasn't.[24]

This perspective was all the more important given Mary Robinson's status as a constitutional lawyer, and she went on to deliver on her promise, acting with notable independence in areas where she was not explicitly constrained by constitutional considerations. This model of a more assertive presidency was followed also by her successor, Mary McAleese (1997–2011). It has been argued that these two women Presidents 'brought a fresh energy to what had become a staid office' (Galligan, 2012: 610). This new vision of the presidency appears to be shared, too, by their successor, Michael D. Higgins, who has been notably outspoken in commenting on contemporary social and political issues.

The presidency in the 2010s has, then, changed greatly since the 1930s. Part of the difference arises from the extended range of the presidential office, with the conferring on the President of functions in the area of international affairs in 1949. But the personalities of the incumbents of Áras an Uachtaráin, the political context within which they operated and the nature of their relationships with the government also served to bring about a steady transformation in the character of the office. The electoral system also left its mark: before 1990, uncontested returns had been more common than elections, but each president since then has enjoyed the mandate of having won in a tough electoral battle.

The President and politics

As we have seen above, the Irish President in practice has few discretionary powers. There are some, such as the right to convene a meeting of the Oireachtas, which the President can exercise relatively freely, but they are of themselves of little consequence (this one has never been used). There are others, such as the right to refer a bill to the people, that are of greater political significance, but can be exercised only if the President is invited to do so by some other body (in this case, the Seanad; but such an invitation has never been issued). There are only two constitutional powers that give the President a significant political role in practice: the right to refer bills to the Supreme Court, and the right to withhold a dissolution from a Taoiseach who has lost the confidence of the Dáil. In addition to these constitutional powers, though, two other arenas of presidential activity need to be explored: the more indirect capacity of the President to exercise political influence, and the broad social and symbolic role of the office. Finally, the capacity of the government to restrict the President's freedom of action needs to be considered.

Referral of bills to the Supreme Court

The most visible and widely used of the President's powers is that of referring a bill to the Supreme Court to test its constitutionality. In all, presidents have exercised this power on 15 occasions, with the Supreme Court finding the bill incompatible with the constitution on seven occasions and clearing it on the remaining eight (Gallagher, 2012: 529–32). Governments did not necessarily always find such referrals entirely unwelcome: referral puts a statute beyond future dispute, since once a bill has been referred in this way and cleared by the Supreme Court, its constitutionality can never again be challenged (art. 34.3.3º). But there have also been occasions where the government has been annoyed at the President's action, and one, in 1976, where the government's irritation was so intense that the resignation of the President was ultimately forced, as discussed above.

Withholding a dissolution of the Dáil

Although the President's other main constitutional power, that of withholding a dissolution to a Taoiseach who has lost the confidence of the Dáil, has never been used, it appears to have influenced the course of events on several occasions. In the Irish Free State, it was the Executive Council (not its President) that had the right to seek an early dissolution; but the Governor-General had no discretion. He was obliged to grant a dissolution if the government enjoyed the confidence of the Dáil, and was precluded from doing so otherwise. Thus, when Fianna Fáil abandoned its policy of abstention and took its seats in the Dáil shortly after the June 1927 general election, the political arithmetic was transformed. A vote of no confidence in the government was defeated on the casting vote of the Ceann Comhairle, so the government was able to call a general election and strengthen its position. Had the confidence vote been lost, a general election could not have been held, and a minority Labour–National League coalition with support from Fianna Fáil would have been the most likely outcome (O'Sullivan, 1940: 219–20). In a second little-known example, on 27 March 1930 the government was defeated 66–64 on the Old Age Pensions Bill introduced by the Fianna Fáil opposition. President Cosgrave resigned, but the calling of an election was impossible; instead, on 2 April the Dáil gave Cosgrave a mandate to form a new government.[25]

It is clear from the debate on the draft constitution in 1937 that de Valera was trying to broaden the options for a defeated Taoiseach by opening a door that up to then had been closed—the calling of an election.[26] Since 1937, six occasions could be identified on which a defeated Taoiseach requested a dissolution; on each occasion, this was granted (on the first and last of these occasions, by the Presidential Commission).

- On 26 May 1938, the government was defeated 51–50 on an opposition resolution calling for the introduction of an arbitration system to deal with civil service disputes; de Valera requested a dissolution the following day.
- On 9 May 1944, the government was defeated 64–63 on the second stage of the Transport Bill, 1944; de Valera requested a dissolution the following day.
- On 27 January 1982, the government was defeated 82–81 on a clause of the budget; FitzGerald immediately requested a dissolution.
- On 4 November 1982, the government was defeated 82–80 on a motion of confidence; Haughey immediately requested a dissolution.
- On 26 April 1989, the government was defeated 72–59 on an opposition resolution calling for assistance for AIDS sufferers, the sixth such defeat since the formation of the government; this was seen as causing the Taoiseach, Charles Haughey, to seek a dissolution on 25 May.
- On 5 November 1992, the government was defeated 88–77 on a motion of confidence (the Fianna Fáil–Progressive Democrat coalition had broken up); Reynolds immediately requested a dissolution.

It has been argued that assessing whether or not the Taoiseach has lost the confidence of the Dáil does not necessarily require defeat in a confidence vote, but that 'by reason of developments inside and outside the House, it is clear that the Taoiseach has lost his majority' (Hogan, 1989). On three occasions (twice in 1982, and in 1992), the government had clearly lost the confidence of the Dáil, so the ultimate decision was the President's; but on two of these (November 1982, and 1992) the defeated Taoiseach used a form of language that implied that the granting of a dissolution was inevitable.[27] Successive Presidents seemed reluctant to contemplate use of this power. Even de Valera reportedly adopted a very cautious view as to whether a dissolution should be withheld from a defeated Taoiseach: 'it would be a very foolish President who would do that' (Walsh, 2008: 473). This view was shared by President Hillery, who felt that the constitution barred the President from involvement in any discussion on the formation of an alternative government, that the President should not 'intervene' as this 'would create a political crisis rather than solving one', and that it was therefore 'of the first importance not to consult or discuss with anyone', as this would draw the President into party politics (Walsh, 2008: 475).

Notwithstanding the overt evidence, it is clear that the President retains considerable discretion. Fianna Fáil leader Charles Haughey sought to exploit this in January 1982 following the FitzGerald government's defeat, when he not only offered to make himself available for consultation with the President, but brought inappropriate pressure to bear on him, encouraging phone calls to the Áras from colleagues and ultimately seeking to insist on an immediate meeting with the President (Walsh, 2008: 477–8). President Hillery resisted this pressure and sought to protect his staff against possible retribution. In 1987, however, President Hillery and the outgoing Taoiseach, Garret FitzGerald, discussed various government formation options in some detail (Walsh, 2008: 493–4), suggesting that the President need not remain entirely aloof from the process. Mary Robinson's energetic redefinition of the presidency extended to this area too: when the Labour Party withdrew from its coalition with Fianna Fáil in 1994, she let it be known by certain gestures that the Taoiseach, Albert Reynolds, could not assume that a dissolution would be granted automatically. In these circumstances, the Taoiseach did not risk rejection, and his government was replaced, without a general election, by a Fine Gael–Labour–Democratic Left coalition (Gallagher, 2012: 529).

To what extent may the President be more proactive than simply withholding a dissolution? Refusal to dissolve would no doubt be based on a President's informed understanding of the position in the Dáil, reinforced by contact with politicians there. Following criticism of President Hillery's decision in November 1982 to dissolve the Dáil for a third time in 18 months (Coakley, 1982), an *Irish Times* editorial (17 November) suggested that the President could go further, inviting the leader of the opposition, or some other politician, to form a government. Constitutional lawyers have, however, reacted negatively to this proposal. Unlike heads of state elsewhere, from this perspective, the Irish President has 'no constitutional authority' to do this (Forde, 1987: 107), the view that he can do so is 'quite inaccurate' (Casey, 1992: 80), or a 'misconception' without any basis in the constitution, and a President acting in this manner might be exposed to the charge of having acted outside his or her powers (Kelly et al., 2003: 209). This restrictive interpretation is discussed further in the next section.

Presidential influence

Early presidents undoubtedly accepted a narrow interpretation of their role, which one cabinet minister described as 'little more than shaking hands with visiting golfers' (Siggins, 1997: 14). President Hillery, before agreeing to be nominated for the post, described the President as 'a prisoner in the Phoenix Park' (Walsh, 2008: 418). But subtle presidential interventions in politics were not unknown. President O'Kelly planned a meeting between members of the government and of the Irish Catholic episcopate in 1953 in an effort to resolve differences over the Health Bill inherited from Noel Browne; and de Valera in 1969 succeeded in delaying Kevin Boland's resignation as minister (Duffy, 1990: part 2).

After the accession of Mary Robinson in 1990, a more assertive, quasi-political presidential role emerged. This was reflected in well-publicised statements on political matters, typically reflecting consensual values. On some occasions, though, the President was accused of stepping outside the consensus. This was alleged in respect of Mary Robinson's rather unspecific remarks about the 'X' abortion case in 1992 (Horgan, 1997: 171–3), her comments in Japan in 1995 showing some sympathy for the unionist position in respect of the British–Irish Framework Documents of that year (Horgan, 1997: 182–3), and apparent support for the 'yes' side in the 1995 divorce referendum (Siggins, 1997: 181–3). A leading constitutional lawyer argued that the President 'plainly transgressed' on the last of these occasions (Morgan, 1999). President Robinson, however, proved herself capable of confronting and annoying governments even more effectively without opening her mouth: by meeting the Dalai Lama in Dublin in 1991, against the initially determined opposition of Taoiseach Charles Haughey; by visiting

West Belfast and shaking hands with Gerry Adams in 1993, before the IRA ceasefire; and by simply attending mass in Gort during serious flooding in 1995, thereby hinting at government inactivity (O'Leary and Burke, 1998: 154–6, 207–16, 233). The most significant of these events was the West Belfast visit, which Foreign Minister Dick Spring saw as conflicting with government policy; but the Taoiseach was not prepared to block this trip to Northern Ireland, professing to see 'no reason to be concerned' (Reynolds, 2009: 263).

Symbolic role

This willingness to offer an independent voice on policy matters, one that substantially remained within the boundaries of wide political acceptability, undoubtedly helped to enhance the status of the President since 1990. But Irish Presidents, like heads of state elsewhere, also play a wider societal role, notably in symbolising and promoting national unity. For Douglas Hyde, this meant acknowledging the importance of the Protestant tradition as well as the Catholic one, promoting the Irish language alongside English, and supporting such sports as soccer as well as Gaelic games, though he was removed from his position as patron of the Gaelic Athletic Association in 1938 over attending a soccer international (Ó Glaisne, 1993: 616–18). Sean T. O'Kelly consciously sought to bridge the gap between the two main 'civil war' parties, as we have seen. Erskine Childers hosted private visits to Áras an Uachtaráin by former Northern Ireland prime minister Terence O'Neill in 1973 and 1974 (O'Neill's grandfather had lived there while Lord Lieutenant in 1892–95), and became the first president to greet a member of the British royal family in 1974, when he met Lord Mountbatten in Sligo (Young, 1985: 192, 200).

This representative role was to expand remarkably after 1990, especially as regards Ireland's closest neighbours. The traditional position has been described as one where the President was 'retained in a time-warp'; while government ministers could travel freely to Britain and Northern Ireland, 'the head of state was expected to stay at home and radiate disapproval, an official nationalist skeleton which could be rattled whenever the British got too complacent' (O'Leary and Burke, 1998: 175). Mary Robinson broke this taboo: in all, she made 15 visits to Britain (Siggins, 1997: 217), including a private visit to the Queen in 1993 and an official visit in 1995, as well as a number of meetings with other members of the royal family. This was continued by Mary McAleese, whose term concluded with a historic state visit to Ireland by Queen Elizabeth II in 2011.

Visits to Northern Ireland also became commonplace: Mary Robinson made the first-ever official visit there in 1992, and in all visited Northern

Ireland on 18 occasions. These visits resulted in a certain level of unionist disquiet, and a request from the British Foreign Office that they be more closely controlled, and restricted to no more than three per year (O'Leary and Burke, 1998: 216–18). The formal standing of the visits was as unclear as was the status of Northern Ireland in the Irish constitution, but following the Good Friday agreement of 1998 they were unambiguously visits to another state. President McAleese, both directly and through the work of her husband Martin, played an important role in establishing channels of communication with both communities in Northern Ireland, to which she had made 97 official visits by 2008 (McGarry, 2008: 241). Important symbolic gestures were made by both presidents also towards minority groups within Ireland, and towards Irish emigrant communities abroad.

Restrictions

Notwithstanding the new, proactive role of Irish presidents, the government possesses formidable resources that can be used to keep a President in check. The first is control over the President's secretariat. The Presidential Establishment Act, 1938, made clear the extent of the Government's role in Áras an Uachtaráin: the President's secretary (now, secretary-general) is a civil servant appointed by the Government (though normally after consultation with the President), and the other staff are also appointed by the Government, on conditions determined by the Minister for Finance. Simply restricting the size and budget of the President's office limits the role of the President. This was a source of continuing frustration to President Hillery, who, in an increasingly media-conscious age, had no press officer and had generally inadequate resources (Walsh, 2008: 430–2, 490). He was, however, able to secure the appointment of a secretary of his own choice, over the preferred government nominee.[28] Mary Robinson also secured replacement of the secretary by someone of her own choosing (O'Leary and Burke, 1998: 150–1). Her new broom extended to other employees, including the 10 members of the household staff, whose role in the Áras was brought to an end amid some controversy (Horgan, 1997: 168).

In the first five decades, the civil service kept a tight rein on the President, taking 'a very restrictive view of the office' (Horgan, 1997: 164). Invitations to the President were filtered by civil servants, and the President's speeches were vetted and approved before delivery (Young, 1985: 190). The outcome was that the typical early Irish president was 'a political Trappist, silent on any matter that could conceivably be thought of as political' (Chubb, 1978: 28). In this, civil servants may well have been exceeding their authority; the right of the government to approve the President's speeches appears to have 'no basis in law' (Duffy, 1990, part 1). Here, once again, 1990 proved to be a pivotal year. In addition to securing additional resources for the office (including appointment of a special adviser), President Robinson asserted her right to speak freely, without government approval. She won a signal victory over Charles Haughey in the course of one meeting at which he produced opinions from two former Attorneys General to the effect that all presidential statements are covered by the blanket provision in respect of addresses to the nation, which require government approval. As a constitutional lawyer, she was able to argue to the contrary, leaving Haughey with little room to fight back (Siggins, 1997: 159).

Governments have also been prepared to use the eccentric provision that the President may not leave the state without permission as a way of restricting presidential freedom of action. Thus, a Costello-led coalition government refused to allow President O'Kelly to make a state visit to the USA (Duffy, 1990: part 2), though a Fianna Fáil government later permitted this; Haughey prevented President Hillery from travelling to Armagh for the inauguration of Archbishop Armstrong in 1980 (Walsh, 2008: 466), and he refused President Robinson permission to travel to London to deliver the Dimbleby lecture in 1991 (Horgan, 1997: 170–1). Unlike the potential implications of an invitation to the wedding of the Prince of Wales in 1981, none of these occasions entailed any politically controversial words or actions on the part of the President, and the rationale for preventing the President from travelling was unclear.

The subordinate role of the President before 1990 was also influenced by the position taken by the Taoiseach of the day. It is likely that de Valera and his successors as Taoiseach saw themselves, in varying degrees, as competing with the more formally prestigious office of President. The practice of monthly visits to Áras an Uachtaráin by the Taoiseach to 'keep the President generally informed on matters of domestic and international policy', as the constitution puts it, followed the pattern of the weekly visits of the British Prime Minister to the Queen. Already by the 1950s, John A. Costello's briefings of the President were, in his own words, 'ten-minute chats' (Duffy, 1993: 158). Taoiseach Jack Lynch visited the Áras infrequently in the 1970s, and during the two-year term of office of President Ó Dálaigh, the Taoiseach, Liam Cosgrave, visited him on only four occasions, for meetings that the President described as 'bright, breezy, chatty, but carefully non-communicative on policy matters' (Rafter, 2012: 585). It has been said of Liam Cosgrave that he apparently 'did not understand the constitution' (Duffy,

1990: part 3). If he did understand it, he chose not to comply with its requirement that he keep the President 'generally informed' on policy matters. For
Charles Haughey, by contrast, the tension arose apparently from his own self-
image. In one view, he saw the President as 'a potential competitor, who might
detract from the position of the Taoiseach' (Walsh, 2008: 465). It has been
argued that Haughey, with his 'imperial' lifestyle, 'saw himself as the real
President of Ireland' (O'Leary and Burke, 1998: 147). He resolved potential
clashes with the President by preventing President Hillery from accepting
invitations to events that he proposed to attend himself; but in the face of
Mary Robinson's refusal to accept such 'guidance', the only way to maintain
his own presidential pretensions was to remain away from events that she
proposed to attend (Horgan, 1997: 169).

ASSESSING THE PRESIDENCY

A comprehensive study of the Irish presidency by Jim Duffy (1993: 177)
described the office of President of Ireland as 'inherently unsatisfactory'; he
saw it as 'a decorative feature created by de Valera to symbolise his break with
British constitutional theory and the monarchy, but which never had a clear-
cut role to play in the eyes of the people of Ireland or their politicians'. The
20 years since these words were written have seen a profound transformation
in the role of the Irish presidency, one that may be traced back to 1990. It is
worth reviewing these changes and the debate about the role of the
presidency that they have generated, before looking at constitutional options
for this office.

The debate on the presidency

Conventional political science texts tend to identify a single or composite
institution corresponding to the executive function in the modern state, and
to largely ignore ceremonial office holders. For example, a leading British text
on comparative politics (Hague and Harrop, 2008: 333–4) presents the head
of state in parliamentary democracies as a harmless though occasionally useful
ceremonial figure who brings a dimension of dignity to the work of the real
or effective government headed by the prime minister. The most influential
names in American studies of comparative politics (Almond, Powell and
Mundt, 1996: 143–4) similarly relegate the ceremonial head of state in
parliamentary democracies to a position as symbolic appendage to the
effective executive, even though their theoretical framework leaves space for a
central role for this office (in respect of the legitimacy of the political system).

In assessing the Irish presidency, it is useful to recall the old distinction between the 'dignified' parts of a constitution, 'those which excite and preserve the reverence of the population', and its 'effective' parts, 'those by which it, in fact, works and rules' (Bagehot, 1928 [1872]: 3–4). This distinction is usually used to explain the significance of the prime-ministerial position; but the importance that Bagehot attributed to the 'dignified' component is frequently overlooked. The Irish President plays an important role that is not encoded in the constitution by acting as a national symbol and as a non-political voice (Duffy, 1993: 177). It is no doubt the discharge of such functions that is responsible for the extremely high levels of reported satisfaction with the President in opinion polls—an outcome that both firewalls the presidency against political attack and creates the space in which it can play a creative role, even if that is difficult to define.

Jim Duffy has made a perceptive distinction between two models of ceremonial head of state: the 'nominal chief executive', such as the British Queen or Commonwealth Governor-General, who is officially head of the executive and thus must be formally involved in all aspects of government activity, and the 'non-executive head of state', such as the President of Ireland, who is formally separate from the government, in which executive power is unambiguously vested by the constitution (Duffy, 1993: 133, 154). This distinction has important implications for the President's freedom of speech—strictly curtailed in the former model, since the head of state always speaks on behalf of the government, but to be interpreted pragmatically in the latter model. This is not to argue that the President's pronouncements should be unconstrained; as it has been appropriately put, aside from addresses to the nation or to the Oireachtas, 'there is a blank cheque—not entirely blank, perhaps, because it is limited by the understanding that the President should never be involved in political controversy of any partisan kind and by a general sense of constitutional good manners' (Horgan, 1997: 170).

In this context, the provision requiring government consent for travel outside the state seems anachronistic. It may have made sense for earlier British kings to prevent their Irish lords lieutenant from simply appointing a deputy to discharge their duties in Ireland, and for ensuring their presence to deal with unexpected developments such as rebellion, or to force colonial governors-general to take up residence in the territories to which they were appointed; but the point of giving the government a veto is less clear when it comes to President Hyde taking his dying daughter abroad, President Hillery sailing outside Irish territorial waters in his yacht, or President McAleese visiting her family in Northern Ireland (see Duffy, 1993: 131–2).

When we consider the substantive and not just the formal powers of the President, we encounter a grey area. Constitutional lawyers tend to take a conservative position on the extent of the President's powers in areas where the constitution is silent. Thus, Michael Mee (1996a) argued that 'unless a power or function has been conferred by the Constitution or by legislation the President cannot perform it'. The detail in which the constitution spells out the President's functions has been interpreted as an indication that 'the President has no implied powers' (Hogan, 1989), and that 'there can be no room for implying any additional powers' (Casey: 1992: 81).

From a comparative political perspective, it is difficult to defend these judgements: presidents and other office holders throughout the world regularly act in areas where the constitution is silent, or act in (at least) implicit violation of constitutional provisions. Even from a legal perspective, it is appropriate to see all constitutions as having an 'unwritten' component, of varying levels of importance, alongside the written text, rather than to follow the dichotomous distinction between written and unwritten constitutions.[29] In several older monarchical constitutions, although the formal position of the head of state is extremely powerful, there is an expectation that the monarch will not exercise these powers independently. But the hazards of 'unwritten' norms are clear. An outstanding example is provided by the Australian experience of 1975: Governor-General Kerr dismissed Prime Minister Whitlam using his enormous powers under the written constitution, but a constitutional crisis was provoked by the fact that under an unwritten constitutional understanding the Governor-General had no such power in respect of a prime minister who retained the confidence of the House of Representatives, and was expected to act in the same manner as the Queen in the United Kingdom (Archer and Maddox, 1976; Galligan, 1980).

In the Irish case, it could be argued that the reality of direct election implies that the President would have considerable discretionary capacity; as de Valera put it, 'nobody would propose getting the whole people to elect a person unless it was proposed to give him substantial powers'.[30] In any case, as in other countries, it is not clear what could be done if the President were to act in areas in which the constitution is silent, or even in areas where a particular function is specifically withheld, or given to another institution of the state. The weapon of impeachment is of course available for 'stated misbehaviour', but requires in effect a two-thirds majority in the Dáil and the Seanad, and in any case would normally be justified only by reference to some kind of serious criminal activity or clearly unconstitutional behaviour. Furthermore, the constitution states that the President is not answerable to any other state institution, including the courts, for 'any act done *or purporting to be done* by him' (emphasis added) in connection with the powers and functions of the office—a far-reaching provision.

This suggests that the power of the President in the main area where this has been disputed—the right to withhold a dissolution requested by a Taoiseach who has lost the confidence of the Dáil—is considerable, and flexible. Its significance is likely to depend on political perspectives, of which we may identify two ideal types. In the case of the set of three elections that took place in quick succession in June 1981, February 1982 and November 1982, the first perspective (which might be labelled the traditional 'Westminster' one) would identify the problem as lying in Ireland's proportional electoral system, which typically prevents the largest party from winning an overall majority. Instead, it results (as in June 1981 and February 1982) in a 'hung' parliament, with no party capable of forming a government on its own, and the only available coalition (a Fine Gael–Labour one) also falling short. The solution—short of changing the electoral system—is to get the people to vote again. Indeed, the logic of this view is that a sequence of elections should be held until the people 'get it right' by producing a winner, and the President should be prepared to grant dissolutions as often as it takes.

The second (broader European) perspective would suggest that in these circumstances it is not the people but the politicians who constitute the obstacle to governmental stability. The people spoke in June 1981, by indicating their relative support for three parties whose policy positions were quite close to each other. It is then up to the parties to work with the existing political arithmetic and do whatever deals are necessary, rather than introducing artificial constraints on coalition formation (such as Fianna Fáil ruling out coalition with any other party, and Fine Gael and Labour in any case refusing to do a deal with Fianna Fáil). In these circumstances, there are strong arguments in favour of the President's not granting a dissolution, and shifting responsibility back to the parties to come to an agreement—as his predecessor, the Governor-General, would have been forced to do.

Constitutional options

The office of President has been examined in some detail in the various constitutional reviews. The Committee on the Constitution (1967: 8) presented arguments for and against retaining the office, but later reports by implication accepted its value. The main recommendations on specific points were as follows.

- Reduce the age of eligibility from 35 to 18 years (All-Party Oireachtas Committee on the Constitution, 1998: 12); the Convention on the Constitution (2013a) voted narrowly (50 to 47, with three abstentions) in favour of reducing the age.
- Eliminate the right of former presidents to self-nominate as candidates (Committee on the Constitution, 1967: 11).
- Grant the right of nomination of candidates to 10 members of the Oireachtas, or 10,000 registered electors (All-party Oireachtas Committee on the Constitution, 1998: 9); the Convention on the Constitution (2013a) voted strongly in favour of giving citizens a say in the nomination process (94 to 6).
- Reduce the President's discretion by ensuring that a Taoiseach could only be deposed by a 'constructive' vote of no-confidence, which would designate a successor (Constitution Review Group, 1996: 31–3).
- Reduce the President's discretion by linking the right to dissolve the Dáil to different ways in which the Taoiseach might lose the confidence of the Dáil (All-party Oireachtas Committee on the Constitution, 1997a: 53–6).
- Give the President the right to confer titles of honour (All-party Oireachtas Committee on the Constitution, 1998: 12).

Other suggestions that have drawn active or passive agreement include rectifying such technical defects as the inaccurate description of the electoral system as 'proportional representation', and the inconsistency in the English version of the constitution which specifies 34 as the age for eligibility. The Constitution Review Group (1996: 28–9) considered arguments for scrapping direct election in favour of election by the Oireachtas, but was divided on the issue. The Convention on the Constitution (2013a) was asked to consider whether the presidential term should be reduced to five years, but voted 57–43 against this. The electoral system itself seems to be widely accepted, even if the rest of the world is out of step with Ireland in using the two-ballot rather than the alternative vote system (bringing people to the polls to vote not once but twice, the norm in countries with an elected president, looks like an extravagant investment, especially in countries where the president has few powers).

There are several ways in which the future role of the President might be modified. The description of the office could be amended by constitutional change; it could be adjusted, as regards ceremonial functions, by law; and it could be altered less formally, through actions of the President or of those with whom the President interacts (Mee, 1996b). Even without constitutional change, there is a case for recognising the exceptional role—perhaps even a proactive one—that a president may play when a defeated Taoiseach seeks to call a general election, for accepting the right of the President to speak more freely on policy matters (subject to commonsense restrictions), and for acknowledging the power that lies in the hands of the President when a government wishes to have a bill signed urgently. With or without reform, it appears that the office remains largely unchallenged as a centrepiece of Ireland's constitutional system.

CONCLUSION

The office of President of Ireland, once written off as largely a rubber-stamping one, was transformed by President Robinson through her assertion of the President's right to speak without government approval, and through her implicit revival of the power to withhold a dissolution of the Dáil to a Taoiseach who had lost its confidence. It may be that further implicit powers lie in the presidency. For example, the President was presumably kept informed on the issue of the Irish Bank Resolution Corporation Bill, 2013, which passed all stages in the Dáil and Seanad on the night of 6 February 2013. Given the urgency of the bill (which, the government argued, needed to be enacted before business opened the next morning), it was subject to an 'early signature' motion in the Seanad—a government request, endorsed by the Seanad, that the President sign the bill before the constitutionally mandated expiry of five days. Since the President has discretion in such cases, the government would be exposing itself to a charge of gross recklessness were it to fail to keep the President fully informed of the relevant circumstances, and to persuade him or her of the need to go along with the proposed course of action. Thus, while regular visits by the Taoiseach to the President continue to be a constitutional requirement, they appear also now to be a political necessity. Given the obvious need for policy coherence and the independent perspective of the President, maintaining distance between Merrion Street and Áras an Uachtaráin risks not just isolating the President but also compromising government policy. Even without constitutional reform, then, the office of President of Ireland contains considerable potential for development and for a creative role within the political system.

NOTES

1. An earlier version of some of this material appeared in Coakley (1998).

2. The term 'semi-presidential' is used here in Duverger's original sense, and as understood in mainstream comparative politics texts. As Hague and Harrop (2008: 334) define it, 'semi-presidential government, or the dual executive, combines an elected president performing political tasks with a prime minister who heads a cabinet accountable to parliament. The prime minister, usually appointed by the president, is responsible for day-to-day domestic government but the president retains an oversight role, responsibility for foreign affairs and can usually take emergency powers.' Derbyshire and Derbyshire (1996: 39–51) also use three major categories, 'parliamentary', 'dual' and 'limited presidential', but define these rather differently, and they identify a further four categories ('communist', 'unlimited presidential', 'military' and 'absolute' executives). Some other scholars, notably Elgie (1999, 2011, 2012), use 'semi-presidential' to refer simply to countries headed by a president who is directly elected.

3. This and much of the later comparative analysis in this section relies on an important comparative dataset developed by Zachary Elkins and Tom Ginsburg, the Comparative Constitutions Project; see www.comparative constitutions project.org [accessed 2 May 2013].

4. Examples include the King or paramount ruler of Malaysia, elected from among their number by the hereditary rulers of nine Malaysian states; the King of Cambodia, elected from members of the royal family by a seven-member Throne Council; and the President of the United Arab Emirates, selected from among their number by the traditional rulers of the component emirates. In practice, the last position has been held by the Emir of Abu Dhabi since the creation of the federation in 1971. This resembles the pattern in respect of the Holy Roman Emperor, selected by a handful of constitutionally defined 'electors' until the empire's demise in 1806: the post was monopolised by the Austrian Habsburg dynasty in its latter years.

5. In Finland vote-trading and negotiation in the electoral college were common, but in the USA, with its two-party system, whoever won a plurality of the popular vote almost always became president. In three cases (1876, 1888 and 2000), the defeated candidate had won in the popular vote, while in 1824 the electoral college was more deeply divided and the candidate ranked second in the popular vote was selected by the House of Representatives. For full results of electoral college votes in all elections, see www.archives.gov/federal-register/electoral-college/votes/index.html [accessed 2 May 2013].

6. Based on the Comparative Constitutions Project (www.comparative constitutionsproject.org). The distribution of presidential election systems is

discussed in Blais, Massicotte and Dobrzynska (1997); for an assessment of the various systems, see Dummett (1997).

7. For background information and collections of relevant texts, see Keogh and McCarthy (2007) and Hogan (2012b).

8. Jim Duffy (1993: 136) points out that the restrictive nomination process prevented small, extremist groups from using a presidential election campaign as a mechanism for advancing their cause, a not unimportant consideration in the Europe of the late 1930s.

9. The President's functions were first outlined systematically in McDunphy (1945), and are reviewed in Gallagher (1988, 1999, 2012), and in an important study by Jim Duffy (1993); they are discussed in detail in a range of constitutional law texts, including Kelly et al. (2003: 193–228), Doolan (1984: 36–46), Forde (1987: 100–111), Casey (1992: 67–84), Morgan (1985: 46–53) and Ryan (2008: 55–62).

10. Several hundred early signature motions have been presented since 1938; there have been no reports of a president refusing to comply.

11. In the event, the King was able to salvage his conscience by use of an unusual constitutional device: parliament declared the throne vacant, due to the King's incapacity to govern; the government (designated by the constitution as entitled to replace the King in such circumstances) ratified the bill; and on the following day parliament declared Baudouin once again fit to govern (Charlier, 1991).

12. *Dáil Debates*, 9 June 1937, vol. 68, col. 133.

13. In Canada, the letters patent of 1947 warned that 'whereas great prejudice may happen to Our Service and to the security of Canada by the absence of Our Governor General, he shall not quit Canada without having first obtained leave from Us for so doing through the Prime Minister of Canada' (*Canada Gazette*, *Extra* 81 (12), 1 October 1947). In New Zealand, the original letters patent of 1917 contained a similar prohibition, but this was relaxed in 1983 and abolished in 2006 (information from Mr Antony Paltridge, Public Affairs Manager, Government House, Wellington, New Zealand).

14. In the Irish case, this provision was in the 'Instructions' rather than in the 'Letters patent'; see 'Instructions passed under the Royal Sign Manual of Signet to the Governor-General of the Irish Free State', appendix B, in Sexton (1989: 183–4).

15. C.M. Martin-Jones, Home Office, to A. Newton Anderson, Law Courts, Belfast, 21 March 1928, Home Office Papers, National Archives of the UK, HO45/14167.

16. See royal.gov.uk/theroyalhousehold/overview.aspx; www.koninklijkhuis.nl/globale-paginas/taalrubrieken/english/organisation; kongehuset.dk/english/Organisation-and-Contact/Employees [accessed 2 May 2013].

17. These figures are based on staff lists available at www.bundespraesident.at/

aufgaben/praesidentschaftskanzlei/mitarbeiterinnen/#c11,www.president.ee/en/53
81-staff/ and www.predsjednik.hr/officeofthe [accessed 2 May 2013].

18. Based on information from Mr Antony Paltridge, Public Affairs Manager, Government House, Wellington, New Zealand. For a comparison of the two offices, see Harris (2009).

19. *Appendix to Report from Select Committee on Civil Government Charges* (1831), p. 64, in *British Parliamentary Papers* 1831 (337) vol. 4, which describes the functions of the various officials. The salary was temporarily increased to £30,000 from 1810 to 1831; it was temporarily reduced to £18,000 in 1916; see *Return, Revenue and Expenditure (England, Scotland, and Ireland)*, 1910–11 to 1920–21, in *British Parliamentary Papers* 1911 (220) vol. 45, etc.

20. *Dáil Debates*, 14 July 1933, vol. 48, col. 2755.

21. The relevant acts are the Presidential Establishment Act, 1938 (no. 24); and the Presidential Establishment (Amendment) Acts, 1947 (no. 22), 1973 (no. 18) and 1991 (no. 10).

22. republic.org.uk/valueformoneymyth.pdf [accessed 2 May 2013].

23. Computed from New Zealand, 2012, output class II and schedule of non-departmental expenses.

24. www.hotpress.com/archive/415947.html [accessed 2 May 2013].

25. *Dáil Debates*, 27 March–2 April 1930, vol. 34, cols 179–468.

26. *Dáil Debates*, 26 May 1937, vol. 67, cols 1204–1213.

27. The wording used on the two occasions in 1982 was revealing. FitzGerald properly stated that he would 'proceed immediately to Áras an Uachtaráin to seek dissolution from the President'; Haughey announced more definitively that 'I will now go to the President and advise him to dissolve Dáil Éireann. At the conclusion of this, the 23rd Dáil, may I convey … every good wish and every blessing for the future', thus giving the impression that the President had no discretion; *Dáil Debates*, 27 January 1982, vol. 332, cols 413–14, and 4 November 1982, vol. 332, col. 1057. In 1992, all parties seemed agreed that the life of the Dáil had come to an end.

28. Interview with Dr Patrick Hillery, 4 January 2001.

29. The All-Party Oireachtas Committee on the Constitution (1997a: 53) took the view that such an unwritten norm had already developed in Ireland in respect of the President's right to withhold a dissolution from a defeated Taoiseach: 'No President has used this discretion … Constitutional tradition, then, has given Taoisigh the facility to have the Dáil dissolved on request to the President.' Events following the collapse of the Reynolds government in 1994 were, however, to disprove this.

30. *Dáil Debates*, 11 May 37, vol. 67, col. 38.

4
THE SEANAD: REFORM
OR REDUNDANCY?

Second chambers of parliament generally tend to have a low profile. Sometimes we hear about them only because they are about to disappear, as in Denmark in 1953, Sweden in 1969 and Turkey in 1980. On other occasions, there is a prolonged public debate on second chamber reform, of a kind that has been proceeding painfully in respect of the British House of Lords since the 1990s. More rarely, a subordinate second chamber suddenly flexes its muscles with surprising effect, as in the role of the Australian Senate in defeating the government in 1975 and precipitating the controversial dismissal of the prime minister by the Governor-General.

The Irish senate has certainly attracted a degree of controversy. On one occasion, this led to its constitutional abolition, in 1936; and the new senate that appeared in the 1937 constitution has drawn its share of criticism. Seanad Éireann was one of the leading targets of commentators and others who were critical of the quality of Irish political institutions. Indeed, in the run-up to the 2011 general election parties competed in their anxiety to bring this institution to an end. In October 2009 Fine Gael leader Enda Kenny proposed abolition of the Seanad, and this policy was written into his party's election manifesto. At the beginning of January 2011, Fianna Fáil went a step further, proposing to hold a referendum on Seanad abolition on the same day as the general election (Magee, 2011). Given the pace of political developments, this idea quickly became an obvious non-starter, but the party incorporated a more nuanced policy in its election manifesto, proposing abolition as part of a broader reform package. The Labour Party, too, climbed on board the abolitionist bandwagon, promising that 'Labour will abolish the Seanad'. The fate of the second chamber appeared sealed when a Fine Gael–Labour coalition took office in March 2011 on a programme that included Seanad abolition as a matter of urgency (Labour Party, 2011: 18), and later statements by the Taoiseach indicated that this item remained high on the political agenda. Finally, on 13 June 2013 a complex bill designed to provide for a referendum to abolish the Seanad was introduced in the Dáil.

Given this apparent shift in Irish elite opinion on the merits of a second chamber, it is worth reviewing the standing of the Irish senate and placing it in both comparative and historical perspective. The present chapter aims to do this. It begins by looking at the emergence of bicameralism in comparative perspective, including the normative arguments that have been advanced in its favour. The chapter goes on to look at the historical evolution of the second chamber in Ireland, reviews the functioning of Seanad Éireann, and concludes with an analysis of the debate about the relevance of Ireland's second chamber.[1]

BICAMERALISM: A COMPARATIVE PERSPECTIVE

The appearance of second chambers of parliament forms part of the story of the emergence of parliament itself. This development is considered in the first part of this section, which reviews the evolution of second chambers and notes the philosophical justifications for their role in the political process. Having considered the broad profile of these bodies, the second part of the section looks at the composition of second chambers: the characteristic principles in accordance with which their members are selected. The third deals with their political role, and, in particular, their powers in relation to the first chamber. Most of this section offers a stock-take that reviews the position of contemporary second chambers against the benchmark of an earlier survey (Coakley and Laver, 1997; Coakley, 1997). It rests on an appendix summarising some of the crucial features of the world's second chambers in 2012 – an appendix that also updates an earlier dataset that reflected the position in 1996 (Coakley and Laver, 1997: 95–8; Coakley, 1997).

The origins of second chambers

The phenomenon of bicameralism is commonly interpreted as an expression of a philosophical commitment to the principle of 'balanced' government that may be traced back to the classical world (Preece, 2000: 68–9; Shell, 2001b: 6). In translating this principle into contemporary practice, the contribution of the British parliament is generally acknowledged, with its division into Lords and Commons acting as 'the main model for almost all the bicameral legislatures of today, either directly or indirectly' (Preece, 2000: 69). Whatever its merits as a theory, though, it is important to see this interpretation as a potent political myth—an 'ideologically marked narrative which purports to give a true account of past, present, or predicted political events and which is accepted as valid in its essentials by a social group' (Flood, 2002: 44). This is not to suggest that the myth is devoid of factual basis; rather, it is to stress that its significance rests on the degree to which it is accepted, not the extent to which it is accurate. It was the strength of the myth of mixed government, not the reality of British bicameralism, that was to have such a profound impact on other countries, whether by imposition, as in Britain's own former colonies, or by serving as a model, as in much of the rest of Europe and in the United States, or indirectly, as a consequence of the export of the British model to most of Latin America.

Notwithstanding Britain's undoubted contribution to the adoption of bicameralism elsewhere, though, this myth is potentially misleading. British bicameralism was never deliberately designed to match a particular philosophical model, but rather emerged as a consequence of historical accident (Shell, 2001b: 7–9). In important respects, indeed, widely accepted accounts of the British experience (describing a lower house being steadily democratised, and an upper house that retained its conservative composition while being shorn of power) obscure a much simpler key to the transition from medieval to modern parliaments. The process that took almost two centuries in Great Britain (from about 1832 to 1999) occurred more precipitously in such countries as France (1789): there, the notion of parliament as a collection of social orders or 'estates' was replaced abruptly by the idea of parliament as comprising representatives of individual citizens.

Rather than seeing early parliaments as potentially including one chamber that would ultimately be democratised, it is more fruitful to see them as forums where the key social groups into which medieval society was legally divided came together: the clergy (internally differentiated between bishops, senior monastic officials and lower clergy), the nobility (also finely graded, from princes through intermediate ranks, to gentry, titled or untitled), and other social groups, such as the bourgeoisie and other urban classes, and, perhaps, certain categories of free peasants (Myers, 1975: 23–9).

Parliaments varied in the extent to which they were open to all of these groups, and in the formula by which they assembled. Originally, in many cases, some or all of these groups came together in a single assembly. The pre-Reformation parliament of Scotland was an example—it brought together the three estates (prelates, lairds and burgh representatives), an arrangement that was redefined after the Reformation but survived up to the Union of 1707 (Goodare, 1996). This unicameral arrangement was the norm in England until the fourteenth century, when the Commons (representing the gentry and the bourgeoisie—the 'knights of the shires, citizens and burgesses') began to meet separately from the Peers (the upper nobility and the upper clergy—the 'lords spiritual and temporal'), with the lower clergy lying outside the parliamentary structure. A similar development took place in Hungary, where the Table of Magnates became a separate house in 1608 (Temperley, 1910: 86–9). But the bicameral formula was not the only alternative to unicameralism: the French Estates General constituted a well-known example of the very common tricameral formula of clergy, nobility, and 'third estate', the last corresponding to the English Commons (Marongiu, 1968: 226–8). Parliamentary organisation could even take quadricameral form, as in Sweden until 1866, with the clergy, nobility, bourgeoisie and peasants each meeting in a separate chamber.

For radicals and socialists in the nineteenth century, estate-based representation and restricted suffrage were anathema; they demanded introduction of the 'four tails' (direct, equal, universal, and secret voting). The most dramatic transition took place in Finland in 1906. The old Diet comprised four houses, on the Swedish model, representing the nobility (0.1% of the population in 1890), clergy (0.3%), bourgeoisie (3.1%) and peasants (26.1%), with 70.4% of the population—including urban workers, rural labourers, landless cottiers and others—altogether excluded from representation (Finland, 1894: 39). At a stroke, the Parliament Act of 1906 ushered in Europe's first fully democratic unicameral parliament, a 200-member body elected by the list system of proportional representation incorporating the 'four tails', a chamber that survives in virtually unaltered form to the present. This constitutional revolution was all the more remarkable because of the acquiescence of the head of state, the Grand Duke of Finland—who was also the autocratic Tsar Nicholas II of Russia, with which Finland had been linked since 1809 in a personal union.

Elsewhere, the installation of a parliamentary chamber representing all the people and incorporating the 'four tails' progressed rapidly in the early twentieth century (Nohlen, 1969). Where a second chamber still existed or was created, this was supplementary to the popularly elected one. The United Kingdom, uniquely, retained the formal remnants of estate-based representation, with one chamber representing the 'Commons' (accounting for the non-noble population), and the second chamber continuing to represent those social groups that were excluded from the Commons, the Lords Spiritual and Temporal. This came to an end only in 1999, when membership of the House of Commons was extended to the (overwhelmingly hereditary) nobility and upper clergy, whose own chamber was fundamentally restructured.

Whatever the route by which stable bicameralism was reached, and regard-less of the role played by historical accident, justifications for this component in modern constitutions were forthcoming. Arguments for bicameralism may be placed under two headings that correspond to two major roles played by second chambers: acting as forums of representation, and as venues for reflection (Norton, 2007: 6–8; see also Baldwin, 2001).

The first argument centres on the representative character of the second chamber. The concept of representation, as is well known, is complex, and may refer to several rather different approaches to the relationship between office holders and those who have placed them in office (Pitkin, 1972). Indeed, study of the UK House of Lords suggests that peers vary widely in their understanding of the kind of representation they offer (Bochel and Defty, 2012), and the extent to which chambers vary in respect of represen-tation is explored further below. As Wheare (1968: 140–6) pointed out, the second chamber may be one where 'special interests' can secure a voice. Of course, such 'interests' may be precisely that—vested interests resisting social reform, yet using their traditional authority to legitimise their position, as in the case of the old British House of Lords and the pre-1918 Hungarian Table of Magnates (Bryce, 1921: 445–8). Nevertheless, distinctive groups with a potentially important national contribution (such as ethnic, linguistic or religious minorities, persons with special expertise, or underprivileged groups) may be given at least symbolic representation by this means (see discussion in Lijphart, 1984: 90–105).

Of 'special' groups that might find representation in a second chamber, regional ones are particularly important. Given the central role played by regional interests in federal states, it is not surprising that a distinctive rationale for bicameralism exists in such cases: the first chamber represents the people of the federation, the second chamber its component member states. The *Federalist Papers* described the equal representation of states in the US Senate as 'at once a constitutional recognition of the portion of sovereignty remaining in the individual states, and an instrument for preserv-ing that residuary sovereignty' (Hamilton, Madison and Jay, 1970 [1787–8]: 316). Much later, Wheare (1953: 92–6) argued that while equal representation of states in such circumstances might not be essential, it was certainly desirable, a view shared by Laundy (1989: 5). As Fiseha (2007: 139–46) put it, the second chamber in federal systems can represent the diversity of the state, while the lower house represents its unity. Indeed, it has been claimed that while most legislatures in unitary states have only one chamber, 'there is no significant federal democracy without a second chamber' (Swenden,

2004: 25). This rather overstates the position. As will be seen below, a number of federal states cope without second chambers, and Watts (2008: 1) suggests that bicameralism is not a definitive characteristic of federation.

The second argument has to do with efficient government. William Riker (1992) has defended the merits of bicameral solutions, rather than such devices as supermajorities, to problems of collective decision making. Others have pointed to the capacity of a second chamber to take pressure from the first chamber. Walter Bagehot (1928 [1872]: 95–8), no apologist for second chambers, saw that there were circumstances where they could lighten the burden of work in the first chamber. James Bryce (1921: 450–5), similarly, pointed out that first chambers were highly partisan and encumbered by so heavy a load that their members had little time to consider legislation, leaving room for a second chamber consisting of members with special expertise. This was the view also of Kenneth Wheare (1968: 140–3), who noted the capacity of second chambers to bring a less partisan perspective to bear on legislation and to provide special skills.

Of course, the argument that a second chamber is needed to correct the potential 'excesses' of the first implies a need to put a brake on democracy, an argument attractive to traditional conservatism. As the *Federalist Papers* put it in the 1780s, a second chamber can be an important component in a system of checks and balances, especially given the propensity of lower houses 'to yield to the impulse of sudden and violent passions, and to be seduced by factious leaders into intemperate and pernicious resolutions' (Hamilton et al., 1970 [1787–8]: 316–17). This argument found lukewarm support from John Stuart Mill in the nineteenth century, when he argued that a second chamber would remind the popularly elected house that it was not the sole power in the land, and thus prevent it from becoming 'despotic and overweening' (Mill, 1912 [1861]: 336). In the era of modern political parties, however, it is likely that most decisions of the lower chamber will be more calculating than hasty, and the case for having another body that could block them in a modern democratic state is hard to make. Indeed, the 'checks and balances' argument may simply disguise sectional self-interest; Finer (1946: 677) argued that 'all second chambers have been instituted, and are maintained, not from disinterested love of mature deliberation, but because there is something their makers wished to defend against the rest of the community'. In any event, there are means other than a second chamber for moderating the potential excesses of a unicameral legislature, with the courts system and a powerful head of state as obvious examples.

Critics of bicameralism have been articulate, undermining arguments for its retention, especially in unitary states. A much-cited judgement attributed to the Abbé Sieyès during the early stages of the French revolution sums up the dilemma: 'if a second chamber dissents from the first, it is mischievous; if it agrees with it, it is superfluous' (cited in Marriott, 1910: 1). This was echoed by later critics, with Jeremy Bentham, for instance, arguing that 'if a second chamber represents the general interest, it is useless; and if it represents only a particular interest, it is mischievous' (Rockow, 1928: 577–8). For critics of the notion of a powerful second chamber, this was simply an anti-democratic device; it was 'part of the defensive armory of the present property system' and 'a bulwark against the aims of the first chamber' (Rockow, 1928: 589–90).

The composition of second chambers

The distinction between unicameral and bicameral parliaments is not cut and dried (Norton, 2004). Sometimes it may be difficult to distinguish between a second chamber and an intergovernmental council (such as the German Federal Council, the *Bundesrat*), or a consultative body (such as the Slovene National Council). Sometimes a unicameral body behaves like a bicameral one: the Norwegian *Storting*, for instance, is elected as a single chamber, but until 2009 it bifurcated for operational reasons into a *Lagting* (made up of one fourth of the total) and an *Odelsting* (the remainder), and until 1991 the Icelandic *Althing* was organised along similar lines. While acknowledging these difficulties, it is nevertheless possible to arrive at a list of 76 current second chambers, using the criterion of recognition by the Inter-Parliamentary Union (see appendix at the end of this chapter). This represents an increase on the number and proportion of bicameral parliaments since 1996, suggesting that the long-term pattern of decline in bicameralism was arrested around the turn of the twenty-first century.[2]

Table 4.1: Second chambers in unitary and federal states, 2012

Type of state	Unicameral legislature	Bicameral legislature	Total
Unitary	108	57	165
Federal	6	19	25
Total	114	76	190

Note: These data refer to countries on which information is maintained by the Inter-Parliamentary Union. *Source:* Appendix.

There is a strong association between federalism and bicameralism, as may be seen in Table 4.1, which breaks bicameral systems down by state structure. It will be noted that 76% of federal states (19 out of 25) have second chambers, by comparison with 35% of unitary states (57 out of 165). This shows a significant change from 1996, when 82% of federal states and 26% of unitary states were bicameral. The diminishing gap between the two state types arises in part from the renewed popularity of the bicameral formula in unitary states but also, even more surprisingly, from a move away from bicameralism in federal states. In 1996, the only four federal states that had unicameral parliaments were small: three (Comoros, Saint Kitts and Nevis, and the Federated States of Micronesia) had populations of less than half a million, while the fourth was also small (United Arab Emirates, though its rapidly expanding population exceeded four million by 2008). But these four states were joined by two much larger federations that dropped their second chambers: Venezuela (1999) and Nepal (2008).

Unlike first chambers of parliament, second chambers tend to vary enormously in their composition. The Inter-Parliamentary Union's summary (1986: 16) of the bases of composition of second chambers distinguished six paths: direct election, election by local units, election by the other chamber, election by other bodies, appointment by the head of state, and *ex-officio* membership (it also identified a seventh hybrid formula). Coakley and Laver (1997), taking account of a larger number of cases, reformulated these, identifying seven principles of representation: direct election, indirect election, appointment, heredity, corporate representation, selection by the lower house, and *ex-officio* membership, with university representation and co-optation as partial approaches. This classification was followed by other authors (for example, Russell, 1999, 2000: 29–32; Borthwick, 2001). In fact, though, this approach merges two quite distinct dimensions: the representation criterion narrowly speaking (the set of people or interests whose representation in the second chamber is intended) and the selection formula (the electoral or other arrangements designed to give effect to this principle).

The *representation criterion* may closely resemble that in the first chamber—the second chamber may also be designed to reflect the views of the population at large. More commonly, though, it is not the people of the state, but the territories which make it up, that are intended to be represented. This is particularly the case in federal systems, where the 'stock type of federal parliament' has been described as having a second chamber where the territorial units are equally represented, regardless of their size and population, and whose powers are equivalent to those of the first chamber (Inter-

Parliamentary Union, 1962: 4–7). Often, though, there is a compromise between the population and territorial criteria, so that territories are indeed represented, not strictly on the basis of their population, but with a weighting that takes account of population. Sometimes the representation criterion is more selective: it may be based on social or corporate groups, on elite groups, or on specific privileged components of the population.

The *selection formula* is similarly varied. The most obvious is direct election, whether on the same basis as the first chamber or using an alternative set of rules. Very commonly, though, election is indirect, with local councillors typically making up the electorate—a formula that, perhaps surprisingly, tends to promote even closer links with provincial interests than direct election (National Democratic Institute, 1996: 7; Russell, 2001: 116). Third, members of the second chamber may be nominated by the head of state, or they may be appointed by some other means, such as co-optation by the chamber itself, selection by the first chamber or membership by virtue of some kind of *ex-officio* or hereditary status.

A summary of the manner in which the world's second chambers are composed in respect of these two approaches is given in Table 4.2. It should be noted that in some cases allocation of the chamber to one category rather than another is problematic, and that in 27 cases a mixture of approaches is in operation; the data here refer to the *predominant* approach. In one case (the Council of the Federation in Russia) two selection formulas, indirect election and appointment, are of equal importance.

Table 4.2: Predominant principles of representation and selection in second chambers, 2012

Representation criterion	*Selection formula*						
	Direct election		*Indirect election*		*Nomination/ other*		*Total*
People	10		4	(1)	–		14 (1)
Territories—weighted	2	(1)	5	(4)	–		7 (5)
Territories—equal	16	(8)	17	(3)	1	(1)	34 (12)
Other	–		2		19	(1)	21 (1)
Total	28	(9)	28	(8)	20	(2)	76 (19)

Note: Numbers in parentheses refer to federal second chambers. *Source:* Appendix.

Direct election

In all, 28 of the 76 second chambers considered here are directly elected. Of these, 10 match the classic criterion of popular representation: the second chamber, like the first, is intended to represent the entire population. Sometimes (as in Colombia, Italy, Paraguay and Uruguay) the most representative system, the party list form of proportional representation, is used for both houses. Romania and Japan use a mixed system for both (with some members elected in single-member districts, a more proportional top-up at national level, and, in Japan, some use of the limited vote in second chamber elections). The Czech Republic and Poland use different formulas for the two houses (the list system for the first chamber, and single-member districts using the majority or plurality system for the second chamber). In the two remaining cases, Palau and the Philippines, the unusual block vote system is used in second chamber elections, with the plurality system and the mixed plurality–list system used respectively in the first chamber.

In an even larger subgroup, however, 16 in all, direct election is used not to represent the population but to represent the territories of which the state is made up: each is equally represented in the second chamber, regardless of population. This is not particularly surprising in federal states. Thus, in Switzerland and the United States the component units of the federation return two members each to the second chamber regardless of population (the Swiss picture being complicated by 'half-cantons' that return a single member), in Argentina, Brazil and Nigeria they return three, while in Australia they elect 12 each. This principle can apply also in unitary states, where the main upper tier of local government units may be represented equally in the second chamber: Bhutan's 20 districts and the Dominican Republic's 31 provinces (one member each), Liberia's 15 counties (two members each), Haiti's 10 provinces (three members each), Bolivia's nine departments (four members each) and Zimbabwe's 10 provinces (six members each).

These two patterns may be reproduced in rather more complex forms elsewhere. To start with, the predominant formula described above may be challenged by approaches of another kind. In Thailand, for example, regional representatives have a bare majority, while 49% of the members of the second chamber are nominated by the Senate Selection Commission (a group of five senior officials) to represent other interests, notably the academic, public, private and professional sectors. In Myanmar, while regional representation predominates, 25% of the members of the second chamber are nominated by the army commander. In Spain, while most senators are elected on the basis of equal representation of the country's 52 provinces, 21% are elected indirectly to represent the 17 autonomous communities that make up the federal system—but on the basis of their populations, not on that of equality between them. Indeed, in two cases the directly elected component does not represent either populations or territories unambiguously; rather, while territories are represented, their share is weighted according to population. This is the case in Chile, where each region returns either two or four senators depending on population, and even in federal Belgium, where the directly elected component of the Senate is selected by two electoral components, one returning 25 Dutch-speaking and the other 15 French-speaking senators.

Indirect election

There are many countries—in 2012, 28, exactly the same as the number of those directly elected—in which the second chamber is said in common parlance to be indirectly elected: the people do not select its members directly, but their representatives do so on their behalf. Strictly speaking, no second chamber fully conforms to this format; there is none for which an electoral college or colleges mandated to select senators is specifically elected for this purpose, on the model of the electoral college that selects the President of the United States. Yet in some cases (five in all) a system is used that is intended to produce a second chamber that is indirectly representative of the population. Thus, in the Netherlands, members of the 12 provincial councils function as an electoral college, their votes weighted by population, to select the First Chamber. This can apply even in federal states: in India, for example, members of the Council of the States are selected by the legislative assemblies of the states and territories, but are distributed between those substantially on the basis of population.

Much more commonly, however (indeed, in 17 cases), seats in the second chamber are distributed equally among the top-tier local government units, whose councillors typically elect them. In Belarus, for example, councillors in each of the seven regions select eight members of the Council of the Republic, in the Congo (Brazzaville) in the six regions they select 12 senators each, in Kazakhstan in the 16 regions they select two senators each, and in Uzbekistan in the 14 districts they elect six senators each. This can also apply in the case of federal states. The South African National Council of Provinces comprises nine members selected by each of the country's 10 provincial legislatures, while Pakistan's four provincial assemblies each return 22 members to the Senate.

As in the case of direct election, the picture may in reality be a good deal more complex than this. In Russia, for example, the Council of the

Federation comprises one representative of each of the 83 republics and regions on which the federation is based, selected by its legislative assembly; but these are matched by the same number of nominees of the governments of the republics or regions. In Bosnia and Herzegovina, the two 'entities' (the Bosnian-Croat Federation and the Serb Republic) are not equally represented in the House of Peoples: the assembly of the former returns 10 members (five Bosnians and five Croats) while the assembly of the latter returns five, so that it is the three nationalities, not the two federated entities, that are equally represented. Of particular interest are five cases where the 'indirect' procedure is not designed to represent the territories on a basis of equality, but a population weighting is introduced. Thus, the French Senate is elected by local councillors to represent *départements* and comparable units, and the distribution by population is modified by the requirement that each *département* have at least one senator.

Three federal states give rise to particular issues in light of the common assumption that the territorial building blocks in federal states should be equally represented in the second chamber. In Ethiopia, members of the House of the Federation are selected by the nine state councils, but the representation of each state is weighted by population. The Austrian Federal Council is similar, with the assemblies of the nine provinces returning between three and 12 members each. The remaining case is perhaps the most misunderstood of all. The German Federal Council is often described as an indirectly elected second chamber, but its members are not elected at all. In one interpretation, they may be seen as a set of delegations appointed by Germany's 16 *Land* governments, numbering 69 in all, and ranging in size from three to six, depending on the *Land* population. An alternative interpretation might see the Federal Council as comprising 16 members, one from each *Land*, each with a single vote of varying weight but with delegations of different sizes (members of *Land* delegations must vote *en bloc*, and the number of members present is irrelevant to the weight of any one delegation's vote).

There are times when indirect election is designed to represent neither the population nor the territories of the state. One of the most unusual principles is that of corporate representation—close in its origins to traditional estate representation, but representing a modernised form of this. This developed most fully in certain Catholic societies in the interwar period, as in Portugal (the Corporative Chamber, 1933–74), Austria (the Economic and Cultural Councils, 1934–38) and Italy (the Chamber of Fasci and Corporations, 1939–43). During the closing years of authoritarian government in Estonia

(1938–40), a National Council constituted mainly on vocational lines functioned as a second chamber (Uluots and Klesment, 1937). Until 1999, one German *Land*, Bavaria, had a bicameral system with a senate selected on vocational lines.

There are two contemporary expressions of this principle. The Irish senate was designed in 1937 to secure the representation of 'vocational' interests, defined as culture and education, agriculture, industry and commerce, labour, and public administration, but since the electoral college that elects these 43 senators is dominated by local councillors the senate in reality represents party interests, not 'vocational' ones as will be seen later. The National Council of Slovenia is a second example: it consists of 18 representatives of functional groups (social, economic, trade and professional interests), together with 22 representatives of local interests. The House of Councillors in Morocco makes a gesture in the same direction: 108 of its 270 members (40%) are elected by representatives of professional chambers in the areas of agriculture, commerce, industry and services, the craft industry, marine fisheries and trade unions.

Appointment and other forms of selection

The remaining second chambers, 20 in all, form the final category, with nomination or appointment as the dominant principle. In the past, heredity played a particularly important role in this group: members of the titled nobility sat in this chamber not necessarily by virtue of their own talents but often thanks to the achievements of their ancestors. This is still the case in Lesotho, where two thirds of the membership of the Senate is made up of the principal chiefs, and chiefs are also represented in the Zimbabwe Senate. The best-known prototype was, however, the UK House of Lords, most of whose members up to 1999 were hereditary peers. Following the 1999 reform, the number of hereditary peers was reduced; by 2013 there were 88 hereditary peers, with life peers accounting for 642 members and archbishops and bishops of the Church of England making up the remaining 25.

The kind of nominated second chamber that eventually evolved in the UK had in fact already been installed in much of the Commonwealth. In eight small states in the Caribbean area, the senates are appointed; the Governor-General (or, in one case, the President) acts on the advice of the prime minister for most appointments, and on that of the leader of the opposition for others. In these cases, provision is sometimes made for appointments based on advice from other bodies, or at the head of state's own discretion (as in Trinidad and Tobago), and similar arrangements are made in other countries, such as Bahrain and Yemen, though with fewer formal restrictions on the discretion of the head of state.

It is difficult to describe the representation criterion in these cases, since members of the second chamber are intended to represent elite groups within the population at large. In Canada senators are appointed until the age of 75 by the Governor General on the advice of the Prime Minister, but the notion of regional representation is retained: the two largest provinces are represented by 24 senators each, and the remainder by smaller numbers. In a second case, the vocational principle rules: in Oman, the Sultan appoints members of the State Council from defined groups (including science, the arts, business and administration). Elsewhere, it is the politically dominant groups that are represented, as in Jordan, where the King makes the appointments from senior politicians, military officers and other select groups, and in Madagascar, where the Transitional President nominates on the proposal of the political parties.

Aside from the bodies mentioned above, which are entirely appointed, the appointive principle is the dominant but not exclusive one elsewhere. Two clear examples are Malaysia, where the Supreme Head of the Federation appoints most of the senators (43; 26 are indirectly elected) and Swaziland, where the King appoints a majority (20; 10 are selected by the House of Assembly). In yet other cases, the head of state makes a small number of appointments to chambers that are selected predominantly on some other basis—in respect of five senators in Bhutan, Italy and Zimbabwe, eight in Belarus and Tajikistan, 11 in Lesotho, 12 in India and 16 in Uzbekistan. We may add to these the peculiar case of Ireland where, uniquely, the appointive function rests with the head of government rather than with the head of state: the Taoiseach appoints 11 senators.

Election (whether direct or indirect) and appointment do not exhaust the range of formulas used in the formation of second chambers. In Cambodia two senators and in Swaziland 10 of the 30 senators are selected by the first chamber (whose members elsewhere often participate also in indirect elections, but are swamped by local councillors, as in Ireland and France). *Ex-officio* membership of the UK House of Lords has already been mentioned, and office holders elsewhere may also be *ex-officio* members: former Presidents in Burundi and Italy, the Vice President in Uruguay and regional governors in Zimbabwe are examples. Ireland's two oldest universities are represented in the senate there, and university staff elect three members of the Senate of Rwanda. This is a survival of an older tradition by which university representation was once relatively common (Meisel, 2011:

148–55). Finally, second chambers sometimes co-opt a portion of their membership: three senators in Mauritania, for example, and 10 in Belgium.

Modifying factors

Whatever the representation criterion or the selection formula, there are at least three other distinctive features of second chambers that set them apart from first chambers. One is *relative size*: the fact that, as the appendix shows, the second chamber tends to be smaller than the first chamber symbolises that body's inferior status, and acquires practical significance when the two chambers meet jointly to resolve disagreements. A second is *age*. The minimum age required for membership of the second chamber is 30 years or more in well over half of all cases (44 of the 71 where an age limit is specified). As regards differences between the age requirement for membership of the two houses, bicameral parliaments fall into three categories of more or less equal size. In 24, there is no difference; in 22 the second chamber has a higher age requirement, but the gap is less than 10 years; and in 25 cases the difference is 10 years or more. Interestingly, this is formally recognised in such cases as Afghanistan, where the second chamber is called the 'House of Elders'.

The third distinctive feature of second chambers is *term of office*. In many cases the second chamber has the same term of office as the first chamber: four and five years are by far the most common terms, accounting for most second chambers. In some cases these are fixed terms; in others provision is made for premature dissolution. However, terms of six, eight and nine years also occur. Especially when the term is long, provision may be made for partial renewal, as may be seen in Table 4.3. When senators have a term of six years, the chamber is normally renewed in stages: either one third retire every two years (as in the USA) or half retire every three years (as in Japan), though in such cases as Mexico all are elected simultaneously. When the term is eight years, there may be provision for renewal of half of the membership ever four years (as in Brazil), but Rwanda is an exception, with simultaneous election. In Morocco the term is nine years, with one third renewed every three years. The remaining cases are more diverse. In Liberia, senators serve for nine years, but renewal is staggered at six- and three-year intervals. In other cases, members of second chambers have an indefinite term of office: for life, normally, in the British House of Lords, and until the age of 75 in the Canadian senate. In certain federal states, the term of office is laid down by the component units of the federation rather than by the constitution: Austria, Germany, the Russian Federation and Switzerland are examples.

Table 4.3: Terms of office of members of second chambers, 2012

Term	Unitary states	Federal states	Total	Example
4 years	11	5	16	Poland
5 years	26	2	28	Italy
6 years	3	1	4	Mexico
6 years (1/2 renewed every 3 years)	6	2	8	Australia
6 years (1/3 renewed every 2 years)	3	3	6	USA
8 years	1	0	1	Rwanda
8 years (1/2 renewed every 4 years)	1	1	2	Brazil
9 years (1/3 renewed every 3 years)	1	0	1	Morocco
Variable, continuous, other	5	5	10	United Kingdom
Total	57	19	76	

Note: In the case of those chambers that make provision for full renewal, the terms above may be either fixed or (if there is provision for premature dissolution) maximum. *Source:* Appendix.

Finally, it is worth commenting on the extent to which one particular historically disadvantaged group, women, are represented in second chambers. In bicameral systems, the two chambers range widely as regards their proportions of women members, but overall, and notwithstanding the existence of generous quotas in certain countries, the proportion of women in second chambers is slightly less than in first chambers (the median value for the former is 15%, for the latter 17%). The percentage of women in the first chamber exceeds that in the second chamber in a majority of cases (41 out of 76)—a surprising outcome, given common reliance on second chambers precisely to redress such imbalances.

The powers of the second chamber

The power of a second chamber will obviously be in part a function of the power of parliament more generally. Measuring this presents formidable difficulties, though a major initiative at surveying the strength of parliaments worldwide has yielded important data. Fish and Kroenig (2009) based their research on expert country specialists as well as on constitutional documents, and, using 32 closely defined areas where parliament potentially has a role, offered ratings of the strength of the world's parliaments. Their scores are reproduced in the second column of the appendix at the end of this chapter, where a high score means that parliament has a role to play in a large number of areas (in Argentina, for example, the score of 0.50 means that in 50%, or 16 out of the 32 areas, parliament possessed specific power).

Comparing the relative strength of the two chambers in bicameral parliaments might appear rather easier, since constitutions normally define the powers of the two houses relatively clearly. If we focus on a central parliamentary function, the legislative process, for instance, we will typically find that the second chamber's role is circumscribed, in that its assent to legislation is not necessarily required, and its capacity to influence money bills is less than that of the first chamber. The two chambers may also have exclusive jurisdiction in specific areas that it is difficult to compare: the US Senate, for instance, has a particular role in the area of foreign policy and in cabinet and other presidential appointments, the Italian Senate has a powerful role in controlling the executive, and the UK House of Lords had a clearly defined judicial function until 2009. Furthermore, regardless of constitutional provisions, there may be important differences in practice in the relative power of the two chambers, ones to some degree subject to measurement (Money and Tsebelis, 1992; Tsebelis and Money, 1997).

The appendix at the end of this chapter incorporates a crude effort to assess the relative power of the second chamber. This is based on a number of detailed country studies (Mastias and Grangé, 1987; Sénat, 2012) as well as on comparative studies that attempt to assess this feature of second chambers (Coakley and Laver, 1997; Patterson and Mughan, 2001; Gélard, 2006; Russell, 2012). This places the second chambers in three crude categories, labelled simply 'high', 'medium' and 'low' in respect of their powers relative to the first chamber, but it should be noted that there is a case for moving some of these into an adjacent category; even experts commonly disagree. This is necessarily no more than a tentative effort to illustrate the range of powers available to second chambers.

The 'high' category includes second chambers whose powers are broadly comparable with those of the first chamber. Indeed, they may sometimes overshadow the first chamber, as is arguably the case in Bosnia-Herzegovina and the United States. The characteristic feature is the fact that their assent to legislation is required, and may not be overridden by the other chamber. This is not to say that the second chamber is itself powerful in any absolute sense: in Zimbabwe, for instance, the low overall score for parliamentary power (0.31) suggests that neither chamber is fully involved in the process of government. The 'medium' category is more difficult to define, and to set apart from the categories on either side of it; it refers to second chambers whose legislative veto may be overridden, but only with difficulty (for example, by means of a joint sitting, as in Uruguay, or an absolute majority in the first chamber, as in Austria). The 'low' category includes the remaining second chambers, whose veto may be overridden by the first chamber by simple majority, as in Ireland and France.

It has been rightly suggested that the power of the second chamber depends to some extent on its selection formula, with popularly elected chambers and those in federal states likely to be relatively more powerful, though conservative senates in traditional regimes may also possess considerable powers (Blondel, 1973: 33). A study of 12 bicameral parliaments in the Americas, however, has suggested that it is not so much federal status as presidential government that matters (Llanos and Nolte, 2003: 75), and this may well be the case more generally (Russell, 2012). The data in the appendix at the end of this chapter seem to offer some support in respect of associations of these kinds. Thus, 46% of directly elected second chambers are classified here as 'high' in respect of their relative powers, compared to 14% of those elected indirectly and none of those selected by other means. Similarly, 32% of federal second chambers, but only 19% of those in unitary states, have been placed in the 'high' category. These figures must, however, be treated with caution in the light of the uncertain quality of the data on which they are based.

Directly elected second chambers may be more willing to challenge governments and the first chamber because of what they see as their democratic mandate. Thus, the Liberal-dominated Australian Senate put an end to Prime Minister Gough Whitlam's Labour government in Australia in 1975 in controversial circumstances, by blocking a money bill. But a nominated second chamber, especially if its members have the security of life-time appointments, need not be reticent in challenging even a democratically elected first chamber. The traditional Conservative dominance of the UK House of Lords was reflected in that chamber's much greater hostility to Labour than to Conservative governments; thus, during the era of Conservative rule from 1979 to 1997 the Lords defeated the government on whipped divisions in 8% of cases; but during the following period of Labour government from 1997 to 2010 they defeated the government in 31% of cases (computed from Purvis, 2011: 7).

These instances highlight the importance not just of the selection formula, but also of its outcome: the political complexion of the two chambers. Their relationship may vary over time, depending on the extent to which they 'cohabit' under the control of different parties, or collaborate in circumstances where the same party or coalition dominates both (Scully, 2001).

Ultimately, assessments of the value of second chambers, at least in unitary states, take us back to the dilemma of Sieyès. If we dichotomise such bodies first in respect of the extent to which they meet conventional criteria of descriptive political representation, and second in the degree to which they may exercise power, and if we cross-classify these dichotomous dimensions, we generate a four-cell grid that permits certain judgements about the role of second chambers in contemporary democratic states. Running through the normative assessments of those who have engaged with the issue of second chambers over the past two centuries are conclusions that may be summarised as follows. If a second chamber is representative and powerful, it duplicates the functions of the first chamber, with which it competes; if it is representative and powerless, it serves no useful function in the decision making system; if it is unrepresentative but powerful, it contravenes democratic principles; and if it is unrepresentative and powerless it is marginal to the political process. From this perspective, then, second chambers in unitary states fall into four categories: respectively, they are disruptive, or redundant, or obstructive, or merely ornamental. Ornaments, however, are by no means necessarily devoid of value; how, it may now be asked, has the Irish state fared in this respect?

BICAMERALISM IN IRELAND

The Irish experience of bicameralism illustrates many of the distinctive features of second chambers that have been discussed above. To start with, over time, those involved in planning Irish institutional structures have experimented with all of the selection mechanisms already discussed, and have grappled with the difficult question of the powers of second chambers. This historical dimension is discussed first below. This is followed by an examination of the immediate predecessor of the present body, the senate of the Irish Free State, and the section concludes with a discussion of the current Seanad.

The historical heritage

Like its counterparts elsewhere, the medieval Irish parliament only gradually acquired definite institutional shape. In the fourteenth and fifteenth centuries, it was tricameral in form: as well as the Lords and Commons, the proctors of the lower clergy constituted another house (Richardson and Sayles, 1964: 76–80, 176–86). With the abolition of the clerical chamber in 1536, following its opposition to Reformation legislation, the Irish parliament came to resemble its English, and later British, counterpart (Bradshaw, 1973: 74). By 1800 the Irish House of Lords consisted of 22 spiritual and 225 temporal peers (McDowell, 1979: 121). Following the merger of the British and Irish parliaments in 1800, Ireland continued to be represented in the British upper house by 28 peers elected by the Irish peerage, and by four Protestant bishops or archbishops.

Perhaps because of the strength of this tradition within the sphere of British political and cultural influence, but also undoubtedly because of circumstances peculiar to Ireland, all 'home rule' legislation proposing the establishment of a separate Irish legislature involved bicameral arrangements. Thus the Government of Ireland (Home Rule) Bill of 1886, defeated in the House of Commons, proposed that, in addition to a popularly elected Second Order of 204 members, there would be a First Order, or upper house, of 103 members (75 elected for a 10-year period by voters with a high property qualification, and 28 representatives of the Irish peerage), though the two orders would normally meet together. The Government of Ireland Bill of 1893, which was passed by the House of Commons but defeated in the House of Lords, proposed that alongside a popularly elected Assembly of 103 members there would be a Council or upper chamber of 48, elected for an eight-year term by electors with a high property qualification; one half would retire every four years. The Government of Ireland Bill of 1912 made similar provision for a popularly elected House of Commons with 164 members and a Senate with 40; senators were to be nominated by the Lord Lieutenant for eight-year terms, with one half retiring every four years. This was amended during the bill's passage to provide for direct election after an initial period during which senators would be nominated; they would then be elected for a fixed five-year term under the existing franchise from the four provinces by the single transferable vote system of proportional representation—14 from Ulster, 11 from Leinster, nine from Munster and six from Connacht (United Kingdom, 1916).

Since this bill was enacted, notwithstanding a suspensive veto in the House of Lords, as the Government of Ireland Act of 1914, it laid the basis for bicameralism in independent Ireland. The replacement of the 1914 act by the Government of Ireland Act of 1920 was marked by the introduction of partition and the installation of parallel parliamentary institutions in Dublin and Belfast. The new act proposed that, alongside the Houses of Commons of Southern Ireland (with 128 members) and Northern Ireland (with 52), there would be a Senate of Southern Ireland (with 64 members) and of Northern Ireland (with 26). The latter body, which survived until 1972, consisted of the Lord Mayor of Belfast and the Mayor of Londonderry as *ex-officio* members, with 24 members elected by the House of Commons for an eight-year term, one half retiring every four years. The Senate of Southern Ireland had a more complex composition, one that was especially interesting in the light of later notions of corporate representation. Its make-up was as follows (senators and those electing them were required to be resident within the Irish Free State, or, in the case of the bishops and archbishops, to have dioceses extending into that territory):

- three *ex-officio* members (the Lord Chancellor and the Lord Mayors of Dublin and Cork)
- 17 members nominated by the Lord Lieutenant to represent commerce (including banking), labour and the scientific and learned professions
- four Catholic bishops, elected by the Catholic bishops
- two Church of Ireland bishops, elected by the Church of Ireland bishops
- 16 peers, elected by the Irish peerage
- eight privy councillors, elected by the Irish Privy Council
- 14 county or county borough councillors, elected on a provincial basis (four each from Leinster, Munster and Connacht and two from the three Ulster counties).

This body met on only two occasions; its legitimacy was seriously undermined by the fact that Sinn Féin took 124 of the 128 seats in the House of Commons and simply refused to work with the institutions of 'Southern Ireland', choosing to interpret the northern and southern House of Commons elections as elections to the second Dáil. Nevertheless, the notion of a second chamber was retained in the Anglo-Irish treaty of 1921 and in a settlement arrived at between the new Irish government and representatives of the southern unionists. For the latter, the notion of bicameralism was seen as 'a guarantee against too much democracy on the one hand and too much nationalism on the other' (Bromage and Bromage, 1940: 520).

The senate of the Irish Free State

The 60-member senate established by the 1922 constitution was to be directly elected for a 12-year period, one quarter of the senators retiring every three years (Kohn, 1932: 190–5). Candidates were to be nominated by the Dáil and, in due course, by the Seanad 'on the grounds that they have done honour to the Nation by reason of useful public service or that, because of special qualifications or attainments, they represent important aspects of the Nation's life', and were required to be at least 35 years of age. This was an oblique but not necessarily effective mechanism for complying with a commitment that the southern Protestant minority would receive adequate representation in the second chamber (Buckland, 1972: 318–24). As a special transitional measure, the first senate in 1922 was partly elected by the Dáil (30 senators) and partly appointed by the President of the Executive Council, W.T. Cosgrave (30 senators).

The first triennial popular election took place in 1925. Because of casual vacancies, the number of places to be filled had increased from 15 to 19, and these were to be elected by a general vote of all those aged 30 or more, by means of the single transferable vote system of proportional representation, with the whole territory of the Irish Free State as a single constituency. There were 76 candidates on the enormous, four-column ballot paper, and 67 counts were required to complete the electoral process. Although only 24% of the electorate had voted, the counting of the votes took three weeks to complete (Coakley, 2005). Before the next triennial elections fell due in 1928 the constitution was amended: the term of senators was reduced to nine years, one third of them were to retire every three years, and the general electorate was abolished, to be replaced by an electoral college consisting of Dáil deputies and existing senators.

Table 4.4: Party representation in Seanad Éireann, 1922–34

Year	Progressive Group/ CnaG/FG	Independent Group	Fianna Fáil	Labour	Unaffiliated	Total
1922	–	–	–	–	60	60
1925	15	*	–	5	40	60
1928	19	12	7	6	16	60
1931	21	10	13	6	10	60
1934	22	7	19	7	5	60

Note: 1925 data are approximate only. 'CnaG/FG' refers to Cumann na nGaedheal/Fine Gael. *Included with unaffiliated senators. *Source:* O'Sullivan, 1940: 266–9, 446–8.

The senate of the Irish Free State left a creditable legislative record. If this is measured by amendments made to bills, the raw figures are high. In all, amendments affected 37% of bills during the life of the first senate (1922–36), and eight bills were rejected, of which two were subsequently dropped by the government—a much more assertive record than that of the post-1937 Seanad, as will be seen below. The historian of the first senate, like many others, paid tribute to its effective role as a forum for debate (O'Sullivan, 1940; see also Dooge, 1987).

One feature of the first Irish senate was that its political composition contrasted sharply with that of the Dáil. Of its initial members, only 36 out of 60 were Catholics, and the landed gentry and the ex-unionist community were strongly represented. This was reflected in the fact that the first Cathaoirleach (chair) of the Seanad, Lord Glenavy, had been a prominent unionist and supporter of Edward Carson. But this pattern of composition also planted the seeds for serious conflict with the first chamber. Formally organised parties developed only slowly in the senate in the 1920s. A pro-Cumann na nGaedheal 'Progressive Party' was formed in the mid-1920s, but was replaced by a formally organised Cumann na nGaedheal group; a group of conservative senators formed an 'Independent Group'; the Labour Party established a minor presence; and Fianna Fáil slowly expanded its small group of senators, as may be seen in Table 4.4. This illustrates the slow pace at which the composition of the chamber changed; even after Fianna Fáil's accession to power in 1932, the Seanad continued to have a substantial non-republican majority. Disagreements between the houses were of minor political significance while the pro-Treaty Cumann na nGaedheal government held office up to 1932, but after that clashes with the Dáil became more serious in their implications, as de Valera sought to effect fundamental changes in the constitution. The long-term consequence was the abolition of the senate in 1936, and the introduction of a brief period of unicameralism.

The creation of the new senate

No sooner had the senate been abolished, however, than the government began to consider mechanisms for its replacement in the new constitution then being drafted. A commission was appointed to examine the possible powers and composition of a second chamber, should one be established. The commission recommended that any new senate should have powers similar to the old one (though with a reduced capacity to delay legislation); that its life-span should coincide with that of the Dáil; and that it should consist of 45 members, of whom 15 would be nominated by the President of the Executive Council and 30 would be elected from a panel drawn up by a nominating authority elected by the Dáil. In the case of elected members, it proposed that nominations should, as far as practicable, have regard to specific public interests and services (national language and culture; the arts; agriculture and fisheries; industry and commerce; finance; health and social welfare; foreign affairs; education; law; labour; and public administration).

These 30 members would be elected by an electoral college consisting of all candidates at the previous Dáil election.

An important minority report, which had more influence on the subsequent shape of the constitution than that of the majority, recommended a slightly different scheme. It proposed a 50-member second chamber whose duration would be linked to that of the Dáil. Ten members would be nominated by the President of the Executive Council, specifically to represent four designated areas (national language and culture with three, public administration, economics and foreign affairs with four, public health and social services with two, and literature and the fine arts with one). The remaining 40 members would be elected by the Dáil from four panels of candidates put forward by various vocational or functional interests: farming and fisheries, labour, industry and commerce, and education and the learned professions (Second House of the Oireachtas Commission, 1936).

The new constitution of 1937 reintroduced a second chamber, following the broad lines of the minority report of the Commission. The number of nominated members was increased to 11, and the number of vocational members to 49, with the addition of a fifth area, public administration. Apart from specifying the minimum and maximum size of each panel (none was to have fewer than five or more than 11 members), the constitution provided that six of the vocational members be elected by graduates of the two existing universities (a provision compatible with the long tradition of university representation in parliament), but otherwise left open the system of nomination and election. Those elected were to have 'knowledge and practical experience' of the panel with which they were associated, but the constitution was otherwise silent on the manner of election (Garvin, 1969; Smyth, 1972; Grangé, 1987).

It was, then, apparently the original intention of the 1937 constitution that these members would represent so-called 'vocational' interests. This view derived in part from Catholic social teaching, but also from the ideas of Italian fascism and from the guild socialist ideas of the Fabians (Garvin, 1969: 8). The encyclical *Quadragesimo Anno* of Pope Pius XI (1931) illustrates one powerful influence. This had stressed, as an alternative to the class conflict recognised in Marxist ideology, an institutionalisation of sectoral divisions based essentially on groupings of occupations and of other major social interests. As the encyclical put it:

> True and genuine social order demands that the various members of
> a society be joined together by some firm bond. Such a bond of union

is provided both by the production of goods or the rendering of services in which employers and employees of one and the same vocational group collaborate; and by the common good which all such groups should unite to promote, each in its own sphere, with friendly harmony. (cited in Commission on Vocational Organisation, 1943: 8)

This thinking had a major impact on Irish political perspectives in the 1930s and 1940s (O'Leary, 2000). The Seanad Electoral (Panel Members) Act, 1937, which sought to give flesh to the constitutional provisions, introduced some features that have persisted to the present. First, it fixed the number of members allocated to each panel at the figure at which it remains today (five on the Cultural and Educational panel, seven on the Administrative, nine on the Industrial and Commercial, and 11 each on the Agricultural and Labour panels). Second, it provided for an extremely complicated system of candidate nomination that distinguished between (1) a subpanel of candidates proposed by special 'nominating bodies' authorised to put forward names and (2) a subpanel of candidates proposed by Dáil deputies. Third, it provided for an electorate to consist of a mixture of Dáil deputies and local councillors. Early difficulties with the implementation of the act led to minor changes in the system of nomination and to major changes in the system of election.

The biggest problem with the original system of election was that the electoral quota (the number of votes needed for election) was so low that it encouraged electoral abuses and there were allegations of bribery and vote-buying. All 43 panel seats were to be filled as if they were part of a single constituency, and the electorate was relatively low (it consisted of newly elected members of the Dáil and seven representatives from each county and county borough council)—a total of 354 people in 1938, of whom 330 voted (*Irish Times*, 29 March 1938). This meant that the electoral quota amounted to a little over eight votes. The ballot paper was huge: it was three feet long in 1938. The Seanad Electoral (Panel Members) Act, 1947, provided, however, for five separate elections, one for each panel, and extended the electorate to include all members of county and county borough councils, as well as outgoing senators—who were also given the right to nominate candidates. Minor changes were made by the Seanad Electoral (Panel Members) Act, 1954, whose main effect was to abolish the 'nomination committees' established by the 1947 act to review candidates in each of the five panels. These changes aside, the formal structure of the Seanad has remained the same ever since.

THE FUNCTIONING OF THE SEANAD

Given its status as the world's longest-surviving house of parliament that is based on functional representation, analysis of the role of the Seanad since 1938 is of particular interest. This section begins by looking at the manner in which the Seanad is composed, focusing in turn on its three main components: the 43 senators returned to represent the five 'vocational' panels, the six university senators, and the 11 nominees of the Taoiseach. The section concludes with a review of the powers of the Seanad.

The panel members

Unlike its predecessor under the 1922 constitution, and many of its counterparts elsewhere, the life of the Seanad is tied to that of the Dáil (though the life-spans of the two chambers may overlap): a new senate must be elected within 90 days of the dissolution of the Dáil, with the election of the 43 panel senators of greatest importance. Because of the extent to which it takes place behind closed doors rather than involving the public, it has been dubbed a 'silent' or 'subterranean' election.

Unlike Dáil elections, 'constituencies' in senate elections are functional, not territorial. The lines of division do not follow the units of area recognised in the population census, but rather a kind of 'industrial' classification of the population. Each candidate must possess, to the satisfaction of the returning officer, 'knowledge and practical experience' of designated areas of activity with which his or her panel is associated. This concern with maintaining the identity of separate panels is reflected in arrangements for the nomination of candidates. Each panel is divided into two 'provisional subpanels'. On one of these, only specially approved 'nominating bodies' may propose candidates; on the other, candidates are proposed by four members of the Oireachtas. Each subpanel is required to return a minimum number of senators (two on the five-member panel, three on the seven- and nine-member panels, and four on the 11-member panels). To ensure that a reasonable contest takes place, the electoral law provides that the number of candidates on any subpanel must be at least two more than the maximum number of members that may be elected from that subpanel; should the number of nominees be too low, the Taoiseach is required to nominate additional candidates to make up the numbers, as occasionally happens (in 2002 the Taoiseach nominated two candidates and in 2007 three to different Oireachtas subpanels; but their special status was known, and none received any votes in 2002, and only one did in 2007, getting a single vote).

The nominating bodies themselves are registered annually by the Seanad returning officer (since 1947, the Clerk of the Seanad). In 1938, 45 bodies were included in the register; by 2011 this number had more than doubled, to 104. The composition of the register has been relatively stable, with steady changes reflecting the evolving character of Irish society. The Industrial and Commercial panel is the largest. It had 15 bodies in 1938, but by 2011 it numbered 43, ranging from the Society of the Irish Motor Industry (registered since 1938) to the more recent National Off-Licence Association. The Cultural and Educational Panel has for long been second largest. It had 15 bodies in 1938, increasing to 33 by 2011. Three of the original bodies (such as the Catholic Young Men's Society) have fallen off, but 12 have survived since then, including such well-known entities as the Royal Irish Academy, the Royal Society of Antiquaries of Ireland, the Law Society, the Bar Council and certain other professional associations. The Agricultural Panel began with eight bodies, and had increased to a modest 11 by 2011 (the Royal Dublin Society, registered since 1938, is an example). On the Administrative Panel there were originally four bodies, rising to 15 by 2011, and including such enduring members as the Association of County Councils and the Association of Municipal Authorities. The Labour Panel has always been smallest in membership, with only two very unevenly matched bodies in 1938: the Trade Union Congress and the Ballingarry Cottage Tenants' and Rural Workers' Association. The status of the latter, based in a village of 500 people and having allegedly no rules, no staff and an income of £11 over two years, caused the Labour Party to object unsuccessfully to the whole process, and then to boycott the first Seanad election because of this 'manifest absurdity' (O'Sullivan, 1940: 571). The Ballingarry association disappeared in due course, and the number of nominating bodies eventually increased for a time to three, but it has for long been stable at two bodies, with the Irish Conference of Professional and Service Associations joining the Congress of Trade Unions. Between them, these two bodies control nominations to the nominating bodies subpanel and are assured of at least four seats (though while the two union bodies propose, it is the political parties in the electoral college who dispose).

One feature of earlier panel elections was the tendency for the Oireachtas subpanels to be filled first, and for the nominating bodies subpanels to reach only their minimum representation of 16. This may be seen from Table 4.5, the right-hand side of which shows the numbers of senators representing each subpanel at each election since 1938. In the first four elections the allocation of seats to subpanels was fixed by legislation, but the 1947 act only specified the minimum representation required for each subpanel (16 in all), leaving 11 'floating' seats that might go to either subpanel. The number of Nominating Body senators dropped from its fixed number, 21 (1938–44) to 18 in 1948 and to 17 in 1951; from 1954 to 1977 it remained at its minimum permitted level (16). In the course of the 1980s this trend was reversed, but the 1993 result showed a swing back to the original pattern, with the Oireachtas nominees dominating. The conventional explanation for this tendency has been the typically higher political profile of Oireachtas nominees. Analysis of the 1981 senate election concluded that this was indeed an important factor, but that even when strength of political profile is controlled for, Oireachtas nominees tend to perform better than nominating body ones (Coakley, 1987).

While provisions for the nomination of Seanad candidates are relatively open, and allow nominating bodies to propose, say, their presidents for membership of the Seanad, the composition of the electorate negates this: it is highly party political. It consists of all members of county and county borough councils, of all members of the outgoing Seanad and of all newly-elected Dáil deputies. Before the abolition of the 'dual mandate' (which allowed TDs and senators also to serve as councillors) in 2003, there was a prohibition on electors voting in respect of more than one qualification. Thus Dáil deputies and senators were entitled to only one vote, although a considerable number were also county or county borough councillors (in 2002, 93 deputies and 29 senators were also councillors). The overall size of the Seanad electorate consequently increased, from 971 in 2002 to 1,096 in 2007. Unlike the division of the Dáil electorate between constituencies, every panel elector is entitled to vote on all five panels.

The actual mechanics of the Seanad electoral system differ from those of the Dáil. To start with, polling is by mail, and is governed by regulations designed to prevent corrupt practices, such as provisions for validating the identity of the voter. Although the single transferable vote system of proportional representation is used for both houses, vote counting procedures are more complex in Seanad elections. This is because the procedure for distributing surplus votes in Dáil elections introduces a random element in certain circumstances, but this is usually of little consequence when the number of ballot papers is large. Because of the much smaller size of the senate panel electorate, each ballot paper is treated as if it had the value 1,000, but when a surplus distribution of the kind mentioned above arises all of the ballot papers in question are transferred physically, but at reduced value, rendering the random element insignificant. Furthermore, additional counting rules ensure that a balance is maintained between the two subpanels in the case of each panel. These rules prevent the elimination of candidates from a subpanel when this would result in that subpanel failing to attain its minimum share of seats, and provide for the elimination of candidates of a subpanel that has already won its maximum number of seats. It is thus possible for a candidate to be eliminated even though he or she has more votes than other, continuing candidates, and this commonly happens.

Table 4.5: Results of panel elections by party and subpanel, Seanad Éireann, 1938–2011

Year	Party affiliation				Subpanel		Total
	Fianna Fáil	Fine Gael	Labour Party	Others	Nominating body	Oireachtas	
1938–1	25	14	1	3	21	22	43
1938–2	21	14	5	3	21	22	43
1943	21	13	7	2	21	22	43
1944	22	14	5	2	21	22	43
1948	17	14	7	5	18	25	43
1951	23	12	5	3	17	26	43
1954	19	12	7	5	16	27	43
1957	20	16	5	2	16	27	43
1961	23	11	7	2	16	27	43
1965	23	13	6	1	16	27	43
1969	20	17	5	1	16	27	43
1973	18	18	6	1	16	27	43
1977	20	18	5	0	16	27	43
1981	19	19	5	0	18	25	43
1982	20	18	5	0	21	22	43
1983	19	19	5	0	21	22	43
1987	24	16	3	0	23	20	43
1989	24	14	4	1	24	19	43
1993	19	16	5	3	19	24	43
1997	23	16	4	0	23	20	43
2002	24	15	4	0	24	19	43
2007	22	14	6	1	22	21	43
2011	14	18	8	3	23	20	43

Source: Coakley and Laver, 1997: 103; Coakley and Manning, 1999; Gallagher and Weeks, 2003; Reidy, 2008; Coakley, 2011.

Figure 4.1: Distribution of Seanad Éireann panel electorate, 1977–2011

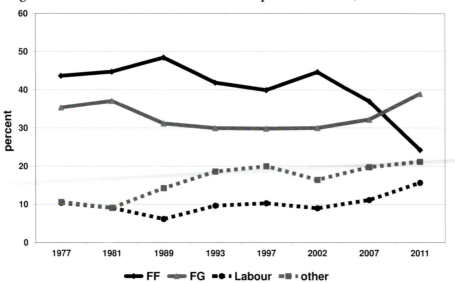

Source: Coakley (1980b, 1987, 1990, 1993), Coakley and Manning (1999), Gallagher and Weeks (2003), Reidy (2008), Coakley (2011).

In reality, it is party political rather than vocational considerations that actually count in Seanad elections. The Seanad electorate has, from the beginning, been dominated by the political parties. The composition of the electorate in selected years since 1977 is summarised in Figure 4.1. If we consider 2002 as representing the traditional voting relationship between the three main parties, with a familiar Fianna Fáil–Fine Gael–Labour ranking similar to the pattern in Dáil elections, the striking changes since then are a drop in Fianna Fáil support from 45% to 24%, and corresponding increases in support for Fine Gael (30% to 39%), Labour (9% to 16%) and others (16% to 21%). Recent data may slightly under-represent Fianna Fáil strength, since it is clear that in the 2009 local elections many long-standing party figures began to distance themselves from their increasingly unpopular party, in some cases contesting the local elections as independents, but nonetheless remaining potential supporters of the party at Seanad elections.

The parties themselves work hard to maximise their position in the second chamber: for the government party or parties, having a secure majority in the Seanad makes life easier, and for the opposition having a strong foothold there opens potential opportunities to embarrass the government. For all parties, too, the Seanad offers a forum for rewarding defeated Dáil candidates and for helping to build up the reputation of future candidates in Dáil elections. Since party affiliations are not indicated on the ballot paper, each party normally circulates a list of its candidates (usually in the form of a mock ballot paper) to party voters (Fine Gael prepared a detailed booklet for the information of its supporters in 2011). Party organisations also make strong efforts to ensure that everyone turns out to vote, offering guidance at meetings of party councillors. Since the political composition of the electorate is known, each party can compute the number of electoral quotas available to it on each panel, and plan the deployment of potential unaffiliated votes. While smaller parties and independent candidates are thus normally seen as a voting resource for the larger parties, there are circumstances where (as in the case of the Progressive Democrats in 1989–93 and Sinn Féin in 2007–11) small parties may be able to win seats with the help of vote-trading arrangements.

Unlike Dáil elections, those to the Seanad attract little public interest— the public, after all, is not directly involved. Instead, candidates travel all over the country pursuing votes from local councillors. While individual candidates are rarely sure of their prospects, the overall political outcome is predictable: each party tends to win a number of seats very close to its known share of the electorate, with the only doubt centring on which candidates from within each party will be successful. The outcome of panel elections since 1938 is summarised in the left-hand side of Table 4.5. This shows the extent to which, until 2011, Fianna Fáil dominated the process, though much less completely than at Dáil elections: Fine Gael tied with it in 1973, 1981 and 1983, and beat it into second position in 2011. The Labour Party has always trailed behind its larger rivals, with smaller parties typically faring extremely poorly, or winning no seats at all.

The university seats

University representation in legislatures is, as we have seen, venerable in origin, though unusual in modern western democracies. Ireland's two university constituencies had well-established political reputations. The University of Dublin (Trinity College), represented in the Irish House of Commons since the seventeenth century and after 1800 in the United Kingdom House of Commons, had for long returned Tories or Conservatives to that chamber, and after the 1880s these identified overwhelmingly as Unionists. The National University of Ireland (NUI) was given representation in the House of Commons in 1918. This university representation was transferred to the House of Commons of Southern Ireland in 1921, where each university was given four seats, and this was carried over to the Dáil under the 1922 constitution, though each university's representation was now reduced to three. Dublin University representation was dominated by three independent former Unionists, Professors Alton, Thrift and Craig, who were returned to the Dáil at each general election, 1923–33. NUI representation initially reflected strong Cumann na nGaedheal influence, but by 1933 the same kind of shift as was taking place in the general electorate gave Fianna Fáil a majority there too.

In 1936 the constitution was amended to bring university representation in the Dáil to an end, but when the new Seanad was established this representation was reintroduced in the second chamber in identical form. Like 'panel' senators, university senators are also elected by postal ballot. Here, though, the electorate is much larger and less concentrated: it comprises all graduates who are Irish citizens and have registered as electors. A candidate must be proposed by two registered senate electors, with the assent of eight others. The rules for counting votes are the same as those used in Dáil elections.

In the first election to the new Seanad in 1938, two former Dublin University TDs simply moved across to the senate, where they were joined by a third independent. They were succeeded in due course by other senators who remained detached from party politics. The major exceptions were Mary Robinson (1969–89), who accepted the Labour whip for most of her time in the Seanad, and Ivana Bacik (2007–), also a Labour senator. On the NUI side, one of three former NUI TDs, Helena Concannon, a Fianna Fail supporter, was elected in 1938 and continued to represent the NUI until her death in 1952. Other long-serving NUI senators were close in political outlook to Fine Gael or even prominently identified with that party, even if they were formally independent: Michael Tierney (1938–44), George O'Brien (1948–65), Bryan Alton (1965–73), Gemma Hussey (1977–82) and James Dooge (1982–87), for example. Supporters of other parties were rarer, but included Labour supporters Michael D. Higgins (1983–87) and Brendan Ryan (1982–92 and 1997–2007).

The pattern by which the university senate electorate has expanded reflects the history of a developing Irish university system. The NUI electorate was a little more than 8,000 in 1938, but had grown to over 30,000 by 1969 and 102,000 in 2002; since then it has fallen. The University of Dublin electorate grew from about 3,000 in 1938 to 38,000 in 2002, and thereafter continued to expand. Turnout levels, however, have in general been dropping. In the NUI turnout remained well above 50% until the mid-1960s, but since then has been declining, to 32% in 2002. In the University of Dublin the 2002 turnout was a little higher, at 37%. In 2011, the turnout levels were 36% in the NUI and 29% in the University of Dublin.

The whole question of university representation has, however, become a subject of considerable debate. By 2009, the NUI accounted for only 32% of all those graduating from undergraduate courses, and Trinity College for just 6%; other university-level institutions accounted for 14% and the institutes of technology for 48%.[3] Despite apparent consensus on reform, no action has been taken to implement the changes promised in 1979, when the constitution was amended by referendum (with a huge majority of 92% voting in favour) to allow university representation to be regulated by ordinary legislation.

Table 4.6: Distribution of university electorate for Seanad Éireann by period of first qualification and region, 2011

Area	Dublin (%)	Rest of Republic of Ireland (%)	Northern Ireland (%)	Great Britain (%)	Rest of world (%)	Total
National University of Ireland						
Before 1960	41.0	52.6	2.3	2.5	1.7	6,261
1960–69	36.9	57.7	1.5	1.6	2.2	9,944
1970–79	32.4	64.2	0.9	1.1	1.4	19,813
1980–89	28.6	68.1	0.7	1.3	1.4	24,552
1990–99	28.5	69.1	0.5	1.0	0.9	22,146
2000–09	29.3	69.4	0.4	0.4	0.5	14,535
Total	31.1	65.7	0.8	1.2	1.3	97,251
University of Dublin						
Before 1960	21.7	12.6	23.0	27.8	14.9	1,983
1960–69	31.0	21.0	16.4	19.2	12.4	1,664
1970–79	44.2	24.2	8.8	11.4	11.4	3,839
1980–89	48.0	30.9	2.7	9.3	9.1	11,024
1990–99	49.4	39.6	2.0	4.3	4.7	17,447
2000–09	49.3	44.3	2.8	1.7	1.9	17,633
Total	47.1	36.7	4.1	6.3	5.8	53,590

Note: The data exclude two electors in the NUI constituency whose qualifications were awarded after 2009 and 481 whose deaths were recorded only after publication of the register, and 75 electors in the University of Dublin constituency where information in respect of region or year of qualification was missing. The full electorates in the respective constituencies were 97,734 and 53,665. *Source:* Computed from anonymised registers supplied by the Registrar, National University of Ireland, and the Vice Provost, Trinity College Dublin (University of Dublin).

Given the debate on the allegedly unrepresentative nature of university representation, it is worth looking in greater detail at its composition. As may be seen from Table 4.6, there are quite significant differences between the two universities, and these were much greater in the past. The NUI electorate broadly reflects the distribution of the Irish population, though with a stronger Dublin bias (this accounts for 31% of the electorate, as compared to 28% of the overall population). In the earlier years, the Dublin share was rather higher. The proportion resident outside the state, 3%, has been shrinking over time. The University of Dublin, perhaps not surprisingly, lives up to its name in having a much stronger Dublin orientation (47% of the electorate). A much higher proportion are resident outside Ireland than in the case of the NUI (16%); but in the past this proportion was higher still. Of those receiving their degrees before 1960, for example, 66% are now resident outside the Republic, though their presence in the register indicates that they are Irish citizens. This is probably a consequence of Trinity College's long but now less marked tradition of recruiting students from Northern Ireland and Great Britain. It is likely that getting qualified graduates to register for Seanad elections poses a considerable challenge, especially in the NUI, where the electorate has not kept pace with the growing pool of graduates. This no doubt reflects the university's own diverse structure, with large campuses spread across the country, but also its uncertain future (given proposals to abolish it), and the debate about the appropriateness of such representation at all.

The Taoiseach's nominees

The Irish prime minister is unique in having the right to appoint members to the second chamber, though this uniqueness is more formal than substantive. Elsewhere, the prime minister may enjoy such a right in practice, but in theory he or she has to operate by advising the head of state to make specific appointments rather than by making them directly. In the Irish case, the Taoiseach can use these nominations to reinforce the government's position in the second chamber, and this has been the trend from the beginning. Subject to an expectation that Taoiseach's nominees will support the government in critical votes, especially when they accept a party whip, efforts have also been made to use this set of senators to secure the representation of special interests.

In the Seanad's early years, the considerations that influenced the Taoiseach's choice recalled the formulation used in the 1922 constitution, with its reference to senators as representing 'important aspects of the

Nation's life'. These included the Protestant minority and the Anglo-Irish community. The Taoiseach's initial nominees in 1938 included Protestants associated with nationalist causes, such as Douglas Hyde and David Lubbock Robinson, and members of the Anglo-Irish gentry, such as Sir John Keane, a politically independent Protestant, and Col. Maurice Moore, a nationalist Catholic. At the opposite end of the political spectrum, they also included persons linked to the Irish language revival movement, such as Peadar Mac Fhionnlaoich, President of the Gaelic League. Later icons associated with the nationalist tradition appointed by Fianna Fáil Taoisigh included Margaret Pearse (1943–69), sister of the executed 1916 leader Patrick Pearse, and Nora Connolly O'Brien (1957–69), daughter of James Connolly, also executed in 1916.

Although prominent representatives of the Protestant minority and of the Irish language movement continued to be appointed, by the latter part of the twentieth century the perceived importance of these traditions had diminished greatly. New priorities emerged. One of these was Northern Ireland: in a revival of an older practice that had begun in 1948 with the appointment of Denis Ireland (1948–51), more consistent efforts were made to secure Northern Ireland representation during the period 1982–2007. Seven different senators from Northern Ireland were appointed during this period. These included prominent SDLP politicians Seamus Mallon (1982–83) and Brid Rogers (1983–87); independent voices from a Protestant background, such as John Robb (1982–89) and Gordon Wilson (1993–95); a former trade unionist, Stephen McGonagle (1983–87); a former civil servant of Catholic background, Maurice Hayes (1997–2007); and a Fianna Fáil supporter, Edward Haughey (1993–2002), who, appointed to the House of Lords in 2004 as Lord Ballyedmond, sat there first as a Unionist peer and then as a Conservative. A second consideration has been gender. Like the Dáil, the Seanad has been ranked low among parliaments of the world in representing women. At certain times in the past, the Taoiseach's nominees helped to rectify this, but the most dramatic moment was in 2011 when, perhaps in reaction to complaints about a notably male-dominated cabinet, the Taoiseach's 11 nominees included seven women.

The 'Taoiseach's Eleven' are not just another mechanism for facilitating the symbolic presence of particular groups; they are of considerable political significance. For party leaders, they are an important source of patronage, and may be used to reward loyal party workers (whether politicians or officials), to offer a forum for upcoming Dáil candidates, and even to appoint potential government ministers (see Chapter 7). In coalition governments, the allocation of these 11 positions forms part of inter-party haggling in the course of which they enter the negotiating pot alongside ministerial positions, other senior appointments, and policy considerations—a status they have had since the formation of the very first coalition government in 1948.

The power of the Taoiseach in this respect may also have unexpected political consequences. Following the Dáil election of 1992, which brought a Fianna Fáil–Labour coalition to power, Taoiseach Albert Reynolds used his position to appoint one independent, six Fianna Fáil and four Labour senators, thus helping to secure the government's position in the second chamber. But when the coalition collapsed in 1994 and was succeeded without a general election by a Fine Gael–Labour–Democratic Left coalition, this constitutional provision placed the new Taoiseach in a difficult position: John Bruton was now saddled with a group of hostile Fianna Fáil Taoiseach's nominees, in circumstances where every other Taoiseach had been able to rely on this group. This posed a particular difficulty in respect of management of government business in the Seanad for the next three years, since the government lacked a majority there.

Powers of the Seanad

As we have seen, the Irish senate forms part of a cluster of relatively powerless second chambers across the globe. Like most of its counterparts, it has no role to play in selecting, approving or removing the government, it has a limited role in the legislative process, and it has few other powers of any significance. It must consider all legislation, but if it amends a bill the Dáil can refuse to accept its amendments and pass the bill over the heads of the senators after 90 days, or about three months. This is much lower than in the case of the senate of the Irish Free State, where the original delay period was 270 days, or about nine months; but as part of a parcel of changes in 1928–29 that abolished the senate's power to trigger a referendum, the delay period was extended to 18 months to compensate for this (Mansergh, 1934: 97). In the case of financial legislation—money bills—the Seanad can only make recommendations which the Dáil is not required to accept, and the Dáil may insist on the bill's passage after 21 days (see Casey, 2000: 123–8). The Seanad has certain little-known additional powers: a special role in respect of private bills (those affecting a single individual or entity), for instance, and in referring bills to the President to consider whether the views of the electorate should be sought. The Seanad has a relatively toothless power to discuss policy matters by means of motions directed specifically at government performance. It plays an important role, however, in providing personnel for other purposes: its chair (Cathaoirleach) is *ex officio* a member of the Council of State and of the Presidential Commission, up to two of its members may be appointed government ministers, and joint Oireachtas committees rely heavily on participation by senators.

If we look at the actual work of the Seanad, at first sight its contribution to the policy process seems slight. In the past, it met infrequently. During the years 1923–35 the Free State senate sat on average 40 days per year, and its successor for long continued to meet at about this level. Towards the end of the century, however, plenary sessions became much more common; since 2000, the Seanad has typically met on about 90 days each year (MacCarthaigh and Manning, 2010: 474). But data on days sitting offer a quite misleading picture of the work of senators (as, indeed, do similar generalisations about the work of Dáil deputies, and criticisms of their allegedly excessive 'holidays'). In reality, plenary debate takes up a relatively small proportion of the time of a typical parliamentarian. As the work of joint committees of the two houses expanded greatly in the wake of the installation of a comprehensive set of committees spanning all areas of government after 1992 (Martin, 2010: 296–7), the role and visibility of senators, as of Dáil deputies, was greatly expanded.

During the Free State period, the Seanad's impact on legislation was considerable. It flatly rejected six bills in all, and delayed four others (O'Sullivan, 1940: 622–5). By contrast, only two bills have been voted down by the Seanad since 1937, a constitution amendment bill in 1959 and the Pawnbrokers Bill in 1963, though in the latter case poor management on the Government side was responsible (Manning, 2010: 160). When it comes to amending bills, the pattern is similar. During the Free State period, the Seanad amended 37% of all bills; in 1938–69 its successor amended 22% of the bills it considered; and in the period 1970–94 the Seanad amended only 13% of the bills coming before it. Of course, it would be dangerous to read too much into these statistics, since part of the change no doubt arose from improved legislative drafting and circumstances other than the level of engagement of senators. Furthermore, intervention by senators may have a decisive effect, as in 2001, when the Government withdrew an Electoral Amendment Bill due to serious drafting defects that were identified in the course of its passage through the Seanad (MacCarthaigh, 2005: 135).

Since 1922, the Seanad has processed only 72 private bills, almost half of these in the 1920s and 1930s. Since 1980, it has enacted only five, the most recent being the Royal College of Surgeons in Ireland (Charter Amendment) Act, 2003. The Seanad has never referred a bill to the President to test whether the views of the electorate on it should be sought. But private bills have a role only in relation to specific needs, and these have arisen rarely; and the government almost always has sufficient support in the Seanad for any referral to the President to be out of the question. In its legislative record, as in its stable principle of representation, the performance of the Seanad is conditioned mainly by circumstances outside its control.

ASSESSING THE SEANAD

The Seanad's apparent unpopularity with the electorate, as illustrated in the outcome of opinion polls in 2011–13, the willingness of political leaders to call for its abolition and the volume of reform proposals that have been gathering dust over the past decade, augur ill for the future of Ireland's second chamber. The fact that the Government introduced a bill on 13 June 2013 providing for a referendum to abolish the Seanad suggests that the second chamber's days may well be numbered. Yet it is worth reviewing the debate on the future of the Seanad, and looking at the constitutional options.

The debate on reform

Seanad Éireann, as currently constituted, has come under threat from two directions. First, the state's major parties were committed to its outright abolition (though Fianna Fáil, which initially supported this in the context of an overhaul of structures of government, has reversed its stance). Such demands go back to the 1950s: there were voices at that time calling for the abolition of the Seanad, at least 'as at present constituted' (Garvin, 1969: 78–80). In 1988 the Progressive Democrats proposed abolishing the second chamber (Collins, 2005: 83), but the party moderated its position as some of its own members found an apparently comfortable niche in this quarter of Leinster House (Manning, 2010: 165). The very attractiveness of the Seanad to politicians as 'a convenient berth for political hopefuls on the way up (or down)' undermined political interest in reform (Laver, 2002: 58).

By contrast to straightforward calls for abolition, in respect of which few efforts at justification have been made, the second challenge to the Seanad in its current shape comes from a range of carefully considered reports on the subject. Critics of the Seanad claimed that there were 12 of these, and that they had been ignored (Weeks, 2010: 126). This, however, seems to be a misinterpretation of a 2004 report, which simply listed 11 reports that had been compiled earlier (Seanad Éireann, 2004). One of these was of purely historical interest, as it dealt with the electoral system of the senate of the

Irish Free State (Oireachtas Éireann, 1928); one considered the options for a new senate (Second House of the Oireachtas Commission, 1936), and one examined vocational organisation as a general principle of social organisation, recommending the creation of a consultative, non-partisan 'national vocational assembly' alongside the existing Seanad (Commission on Vocational Organisation, 1943: 310). Three further reports examined technical aspects of electoral law (Dáil Éireann, 1937; Oireachtas Éireann, 1947; Seanad Éireann, 1952). A more radical proposal was made in 1959, though this was never followed up: it was suggested that senators nominated by nominating bodies could be elected by electoral colleges comprising members nominated by the nominating bodies themselves (Seanad Electoral Law Commission, 1959: 16–20). Two later comprehensive reviews of the constitution came to only general conclusions regarding the Seanad. The Committee on the Constitution (1967: 29–31) endorsed retention of a second chamber 'on vocational or functional lines' but recommended little by way of reform to bring about this objective. The Constitution Review Group (1996: 65–71) concluded that 'the Seanad does not appear to satisfy the criteria for a relevant, effective and representative second house', but took the view that there was insufficient time to consider so complex an issue in detail. The second progress report of the All-Party Oireachtas Committee on the Constitution (1997b: 12), the seventh progress report of the same committee (2002: 38) and a Seanad subcommittee on reform (Seanad Éireann, 2004: 9–13) each recommended retention of the Seanad, but with transformed membership (the three reports differed on the system proposed for selecting senators, as discussed below).

Of course, alongside the two options already discussed, abolition and reform, there is a third: retention in its present form. The idea of a vocational senate had its supporters in the 1930s, as we have seen, and some of these expressed their ideas in extended form (Binchy, 1936; O'Rahilly, 1936). For some, the notion of bicameralism is in itself valuable. Thus Denis O'Keefe (1936: 209) turned Sieyès's dictum on its head: 'if a second chamber agrees with the first, it is an added guarantee of wisdom; if it disagrees, it certainly establishes a case for reconsideration'. Later, critics of the Seanad focused for long not on the constitutional provisions for the composition of the Seanad but on the manner in which these were given legislative effect, suggesting mechanisms by which the quality of vocational representation might be improved (Sutton, 1958). But the battle for a vocational senate has for long been over. Over half a century ago, Basil Chubb (1954) dismissed the view that it would be possible to base a second chamber on this principle in circumstances where society was not so structured, and this view has been widely accepted since then. Indeed, if the concept of a vocational senate could not be realised in the late 1930s and the 1940s, when 'vocational' thinking was at its height, it was likely to be even more problematic with the demise of corporatist thinking after the Second World War (O'Leary, 2000: 189).

Arguments that a second chamber could be 'non-political' have been similarly fraught. If a second chamber is to be truly non–political, it would have to be shorn of so much power that its role as part of parliament would be called into question; once it acquires substantive powers, it becomes inevitably political, if not necessarily fully partisan (Seanad Electoral Law Commission, 1959; McGowan-Smyth, 2000: 150). As the dilemma has been summarised,

> A functional or vocational chamber can work as such in association with a party legislature only in an advisory capacity. If it is intended to be an integral part of the legislature, its party composition becomes a matter of concern to the party politicians of the lower house and it will be converted sooner or later into another party chamber. Vocational chambers, whether as second or as third chambers, in societies where politics are conducted on a free party system, cannot function effectively as an integral part of the legislature. Their proper sphere lies outside the legislature. (Wheare, 1968: 146)

Problematic though the principle of representation may be, it is hard to find an ideal system. It has for long been acknowledged that a directly elected second chamber would be disposed to argue that its mandate matches that of the first chamber, or, if it has been more recently elected, surpasses it (Bryce, 1921: 442–3). Indirect election tends to produce highly partisan second chambers, given the nature of the electorate. Nomination poses problems too; as James Bryce (1921: 443) drily put it, 'there are countries in which secretly rendered political services or liberal contributions to party funds are believed to open the door of the Chamber to those whose merits the public had failed to discover'. In such circumstances, he added, a government may be tempted to use its power of appointment 'to reward its elderly supporters, who, weary of courting constituencies, gladly subside into a dignified armchair' (Bryce, 1921: 443).

Constitutional options

Options currently on the table for the future of Seanad Éireann range from relatively innocuous proposals that do not require constitutional change, such as using the Taoiseach's nominees to include three representatives of the diaspora (Department of the Environment, 1996), or reforming university representation, to more radical proposals, such as outright abolition of the second chamber. What are the alternatives to this?

In the light of plans to abolish the Seanad, the Government has no interest in considering issues of reform, and the topic was not placed on the agenda of the Convention on the Constitution (which in any case voted against considering this matter). Nevertheless, it is worth discussing further the three parliamentary reports that drew up specific and detailed recommendations on the Seanad.

- The All-Party Oireachtas Committee on the Constitution, in its second progress report (1997b: 10–12), suggested a 60-member body with 15 senators elected from European constituencies in the same manner as MEPs, 14 elected by Dáil deputies, 14 by local councillors, six by university graduates, and 11 Taoiseach's nominees.
- A reconstituted All-Party Oireachtas Committee on the Constitution, in its seventh progress report (2002: 38–39), suggested a 60-member body with 48 members elected from a single state-wide constituency by means of the list system, and 12 Taoiseach's nominees.
- A Sub-Committee on Seanad Reform of the Seanad's own Committee on Procedure and Privileges (Seanad Éireann, 2004: 9–13) suggested a 64-member body with 26 members elected from a single state-wide constituency by means of the list system on the same day as the European and local elections, six elected by university graduates on the same day, 20 elected by an electoral college made up of newly elected Dáil deputies, outgoing senators and county and city councillors, and 12 Taoiseach's nominees.

Notwithstanding the careful consideration that has been given to the issue, no consensus has emerged on the shape that a reformed Seanad might take. This is reflected in the failure of the All-Party Group on Seanad Reform in 2008–10 to find common ground between the parties.[4] Neither is it clear, though, that sufficient consideration has been given to the implications of simply abolishing the Seanad, a move that would entail a wide range of constitutional changes. The expression 'Seanad Éireann' occurs 65 times in the text of the constitution, and substantive references extend over 16 articles. These of course include articles 18 and 19 which describe the structure and role of the Seanad itself, and a further 10 articles that deal with aspects of the legislative or other control functions shared with the Dáil. Abolishing the Seanad and allocating exclusive responsibility to the Dáil in these areas might pose few formal problems. But there are areas where there are implications for other institutions of state (such as the Council of State and the Presidential Commission), and the Government has had to devise alternative arrangements in these areas in the bill designed to abolish the Seanad.

CONCLUSION

It would be hard to argue that any 'debate' on the future of the Seanad took place between the time its abolition jumped onto the political agenda and the introduction of the abolition bill in the Dáil. Up to that point, no considered case for abolishing the Seanad was made, nor were the implications of abolition assessed in any degree of detail. The bold commitment of the Fine Gael–Labour coalition to getting rid of the Seanad as one of three 'urgent parliamentary reform issues' implicitly ignored the painstaking deliberations (extending over the past 16 years) of earlier parliamentary evaluations of the composition and role of the second chamber, and sidelined the Convention on the Constitution. In the light of the long discussion of the merits of second chambers inside and outside Ireland, the fate of Seanad Éireann surely deserved more sustained and balanced consideration before the Dáil began to discuss practical arrangements for consigning it to history.

NOTES

1. This chapter is based on Coakley, 1997; Coakley, 2011; and other items cited here.
2. Surveys by the Inter-Parliamentary Union showed the proportion of bicameral parliaments dropping to 59% in 1961 (17 out of 41), 46% in 1976 (26 out of 56), 34% in 1986 (28 out of 83) and 33% in 1996 (59 out of 178; Inter-Parliamentary Union, 1962: 12–13; 1986; Herman 1976; Coakley and Laver, 1997: 35–7; see also Ameller, 1966). Observers noted a levelling in this decline in the last two decades of the twentieth century (Massicotte, 2001: 153–4; Shell, 2001a: 1; Norton, 2007: 18).
3. Computed from HEA statistical data for 2009, available at www.hea.ie/en/statistics
4. See minutes of the meetings of the group at www.environ.ie/en/publications/localgovernment/voting

APPENDIX A: FEATURES OF 76 SECOND CHAMBERS OF PARLIAMENT, 2012

Country, chamber	Parl. power index	Second chamber						First chamber		Population 2010	
		Power	Size	Rep. principle	Sel. formula	Term	Min. age	Size	Ratio	Total (000s)	Ratio
Afghanistan House of Elders	0.38	low	102	territory (equal)	I 68 A 34	na	35	249	41	24,486	240
Algeria Council of the Nation	0.25	high	144	territory (equal)	I 96 A 48	6–3	40	389	37	35,978	250
Antigua and Barbuda Senate	–	low	17	unspecific	A	5	21	19	89	86	5
Argentina* Senate	0.50	high	72	territory (equal)	D	6–2	30	257	28	40,519	563
Australia* Senate	0.63	medium	76	territory (equal)	D	6–3	18	150	51	22,342	294
Austria* Federal Council	0.72	low	62	territory (weight)	I	na	21	183	34	8,390	135
Bahamas Senate	–	low	16	unspecific	A	5	30	41	39	347	22
Bahrain Shura Council	0.19	medium	40	unspecific	A	4	35	40	100	1,178	29
Barbados Senate	–	low	21	unspecific	A	5	21	30	70	276	13
Belarus Council of the Republic	0.25	medium	64	territory (equal)	I 56 A 8	4	30	110	58	9,491	148
Belgium* Senate	0.75	medium	71	territory (weight)	D 40 I 21 C 10	4	21	150	47	10,879	153
Belize Senate	–	low	13	unspecific	A	5	18	32	41	333	26
Bhutan National Council	0.22	medium	25	territory (equal)	D 20 A 5	5	25	47	53	696	28
Bolivia Senate	0.44	medium	36	territory (equal)	D	5	35	130	28	10,426	290
Bosnia and Herzegovina* House of Peoples	0.63	high	15	territory (weight)	I	4	18	42	36	3,844	256
Brazil* Federal Senate	0.56	medium	81	territory (equal)	D	8–4	35	513	16	193,253	2,386
Burundi Senate	0.41	medium	41	territory (equal)	I 34 E 7	5	35	106	39	7,384	180
Cambodia Senate	0.59	low	61	people	I 57 P 2 A 2	6	40	123	50	14,303	234
Canada* Senate	0.72	low	105	territory (weight)	A	na	30	308	34	34,109	325

Country, chamber	Parl. power index	Second chamber						First chamber		Population 2010	
		Power	Size	Rep. principle	Sel. formula	Term	Min. age	Size	Ratio	Total (000s)	Ratio
Chile Senate	0.56	medium	38	territory (weight)	D	8–4	35	120	32	17,094	450
Colombia Senate	0.56	medium	102	people	D	4	30	166	61	45,508	446
Congo, DR Senate	0.25	low	108	territory (equal)	I	5	30	500	22	65,966	611
Congo Senate	0.38	medium	72	territory (equal)	I	6–3	45	137	53	3,752	52
Czech Republic Senate	0.81	low	81	people	D	6–2	40	200	41	10,520	130
Dominican Republic Senate	0.41	high	32	territory (equal)	D	4	25	183	17	9,884	309
Ethiopia* House of the Federation	0.50	low	135	territory (weight)	I	5	21	547	25	79,221	587
France Senate	0.56	low	348	territory (weight)	I	6–3	30	577	60	62,968	181
Gabon Senate	0.44	low	102	people	I	6	40	120	85	1,313	13
Germany* Federal Council	0.84	medium	69	territory (weight)	I†	na	18	622	11	81,776	1,185
Grenada Senate	–	low	13	unspecific	A	5	18	15	87	109	8
Haiti Senate	0.44	high	30	territory (equal)	D	6–2	30	95	32	10,085	336
India* Council of States	0.63	medium	245	people	I 233 A 12	6–2	30	545	45	1,182,105	4,825
Ireland Senate	0.66	low	60	other	I 43 A 11 O 6	5	21	166	36	4,474	75
Italy Senate	0.84	high	322	people	D 315 A 5 E 2	5	40	630	51	60,483	188
Jamaica Senate	0.63	low	21	unspecific	A	5	21	63	33	2,702	129
Japan House of Councillors	0.66	low	242	people	D	6–3	30	480	50	127,450	527
Jordan Senate	0.22	low	60	other	A	4	40	120	50	6,113	102
Kazakhstan Senate	0.38	high	47	territory (equal)	I 32 A 15	6–3	30	107	44	15,900	338
Lesotho Senate	0.53	low	33	other	H 22 A 11	5	21	120	28	1,892	57

Country, chamber	Parl. power index	Second chamber						First chamber		Population 2010	
		Power	Size	Rep. principle	Sel. formula	Term	Min. age	Size	Ratio	Total (000s)	Ratio
Liberia Senate	0.44	high	30	territory (equal)	D	9†	30	73	41	3,477	116
Madagascar Higher Transitional Council	0.41	low	90	other	A	na		256	35	18,865	210
Malaysia* Senate	0.34	medium	70	other	A 44 I 26	na	30	222	32	28,250	404
Mauritania Senate	0.31	low	56	territory (equal)	I 53 C 3	6–2	35	95	59	3,162	56
Mexico* Senate	0.44	high	128	territory (equal)	D	6	25	500	26	107,551	840
Morocco House of Councillors	0.31	low	270	territory (equal)	I	9–3	30	395	68	31,851	118
Myanmar House of Nationalities	0.00	medium	224	territory (equal)	D 168 A 56	5	30	436	51	58,377	261
Namibia National Council	0.50	medium	26	territory (equal)	I	5	21	78	33	2,143	82
Netherlands Senate	0.78	medium	75	people	I	4	18	150	50	16,615	222
Nigeria* Senate	0.47	high	109	territory (equal)	D	4	35	352	31	140,004	1,284
Oman State Council	0.16	low	83	other	A	4	40	84	99	3,174	38
Pakistan* Senate	0.44	medium	100	territory (equal)	I 88 P 12	6–3	30	342	29	165,150	1,652
Palau Senate	–	high	13	people	D	4	25	16	81	21	2
Paraguay Senate	0.56	high	45	people	D	5	40	80	56	6,451	143
Philippines Senate	0.56	high	23	people	D	6–3	35	280	8	94,013	4,088
Poland Senate	0.75	low	100	people	D	4	30	460	22	38,184	382
Romania Senate	0.72	high	137	people	D	4	33	334	41	21,438	156
Russian Federation* Council of the Federation	0.44	low	166	territory (equal)	I 83 A 83	na		450	37	142,938	861
Rwanda Senate	0.47	high	26	territory (equal)	I 14 A 12	8	40	80	33	10,413	400
Saint Lucia Senate	–	low	11	unspecific	A	5	21	18	61	168	15

Country, chamber	Parl. power index	Second chamber						First chamber		Population 2010	
		Power	Size	Rep. principle	Sel. formula	Term	Min. age	Size	Ratio	Total (000s)	Ratio
Senegal Senate	0.44	low	100	other	A 65 I 35	5	35	150	67	12,509	125
Slovenia National Council	0.75	low	40	other	I†	5	18	90	44	2,049	51
South Africa* National Council of Provinces	0.63	medium	54	territory (equal)	I	5	18	400	14	49,991	926
South Sudan Council of States	–	medium	50	other	A	4		332	15	8,260	165
Spain* Senate	0.72	low	264	territory (equal)	D 208 I 56	4	18	350	75	46,071	175
Sudan Council of States	0.22	medium	32	territory (equal)	I	5	21	346	9	30,890	965
Swaziland Senate	0.25	medium	30	other	A 20 P 10	5	18	66	45	1,146	38
Switzerland* Council of States	0.72	high	46	territory (equal)	D	4	na	200	23	7,826	170
Tajikistan National Assembly	0.31	medium	34	territory (equal)	I 25 A 8 E 1	5	35	63	54	7,295	215
Thailand Senate	0.59	low	150	territory (equal)	D 77 A 73	6	40	500	30	67,312	449
Trinidad and Tobago Senate	0.53	low	31	unspecific	A	5	25	42	74	1,318	43
United Kingdom House of Lords	0.78	low	733	other	A 616 H 92 E 25	na	21	650	113	62,222	85
United States of America* Senate	0.63	high	100	territory (equal)	D	6–2	30	434	23	309,051	3,091
Uruguay Senate	0.66	medium	31	people	D 30 E 1	5	30	99	31	3,357	108
Uzbekistan Senate	0.28	medium	100	territory (equal)	I 84 A 16	5	?	150	67	25,568	256
Yemen Consultative Council	0.44	low	111	other	A	na	40	301	37	23,154	209
Zimbabwe Senate	0.31	medium	100	territory (equal)	D 60 E 28 A 5 O 7	5	40	214	47	12,260	123

Note and sources. *Federal system (Forum of Federations, 2012). **Chamber name**: English version used by the Inter-Parliamentary Union (2012). **'Parl. power'**: Fish–Kroenig (2009) index of parliamentary power. **'Power'**: crude estimate of the power of the second chamber in relation to the first, compiled as follows: in 30 cases, based on Patterson and Mughan, 2001, who use five categories of overall power, here grouped: co-equal (high); co-equal with restrictions; limited exclusive powers, veto (medium); delay and advisory; subordinate (low); in a further 26 cases, based on Russell, 2012, who offers a more complex and sophisticated categorisation according to role in the legislative process, with six major categories and some subdivisions within these, here grouped: absolute veto (high); absolute veto with qualifications, joint sittings or supermajority in lower house can override (medium); upper house can be overridden by normal or absolute majority in lower house (low); in nine cases not covered by either of these, based on Sénat, 2012, following the same principles as in respect of Russell, 2012; eight Commonwealth senates in the Caribbean with British-style constitutions were coded 'low'; and in the three remaining cases classification was based on an examination of specific documents: the Transitional Constitution of South Sudan (2011), the Interim Constitution of Sudan (2005) and the Constitution of Swaziland (2005). **'Rep. principle'**: representation criterion at which the chamber seems to aim. **'Sel. formula'**: selection formula (A: appointment; C: co-optation; D: direct election; E: *ex officio*; I: indirect election by local councillors or equivalent; O: other; P: selection by first chamber; when more than one formula is used, the digits indicate the number of members selected in accordance with each; †the description over-simplifies). **'Term'**: term of office, where, when a dash appears, the first digit refers to the term of office of senators, the second to the number of years between partial renewals. **'Min. age'**: minimum age for membership. **'First chamber: ratio'**: number of members of the second chamber for every 100 members of the first chamber. **'Population: ratio'**: mean population (thousands) for each member of the second chamber (derived from United Nations, 2012). **Other sources** used include Mastias and Grangé, 1987; Coakley and Laver, 1997; Gélard, 2006; the constitutions of certain countries.

5

THE DÁIL ELECTORAL SYSTEM: DEMOCRACY OR EFFICIENCY?

There can be no doubting the significance of an electoral system for political outcomes. To cite some famous examples of the immediate, radical impact of change in electoral law, we could recall the abolition of proportional representation in Italy in 1993, which helped to bring the traditional party system to an abrupt end and replace it by a more fluid set of alliances. The reintroduction of the two-ballot system in France in 1958, which decisively marginalised the powerful Communist Party, was an important instrument in facilitating Gaullist rule. The Acerbo Law in Italy in 1923, which provided that the party winning most votes would be awarded two thirds of all seats in parliament (provided it won at least a quarter of votes cast) handed a huge majority to the Fascist Party.

Undoubtedly, Ireland would have suffered similar trauma after 1959 or after 1968, had government proposals to replace the existing electoral system been accepted by voters: Fianna Fáil would have become entirely dominant in the Dáil, at least in the short term. It appears, though, that the electoral system continues to be relatively popular; none of the several official reviews have recommended its abolition, and some have dismissed the case against it. Nevertheless, the recurring debate on electoral reform in Ireland suggests that notwithstanding apparently decisive verdicts on the system in the past, dissatisfaction with certain of its consequences has ensured that the future of the current system cannot be entirely taken for granted. Thus, for example, Garret FitzGerald argued that an electoral system based mainly on single-member districts would relieve deputies of a great deal of their constituency work and leave them freer to concentrate on their legislative roles (FitzGerald, 2008). The electoral system has also been criticised vigorously by an experienced then government minister (Dempsey, 2010) and, in a more undiscriminating way, by a former university president (Walsh, 2010). As another ex-minister put it, the present system 'almost ensures that a broad range of the best brains and achievers in the country will never see the inside of Leinster House, much less the Cabinet room' (Hussey, 2009).

The object of this chapter is not simply to add further to this debate, as it has been exhaustively reviewed in the academic literature as well as in public discourse, but rather to address a simple question: what might the Irish party political landscape look like if we were to move to one of the several well-known electoral systems that have been canvassed in the past? Indeed, the question is narrower than this: it aims to address not the general con-sequences of change in electoral law (such as the creation of an alternative incentive structure that might encourage deputies to spend less time on constituency work) but the more specific probable impact of change in the electoral formula on the party political composition of the Dáil.[1]

The chapter begins by reviewing the main alternatives that have been proposed to the present electoral system (in fact, all major electoral systems have been suggested on some occasion or other). It offers an overview of the mechanics and known political consequences of the most important of these. It continues by looking at the introduction of the single transferable vote (STV) system to Ireland in 1920, and at the debate about its consequences. It then describes an approach to simulating outcomes under different electoral systems on the basis of the 2007 and 2011 election results (making use also, for technical reasons, of the 2009 local elections results), and reviews the consequences of these various systems for the distribution of seats between parties. It concludes by speculating on the probable longer-term consequences of adoption of any alternative system and sets this in the context of possible constitutional change.

ELECTORAL SYSTEMS: A COMPARATIVE PERSPECTIVE

In understanding the Irish electoral system, there are two broader contexts that need to be considered. The first has to do with its rather unusual mechanical properties as a device for translating voter preferences into parliamentary seats, which set it apart from the other more widely used electoral systems. The second concerns the political consequences of these systems, whether direct or indirect. These are considered in turn in this section.

Types of electoral system

We may set the Irish electoral system in context by locating it within the wider world of electoral systems globally. Already a century ago, a lawyer and activist in the Proportional Representation Society, John Fischer Williams, expressed the view that 'there are said to be some 300 systems [of proportional representation] in existence, and the ingenuity of inventors shows no sign of exhaustion' (Williams, 1914: 30). It was not, however, the imagination of those who devised such systems but rather hard-headed political choices by state elites that led to the configuration of electoral systems that was ultimately to emerge. These have tended to centre on a relatively small number of electoral formulas, as described in Table 5.1, which provides an overview of the distribution of the electoral systems of the countries of the world. The table makes clear the dominance of two particular types of electoral formula: the party list system of proportional representation, and the plurality system and its relatives. The dominance of these two types is all the more striking when the size of the countries in question is taken into account: the large countries of the world, as measured by population, fall overwhelmingly into these two categories.

The main features of these systems are well known, and have been definitively described in the standard text on electoral systems (Farrell, 2011) and in the major comparative volume that explores these systems and their political consequences (Gallagher and Mitchell, 2009), so it is not necessary to describe them in detail here (see also Reeve and Ware, 1992; Reynolds, Reilly and Ellis, 2005). It is nevertheless important to sketch their main features as these impinge on the fortunes of parties.

In the case of list systems of proportional representation, three features are of particular importance. The first is constituency size. Obviously, the larger the number of representatives returned by each constituency, the greater the potential degree of proportionality, other things being equal. For example, if three parties, A, B and C, win respectively 50%, 30% and 20% of the vote in a constituency in a typical proportional system, then in a single-member constituency A will win the seat, in a three-member constituency A will probably win two seats and B one, and in a 10-member constituency the respective parties will win 5, 3 and 2 seats. The proportionate distribution of seats between the parties in the three scenarios is, then, 100–0–0, 67–33–0 and 50–30–20, with only the last one representing true proportionality. In practice, constituency size in list systems ranges from the modest (as in Belgium or Spain) to the very large (as in the Netherlands and Israel, where the whole territory of the state is treated as a single constituency).

Table 5.1: Distribution of world's electoral systems, 2010

System	Countries	Examples
Proportional		
List proportional representation	75	Spain, Switzerland
Single transferable vote	2	Ireland, Malta
Single-member non-proportional		
Plurality	49	UK, USA
Two-round system	19	France, Belarus
Alternative vote	3	Australia, Fiji
Multi-member non-proportional		
Single non-transferable vote	2	Afghanistan, Vanuatu
Limited vote	1	Gibraltar
Block vote	14	Kuwait, Laos
Mixed		
Mixed proportional	7	Germany, New Zealand
Mixed parallel	26	Japan, Korea
Single non-transferable vote and list PR	1	Jordan
Other		
Party block vote	3	Singapore, Chad
Borda count	1	Nauru

Note: Data appear to refer to different dates and predominant systems. *Source:* International Idea, 2010 (accessed 18 October 2012).

The second feature is the formula for translating votes into seats for parties. In list systems in general, each party gets at least as many seats as it has Droop quotas (a concept that is familiar in Ireland, since it forms the basis of the STV system; it is defined as the number of valid votes divided by one more than the number of seats, with any fractional remainder rounded up). But even if the allocation of seats follows Droop quotas exhaustively, some seats will remain unallocated, and list systems differ in the manner in which they deal with this. There are three main approaches, as discussed further in Chapter 6 in relation to allocation of seats to constituencies. The simplest and most intuitively obvious is the largest remainder system: remaining seats in a constituency are allocated to parties in order of their remaining votes once Droop quotas that have been used up have been subtracted, as in South Africa. A second approach (the Sainte-Laguë system) is to adjust the size of the quota until a point is reached at which the proportions of seats due to the various parties, *when rounded*, total exactly the number of seats in the constituency, as in the Scandinavian countries (where, however, this system is applied in modified form that raises the threshold for smaller parties). The third approach (the D'Hondt system) is similar: the size of the quota is adjusted until a point is reached at which the proportions of seats due to the various parties, *when truncated*, total exactly the number of seats in the constituency, as in Belgium.[2]

The third broad consideration is the mechanism for allocating seats to candidates within party lists. Here, the extremes are represented by 'closed' list systems, as in Spain, where seats are allocated to candidates in an order predetermined by the party, and 'open' ones, as in Switzerland, where personal votes determine the outcome. In typical list systems that allow personal voting, many voters in practice do not take up this option, and their votes are automatically allocated to candidates beginning at the top of the list of the party they support. Under these arrangements, personal votes have an impact only in marginal circumstances, since in the case of major parties candidates at the top of the list are certain of election, while those at the bottom will almost certainly not be elected.

The STV system differs from the party list one in that parties need not be present (indeed, party affiliations of candidates were not indicated on Irish ballot papers before 1963). Ranking of candidates can proceed in accordance with whatever criterion the voter wishes to use, and personal votes entirely determine the outcome. Nevertheless, the system can allow considerable influence to parties: candidates may be grouped by party rather than simply being listed alphabetically, as in Malta; or voters may be allowed to select a predetermined candidate ranking favoured by a particular party rather than themselves ranking the candidates, as in Australian Senate elections, where voters can tick 'above the line' to signify their support for the preference ordering offered by a particular party (Farrell and McAllister, 2006: 65–7). The complexity of the voting and especially counting process may give rise to difficulties if the number of vacancies is large. In 1925, for example, the only occasion on which a portion of the Irish senate was elected directly by the people, such an experiment took place: the whole territory of the state became a vast constituency for the election of 19 senators by STV. There were 76 candidates, whose names appeared in four columns on a huge ballot paper, and it took 67 counts over three weeks to complete the election, an outcome that attracted a great deal of criticism (see Coakley, 2005).

The older plurality system is easier to describe, and more familiar, due to its widespread use in the past (as in parliamentary elections in Ireland from

1885 to 1918, and elections to the Northern Ireland House of Commons from 1929 to 1969), and its use to the present in UK House of Commons elections. It is often misleadingly labelled the 'first past the post' system, implying an analogy with racing, where the winning runner has demonstrated his or her capacity to out-run all other competitors in the race. This quality is not necessarily shared by winners under the plurality system: the rule that whoever wins a plurality (i.e. more votes than any other candidate) is returned does not necessarily ensure the election of a candidate capable of beating each of the others in a two-way contest. The system is also strikingly disproportional. Two related systems share this feature (disproportionality), but at least offer a more easily justifiable result at local level. Under the two-ballot system, as in France, if no-one wins an overall majority (50% or more) in a first round of voting, a run-off ballot takes place between the leading candidates. Under the alternative vote system, as in Australia, and in Irish by-elections, voters rank candidates, and, if no candidate has an overall majority, candidates are eliminated in inverse order of popularity and their votes are distributed to other candidates in accordance with their lower preferences until some candidate reaches 50%, or only one candidate is left.

The three electoral systems described as 'multi-member non-proportional' have in common the fact that they are based on multi-member constituencies with categorical voting. The single non-transferable vote and the limited vote, which give the voter respectively one vote and a number of votes less than the number of seats, allow for a level of minority representation in a constituency and soften some of the disproportionality that is inherent in the plurality system. The block vote, however, where voters have as many votes as there are vacancies, aggravates this disproportionality in the context of partisan elections; widespread use of this system at local elections in Northern Ireland up to 1967 further discredited a formula that was seen as copper-fastening majority dominance there. The remaining formulas, the party block vote (a list system, where whichever party wins a plurality gets all seats) and the Borda count (a preferential system where voters' rankings of candidates are given numeric weightings), are confined to a very small number of countries.

In the case of list systems of proportional representation, there is commonly a two- or even three-tiered approach, with an initial allocation of seats in relatively small constituencies, a further corrective allocation at regional level, and occasionally even a final allocation at national level to maximise proportionality. But sometimes a fully-fledged hybrid system is used, with each elector given two votes, one for constituency candidates and the other for regional lists. Germany is an important example: half of the members of the Bundestag are elected from single-member constituencies using the plurality system; the remainder are elected from regional lists, but seats are allocated in such a way as to compensate for the disproportionality of the lower tier. New Zealand, Scotland and Wales moved to similar systems. In most hybrid systems, though, the regional tier plays no role in correcting for absence of proportionality in the lower tier; in such cases as Japan, the upper tier simply adds a proportional allocation of regional seats to a disproportional constituency level.

Consequences of electoral systems

While there is agreement that electoral systems have a big impact on the shape of the political system more generally, efforts to assess their consequences vary from author to author, depending on the criteria that each sees as important (for a comprehensive overview, see Gallagher, 2009: 566–75). It is possible to arrive at some generalisations about the immediate or proximate consequences of the electoral systems presented in Table 5.1. These are summarised in Table 5.2, which focuses on those which are most important numerically, or which have been advocated as alternatives to Ireland's current system. Four dimensions are considered: the extent to which the system meets criteria of proportionality of representation, accountability of those elected, simplicity from the perspective of the voter, and spatial or geographical representation of the population. Of course, the entries in this table are generalisations, and the description 'varies' might replace 'low' or 'high' in more cells than is the case here.

The criteria listed in Table 5.2 are designed to assess 'proximate' or immediate consequences of an electoral system. 'Proportionality' refers to the accuracy with which the system translates divisions in the electorate into groups in parliament. 'Accountability' refers to the extent to which voters have the capacity to influence an elected member. Usually, this extends no further than the right to punish him or her when voting at the next election, and is likely to be at its lowest under closed list systems, where it is typically parties rather than voters that have a determining say as to who is elected. 'Simplicity' refers to the ease with which the voter may complete a ballot paper (but not to the process by which votes are counted, which is the responsibility of the returning officer, and may sometimes be quite complex, as in the case of STV). Here, systems that require voters to rank candidates, or to cast a double or otherwise compex vote, are rated as less simple than

Reforming Political Institutions

Table 5.2: Selected properties of electoral systems

System	Proportion-ality	Account-ability	Simplicity	Spatial representation
Party list system	High	Low	*Varies*	Low
Single transferable vote	High	High	Low	Medium high
Mixed proportional	High	*Varies*	Low	High
Mixed parallel	Varies	*Varies*	Low	High
Plurality	Low	High	High	High
Two-round system	Low	*Medium*	*Low*	High
Alternative vote	Low	High	Medium	High

Source: Derived from Reynolds, Reilly and Ellis, 2005: 49, 76–8, 119–20; elements in italics added by author.

those where the voter makes a single categorical choice. The two-ballot system is indeed simple on each occasion that the voter votes, but it has been categorised as difficult here to take account of the fact that the voter may have to turn out to vote twice. 'Spatial representation' refers to the extent to which there is a link between candidates and particular territories, with small (and especially single-member) districts ensuring that this link is strongest of all.

The most widely discussed criterion, however, is the first one—the extent to which the various systems are proportional. Here, there is a good deal of variation within proportional systems, a function of constituency size, the actual electoral formula used, and such issues as the existence of a threshold clause (requiring a party to reach a certain share of the vote if it is to be allocated any seats at all). Proportionality, also, tends to be measured in a unidimensional way: the share of seats won by a party is compared with its share of votes. This makes perfect sense for list systems, but for Ireland's STV system it is less appropriate, since first preference votes are not categorical party choices; voters may have ranked candidates along some kind of nonpartisan criterion, such as gender or geography. Nevertheless, making the simplifying assumption that a first preference vote indicates a voter's preferred party, the record of Ireland's electoral system is compared in Table 5.3 with the position in other selected countries since 1945. This reports the most widely used index of proportionality, the Gallagher index, where 0 represents perfect proportionality and higher figures represent deviations from this (for example, an index of 10.0 would arise if, in a two-party state, party A won 70% of the seats with 60% of the votes). On balance, STV in

Ireland is less proportional than in Malta, or in Northern Ireland since 1973, perhaps because of the small size of constituencies. It falls in the bottom tier of proportional representation systems in general, which range from the Netherlands, the most proportional, to Spain, the least proportional of those listed here. It is much more proportional than either the plurality or majority system, not surprisingly, and falls between the very proportional mixed systems of New Zealand and Germany, on one hand, and the less proportional ones of Scotland and Wales, on the other.

This does not exhaust all of the relevant consequences of electoral systems. Systems based on single-member districts normally require the holding of a by-election or a 'partial' election every time a vacancy occurs; under list systems, the next candidate on the list of the relevant party is awarded the vacant seat, and under STV it is possible to recount votes (though Ireland instead holds by-elections). Single-member systems also require frequent revision of constituency boundaries to ensure equality of representation, since this cannot be done by adjusting the number of representatives per district, and this opens the door to potential gerrymandering (see Chapter 6). Such systems (and especially the plurality system) may also encourage strategic rather than sincere voting, distorting 'real' electoral preferences (for example, supporters of 'no hope' candidates may be tempted to vote for another party rather than 'wasting' their votes). Finally, mixed systems tend to create two classes of representatives, those representing regions (typically beholden to their parties) and those representing constituencies (and therefore dependent on voters). In practice, the high proportion of dual (constituency-list) candidates may reduce the difference between the two types.

Aside from these proximate consequences of an electoral system, however, there is a second layer of less immediate, or 'ultimate', consequences. For example, 'accountability' may also refer to the relationship between elected parliamentarians and government ministers, though this is usually determined more by constitutional provisions and parliamentary procedural norms than by the electoral system. The major ultimate effect of an electoral system is said to be its impact on governmental stability: if an electoral system produces a fragmented parliament, so the argument runs, it is also likely to be associated with unstable governments (though in reality governmental stability may be a product of elite disposition to cooperate rather than of the electorate's willingness to give an overall majority to one party). Quite apart from the effectiveness of an electoral system in delivering a representative parliament and an efficient government, its legitimacy is likely to be an issue:

Table 5.3: Index of proportionality, selected electoral systems, 1945–2012

Country	Period	No. of elections	Value of Gallagher index		
			Minimum	Maximum	Mean
Plurality system					
Canada	1945–2011	22	2.9	21.2	11.6
United Kingdom	1945–2010	18	2.6	17.8	11.7
Majority system					
France (two ballot)	1958–2012*	13	6.6	25.3	15.9
Australia (alternative vote)	1946–2010	26	2.9	14.9	9.1
PR-list system					
Netherlands	1946–2010	20	0.8	1.7	1.3
Denmark	1945–2011	26	0.4	4.2	1.7
Sweden	1948–2010	20	1.0	3.5	2.0
Austria	1945–2008	20	0.9	4.4	2.5
Switzerland	1947–2011	17	1.2	4.4	2.7
Finland	1945–2011	19	1.7	5.0	3.0
Belgium	1946–2010	21	1.9	5.2	3.4
Norway	1945–2009	17	2.7	9.2	4.5
Portugal	1975–2011	14	3.0	6.1	4.8
Spain	1977–2011	11	4.3	10.6	7.2
PR-STV system					
Malta	1947–2008	16	0.3	7.3	2.9
Northern Ireland	1973–2011	8	2.9	5.9	4.0
Ireland (Republic)	1948–2011	19	1.7	8.7	4.3
Mixed PR system					
New Zealand	1996–2011	6	1.1	3.8	2.7
Germany	1949–2009	17	0.5	4.7	2.7
Scotland	1999–2011	4	7.0	7.6	7.3
Wales	1999–2011	4	8.6	11.4	10.2

*Excluding 1986, when PR-list was used.

Note: the Gallagher index is defined as the square root of the sum of the squared deviations of seat share from vote share, with 0 representing perfect proportionality; see Gallagher and Mitchell, 2009: 602–5. *Source:* Derived from dataset produced by Michael Gallagher, 'Election indices', available at www.tcd.ie/Political_Science/staff/michael_gallagher/ElSystems/Docts/ElectionIndices.pdf the extent to which it is *seen as* fair, rather than necessarily being 'fair' as judged by a set of objective criteria. Thus, for typical British and American citizens, apparently, the electoral system is legitimate and seen as 'fair', notwithstanding the widespread incidence of disproportional or otherwise anomalous results.

There is no unanimity as to which electoral system is to be preferred. The plurality system has brought forth a long line of passionate defenders. The major work of Ferdinand Hermens, for example, was a full frontal assault on proportional representation, which he blamed *inter alia* for the collapse of democracy and the victory of fascism and Nazism; and he took the view that 'if PR did not plunge [Ireland] into "Mexican politics" in the past, it still has ample opportunity to do so in the future' (Hermens, 1972 [1941]: 325). But the plurality system has had an equally long line of passionate opponents, who have typically advocated the STV system (for example, see the several works of Enid Lakeman, including Lakeman, 1982). The list system is generally favoured in continental Europe by academics as well as by practitioners (see the implied endorsement in Lijphart, 1994, and the explicit endorsement of the Danish system in Lijphart, 2009: ix). Others have advocated mixed systems as embracing 'the best of both worlds' (Shugart and Wattenberg, 2001: 591). After an exhaustive analysis of electoral systems and their critics, Gallagher (2009: 572) arrived at eight criteria that are widely used in assessing them: their accuracy in representing voter preferences and in producing a socio-demographically representative parliament; their capacity to render parliamentarians accountable to constituents, to maximise voter participation opportunities, and to produce both cohesive, disciplined parties and stable, effective governments; and the degree to which they produce identifiable government options and allow voters an opportunity to vote out a government. But these criteria individually may point in the direction of different electoral systems; as Gallagher argues, there is no 'best' electoral system:

> Those who value stable and ejectable government, and identifiability of alternatives, above all else, even at the expense of performance on several other criteria, will be attracted by a single-member constituency system. Those for whom a high degree of proportionality and disciplined parties are the transcendent virtues will favour a closed-list system in a nationwide constituency. Those prioritising proportionality, a high degree of voter participation, and personal accountability of MPs will logically gravitate towards PR-STV or open list PR. Mixed compensatory systems score well on nearly every criterion. (Gallagher, 2009: 575)

There appears to be a consensus among those who study electoral systems, then, that choice of a system depends on the results that one wishes to be delivered. As it has been put, 'it would stretch credulity to attempt to argue that one electoral system is "best" or "ideal" for all circumstances' (Farrell, 2011: 229–30). Indeed, as van der Eijk and Franklin (2009: 69) argue, 'there is no perfect electoral system, just systems in which the trade-offs that have been made are thought to be appropriate for particular countries, their culture and their people's expectations about what an election should be'. It would, then, be unwise to sit back and try to devise a system that is objectively 'best', ignoring existing institutional and political cultural realities that shape the world of those who will be affected by the system. A new electoral system should not, in other words, be devised in the abstract and be implemented blindly; we need to take account of the costs of change, and they may 'outweigh the benefits of reform' (Reeve and Ware, 1992: 173).

IRISH ELECTIONS AND THE ELECTORAL SYSTEM

The manner in which the Irish electoral system has operated has been thoroughly researched, but it is nevertheless worth reviewing the circumstances behind its introduction in Ireland in 1920 and the arguments behind its subsequent retention. This section therefore begins by looking at the manner in which the STV system became so deeply rooted in the Irish political system, and continues by commenting on its main consequences.

The evolution of the single transferable vote in Ireland

Like many of Ireland's other political institutions, STV was a legacy of British rule in the island. As is well known, electoral reformers in the United Kingdom had been preoccupied with the STV form of proportional representation. The system devised by Thomas Hare in the 1850s was of more interest to theoreticians than to politicians for the remainder of the nineteenth century, although an almost identical system devised simultaneously by Danish mathematician C.G. Andrae was applied in certain Danish elections (Hare, 1859; Sterne, 1871). The first significant practical application of the scheme in the English-speaking world was introduced by the Tasmanian Electoral Act of 1896, which prescribed a set of rules for counting votes that had been elaborated by Attorney-General Clark as a modification of the original Hare system (Piesse, 1913). The Hare-Clark system attracted favourable comment from a Royal Commission of Enquiry into electoral systems established by the British Parliament in 1909 (United Kingdom,

1910). It had already entered the mainstream of British thinking on electoral reform as it had been adopted in the 1880s by the Proportional Representation Society as the favoured electoral system (O'Leary, 1975: 154), and was almost adopted by the British parliament itself in 1917, at least for urban elections (Bogdanor, 1984: 76–77).

As in other matters, the United Kingdom government was more prepared to engage in institutional experimentation in its western island than on the mainland (MacDonagh, 1977: 33–34). As part of the 'Home Rule' or devolved government package for Ireland, it had been intended that the Hare-Clark system be adopted for elections to the Senate and, in some constituencies, to the House of Commons of the Irish Parliament proposed in the Government of Ireland Act, 1914. The collapse of this measure meant that, apart from a 'model election' carried out through the newspapers under the auspices of the Proportional Representation Society of Ireland in 1911, it was not until the local elections in 1919 in the troubled borough of Sligo that Irish people got their first opportunity of using this system.[3] The success of this experiment was followed by the introduction of the same system for all local elections in the country by the Local Government (Ireland) Act, 1919, and for elections to the proposed Southern and Northern Houses of Commons by the Government of Ireland Act, 1920. The regulations then adopted, though dropped in the 1920s for local and parliamentary elections in Northern Ireland when the plurality system and block vote were reintroduced, were built into the electoral law of the Irish Free State by the Electoral Act, 1923, and remain the basic regulations for elections both to the Dáil and to local authorities. They were further extended to govern popular elections to the Seanad on the only occasion on which these took place (1925), and a modified version was applied to indirect elections to the senates of Northern Ireland and of the South.[4]

Why was this electoral system adopted in Ireland? This question may be answered in two stages. First, if proportional representation were to be adopted at all, it was almost inevitable that it would be the STV system—the 'British' system of proportional representation, which dominated the ideas of electoral reformers at the beginning of the twentieth century. The second stage has to do with explaining why any form of proportional representation was considered necessary. Two factors seem to have been important here. First, the British government favoured proportional representation in Ireland with a view to strengthening the position of conservative forces (the moderate nationalist party, which up to then had controlled almost all of the parliamentary seats in southern Ireland, lost all but two of them to the radical nationalist Sinn Féin party in 1918 in an election fought under the plurality system), and in particular in order to protect the position of the small Protestant minority. It was for this reason that proportional representation was introduced in the Government of Ireland Act of 1920, and, although its retention was not covered by the terms of the Anglo-Irish Treaty of 1921, its continued application was taken for granted.

The second factor was the attitude of the Sinn Féin party, the dominant political force after the 1918 election. Already before the First World War, when it was a minor group without parliamentary representation, Sinn Féin had endorsed the principle of proportional representation, and its leader, Arthur Griffith, was a founder member of the Proportional Representation Society of Ireland. When proportional representation was written into the 1922 constitution, it seems to have been assumed that this would be the STV version. But the 1937 constitution went further, specifying STV. Though it was thus embedded in the constitution by de Valera and his Fianna Fáil government, Fianna Fáil's attitude to electoral law later changed. Two Fianna Fáil-sponsored referenda designed to amend the Constitution to replace STV by the plurality system were, however, defeated in 1959 and 1968 by majorities respectively of 51.8% and 60.8%.

The effects of the single transferable vote

Because of its sophistication as a device for maximising the subtlety with which the voter may pass verdict on candidates, STV has attracted a good deal of attention from collective choice theorists, not all of it favourable; see, for instance, the assessment by Hannu Nurmi (1983), which judges this system to be compatible with only three of the nine evaluation criteria he used, whereas even the plurality system is judged compatible with six. The concern of the logician and the mathematician to evaluate electoral systems and to pinpoint the ideal one is far removed from the preoccupation of the political scientist with analysis of mechanisms by which political groups seek to gain or hold power. A comparison of two lengthy bibliographies in books dealing with voting systems, one by a mathematician, the other by a political scientist, showed strikingly that the two had only a single author, John Stuart Mill, in common (Dummett, 1984: 294–5). The relatively harsh verdict of social choice theorists on STV must be seen in context: it is at least the voting system used for the election of national parliaments that they take most seriously, not because of the seat allocation formula it uses but rather because it is based on the theoretically demanding notion of preferential voting.

The principal theoretical and mathematical battles over STV were fought out in its home, Tasmania, a century ago (Piesse, 1913), but many of the issues raised then have continued to recur in political debate, and practical difficulties not foreseen at that time have generated further discussion. Analyses of the application of STV in Ireland have addressed many of the questions that have been extensively discussed in the Australian and Tasmanian contexts. On the positive side, observers have been impressed by the extent to which the system is multidimensional, allowing for the representation of competing groups within parties, or indeed regardless of parties. These include women (Engstrom, 1987), local interests (Parker, 1982), and individual bailiwicks and religious minorities (Sacks, 1976). Criticisms have, however, been more common. It has been demonstrated, for instance, that there is significant 'alphabetical' voting bias, with candidates whose surnames take them to the top of the ballot paper enjoying an advantage over others (Robson and Walsh, 1973). This phenomenon has been labelled the 'donkey vote' in Australia, where voters often react to a compulsory voting system with mandatory ranking of all candidates by simply ranking candidates from top to bottom in the order in which they appear on the ballot paper. This is not intrinsic to the STV system, and could be neutralised by altering ballot paper design. The system has an acknow-ledged problem with a random element that sometimes arises following the distribution of surpluses, so that successive counting of the ballot papers, without error, could result in a different outcome (Coakley and O'Neill, 1984; Gallagher and Unwin, 1986). The Irish system has also been criticised on the grounds that it does not eliminate tactical voting: the extent to which the system is sensitive to candidate nomination strategies on the part of parties has for long been the subject of comment (Cohan, McKinlay and Mughan, 1975; Lijphart and Irwin, 1979; Gallagher, 1980; Marsh, 1981; Katz, 1981).

The debates around these issues are entirely overshadowed, however, by two other matters: the link between the electoral system and political stability, and the system's consequences for the work patterns of parliamentary representatives. On the first point, early analysis in Ireland sometimes argued that the STV system commonly left governments short of an overall majority and unhealthily reliant on independent deputies or small groups to form a government, raising risks of governmental instability and inappropriate policy compromise (O'Leary, 1979). More recently, however, a near-consensus has emerged on the relatively benign consequences of STV for the conversion of voters' preferences into Dáil seats. Though tending to give an advantage to larger parties, STV is by comparative standards relatively proportional. Research in the late 1980s showed Ireland as being at an intermediate point in the league table of proportionality, however measured (Gallagher, 1987: 29; Gallagher, 1991: 40).[5] As Table 5.3 shows, this has continued to be the case up to the present; the mean value of the Gallagher index of proportionality in Dáil elections since 1945 (4.3) lay somewhere in the bottom half of party list systems, where the index ranged from 1.3 to 7.2. Furthermore, there is little evidence that this proportionality damages government stability or policy coherence. Though it is associated with the appearance of a multi-party system, the extent to which it promotes political fragmentation is, again from a comparative perspective, rather modest (Gallagher, 2009; Sinnott, 2010).

As attacks on the proportionality of the electoral system have receded in Ireland, they have been replaced by warfare on another front: allegations that STV encourages intra-party competition and therefore promotes patronage and clientelism (for the older literature, see Gallagher, 1987; Farrell, 1985; O'Connell, 1981; Carty, 1981: 109–139). While the workloads and diaries of Dáil deputies may indeed give the impression that there is some merit in this argument, extensive research by the main authority in the area suggests that under other electoral systems, too, and especially with open list systems, parliamentarians tend to have heavy constituency workloads (Gallagher, 2009: 557–62; see also Gallagher and Komito, 2010; Farrell, 2010). As in the operation of other Irish institutions, it is likely that the relationship between Dáil deputies and their constituents is a function not just of the electoral system but also of deeply ingrained political cultural attitudes. Quite apart from TDs' diaries, the Dáil debates record an extraordinarily high level of activism by deputies on behalf of their constituents and constituencies. Thousands of examples could be given, but one, chosen almost at random, should be sufficient to convey the flavour; it concerns the efforts of Timothy O'Connor, Fianna Fáil TD for Kerry South, 1961–81, to secure improvements to a harbour in his constituency in 1969:

> Mr. O'CONNOR: asked the Minister for Finance when the boring survey will be carried out in Cahirciveen harbour for the general improvement of berthing facilities at the pier in Cahirciveen which are urgently needed as two new trawlers will be working out of this harbour before the end of the year and two next year.
> PARLIAMENTARY SECRETARY TO THE MINISTER FOR FINANCE (Mr. J. GIBBONS): The survey will be made this summer.[6]

We need not confine ourselves to mere speculation as to how parliamentarians would relate to their constituents were the British plurality system to be reintroduced: we have hard evidence. This system operated in single-member constituencies in Ireland from 1885 to 1918, offering us an abundance of data on the behaviour of MPs with secure seats (incumbent Irish nationalist MPs could typically see off all electoral challenges without difficulty). If we go back a century to 1912, to the time when the momentous third home rule bill was going through the House of Commons, we will find the parliamentary record showing that the 'mother of parliaments' was able also to consider less weighty matters.[7] The MP for South Kerry, John Pius Boland (famous for his achievements during the 1896 Olympics, when he won two gold medals in tennis), found time to avert his gaze from the national question and the Ulster problem—the truly pressing issues of that time—to more local matters:

> Mr. BOLAND: asked the Chief Secretary whether he is aware that, in spite of repeated representations, the Congested Districts Board has not yet undertaken the construction of a boatslip at Caherciveen; and whether steps will be taken to complete it before the autumn fishing season opens?
>
> Mr. BIRRELL: The Congested Districts Board have decided upon not undertaking the construction of a boatslip at Cahirciveen at present, as, in their opinion, other more important works in the county Kerry require earlier attention.[8]

This example could, of course, be multiplied; the pages of *Hansard* are full of such references. It is hard to resist the conclusion that, regardless of electoral law, Irish constituents expect their elected representatives to be particularly vigilant in respect of all local matters, and that their representatives respond accordingly.

SIMULATING ALTERNATIVE ELECTORAL SYSTEMS

One way of assessing Ireland's current system is to ask what would happen if we were to move to an alternative system. Answering this question is not easy, in the absence of the necessary data. Rather than giving up on the effort, however, it is possible to simulate data that may be used to assess the consequences of different electoral systems. Following a discussion of the technical issues involved, this section goes on to estimate the probable outcomes were Ireland to move to one of the other electoral systems that have been proposed.

Generating notional data

In the Irish case, it is difficult to obtain the kind of data that are available in Great Britain for analysis of the implications of the adoption of a new electoral system. In Britain, results of a large survey were used to simulate outcomes under different electoral systems (Dunleavy, Margetts and Weir, 1992). In the absence of detailed survey data of this kind, one option is to go back to cruder methods of estimation, a difficult challenge in the case of single-member districts (it is much more difficult to disaggregate from 43 multi-member constituencies to 166 single-member ones than to aggregate from 166 to 43!). One influential study (Laver, 1998) simulated results for 166 single-member constituencies by assuming that the pattern in each current Dáil constituency would be distributed uniformly throughout that constituency, so that when it is divided into single-member districts the same party wins in each. Thus, estimates for 1997 show all four districts in Galway West going to Fianna Fáil, and all five in Galway East going to Fine Gael—a crude but not unrealistic judgement (Laver, 1998: 52). The approach in this chapter is based on an effort to measure variation in party support below the level of Dáil constituencies, using local election data, along the following lines.

First, analysis focuses on the following electoral systems.

- The plurality system, as used currently in the United Kingdom, and as rejected at Irish referenda in 1959 and 1968: voters indicate support for one candidate in a single-member constituency, and the candidate with the largest number of votes wins.
- The majority system in its alternative vote form, as used currently in Australia and in Ireland in by-elections, as proposed in 1968 as an alternative to the plurality system (the 'Norton amendment'), and as supported later by figures within the two largest parties: voters rank candidates in a single-member constituency, and any candidate with a majority of votes wins; if no candidate has a majority candidates are eliminated in inverse order of votes won and their further preferences are redistributed until one candidate has a majority, or only one candidate remains.[9]
- The party list system, with or without personal voting, as used widely in continental Europe and as used in Great Britain for elections to the European Parliament: voters indicate support for one party in a multi-member constituency, and seats are allocated to parties in proportion to votes won; within party lists, voting for one or

more individual candidates may be allowed and this will have an impact on (but will not necessarily determine) which candidates are elected.

- Some kind of hybrid (or 'mixed member proportional') system, comprising a mixture of deputies elected from single-member constituencies using either the plurality or the alternative vote system and deputies elected from regional lists, as in elections to the German Bundestag, the New Zealand House of Representatives, the Scottish Parliament and the Welsh Assembly; the allocation by party list is not proportional, but designed to correct the disproportionality arising from outcomes in the single-member constituencies, to give an overall result that is as proportional as possible.

In simulating probable outcomes under each of these electoral systems, there are two big difficulties that arise in principle from the nature of the available data, and a third that arises in practice in this case.

First, all currently available data are based on preferential voting, where voters rank candidates rather than opting for a single candidate or party. Using first preference votes as indicators of how voters would behave under the party list system is problematic, since a first preference vote is not the same as a categorical party choice; but we have little option other than accepting this equivalence. STV results are no doubt easier to translate into probable voting patterns under the alternative vote system; but there is a problem in the case of the plurality system, which encourages tactical rather than sincere voting. It is likely that many voters whose first preference would be for a minor party or independent under the current STV system would switch to a major party under the plurality system, to avoid 'wasting' their votes—but this is a difficulty about which little can be done, other than acknowledging its existence.

Second, existing data for Dáil elections are available only at the level of 43 Dáil constituencies, and although informal tallies may be used to measure party support locally, we have no data on the kind of smaller constituencies that would have to be created if the plurality or alternative vote systems were to be introduced. The only low-level data officially available are from local elections: local electoral areas may be combined to produce a set of 166 single-member 'constituencies' (or any number smaller than this). But this creates two further difficulties. One is that voting patterns in local elections are known to deviate from the pattern at general elections. We may counter this simply by taking note of this bias: it is a reality that independents fare better and major parties worse in local elections. The other is that because of extreme variation in the size of local electoral areas, the resulting 'constituencies' would also vary greatly in size. We may counter this by pointing out that extreme variation in the deputy–population ratio is in any case a feature of elections based on single-member constituencies.

Third, contemporary Irish politics presents a particular difficulty that would not have arisen after earlier general elections. After decades during which the electoral relationship between the three largest parties remained substantially unaltered (with the Fianna Fáil–Fine Gael/Cumann na nGaedheal–Labour ranking established in 1932 reproduced election after election), support for Fianna Fáil slumped dramatically, with a corresponding rise in support for Fine Gael and Labour and changes also in respect of other parties and groups. Far from impeding examination of the impact of the electoral system, however, these developments provide a kind of 'stress test', allowing us to assess the implications of profound shifts in electoral loyalties under different regimes of electoral law, using the results of the Dáil elections of 2007 and 2011 and the intervening local and European elections.

The manner in which 'constituencies' were devised and voting strength was estimated is reported in the appendix at the end of this chapter, and may be summarised as follows. First, notional constituencies were created using the following procedures.

- A set of **166 single-member 'constituencies'** was produced by combining certain of the smaller existing local electoral areas, and regrouping the results of 2009 local elections accordingly. Three datasets were produced for these 'constituencies': one based on the actual results in 2009, the second and third based on weighting these data to reproduce the results of the 2007 and 2011 general elections respectively. In other words, the actual results of the 2007 and 2011 elections were also distributed among the 166 'constituencies' in proportion to the electoral support of parties there according to the 2009 local elections.
- A further set of **100 single-member 'constituencies'** was produced in the same way, by further grouping smaller local electoral areas, and estimates of party strength at three points in time were produced as described above.
- The existing **43 Dáil constituencies** were used to produce an estimate of party strength in 2009 by weighting the 2007 strength of each party by an estimate based on 2009 local election data (the 2007 and 2011 Dáil results were left unaltered).

- A set of **four regions** was produced by grouping 2007, 2009 and 2011 data so that results at this level too could be simulated.

The outcome for the various electoral systems was estimated as follows.

For the plurality system, seats were allocated to the party winning the largest number of votes in each of the 166 'constituencies'. There were particular difficulties in the case of independent candidates; seats were not allocated automatically whenever the 'other' (non-party) category comprised a plurality; this was done only when this category contained a particularly strong candidate.

For the alternative vote system, information on the further preferences of party supporters was important. This was based on results of an exit poll in 2007 (Suiter, 2008: 108). It was assumed that the same broad pattern of passing of preferences between parties would be followed in 2009 and 2011. Seats were then allocated in four stages. First, whenever a single party won an overall majority in a 'constituency' it was of course allocated the seat (47 occasions in 2007; 10 in 2009; 29 in 2011). Second, there were circumstances where one party, though falling short of 50% of the vote, was so far in front of any potential challenger that the outcome would be virtually certain (27 cases in 2007; 16 in 2009; 29 in 2011). Third, in most cases the outcome was much less certain; it was estimated on the basis of the probable pattern of vote transfers based on the successive elimination of candidates (76 cases in 2007; 117 in 2009; 83 in 2011). Finally, in some cases the outcome was based on little more than educated guesswork, and there would be a case for calling a different result (but only 16 cases fell into this category in 2007, 23 in 2009 and 25 in 2011).

For the list systems, it was assumed that first preference votes could legitimately be translated into straightforward party votes, an assumption that would undoubtedly have many exceptions, but there is no alternative to this. Under list systems, two 'highest average' formulas stand out as the most widely used; they differ from each other primarily in respect of how they deal with rounding problems, with one formula distinctly more favourable to larger parties and groups than the other. The Sainte-Laguë formula is widely regarded as the more proportional of the two, and it has been used here as the best indicator of 'perfect' proportionality (where it is used in actual list system elections, as in Scandinavia, it is modified to make it more difficult for small groups to gain representation). In addition, outcomes using the D'Hondt system were calculated at three levels: using the whole territory of the state as a single constituency, at the level of four regional constituencies

(Dublin, rest of Leinster, Munster, Connacht–Ulster), and at the level of the existing 43 constituencies.

Finally, there is a considerable range of hybrid or mixed systems whose probable impact in the Irish case might be simulated. The German system, for instance, would imply 83 single-member constituencies elected by the plurality system, with a further 83 elected from regional lists; the Scottish system would imply a 94–72 division between constituency and list seats; the New Zealand division would be 97–69; and the Welsh division would be 111–55. For present purposes a division of 100–66 (60% constituency seats, 40% list seats) has been assumed. This is in line with a suggestion made by Dr Garret FitzGerald (2008) for a division precisely along these lines, with 100 single-member constituencies filled by means of the alternative vote system (as currently used in by-elections) and 66 by means of the list system.[10] In these cases, an 'overhang' problem may arise: a particular party may win more seats from the single-member constituencies than its total proportional entitlement. There are different ways of dealing with this; for example, in Germany a party with an 'overhang' is allowed to retain this, but other parties are still allocated their proportionate share, resulting in a Bundestag which may be larger than its target size. Here, with a view to retaining Dáil size at 166, other parties have not been compensated in this way, so the level of proportionality has been compromised.

Impact of different electoral systems

The outcome of these calculations is reported in the appendix at the end of this chapter. In each case, the most proportional result is indicated by the 'national' Sainte-Laguë estimate. Thus, in 2007, Fianna Fáil's proportional share would have been 69.1 seats; the Sainte-Laguë formula would allocate it 69 (it will be seen that the D'Hondt formula would have been more generous, giving Fianna Fáil 70 seats). The actual results under list systems are reproduced in the rows below this, with 'others' treated as a cohesive block—as an additional notional 'party'. It will be seen that the advantage given to the larger parties increases as constituency size falls. Thus, when we move from a single 166-seat national constituency to four provincial ones, Fianna Fáil strength in 2007 increases to 71, and if the 43 current constituencies were used it would have won 94 seats.

Several points of qualification about this procedure should be noted. First, under the list system, electoral law commonly imposes a threshold clause: a party may be required to win a certain share of the vote if it is to win any list seats at all, and this can be as high as 5%. In the simulations presented here, no threshold is imposed (the impact of such a threshold could be estimated very easily). Second, it is extremely unlikely that the group here described as 'others' would in reality behave as a single block or party. If we divide this into its component groups and interests, some might be ineligible to contest elections under the list system, and others would be too small to win any seat. For this reason, a second set of results is reproduced: this looks at the probable effect of the list system on microparties and independents, who would experience great difficulty in securing any representation. The third panel of each appendix table shows what would probably happen in these circumstances, with the larger parties absorbing seats that would otherwise go to these interests. The 'real' outcome would probably lie somewhere between the extremes reported in this table—extremes represented by the position where 'others' win their full collective share of seats, and that where they win none.

A shift to the alternative vote system would have given the largest party in 2007, Fianna Fáil, 111 seats out of 166, and this would have increased to 134 under the plurality system. Similar dominance by the largest party would have occurred in 2011, though this time with Fine Gael as the most popular party.

Outcomes for two of the many possible hybrid systems are also shown in the bottom panel of Table (a) in the appendix at the end of this chapter. In 2007, if the plurality system were to be used for the single-member constituencies (as is the norm in the countries discussed above, such as Germany, where half of the members of the Bundestag are elected by this means), Fianna Fáil would have won an 'overhang' of 13 seats (it would have won 83 in the constituencies, and even without winning any at national level it would be over-represented, since the D'Hondt system at national level would award it only 70 seats). Under the German system Fianna Fáil would have been allowed to retain these seats, but other parties would have been given their due share, so the overall size of the Dáil would increase to 179. These strikingly different outcomes would be reflected also in the 2009 results, but with the big advantage this time passing to Fine Gael.

Important confirmation of the outcomes described above emerges from a painstaking set of simulations conducted by Kavanagh and Whelan (2013). Using micro-level data (and unofficial tally figures indicating the first preference vote by polling district in 2007 and 2011), they created notional single-member constituencies of the kind discussed above, but more even in population size. They used the tally data to project the probable outcome under the plurality system, and, by taking account also of local transfer patterns, they computed the outcome under the alternative vote system. Their results—shown in Tables (a) and (c) in the appendix—though slightly different from those reported above, are quite close in order of magnitude, confirming by means of a different methodology the results arrived at here. Kavanagh and Whelan also illustrate yet another variant of mixed systems: the classic German model, with an even distribution of seats between constituencies and lists (83 returned by either method), and with a demanding threshold clause (to win any seats from the list system, a party must win at least 5% of the overall vote, or secure three constituency seats). Their conclusions are entirely compatible with the diverging outcomes reported here, based on a different division between the two categories of seats (100–66 rather than 83–83) and without a threshold clause.

ASSESSING THE IRISH ELECTORAL SYSTEM

The likelihood of a change in the Irish electoral system will be conditioned not just by abstract theoretical considerations, but by hard-nosed judgements by politicians about the probable effects of any change, and about the implications of such change for their own future and that of their parties. This section seeks to generalise about the consequences of change, and to consider where this fits into the current debate on constitutional reform.

Consequences of electoral system change

Subject to a range of reservations, the estimates produced in this chapter provide a not unrealistic picture of what the outcome would be under different types of electoral system, taking account of the assumptions mentioned above. The specific consequences are summarised in Table 5.4 for a selection of the systems discussed (the plurality system, the alternative vote, and the most common list system in continental Europe, regional lists using the D'Hondt formula).

The D'Hondt system would result in relatively little change from the inter-party balance under the current STV system. The plurality system, however, would result in wild fluctuations, with Fianna Fáil completely dominating the Dáil in 2007 with 134 seats, but being virtually eliminated in 2011, when it would have won only five seats, and with Fine Gael showing a starkly opposite trend, jumping from 21 seats in 2007 to 119 in 2011. The alternative vote would show a shift in representation on a similar if slightly less extreme scale. These simulations are borne out by the experience of countries that operate the plurality system, such as Canada.

Table 5.4: Party political consequences of selected electoral systems, Ireland, 2007–11

Party	Year	Vote share	Actual seats (STV)	Plurality system	Alter-native vote	D'Hondt* (provincial)
Fianna Fáil	2007	41.6	78	134	111	78
	2009	25.4	49	35	27	52
	2011	17.4	20	5	4	34
Fine Gael	2007	27.3	51	21	39	50
	2009	32.2	60	99	98	66
	2011	36.1	76	119	111	73
Labour	2007	10.1	20	7	13	18
	2009	14.7	23	25	29	30
	2011	19.4	37	29	35	39
Green Party	2007	4.7	6	0	0	6
	2009	2.3	0	0	0	4
	2011	1.8	0	0	0	2
Sinn Féin	2007	6.9	4	1	0	10
	2009	7.4	7	1	1	14
	2011	9.9	14	6	6	18
Others	2007	9.4	7	3	3	4
	2009	18.0	27	6	11	0
	2011	15.3	19	7	10	0

Note: For 2009, 'actual' results refer to the outcome of a nationwide Sainte-Laguë allocation. *Constrained version (no allocation to independent 'others'; allocation to Progressive Democrats in 2007).

Mixed systems based on the German model are also not without their problems. Advocated as a method that would incentivise the emergence of legislators rather than constituency workers, a mixture of single-member constituencies and regional lists would be likely to result in certain anomalies. In principle, it would tend to produce deputies of two quite different types: those elected from party lists, who would be highly dependent on the party organisation but under little pressure to engage in constituency work, and those elected from single-member constituencies, relatively independent of the party but under pressure to work for their constituents (Laver, 1998). In practice, however, as mentioned above, there would be strong incentives for dual list–constituency candidacies, reducing the distinction between the two types and securing the survival of links between deputies and their constituencies. More unfortunately, though, any party with a considerable lead over others would be likely to be entirely dominated by constituency deputies, while its rivals would be made up mainly of members elected under the list system. As Table 5.5 shows, under this system all Fianna Fáil deputies in 2007 would be constituency based, but in 2011 only one would be elected from a constituency, with the remainder elected from party lists. Over the same period, Fine Gael would have moved in the opposite direction, from being a predominantly list-based party to an exclusively constituency-based one. The implications for the role of deputies and for internal party relationships in these circumstances are unpredictable.

It should be stressed in conclusion that the projections made in this chapter are mostly purely arithmetical ones: they make very straightforward, undemanding assumptions about the manner in which votes cast under one system might be translated into votes under another system, equating candidate votes under the plurality system with first preference votes under the alternative vote and STV systems, and with categorical party choices under the list system.

There are particular difficulties with the projections based on single-member districts. To start with, short cuts have necessarily been taken in arriving at these, given data limitations. In addition, no allowance is made for the effect of tactical voting, nor is any account taken of the impact of past experience on current behaviour. In these simulations, the voter does not learn from the outcome of previous elections that some voting choices result in 'wastage', while others may have a big positive effect. Thus, it is extremely unlikely that the pattern of support projected for the plurality system would be reproduced in the long term: supporters of smaller parties would discover quickly that voting for 'no-hope' candidates is a waste of time, and would modify their behaviour accordingly. The net effect is likely to be that the simulations reported here will understate the prospects for the dominant parties—in other words, the real outcome over time would be likely to be even more disproportional than the estimates presented here.

Table 5.5: Probable consequences of mixed plurality–party list system for representative type, Ireland, three largest parties, 2007–11

Party	Election basis	2007	2009	2011
Fianna Fáil	Constituency	83	18	1
	List	0	23	24
Fine Gael	Constituency	8	60	71
	List	32	0	0
Labour	Constituency	7	21	21
	List	9	3	10

Constitutional options

Given the vital importance of the electoral system for Dáil deputies, it is not surprising that it was the subject of extensive discussion in the various constitutional reviews. The Committee on the Constitution (1967: 21–26) looked at arguments for and against moving to the alternative vote system. The Constitution Review Group (1996: 60) noted that the current system 'has had popular support and should not be changed without careful advance assessment of the possible effects', and thought that any alternative should be proportional in effect. The seventh progress report of the All-Party Oireachtas Committee on the Constitution (2002: 14–29) engaged in a detailed study of alternatives to STV, considered several outside submissions, and sought the views of sitting deputies and senators (of whom 59 wanted no change, and 22 supported alternative systems). It concluded that there was no need to move to another system. A similar survey whose results were reported in 2010 showed slightly greater political support for reform, with 53 members of the Oireachtas supporting the status quo, and 40 favouring change; excluding senators, 43 TDs were opposed to change, while 28 supported it (Joint Committee on the Constitution, 2010a). The fourth report of the Joint Committee on the Constitution (2010b: 18), after detailed consideration of the matter, suggested that it be referred to a citizen's assembly. The resulting discussion of the matter by the Convention on the Constitution showed this body to be divided on the issue of electoral reform, but it voted decisively (79–20) against a move to the main system that has been advocated as an alternative to the present one, a mixed system along the lines of that of Germany or New Zealand. Its members, were, however, in favour of smaller changes to the current system (Convention on the Constitution, 2013b).

Notwithstanding failed attempts to change the electoral system in the past, then, it has apparently proved impossible to dislodge the notion of electoral reform from the agenda. For politicians, the electoral system is of central interest, since by definition they are members of the Dáil precisely because the electoral system got them there. Aside from considerations of the common good, politicians will inevitably take a close interest in the probable impact of any other systems on their own electoral prospects and modes of work. In these circumstances, it is probably not surprising that so many deputies are hesitant about change; but in this caution they appear to be at one with a majority of voters, as the opinion poll results presented in Chapter 1 suggest.

CONCLUSION

This chapter has presented stark estimates of the consequences of electoral system change for the character of the representative process in Ireland. Because of the 'learning function' referred to above, however, it is important not to overstate the extent to which we can predict the results of a move to a new electoral system. Quite apart from a probable tactical switch in support from small to large parties under the plurality systems, big parties might themselves be victims of their own success. Put bluntly, expanding this simulation of the effects of the plurality system to the period from 1932 to 2011 would show a Dáil completely dominated by Fianna Fáil, which would enjoy majorities ranging from large to enormous; in reality, though, it is likely that the party would have fractured, or that a fundamental electoral realignment would have taken place, as voters tired of single-party rule. The debate on electoral reform would need, then, to consider not just the near-certain consequences of some aspects of change in electoral arrangements, but also the imponderables that would be associated with this.

NOTES

1. This chapter is based in part on two conference papers: 'The single transferable vote in Ireland: origin, performance and prospects', Annual Meeting of the American Political Science Association, Washington, DC, 1–4 September, 1988; and 'The debate on electoral reform in Ireland: assessing the consequences for parties', Annual Conference of the Political Studies Association of Ireland, Magee College, Derry, 19–21 October 2012.

2. There are many variants of these systems, such as use of the Hare quota (votes divided by seats) rather than the Droop quota in largest remainder systems. The discussion here focuses on the mathematical principle that underlies these

formulas; the generally used rules for counting votes under the D'Hondt and Sainte-Laguë systems (based on division tables) seem at first sight quite dissimilar to the approach described above.

3. The mock election was supposed to be for the parliamentary division of Dublin, and was based on ballot papers containing the names of leading Irish politicians circulated through newspapers. The valid 'vote' was 9,019, and the poll was headed by John Redmond (Nationalist), followed by Sir Horace Plunkett (Independent) and Sir Edward Carson (Unionist); see Meredith, 1913; *Irish Times,* 7 December 1911.

4. The main difference between the system used in the Seanad and the Dáil system is that in the former all votes are treated as if they had the value 1,000; this allows for refined fractional transfers that effectively eliminate random elements (see Coakley and O'Neill, 1984; Gallagher and Unwin, 1986).

5. It should be noted that this discussion rests on the implicit assumption that first preference votes are categorical party choices, an assumption whose validity remains to be demonstrated, though in the absence of evidence to the contrary a not unreasonable one.

6. *Dáil Debates,* 29 April 1969, vol. 240, col. 38.

7. I am indebted to Conor Mulvagh for drawing this form of parliamentary behaviour among Irish MPs to my attention.

8. *House of Commons Debates,* 20 June 1912, vol. 39, col. 1983.

9. This proposal was made by Patrick Norton, an independent (former Labour Party) TD who favoured the plurality system, but felt that 'proportional representation by means of the single transferable vote' in single-member constituencies (a self-contradictory concept) would be easier to sell to the electorate; see *Dáil Debates,* 6 June 1968, vol. 235, cols 667–73.

10. Dr FitzGerald suggested that instead of being selected from lists drawn up by parties, the 'top-up' seats could be allocated to those candidates most narrowly defeated in the single-member districts. Thus if, for example, Labour were to be entitled to 12 'list' seats, these could be awarded to the 12 Labour candidates who came closest to being elected in the single-member constituencies, a mechanism sometimes to be found in continental Europe.

APPENDIX B: SIMULATED OUTCOME OF IRISH ELECTIONS BY VARIOUS ELECTORAL SYSTEMS, 2007, 2009, 2011

The data were computed as follows. Sainte-Laguë and D'Hondt systems at national level are based on actual results in 2007, 2009 and 2011, applying the respective formulas. The constituency-level data are based on actual results in respect of first preference votes in 2007 and 2011, and estimates for 2009 based on the national swing in party support since 2007.

Plurality and alternative vote data were computed as follows. The 171 local electoral areas in 2009 were grouped to form 166 areas by merging certain smaller areas. Drumahaire and Manorhamilton (Leitrim); Ballinamore and Carrick-on-Shannon (Leitrim); Drumlish and Granard (Longford); Boyle and Strokestown (Roscommon); and Ballymote and Tubbercurry (Sligo) were merged to form five single districts or 'constituencies'. It was assumed that support for the five main parties in plurality and alternative vote elections would be the same as the first preference vote in 2009. Minor parties were grouped as a potential sixth party, and 'others' were grouped as a potential seventh party in the alternative vote simulations. In the plurality simulations, a seat was allocated to 'others' only where a single candidate from the 'other' category actually won more votes than any other category. The tables below group 'other' and minor party representatives. In the alternative vote simulation, seats were allocated in the following stages: (1) to any party winning at least 50%; (2) to any party winning at least 45% in circumstances where it would be extremely improbable that that candidate could be overtaken on the basis of transferred votes; (3) on the basis of assessment of the consequences of successive eliminations, taking account of known broad transfer patterns; and (4) in a few cases, on the basis of educated guesswork. For 2007 and 2011, the same 'constituencies' were used, but the data were weighted to take account of the overall swing in party votes from 2009. The level of confidence in the alternative vote estimates may be summarised as follows.

Level of confidence	2007	2009	2011
Certain (winning candidate with 50%+)	47	10	29
Highly probable (winning candidate beyond reach of others)	27	16	29
Probable (based on assessment of transfers)	76	117	83
Most likely (uncertain; based largely on guesswork)	16	23	25
Total	166	166	166

It should be noted that the single-member 'constituencies' resulting from this approach varied greatly in size. On the basis of their 2006 population, they were distributed as in the following table, which shows a big difference in population between the smallest and the largest 'constituency', especially in the 166-constituency model. It is possible that this results in political bias, since Fianna Fáil and Fine Gael are likely to be stronger in the smaller (mainly rural) 'constituencies'.

Statistic	166 constituencies	100 constituencies
Minimum	9,110	25,146
Maximum	60,277	72,414
Mean	25,541	42,398
Median	22,049	41,365
Standard deviation	12,632	10,863

(a) General election, 2007

System	FF	FG	Lab	Green	SF	Other*	Total
Share of votes	41.6	27.3	10.1	4.7	6.9	9.4	100.0
STV (actual result)	78	51	20	6	4	7	166
Proportional systems (unconstrained)							
Sainte-Laguë, national	69	45	17	8	11	16	166
D'Hondt, national	70	46	17	7	11	15	166
D'Hondt, provincial	72	46	18	6	10	14	166
D'Hondt, constituency	94	52	10	1	3	6	166
Proportional systems (exclusion of 'others')							
Sainte-Laguë, national	74	49	18	8	12	5*	166
D'Hondt, national	75	49	18	8	12	4*	166
D'Hondt, provincial	78	50	18	6	10	4*	166
D'Hondt, constituency	95	54	12	1	3	2*	166
Non-proportional systems							
Alternative vote	111	39	13	0	0	3	166
Plurality	134	21	7	0	1	3	166
Kavanagh–Whelan projections							
Alternative vote	114	34	12	2	1	3	166
Plurality	142	18	3	0	1	2	166
Mixed systems							
Plurality + list	83	40	16	6	9	12	166
Plurality	83	8	7	0	0	2	100
List (D'Hondt, national)	0	32	9	6	9	10	66
Alternative vote + list	70	46	17	7	11	15	166
Alternative vote	66	19	13	0	0	2	100
List (D'Hondt, national)	4	27	4	7	11	13	66
Kavanagh–Whelan projections							
Plurality + list	80	53	19	0	13	1	166
Plurality	73	8	0	0	1	1	83
List (national; threshold)	7	45	19	0	12	0	83

*Progressive Democrats classed as a separate party. *Note:* Additional data are from Kavanagh and Whelan (2013: 30, 34), and in mixed systems assume a threshold of 5% of the list vote, or winning a seat in at least three constituencies, for entitlement to list seats.

(b) Simulated general election, 2009 (based on local election results)

System	FF	FG	Lab	Green	SF	Other	Total
Share of votes	25.4	32.2	14.7	2.3	7.4	18.0	100.0
Sainte-Laguë, constituency*	49	60	23	0	7	27	166
Proportional systems (unconstrained)							
Sainte-Laguë, national	42	54	24	4	12	30	166
D'Hondt, national	43	54	24	3	12	30	166
D'Hondt, provincial	43	55	25	3	10	30	166
D'Hondt, constituency	47	61	24	0	6	28	166
Proportional systems (exclusion of 'others')							
Sainte-Laguë, national	51	65	30	5	15	0	166
D'Hondt, national	52	65	30	4	15	0	166
D'Hondt, provincial	52	66	30	4	14	0	166
D'Hondt, constituency	55	72	32	0	7	0	166
Non-proportional systems							
Alternative vote	27	98	29	0	1	11	166
Plurality	35	99	25	0	1	6	166
Mixed systems							
Plurality + list	41	60	24	3	11	27	166
Plurality	18	60	21	0	0	1	100
List (D'Hondt, national)	23	0	3	3	11	26	66
Alternative vote + list	39	63	24	3	11	27	166
Alternative vote	12	63	23	0	0	2	100
List (D'Hondt, national)	27	0	1	3	11	25	66

*It is not possible to give an 'actual' result for 2009, or to simulate the STV outcome, so the Sainte-Laguë formula has been applied at constituency level to approximate this.

(c) General election, 2011

System	FF	FG	Lab	Green	SF	Other	Total
Share of votes	17.4	36.1	19.4	1.8	9.9	15.3	100.0
STV (actual result)	20*	76	37	0	14	19	166
Proportional systems (unconstrained)							
Sainte-Laguë, national	29	60	32	3	17	25	166
D'Hondt, national	29	61	32	3	16	25	166
D'Hondt, provincial	30	61	33	1	16	25	166
D'Hondt, constituency	26	75	31	0	9	25	166
Proportional systems (exclusion of 'others')							
Sainte-Laguë, national	34	71	38	4	19	0	166
D'Hondt, national	34	72	38	3	19	0	166
D'Hondt, provincial	34	73	39	2	18	0	166
D'Hondt, constituency	37	82	38	0	9	0	166
Non-proportional systems							
Alternative vote	4	111	35	0	6	10	166
Plurality	5	119	29	0	6	7	166
Kavanagh–Whelan projections							
Alternative vote	2	114	35	0	5	10	166
Plurality	3	114	32	0	6	11	166
Mixed systems							
Plurality + list	25	71	31	3	14	22	166
Plurality	1	71	21	0	3	4	100
List (D'Hondt, national)	24	0	10	3	11	18	66
Alternative vote + list	26	68	31	3	15	23	166
Alternative vote	1	68	24	0	3	4	100
List (D'Hondt, national)	25	0	7	3	12	19	66
Kavanagh–Whelan projections							
Plurality + list	35	71	38	0	20	2	166
Plurality	0	62	16	0	3	2	83
List (national; threshold)	35	9	22	0	17	0	83

*Including the Ceann Comhairle, returned unopposed. *Note*: Additional data are from Kavanagh and Whelan (2013: 31–2 , 35), and in mixed systems assume a threshold of 5% of the list vote, or winning a seat in at least three constituencies, for entitlement to list seats.

6
DÁIL CONSTITUENCIES: REAPPORTIONMENT OR REDISTRICTING?

Controversy over constituency boundary delimitation rarely breaks the surface in discussions in comparative politics. Nevertheless, there are contexts where it still provokes animated public discussion. The term 'gerrymander' was, after all, coined to describe the inventive efforts of Governor Elbridge Gerry of Massachussetts to devise constituencies that would help his party in the early nineteenth century (the contorted shape of one resulting area, resembling a salamander, gave rise to the term); and such controversy was long to continue in the USA. The unfair drawing of local electoral boundaries in Northern Ireland was one of the grievances that gave rise to the civil rights movement there, a development that ultimately sparked the long-running civil unrest, or the 'troubles'. While such debates have been much rarer in continental Europe, they are not unknown: the controversy since 2003 over the partition of the Brussels-Halle-Vilvoorde parliamentary constituency in Belgium is an example.[1]

In Ireland, bitter division over the manner in which constituency boundaries were drawn was for long a central ingredient in Dáil debates. Much of this had to do with the rupture of long-recognised boundaries, such as county ones. The case of Leitrim is an example. More than 40 years ago, the Council of Irish County Associations in London appealed to the Taoiseach to protect the integrity of Ireland's least populous county:

> Members of this Council deplore the annihilation of County Leitrim under the proposed Electoral Bill, and appeal to the Irish Government to consider alternative proposals which will preserve

County Leitrim as far as possible, as an Electoral Unit, thus enabling the people of Co. Leitrim to enjoy their democratic rights to select and elect Leitrim Deputies to Dail Eireann.[2]

Many similar complaints have arisen from other counties over the years. The negative consequences of frequent, unpredictable changes in constituency boundaries are well documented (Kavanagh, 2003: 93–98). For sitting and would-be Dáil deputies, uncertainty over what the next revision may bring adds further unpredictability to a job that is already quite insecure. For voters, being moved from one constituency to another is potentially confusing and disconcerting, and may rupture long-standing ties with a community to which people are attached. For officials, the process of revision brings yet another heavy and potentially contentious administrative burden that is not necessarily particularly welcome.

This chapter argues that the political turmoil, popular upset and considerable expense (in time and money) that have been associated with the process of constituency boundary revision have been unnecessary. The Irish approach to constituency boundary delimitation is an eccentric Irish solution to a problem that is not Irish, but universal in the world of proportional representation—how to distribute parliamentary seats fairly. The chapter suggests that (subject to constitutional considerations) a great deal of trouble could have been avoided by adoption of a simple formula that is close to being universal in proportional representation systems: definition of 'permanent' constituency boundaries by legislation in the early 1920s, modified by a few minor local adjustments in subsequent years, with seats reallocated between constituencies by means of a simple mathematical formula after each population census. The resource needed for each revision is about half an hour of the time of a junior official in the Department of the Environment who can use spreadsheets; there is no need to take up hours of Dáil time or months of work by a high-powered constituency commission.

This chapter begins by describing the manner in which constituency boundaries are revised and seats are reapportioned in jurisdictions outside Ireland. It continues by outlining the unhappy Irish experience of constituency boundary delimitation. It goes on to illustrate what might have happened had the continental European rather than the British or American approach to constituency boundary revision been adopted. It concludes by assessing the arguments for and against change, and considering the options for constitutional reform.

CONSTITUENCY BOUNDARIES: A COMPARATIVE PERSPECTIVE

The tone of the debate about constituency boundary revision in Ireland bears some resemblance to that in the UK. This is not altogether surprising: shared historical, cultural and linguistic features have made it natural for Irish people—including Irish lawyers—to look eastwards (and, indeed, westwards) to other English-speaking jurisdictions in the pursuit of constitutional, political, cultural and other models. In the area of parliamentary seat allocation, Ireland has opted to follow the approach in Britain, which has handed responsibility for periodic revision of constituencies to a boundary commission since 1944, a responsibility earlier borne by politicians (Pulzer, 1975: 31–35; Gudgin and Taylor, 1979: 8–9; Blackburn, 1995: 113–56). The problem is that the issues raised by the process of seat allocation in Ireland resemble those in continental European countries (where proportional representation with multi-member constituencies is the norm) more closely than those in Britain or the United States (where single-member constituencies are the norm). A very simple, standard approach has been adopted in continental Europe in the pursuit of electoral equity, one far removed from the unending tinkering with boundaries that is necessary to ensure fairness in systems based on single-member districts. This is considered in the first part of this section; the second part looks at the arithmetical formula used in seat allocation.

Constituency boundaries and redistricting

The Irish constitution's insistence on maintenance of a uniform deputy–population ratio is a conventional attempt to protect the principle of suffrage equality, and is commonplace in democratic constitutions. This is a key ingredient in the so-called 'four-tail formula' for modern representative democracy—one of the demands for institutional reform that played so important a part in the struggle for democracy in nineteenth-century Europe. The 'four tails' demand endorsed by nineteenth-century radicals and social democrats finds clear expression in article 1 of the Erfurt (1891) programme of the German Social Democratic Party, which called for 'universal, equal, and direct suffrage, with secret ballot' (other socialist parties, such as the Russian one, followed the same formula). It is also routinely written into contemporary constitutions, generally with the additional requirement that elections be 'free', as in the case of Germany (where article 38 of the constitution requires election of the Bundestag by 'general, direct, free, equal, and secret elections') and Spain (where article 68 of the constitution provides that the Congress of Deputies be elected by 'universal, free, equal, direct, and secret suffrage').

These demands need to be seen in context. Secrecy of the ballot was designed to neutralise inappropriate external influences in elections, of the kind exercised in Ireland by landlords and priests before the passing of the Ballot Act in 1872 ended open voting. Direct voting (an issue of little importance in the United Kingdom) was designed to thwart the imperfectly democratic device of constraining voters to choose an electoral college which would then select parliamentary representatives, by allowing them instead to vote directly for their representatives (the election of the US President is the major surviving example of indirect voting). Universal suffrage stresses the need for the removal of all exclusionary mechanisms so that the whole adult population is enfranchised. Suffrage equality was an effort to ensure that everyone's vote counts equally—to prevent undue parliamentary influence being exerted by small, unrepresentative clusters of powerful people, of which the 'rotten boroughs' in the British parliament were an example. The many tiny boroughs that each returned two members to the Irish House of Commons up to 1800 fall into the same category: such small villages as Doneraile, Dingle and Duleek returned the same number of members as the large counties that enclosed them (respectively, Cork, Kerry and Meath; see Johnston-Liik, 2002, vol. 2). The universal democratic demand for equality of voting power was designed to counteract abuses of this kind, not to promote a fruitless pursuit of arithmetical equality in an arguably inappropriate ratio (uniformity in the deputy–electorate ratio is a more obvious requirement of fairness than uniformity in the deputy–population ratio—one with which it is likely to conflict).

In continental Europe, the formula for constituency boundary delimitation and seat reapportionment is very simple, as we will see if we look at the position in countries facing the same kind of apportionment issues as Ireland. This means leaving aside the UK (single-member districts using the plurality system), France (single-member districts using the two-ballot system) and Germany (where half of the seats are elected from single-member districts using the plurality system, with the remainder elected from regional lists). It also means leaving aside the Netherlands (where the whole country is treated as a single 150-member constituency) and Italy (where seats are not pre-allocated to regions before an election).

In those countries with a single-tier voting system, the design of constituencies and the allocation of seats between them is a simple, automatic process. The basic administrative units become constituencies: in

Switzerland, the cantons; in Spain, the provinces; in Belgium, the provinces, except for Brabant (which has been partitioned in response to problems of linguistic politics); in Luxembourg, four groups of cantons. In each case, seats are allocated between these strictly on the basis of population as measured by the most recent census. In Portugal, administrative districts are used, and in Finland groups of municipalities (which correspond substantially to provinces); but in these two cases the allocation of seats is based on the distribution of the citizen population rather than of the overall population.

In countries with a two-tier system (where most seats are allocated to constituencies, but some are held over to a higher level), the position seems more complex but the principle is the same in allocating seats at the lower level. In Greece, seats are allocated first to 56 pre-defined 'minor' electoral districts on the basis of population. In Austria, seats are apportioned initially on the basis of resident population plus registered but absent electors to 43 'regional electoral districts', or constituencies formed by combining local government areas. In Sweden constituencies are formed out of the country's 21 counties (though two are divided, and three cities constitute separate constituencies), and seats are allocated in proportion to the distribution of the electorate. A similar approach is adopted in Norway and Denmark, but there the allocation formula is more complex: in Norway, population density is taken into account alongside population, while Denmark adds a third consideration: seats are allocated according to a proportionality formula based on population, electorate and area.[3] In the three Scandinavian countries, a small number of seats are reserved for national level allocation, and in Austria and Greece there are two higher-level allocations based on a more complex formula.

What these systems have in common, and what distinguishes them from the Irish approach, is that in each case a two-stage process is followed: definition of constituency boundaries (typically, for the long term) on the basis of existing administrative divisions, and periodic allocation of seats to these on the basis of an automatic formula. The second process typically follows a different cycle from the first: every 10 years in Belgium, for instance (following the decennial population census), but every four years in Sweden (following the electoral cycle, and using electorate rather than population).

Seat allocation formulas

Allocating seats proportionally to constituencies seems at first sight a straightforward arithmetical exercise, but this is not the case. Proportions will almost never result in integer (i.e. whole) numbers of members being allocated to a particular constituency. We may see this from a simple example. Let us suppose that three seats are to be divided between two counties. Red County has a population of 52,000; Green County has 48,000. It makes intuitive sense to divide the total population (100,000) by three, and to use the resulting figure (33,333) as a 'quota', or the population that should be entitled to a single seat (this is generally known as the Hare quota).[4] We may then divide the county population by this figure to give us an indication of the 'fair' number of seats to which it is entitled. In terms of strict proportionality, then, Red County is entitled to 1.56 (52,000 divided by 33,333) seats and Green County to 1.44. All conventional apportionment formulas will allocate the integer portion calculated in this way to the respective counties, so each receives one seat. The simplest formula for allocating the third seat is the 'largest remainder' one: allowing for the two seats already allocated, Red County has a remainder of 0.56 and Green County of 0.48. The third seat is thus allocated to Red County, the one with the largest fractional remainder. This approach can be generalised to deal with larger numbers, so that once integer portions have been distributed, remaining places can be allocated in descending order of largest remainders.

This formula is widely used in allocation systems, but it has certain acknowledged drawbacks. In the example above, Green County could be divided into two smaller units, Dark Green County and Light Green County, with respective populations of 28,000 and 20,000. The three resulting units would then be entitled to representation of 1.56, 0.84 and 0.60 seats. On the largest remainder system, Red County is first allocated the seat to which its integer portion entitles it; and the two remaining seats go in order of largest remainder to Dark Green County (0.84) and Light Green County (0.60), leaving Red County (remainder 0.56) with only one seat—even though it is more populous than the other two combined. This problem might not be too serious when seats are being allocated automatically to pre-existing territorial units, but it leaves proportional representation list systems based on the largest remainder allocation highly vulnerable to manipulation by parties. A further anomaly arises, though. In certain circumstances, even if there are no new units, no boundary changes and no changes in population, a territory may lose representation *even if the overall number of seats available increases*. This anomaly—someone getting a smaller slice of the cake, even though the overall size of the cake increases and there are no extra mouths to feed—is known as the 'Alabama paradox', since the US 1880 census results would have given Alabama eight seats in a 299-member House of Representatives, but if the overall number increased to 300 Alabama would end up with only seven. This system was used over the period 1852–1901 in apportioning seats in the House of Representatives between the states in the USA, where it has been labelled the Hamilton method (Alexander Hamilton had sought unsuccessfully to secure its introduction in the 1790s).[5]

An alternative approach that resolves these problems (but leaves others) is the 'highest average' one. This is based on the allocation of seats in such a way that the seat–population ratio is, as far as possible, the same from one constituency to another (the largest remainder system will not necessarily yield this outcome). This may be described as differing from the largest remainder system in that, following allocation of integer shares of seats on the basis of a quota as discussed above, the remaining seats are allocated to the constituencies with the highest average seat–population ratios in descending order. Seats are allocated initially by truncating proportionate shares (in other words, ignoring fractions). If there is a shortfall in the number of seats to be allocated, the highest average may be arrived at by using the D'Hondt system (calculating population–seat ratios on the basis of new seat distribution scenarios), or by progressively reducing the quota until a point is reached where the sum of the integer portions for all of the constituencies totals the number of seats to be allocated. This has been labelled the Jefferson method, after Thomas Jefferson; it was adopted in the USA in 1791 in preference to the Hamilton method for allocation of House of Representative seats at federal level, and continued in use until 1842. It corresponds to the D'Hondt system, widely used in European list voting systems, and sometimes used in constituency apportionment.

But with this formula there is an added complication: the Jefferson/ D'Hondt approach may violate a 'quota rule' by giving a particular constituency, in certain circumstances, a number of seats greater than its proportionate share rounded upwards (for example, allocating an area whose due share is 7.9 seats nine seats rather than eight)—an intuitively unfair result. A variant of this method has been developed to tackle this difficulty. This initially allocates seats to constituencies by rounding rather than by truncating. If this does not result in allocation of the exact number of seats, the quota is adjusted until a value is found which, when rounded, yields exactly the overall number of seats to be allocated. Labelled the Webster method in the USA after the lawyer-politician Daniel Webster, it was used in US apportionment at federal level for the periods 1842–52 and 1901–41; it corresponds to the Sainte-Laguë method widely used (typically in modified form) in northern European electoral systems. In fact, a minor adjustment to this method has been in use for post-census apportionment in the USA

Reforming Political Institutions

since 1941. This is the Huntington-Hill method, which uses the geometric mean rather than the arithmetic mean as the basis for rounding.[6]

The difference between these approaches may be illustrated by an example: how Ireland's 13 European Parliament seats would have been allocated between the provinces on the basis of 2006 data (for purposes of illustration, the four traditional provinces are retained—Dublin included in Leinster, and Connacht and Ulster as separate provinces; comparable data for 2011 are less useful in illustrating this point).[7] Table 6.1 shows the population of each province according to the 2006 census, and indicates the exact number of seats to which each is entitled on the basis of population. But this number is not an integer: Ulster, for instance, cannot have 82% of a seat: it must have either one seat or none. The largest remainder (Hamilton) system begins by allocating the integer portions to the respective provinces. This accounts for 11 seats. The two remaining seats are allocated to the two provinces with the largest fractions: Ulster (0.82) and Munster (0.60), thus giving Ulster a single seat and Munster a total of four. In the D'Hondt (Jefferson) highest average system, we progressively reduce the size of the divisor (beginning with the Hare quota, 326,142) until we reach a value at which the integer portions sum to 13. Once the divisor is reduced to 286,890, we get this result. Any other divisor greater than or equal to 267,265 will yield a similar result; smaller divisors will allocate too many seats—14 or more. The outcome, a well-known feature of the D'Hondt system's tendency to favour larger

Table 6.1: Three methods of seat allocation by province, Ireland, 2006

Province	Population	Share of seats		Hamilton method				Jefferson method		Webster method	
		Propor-tionate	Total	Integer	Rem-ainder	Added	Final	Seats	Truncated	Seats	Rounded
Leinster	2,295,123	0.541	7.04	7	0.04	0	7	8.00	8	6.85	7
Munster	1,173,340	0.277	3.60	3	0.60	1	4	4.09	4	3.50	3
Connacht	504,121	0.119	1.55	1	0.55	0	1	1.76	1	1.50	2
Ulster	267,264	0.063	0.82	0	0.82	1	1	0.93	0	0.80	1
Total	4,239,848	1.000	13.00	11	2.00	2	13	–	13	–	13

Note: Population figures refer to 2006, and it is assumed that 13 seats are to be allocated. The total share of seats shown in column 4 is based on dividing the population by the Hare quota (total population divided by 13, or 326,142). In the Jefferson method, this quota is progressively reduced to the point where the integer portions total exactly 13 (any number between 267,265 and 286,890, the figure used here, will yield this result). In the Webster method, the quota is adjusted to the point where the rounded figures total exactly 13 (any number between 335,241, the figure used here, and 336,080 will yield this result).

groups, is that Ulster loses its seat and Leinster gains one. The Sainte-Laguë (Webster) system begins with a different logic: finding a divisor which will yield allocations that when rounded (not truncated) will give an integer value of 13. Any number from 336,080 to 335,241 will give this result. As Table 6.1 shows, this produces yet a different outcome from the other two methods.

Of the several methods, specialist study suggests that the Sainte-Laguë (Webster) system—and not its more complex successor in the USA—is the fairest system all round (Balinksi and Young, 2001: 71–78). In continental Europe, though, the largest remainder system is commonly used in allocation of seats to constituencies, though some countries (such as Portugal) use the D'Hondt system.

CONSTITUENCY BOUNDARIES IN IRELAND

The first legislation that made provision for the conduct of elections in independent Ireland, the Electoral Act, 1923, launched a system of constituency delimitation that might indeed have served the country well. The manner in which this fell victim first to vested political interests and then also to the pursuit of narrow arithmetical rather than broader representative criteria is described below. This is followed by a description of the machinery that has governed this process since 1997.

The history of boundary delimitation in Ireland
In the traditional system of political representation in Ireland, which survived the Act of Union of 1800, members of parliament were elected to represent counties or boroughs with little reference to the distribution of the people. In the early 1880s each county still returned two members to the House of Commons, regardless of population. For example, the small county of Carlow, with a population in 1881 of 41,000, returned two members, the same as the huge county of Cork, with a population of 369,000 (almost 10 times the size of Carlow). The inequity of this system was recognised in the Redistribution of Seats Act, 1885, which made a gesture in the direction of equality: Cork was now given seven seats, while Carlow was reduced to one, with other counties allocated two, three or four seats, depending on their population. A price was paid for this: counties were divided into new, single-member constituencies. Thus, for the first time, the new constituencies no longer coincided with counties, but were defined as groups of baronies or in some cases parishes. Indeed, in the case of 10 counties, a much smaller unit, the townland, was used.[8] This system was overhauled by the Redistribution

of Seats (Ireland) Act, 1918, which re-allocated seats and redefined some boundaries, but otherwise retained the same approach.

The introduction of proportional representation by the Government of Ireland Act, 1920, for the two parts of newly partitioned Ireland entailed the creation of multi-member constituencies, and would have permitted a return to counties (or groups of counties) as the basis for new electoral districts. Instead, however, existing constituencies were grouped in peculiar ways to produce a set of 26 territorial units returning between three and eight members each. As well as such entities as King's County–Queen's County (now Laois–Offaly), Carlow–Kilkenny and Longford–Westmeath (later to become familiar combinations), this resulted in peculiar mergers such as Kerry–West Limerick, Waterford–East Tipperary, South Mayo–South Roscommon, East Mayo–Sligo and Leitrim–North Roscommon. Two important elections took place on these boundaries: in 1921 to the House of Commons of Southern Ireland (regarded by Sinn Féin as part of the election of the second Dáil), and in 1922 to the provisional parliament of the Irish Free State (similarly interpreted, at least by the pro-Treaty group, as an election to the third Dáil).

The 1922 constitution made comprehensive provision for the boundary revision process. Article 26 specified the minimum and maximum size of the Dáil (not less than one member for each 30,000 of the population, nor more than one member for each 20,000 of the population), stipulated that the ratio of population to Dáil deputies at the most recent census should 'so far as possible, be identical throughout the country', and required the Oireachtas to revise the constituencies 'at least once every ten years, with due regard to changes in distribution of the population'. These provisions were carried over in the 1937 constitution, except that the revision period was extended from 10 to 12 years, a minimum number of members per constituency was specified (three), and the requirement of an equal deputy–population ratio 'so far as possible' was misrendered in the English version as 'so far as it is practicable', as discussed below. Flesh was given to these provisions by the Electoral Act, 1923, which created a set of 28 territorial constituencies, ranging in size from three to nine members, but returning to the county as the basic unit. The only exceptions were the three double-county constituencies just named (Laois–Offaly, Carlow–Kilkenny and Longford–Westmeath); Dublin city and Mayo county (divided in two by grouping local electoral areas); and Cork county (divided in three on the same basis). The overall distribution of seats under this and subsequent electoral acts is described in Table 6.2.

Table 6.2: Size and population variation of constituencies under electoral acts, Ireland, 1920–2013

Act	Constituencies by size (number of members)								Total TDs	Mean size	Index of variation
	3	*4*	*5*	*6*	*7*	*8*	*9*	*total*			
1920	3	14	4	2	1	2	–	26	120	4.6	29.1
1923	6	4	9	–	5	3	1	28	147	5.3	17.4
1935	15	8	8	–	3	–	–	34	138	4.1	20.5
1947	22	9	9	–	–	–	–	40	147	3.7	27.8
1961	17	12	9	–	–	–	–	38	144	3.8	8.1
1969	26	14	2	–	–	–	–	42	144	3.4	9.8
1974	26	10	6	–	–	–	–	42	148	3.5	9.8
1980	13	13	15	–	–	–	–	41	166	4.0	12.7
1983	13	13	15	–	–	–	–	41	166	4.0	14.6
1990	12	15	14	–	–	–	–	41	166	4.0	14.6
1995	12	15	14	–	–	–	–	41	166	4.0	12.6
1998	16	12	14	–	–	–	–	42	166	4.0	14.1
2005	18	13	12	–	–	–	–	43	166	3.9	15.4
2009	17	15	11	–	–	–	–	43	166	3.9	10.8
2013	13	16	11	–	–	–	–	40	158	4.0	9.9

Note: The 1959 act (which was declared unconstitutional) has been omitted. Data refer to territorial constituencies only, i.e. excluding two university constituencies in 1920 (returning four members each) and 1923 (returning three each). The index of variation is the difference between the largest percentage deviation above the mean and the largest percentage deviation below the mean.

The next revision, introduced in 1934 by Minister for Local Government Sean T. O'Kelly and enacted as the Electoral (Revision of Constituencies) Act, 1935, moved sharply away from the principles of the 1923 act. It reduced average size, leaving only three constituencies with more than five members (these were the seven-seat constituencies of South Dublin, Limerick and Tipperary). But it also fractured existing boundaries liberally: 27 of the 34 constituencies were now based on small units or micro-units such as district electoral divisions or, in Dublin, on complex imaginary lines running between named points. County boundaries were also widely breached: the new constituency of Clare included part of Galway, Leitrim included part of Sligo, and Waterford included part of Cork; Carlow–Kildare excluded a small part of Carlow, which was merged instead with Wicklow; and Meath–Westmeath excluded a sizeable portion of the latter county, which was included (together with part of Roscommon) in the new constituency of Athlone–Longford. The bill attracted intense criticism from the opposition, with the 'mutilation' of county boundaries and suggestions of attempted gerrymander—or 'Kellymander' as an opposition speaker described it—as the most emotive points.[9]

The next electoral act (that of 1947, introduced by Sean MacEntee) rectified the issue of county boundaries by not breaching them in any case (apart from the three well-known double-county constituencies already mentioned), though it continued to use low-level units (district electoral divisions) to define constituencies within counties. Outside Dublin, only six counties were divided: Kerry, Limerick, Mayo and Donegal into two constituencies, and Cork and Galway into three.

The same arrangement was continued by the 1959 act, but this had a fatal flaw. In introducing it as a bill, Local Government Minister Neil Blaney had argued that not just the population but the area of each constituency should be considered, on the ground that 'it should be made as convenient as possible for a Deputy to keep in touch with his constituents'.[10] The act thus allocated proportionally more deputies to the sparsely populated western counties than to built-up areas such as Dublin. Notwithstanding strong opposition, the bill duly passed. But the government victory was short-lived: an opposition senator, Dr John O'Donovan, contested its constitutionality in the High Court, and won his case, causing the act to be struck down on the grounds that, in the words of Justice Budd, 'it has been clearly established that the form of the Act of 1959 has been such as to result in substantial departures from the stipulated ratio of members to population, causing grave inequalities of parliamentary representation, and that it has likewise been demonstrated that there are no relevant circumstances to justify these departures'.[11]

The 1961 O'Donovan case was a landmark, but it turned out to be an unfortunate one. It prevented one form of possible abuse (disproportionate allocation of seats to areas where the governing party was strong), but at the cost of facilitating another (straightforward gerrymandering through boundary manipulation). The High Court judgment was interpreted as requiring very close adherence to a uniform deputy–population ratio, and thus as entailing micromanagement of constituency boundaries. This had the potential to give cover for manipulation of boundaries to optimise the chances of government victory, and such misconduct was alleged immediately in respect of the new Electoral (Amendment) Act, 1961. Allegations of gerrymandering escalated with the next two bills. The 1968 bill, introduced by Local Government Minister Kevin Boland, was described by the opposition as a 'Bolander',[12] and the debate on it extended over more than 1,000 columns in the official report of the Dáil and Seanad debates (about 50 hours of parliamentary time). The 1973 bill, introduced by James Tully, Minister for Local Government in the new Fine Gael–Labour coalition government, was similarly dubbed a 'Tullymander',[13] and took up over 1,600 columns (the equivalent of a big, 800-page volume, or about 80 hours of parliamentary time) before completing its electoral passage in 1974. Like other government bills, these inevitably passed into law, though the latter failed dramatically to enhance the government's position at the next election.

All three of these post-O'Donovan bills were characterised by a willingness to ignore the county as a basic unit. Under both the 1947 and the 1959 acts, 12 constituencies had corresponded to counties, with a further four consisting of two-county combinations. But in the 1961 act, only three constituencies (Cavan, Clare and Wicklow) corresponded to counties, with a further constituency matching the Laois–Offaly combination. In 1969, only one constituency (Wicklow) corresponded to a county, with one other (Laois–Offaly) coinciding with the area of two counties. In 1974, Waterford replaced Wicklow as the only constituency corresponding to a county, and Longford–Westmeath became a second double-county constituency.

The 1974 act was the last to be drafted under political direction. Following its return to office in 1977, Fianna Fáil agreed to the establishment of the state's first-ever constituency commission, to deal with the relatively uncontentious area of elections to the European Parliament. This was followed by a series of ad-hoc commissions to advise on the much more sensitive issue of Dáil constituency boundaries. The first such commission (a non-political body, chaired by a judge and with the Clerk of the Dáil and the Secretary of the Department of the Environment as its other members) was appointed in 1979, and its recommendations were enacted without alteration as the Electoral (Amendment) Act, 1980. Four further ad-hoc commissions on the same model were appointed subsequently, and reported in 1983, 1988, 1990 and 1995.[14] The first and last of these were required to take account of the results of the 1981 and 1991 censuses respectively, and their recommendations were duly translated into law. The 1988 report was based on the results of the 1986 census, but its terms of reference required a set of three- and four-seat constituencies, permitting five-seat ones only 'if necessary to avoid the breaching of county boundaries' (Ireland, 1988: 7). This was seen by the opposition as an attempt to undermine proportionality and to reinforce Fianna Fáil's position; and opposition threats to vote against any bill based on this principle were sufficient to ensure that no such measure was brought forward.[15] Instead, a new commission was appointed, and its report became the basis of the Electoral (Amendment) Act, 1990.

The current system
The final stage in the depoliticisation of constituency boundary revision came with the Electoral Act, 1997, which placed the boundary commission on a statutory basis. This reduced the role of the Minister for the Environment to the purely formal one of establishing a constituency commission (with pre-determined membership and terms of reference) on publication of the official breakdown of census results by area. The five-person commission is headed by a senior judge nominated by the Chief Justice, and has four *ex-officio* members: the Ombudsman, the Secretary General of the Department of the Environment, and the Clerks of the Dáil and Seanad. The commission is constrained by the following terms of reference (in addition to the overriding condition of article 16.2.3 of the constitution, not mentioned in the act, which requires it to observe a uniform deputy–population ratio from constituency to constituency):

(*a*)   the total number of members of the Dáil, subject to Article 16.2.2 of the Constitution, shall be not less than 164 and not more than 168 [amended in 2011 to specify 153 and 160 as the limits];

(*b*)   each constituency shall return three, four or five members;

(*c*)   the breaching of county boundaries shall be avoided as far as practicable;

(*d*)   each constituency shall be composed of contiguous areas;

(*e*)   there shall be regard to geographic considerations including significant physical features and the extent of and the density of population in each constituency; and

(*f*)   subject to the provisions of this section, the Commission shall endeavour to maintain continuity in relation to the arrangement of constituencies.

The provisions of the act have since then been triggered on four occasions, in 1997, 2003, 2007 and 2011, leading to boundary revision acts in 1998, 2005, 2009 and 2013.[16]

The move to an independent boundary commission has resolved two major problems. First, it has promoted wider acceptance of a process that had previously attracted a high degree of public cynicism, as governments were accused of gerrymandering boundaries and pursuing naked electoral self-interest. Second, and related to this, it has saved a great deal of parliamentary time. The last politically driven measure (the 1973 bill) had, as we have seen, taken more than 80 hours of parliamentary time. But the bills that gave legal effect to the recommendations of the first five Dáil constituency commissions took between two and seven hours to secure their passage. The 2005 bill, admittedly, took a great deal longer, but this was because of a range of particular local issues, underscored by grievances over the unrelated matter of electronic voting, and did not reflect on the independence of the commission. The 2008 bill (enacted in 2009), however, attracted a great deal of criticism, with Fine Gael's Michael Noonan offering a trenchant critique:

> My party supports the Bill but I do not welcome it because it is based on a flawed commission report which was carelessly drafted ... The report is careless but the commission arrived at its conclusion and knows that the practice in the Dáil is to accept what the commission decides. If there are other reports like this, that practice itself could break down.[17]

Although the bill covered some other technical areas, it is striking that the debate was so long, extending over about 14 hours.

The new procedure has not, however, resolved a remaining difficulty, and is in effect prevented from doing so by its terms of reference. Conditions (c), (e) and (f) are essentially conservative, in that they collectively promote stability in constituency boundaries (the third of these explicitly, the other two by implication, in suggesting appropriate deference to very stable county boundaries and unchanging geographical features). But there is a tension between these and condition (b) (which sets the number of deputies per constituency at between three and five), when it is taken in combination with article 16.2.3 of the constitution (which requires adherence to a uniform deputy–population ratio). Vindication of the latter principle, if it is narrowly defined, requires careful attention to the issue of boundary revision, and is likely to lead to frequent changes in the shape of constituencies. This has been reflected in the extent to which constituency boundaries have continued to be unstable over the years, as summarised in Table 6.3.

Table 6.3: Basis of formation of constituencies created by electoral acts, Ireland, 1923–2013

Act	Boundaries on which based					No. of words to describe boundaries	Creation of boundaries		
	County	Sub-county			Total		New	Recent	Old
		Large	Small	Micro					
1923	20	8	–	–	28	386	18	10	–
1935	7	–	22	5	34	1,837	28	3	3
1947	16	–	18	6	40	1,725	30	6	4
1961	4	–	23	11	38	2,168	34	2	2
1969	2	–	24	16	42	3,816	37	3	2
1974	3	–	36	3	42	2,708	35	4	3
1980	10	–	21	10	41	2,914	40	–	1
1983	11	–	21	9	41	2,768	4	36	1
1990	10	–	20	11	41	2,616	25	1	15
1995	9	–	21	11	41	3,147	21	8	12
1998	9	–	21	12	42	3,373	22	7	13
2005	5	–	26	12	43	3,244	28	5	10
2009	3	–	38	2	43	3,161	24	9	10
2013	3	–	35	2	40	3,022	29	4	7

Note: The 1959 act (which was declared unconstitutional) has been omitted. 'Large' sub-county units refer to local electoral areas; 'small' units to district electoral divisions, wards, or electoral divisions; 'micro' to townlands and urban street lines. 'New' boundaries are those created for the first time by the act in question; 'recent' refers to those created in the immediately preceding electoral act; and 'old' refers to all others.

Table 6.3 uses three criteria to assess the geographical robustness and stability of constituency boundaries. The first is the extent to which they coincide with well-known administrative divisions. As the table shows, constituency boundaries do not usually coincide with county boundaries, and where they depart from these they typically use low- or micro-level units for purposes of definition, except in 1923, when local electoral areas were used. The problem is that Ireland possesses few administrative districts other than the county, and that use of low-level districts whose boundaries and names evoke minimal levels of public consciousness creates difficulties for popular recognition of the shape of constituencies.

This perspective is reinforced in the second criterion reported in Table 6.3: the number of words used in the schedules to the electoral acts to define constituency boundaries. Except in 1923, this has normally been a long essay.[18] In the case of those constituencies that form part of counties, the description is likely to make sense only to lawyers—and even to them, in a purely formal sense. We may consider the manner in which the division of county Meath into two constituencies was described in the 2013 act:

> **Meath East**: In the county of Meath the electoral divisions of: Drumcondra, Grangegeeth, Killary, in the *former Rural District of Ardee No. 2*; Culmullin, Donaghmore, Dunboyne, Dunshaughlin, Kilbrew, Killeen, Kilmore, Rathfeigh, Ratoath, Rodanstown, Skreen, in the *former Rural District of Dunshaughlin*; Ardagh, Carrickleck, Ceanannas Mór Rural, Cruicetown, Kilmainham, Maperath, Moybolgue, Moynalty, Newcastle, Newtown, Nobber, Posseckstown, Staholmog, Trohanny, in the *former Rural District of Kells*; Ardcath, Duleek, Mellifont, Stamullin, in the *former Rural District of Meath*; Ardmulchan, Castletown, Domhnach Phádraig, Kentstown, Painestown, Rathkenny, Slane, Stackallan, Tara, in the *former Rural District of Navan*; and the town of Kells.
>
> **Meath West**: The county of Meath, except the parts thereof which are comprised in the constituencies of Meath East and Louth; and the county of Westmeath, except the part thereof which is comprised in the constituency of Longford–Westmeath.

This description may be displayed with some clarity on a map; but this does not take from the bewildering wording used formally to define it. Although placenames such as Dunboyne and Duleek will be familiar, it is likely that almost no-one (even local electoral specialists, politicians and their agents) would know the approximate boundaries of the corresponding electoral divisions. This is not surprising, since these units were last used for electoral purposes in 1914 to return poor law guardians and rural district councillors.[19] They do not coincide at all with polling districts, and the rural districts referred to disappeared as administrative units in the early 1920s.

The third criterion used in Table 6.3 is the stability of constituencies. Here, once again, the picture is one of potential difficulty for the electorate: in all electoral acts except one, most of the constituencies that emerged were new, as their boundaries were altered at least slightly. The only exception, that of 1983, was a striking one, in that all constituencies outside Dublin, and most within the capital, continued unchanged from the 1980 act. We may consider some statistics. Since the introduction of proportional representation in

1920, no fewer than 401 new Dáil constituencies have been created. This counts as 'new' any constituency where there was even a marginal change in the boundary (for example, Limerick East in 1980, where the district electoral division of Ballycummin was gained from Limerick West), or where the 'new' constituency had existed previously (for example, Clare in 1980 reverted to its pre-1969 shape). Many constituencies have been used just once, in a single election, before being again adjusted. The record for longevity was held by the venerable constituency of Laois–Offaly, which remained unaltered since it was created in 1920 as the constituency of King's County–Queen's County until it was broken up in 2009. But no other constituency comes close; two others created at the same time, Monaghan and Cavan, survived past the age of 40, but disappeared in 1961 and 1969 respectively.

A final vivid example of the effects of frequent changes on local loyalties is offered by the many revisions that have swept people across county boundaries. Up to 1969, the people of Lisdoonvarna were part of the easily recognisable constituency of their own county, Clare (though from 1935 to 1947 this had protruded far into South Galway). In 1969, however, they were separated from Ennis and the rest of the county, and transferred into the constituency of Clare–South Galway. In 1974 they found themselves in the horseshoe-shaped constituency of West Galway. They were restored to their own county only in 1980. This example could be multiplied, with the partition of tiny Leitrim as the most obvious recent case.

ALTERNATIVES FOR IRELAND

This section argues that Ireland's departure down a lonely and unfortunate path, though largely taken for granted at all levels of Irish society, has not been necessary. The continental European approach could easily have been applied, and this section demonstrates how this might have been done, documenting this in a statistical appendix which illustrates the kind of constituencies that might have existed. It might be objected that this is merely a mathematical exercise that exploits the benefits of hindsight, but it is possible to put the scheme devised here to a realistic 'stress test': it was initially devised and published in 2008 (Coakley, 2008a), so it is reasonable to ask how it would have fared under the population expansion demonstrated by the 2011 census, and the reduction in Dáil size proposed by the government. This issue is addressed in the latter part of the section.

Designing constituencies

It was perhaps natural for Irish lawmakers in the 1920s to consider the British model as the obvious one for constituency boundary delimitation. This was the constitutional system with which most Irish politicians—however radical their republicanism—were overwhelmingly familiar, and the system of proportional representation bequeathed to independent Ireland by the departing British administration was the 'British' single transferable vote (STV) one, not the more common continental European party list system. There was one important practical consequence of adoption of the STV rather than the party list system of proportional representation. The list system delivers a speedy outcome regardless of constituency size (though of course tending to give a more proportional result in constituencies with large numbers of members). But the human cost and administrative incon- venience of STV rise rapidly with constituency size, as we have seen in Chapter 5.

Had the continental European system been introduced in Ireland at the foundation of the state, the original fundamental electoral act would have addressed three questions: (1) the total size of the Dáil, (2) the boundaries of the constituencies to be used in returning deputies and (3) the formula to be used in allocating seats to constituencies.

First, a simple approach would be to set Dáil size at, say, 140; the 1911 census, on which this would have had to be based, would have allowed a minimum of 105 and a maximum of 156 deputies, given the constitutional requirement that the number of such deputies be not less than one for every 30,000 or more than one for every 20,000 of the population. Dáil size could have remained at this level almost until the present, but for illustrative purposes it is assumed here that Dáil size would be increased to 166 following the 1979 census (as indeed it was), and that it would drop to 158 in 2011 (a political decision by the government).

Second, administrative counties in principle become constituencies. There were 31 of these, with a small average population, and some would be entitled to only one or two members—levels too low to permit genuine proportional representation. It is assumed here that three would be set as minimum constituency size (a level in any case set by the constitution in 1937), and that an upper size of nine members would be set, for practical reasons already discussed. To achieve appropriate constituencies, it would be necessary to merge smaller counties with adjacent ones with which they had links at least at the geographical level, and in exceptional cases to divide counties. The formula could thus be that each administrative county would become a Dáil constituency, with the following exceptions, to produce a standard set of 25 constituencies.

- The county boroughs (cities) of Limerick and Waterford would be included in the counties with which they shared their names; the two ridings of Tipperary would together constitute a single constituency; and the small counties of Carlow, Laois, Longford, Leitrim and Monaghan would be merged respectively with the counties of Kilkenny, Offaly, Westmeath, Sligo and Cavan to produce a set of five two-county constituencies.
- The county of Cork would be divided into two constituencies, 'East' and 'West', by merging major local authority districts; Cork county borough (city) would remain separate; and Dublin county borough (city) would be divided into two constituencies, 'North' and 'South', on the same basis; Dublin county would remain separate.

Third, it is assumed that the Sainte-Laguë/Webster highest average allocation system would be chosen (it is acknowledged as the fairest system for allocation of this kind), and that it would be applied after every census. As described above, this entails finding a quota or divisor to calculate each constituency's proportionate share of seats, so that when fractional remainders are rounded up or down, following basic rules of arithmetic, the total number of seats allocated is exactly the number targeted for distribution. Initially, the results of the 1911 census would have had to be used (they did indeed form the basis of the 1923 Electoral Act).

The outcome of this process would be as reported in the appendix at the end of this chapter, part (a) of which indicates the population of each constituency and part (b) the number of seats based on the Sainte-Laguë/Webster system. There would originally have been two large nine-seat constituencies (Cork West and Mayo), and five three-seat constituencies, with others returning intermediate numbers. The appendix shows how the position would have changed following subsequent censuses. For reasons of space, the outcomes in certain intermediate censuses (1951, 1961, 1971, 1981, 1991 and 2002) have been dropped from the appendix; any issues to which these might have given rise are discussed in the text, and the 2011 outcome is discussed later.

As the appendix shows, this arrangement would have been extraordinarily stable. Twenty constituencies (the first 20 listed) could have continued with unaltered boundaries to the present. Five others would, though, have had to be revised. First, population decline would eventually cause Roscommon to fall below the threshold for three seats. It is assumed here that it would have been merged with Leitrim–Sligo following the results of the 1971 census to produce the new constituency of Connacht East. The greater Dublin area presents a bigger difficulty. This would originally have been divided into three constituencies. The extension of the city boundaries that took place in 1930 could have been followed by dividing each of the city constituencies (Dublin City North and Dublin City South) in two, an 'inner' constituency (including areas closest to the city centre) and an 'outer' one (the newer suburbs).[20] This would have been sufficiently robust to last to the present, without further modification. But the growing population of Dublin County would also require attention. A new constituency of Dun Laoghaire–Rathdown would have been created in 1961, with the rest of the county partitioned into northern and southern constituencies following the 1979 census. These areas would correspond with the new administrative counties (Dun Laoghaire–Rathdown, Fingal and South Dublin) created in 1994. But South Dublin would quickly become too large, so it is assumed here that it would be divided into a northern and a southern constituency (we might label them Clondalkin and Tallaght, respectively) following the 1986 census. It should be noted that, with the exception of the division of South Dublin, these changes in Dublin County constituencies would have matched local government reforms, though as envisaged here they would have fallen due before local government restructuring actually took place.

Meeting representation criteria

The data in the appendix at the end of this chapter were compiled and published before the results of the 2011 census became available (Coakley, 2008a). A crucial test of the viability of the proposal here has to do with its applicability in the wake of further population change. Applying the 2011 census data to the same constituencies, this time with the reduced number of TDs (158) for which the most recent constituency boundary report makes provision, would result in a workable outcome. This is illustrated in Figure 6.1, which shows what the position would have been after the 2011 census had the approach discussed here been adopted. The position in Dublin, necessarily omitted from the map, would have changed only slightly since 2006.

This approach, then, gives us a very stable set of constituencies, each with a clearly defined identity and well-recognised boundaries. In some cases, representation would have been virtually unchanged from 1923 to 2011: Carlow–Kilkenny, Laois–Offaly and Wexford as five-member constituencies, for example, though their representation would occasionally have slipped back to four. In others, there would have been a big but gradual drop, though without any need for boundary change: Mayo falling from nine to four, for instance, and Cavan–Monaghan from seven to five. In yet other cases, there would have been an increase in representation: Kildare from three to seven, Meath from three to six, and Wicklow from three to five, for example. The shape of the resulting seat allocation process is summarised in Table 6.4, which facilitates comparison with the existing system, as summarised in Table 6.2.

Figure 6.1: Simulated allocation of seats to fixed-boundary constituencies, Ireland, 1923 and 2013

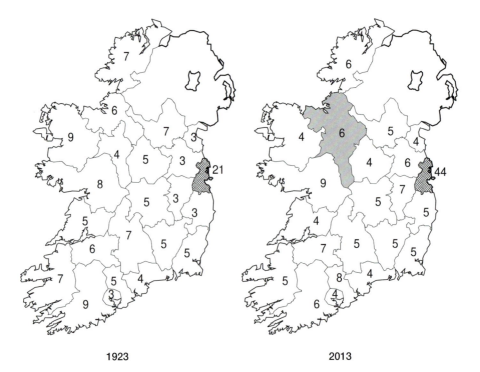

1923   2013

Note: Boundaries are those of counties or groups of counties, except in the case of Cork. Seat allocation is based on the Sainte-Laguë highest average formula, using census data of 1911 and 2011 respectively. Assumed total number of seats is 140 (1923) and 158 (2013). One new constituency is shaded. Dublin constituencies are not illustrated.

Table 6.4: Size, population variation and creation year of notional constituencies, Ireland, 1923–2013

Census	Constituencies by size (number of members)								Total TDs	Mean size	Index of variation
	3	4	5	6	7	8	9	total			
1911	5	2	6	3	5	2	2	25	140	5.6	23.7
1926	4	6	3	1	6	4	1	25	140	5.6	23.4
1936	4	7	4	6	4	2	–	27	140	5.2	20.1
1946	5	5	5	5	6	1	–	27	140	5.2	25.0
1951	6	4	5	6	3	3	–	27	140	5.2	28.8
1956	6	5	5	5	2	3	1	27	140	5.2	22.0
1961	6	7	4	6	3	1	1	28	140	5.0	26.8
1966	5	6	7	6	2	2	–	28	140	5.0	23.8
1971	4	6	5	5	7	–	–	27	140	5.2	29.3
1979	–	5	7	6	6	3	1	28	166	5.9	22.3
1981	–	5	7	7	4	4	1	28	166	5.9	19.7
1986	1	5	9	6	4	2	2	29	166	5.7	21.9
1991	1	5	9	6	4	2	2	29	166	5.7	16.9
1996	1	5	9	6	4	2	2	29	166	5.7	21.6
2002	1	5	9	6	4	2	2	29	166	5.7	19.3
2006	1	5	9	6	4	2	2	29	166	5.7	20.1
2011	2	6	9	6	3	1	2	29	158	5.4	23.9

Note: The index of variation is the difference between the largest percentage deviation above the mean and the largest percentage deviation below the mean.

Three criteria of the suitability of a boundary delimitation and seat allocation system are implicit in these tables: fairness, or the extent to which the principle of suffrage equality is respected; efficiency, or the ease with which the revision process takes place; and legitimacy, or the capacity of the system to produce a result that is widely accepted as appropriate. To what extent are these criteria met by the system proposed here?

First, it must be acknowledged immediately that none of the revisions proposed here conforms literally to the provisions of the constitution regarding maintenance of a uniform deputy–population ratio; all of them conform to its spirit, or intention. But this point must be quickly set in context. *None of the constituency boundary revision measures actually adopted since 1923 has conformed literally to the provisions of the constitution either; and some of them (especially those adopted since maximum constituency size was reduced to five in 1947) have arguably failed to conform to its spirit, or intention.* The first part of this point may be documented statistically. Part (c) of the appendix reports the population per deputy in the constituencies described here. The simplest way to assess compatibility with the principle that the deputy–population ratio shall as far as 'possible' (a word whose significance is discussed later) be the same from one constituency to another is to measure the gap between the lowest and highest ratios. For example, the 2007 commission's recommendations gave Carlow–Kilkenny the highest population–deputy ratio (26,749 people per TD), 4.73% above the national average of 25,541, and it gave Cavan–Monaghan the lowest ratio (24,000), 6.03% below the national average; the gap between these two figures, 10.76%, gives a good indication of the overall deviation. The deviations in the constituencies devised here are reported in part (d) of the appendix. The smallest difference is 16.9% (1991) and the largest is 29.3% (1971), though these particular years have had to be dropped from the appendix. This compares favourably with the position before the 1961 High Court decision (where the range was from 17.4% in 1923 to 27.8% in 1947), but is rather higher than the deviations that have been the norm in later electoral acts (ranging from 8.1% in 1961 to 15.4% in 2005).[21] Furthermore, looking at the balance of under- or over-representation in each constituency over time would rectify some of these anomalies. It is true that two of the constituencies suggested here would have enjoyed significant over-representation over the nine-decade period to 2011: Louth (6.8%, on average) and Longford–Westmeath (5.2%). But all of the other constituencies would have remained within a very tight band, close to the national average, ranging from Limerick (2.9% below the average ratio) to Carlow–Kilkenny (1.9% above).

Second, in respect of efficiency, the proposed set of constituencies is very stable and requires little effort to secure its implementation. Instead of the 401 constituencies that have been created since 1920, there would have been a total of 36 constituencies over time. Furthermore, 20 of these could have survived unchanged from the beginning, and most of the others would have had a long life. Only the constituency of Dublin County South would have been short-lived: created around 1979, it would have been divided by about 1986.

Third, this scheme is designed to enhance the legitimacy of the reapportionment process. The point emerged above that most constituencies created since 1935 have been defined in terms of low-level units, such as electoral divisions, which are unrecognisable to the general public, and that slices of territory from one county are often incorporated with another. In the scheme suggested here, no county boundaries are breached, and only two counties are divided. In the case of Cork, the original division coincides with well-known administrative areas (rural and urban districts) which, though they disappeared in the 1920s, would have left an intra-county border that would by now be quite familiar. In the case of Dublin City, a straightforward, generally recognised division between North and South would have been modified by a further division between 'inner' and 'outer' city areas that would become familiar over time. In Dublin County, changes could have coincided with local government reform, except for the need to divide Dublin County South. The complex wording, similarly, required to define boundaries would no longer be needed: the schedule to the original act would need about 350 words, much shorter than the long essays (typically of more than 3,000 words) that have been the norm more recently. To recapitulate, the only subsequent changes would have been (1) a simple redefinition of the Dublin City constituencies in 1930 in association with the major change in city boundaries as part of the local government reform process, (2) an even simpler amendment merging Roscommon with Leitrim–Sligo around 1971, and (3) a rather more demanding set of changes in Dublin County in 1961, 1979 and 1986 to take account of rapid population growth (the first two of these could have been carried out as part of local government reform).

This proposal possesses the advantage that it is more congruent with notions of territorial identity and powerful local loyalties than the current system. While no such principle is specified in the constitution, it could be inferred from article 5 that as a 'democratic state' Ireland's standing in this respect should be protected, and that the principle of equal representation should not be brought into disrepute by insistence on an excessively narrow interpretation of what quickly become merely historical census data. Furthermore, there is a more persuasive way to reduce inequalities in representation while simultaneously enhancing proportionality: by simply abolishing all small constituencies, and making, say, five the *minimum* number of deputies per constituency, not, as at present, the maximum. The European-style approach suggested here may produce a nominally higher deviation from the average deputy–population ratio than a system where boundaries are continually overhauled, but it is much simpler, more flexible, more responsive to population change, more predictable in its outcome, and more likely in the long term to vindicate the principle of equal representation and to protect the legitimacy of the political system.

ASSESSING THE CONSTITUENCY BOUNDARY REVISION SYSTEM

Given the gap between the practice of constituency revision in Ireland and in continental Europe, it is worth reviewing the key difficulties that would be likely to obstruct a move from the current system to one that would be more familiar on the continent. Having considered the potential debate in this area—and it is no more than a potential one, since few voices are arguing for change—the possible implications for constitutional change are considered.

Debating constituency boundaries

The suggestions in this chapter regarding a new approach to constituency boundary revision may appear so radical that their chances of securing acceptance are slight. It is, however, worth discussing some of the more obvious areas of potential dispute regarding any new system. They correspond to the following questions, of which the first is the most challenging.

- How closely should a uniform deputy–population ratio be pursued?
- How often should constituencies be revised?
- How large should constituencies be?
- To what extent should local government boundaries be adhered to?

Equality of representation

It could be objected in the first place that the constitutional requirement that a uniform deputy–population ratio be maintained entails painstaking revision of constituency boundaries to match the most recent census results. The meaning of the 1937 constitution (which in this respect carries on the provisions of the 1922 constitution) seems clear. Article 16.2.3° provides that 'The ratio between the number of members to be elected at any time for each constituency and the population of each constituency, as ascertained at the last preceding census, shall, *so far as it is practicable*, be the same throughout the country' (emphasis added). But the Irish language text, which takes precedence over this, is much more demanding; it requires conformity to this ratio '*sa mhéid gur féidir é*' ('in as far as *possible*'), thus reproducing the requirement of the 1922 constitution, article 26 of which stipulated conformity to this ratio 'so far as possible' across constituencies.

This is one of the instances where there is a clear conflict between the Irish and English versions of the constitution—not a particularly surprising one, since, as the definitive study of the Irish language text of the constitution points out, 'practically every section of the Constitution contains divergences between the Irish and the English texts' (Ó Cearúil, 1999: 7). This is in line with the reality that there are no two languages between which perfectly accurate translation is possible. For the courts, a literal interpretation of the constitution would have to abandon the notion that the Irish and English texts can always be reconciled, and rest instead on the Irish language version— a singular challenge, since most judges are not fluent speakers of Irish, and there is a perception that the Irish version is a derived document, a translation of the English version that was worked through in the Dáil.[22] Strangely, though, the High Court ruled in 1961 that 'no material discordance exists between the English and Irish texts' of the constitution in this respect.[23]

The implications of this narrower understanding of the constitution are clear. Since 1841, the Irish census has used the townland as its basic enumeration and reporting unit. Census results were published at this level for the whole island until 1911; since then, townland data have been available on request from the Central Statistics Office; and townland data continued to be published in the Northern Ireland census until 1951. Use of this unit (the average population of which in 1911 was 58) permits the fine-tuning of constituency boundaries in such a way that near-mathematical accuracy can be obtained in the deputy–population ratio from one constituency to another.

This strict interpretation is compatible with that in another jurisdiction where the principle of equal representation is constitutionally embedded in respect of the lower house of parliament (see Huckabee, 2001). In the USA, article 1.2 of the constitution provides that 'representatives ... shall be apportioned among the several states ... according to their respective numbers'. There, a two-stage process has been followed. The first is the *apportionment* stage. The Bureau of the Census, which conducts a census every 10 years— originally, primarily to apportion seats in the House of Representatives— reports to the President within nine months on the population of each state; the President informs the Clerk of the House of Representatives of the population and number of representatives to which each state is entitled; and the Clerk passes this information on to state governors within 15 days. The second stage, *redistricting*, then begins: the division of states into the appropriate number of congressional districts.

In the past, the redistricting or constituency boundary revision process was carried out with uneven attention to the principle of equal representation, but a series of Supreme Court judgments brought about a radical change in the position.[24] The result has been a pattern of complete mathematical parity in most states, and of a level close to this in others. To take the example of Colorado, whose 2000 population (4,301,261) is close to that of Ireland: the census showed that it was entitled to seven congressmen, with an average population of 614,466 each. Two of the state's congressional districts (the 4th and the 6th) have precisely this population; two lie above it by one person, with a population of 614,467 (the 3rd and 5th districts); and three lie below it by the same amount, with a population of 614,465 (the 1st, 2nd and 7th districts). Some might consider this impressive; others would regard it as completely pointless. Arithmetical perfection has been achieved in applying the principle of equal representation within states, but at a terrible cost in respect of both geography, with bizarrely shaped districts, and political legitimacy, given the general acceptance that the process is normally driven by considerations of electoral advantage, and a lack of interest by the courts in the extent of gerrymandering.

Focusing on the trees may have caused US legislators and judges to lose sight of the wood. Following the 2000 reapportionment, notwithstanding numerical parity *within* states, there were big disparities *between* them: the gap between the largest deviation above and below the mean was 62.5%, well above any level that would be viewed as acceptable in Ireland.[25] Furthermore, there is a strong perception among observers that the pursuit of arithmetical equality has disguised a deeply partisan procedure, causing redistricting to be described as 'one of the most conflictive political activities in the United States' (Engstrom, 2002: 51). The process and its results have drawn such negative descriptions over the decades as 'disturbing' 'notorious and shameful' and 'invidious' (Hacker, 1963: 2, 20, 120), 'murky', 'crass' and 'seedy' (Cain, 1984: xi, 1, 189), and 'outrageous', 'contorted' and 'scandalous' (Monmonier, 2001: 150, 154, 156).[26]

The contribution of the courts in Ireland to the equal representation debate has been more solidly grounded in broad considerations of democratic theory, though the initial judicial intervention in 1961 had one effect similar to that in the USA, in opening the door to large-scale gerrymandering. In this case, Mr Justice Budd held that the 1959 constituency revision act was 'such as to produce substantial departures from the ratio of members of Dáil Éireann to the population of the Republic prescribed by the Constitution, causing grave inequalities of representation for which no justification or genuine administrative difficulty exists', and that it had also failed to take due account of changes in population distribution; although he adopted a quite restrictive interpretation of how closely a uniform ratio should be followed, he did not insist on mathematical accuracy.[27] This approach was developed by the Supreme Court in ruling on the constitutionality of the new Electoral (Amendment) Bill, 1961:

> Exact parity in the ratio between members and the population of each constituency is unlikely to be obtained and is not required. The decision as to what is practicable is within the jurisdiction of the Oireachtas. It may reasonably take into consideration a variety of factors, such as the desirability so far as possible to adhere to well-known boundaries such as those of counties, townlands and electoral divisions. The existence of divisions created by such physical features as rivers, lakes and mountains may also have to be reckoned with. The problem of what is practicable is primarily one for the Oireachtas, whose members have a knowledge of the problems and difficulties to be solved which this Court cannot have. Its decision should not be reviewed by this Court unless there is a manifest infringement of the Article. This Court cannot, as is suggested, lay down a figure above or below which a variation from what is called the national average is not permitted.[28]

The question whether the deviations that would arise under the scheme proposed here would be compatible with the constitution has no clearcut answer, and would rest ultimately on the position taken by the Supreme Court. A narrow, literal interpretation would lead it to find wanting all boundary revisions to date (including all of those devised by independent boundary commissions). Fortunately, the courts have adopted a much more holistic approach, seeking to identify the principles lying behind particular constitutional formulations rather than spelling out the literal implications of specific clauses, with the 2007 judgment of Mr Justice Clarke as an effective illustration of a judge's appreciation of the broad political principles that must inform constitutional interpretation in a modern democracy.[29] Vindicating the mainstream principle of equal representation should be no more traumatic in Ireland than elsewhere in Europe, and need not violate citizens' sense of geographical identity.

Timing of revision

It could also be objected that the constitutional requirement that the Oireachtas revise constituency boundaries at periodic intervals precludes the transfer of this function to any other agency. This argument has weight, but need not undermine the proposal being made here. Article 16.2.4° of the constitution requires the Oireachtas to 'revise the constituencies at least once in every twelve years'. The Oireachtas has already devolved the spadework entailed by this responsibility to a boundary commission, whose recommendations up to now have been enacted without amendment (with an important qualification in the case of the 1988 commission, whose terms of reference were allegedly politically biased, as discussed above).

The alternative procedure, calculating reapportionment based on a new census, could easily be managed by the Oireachtas—there would be little to debate, other than egregious departures from a uniform deputy–population ratio. The expression 'revise the constituencies' is clearly intended to refer to maintenance of this ratio, and this could be done by reapportionment of seats rather than by alteration of boundaries (which would take place only rarely). This is much more straightforward than current practice; it ensures that the constituencies are still being revised, but it greatly simplifies the process, and allows it to be completed more quickly. Furthermore, there would no longer be any need for significant delay between availability of census data and Dáil seat reapportionment. Notwithstanding the diligent work and judicious recommendations of successive boundary commissions, the outcome of the present arrangement as measured by implementation of policies of electoral fairness has been unimpressive, and it was even less impressive in earlier years when political interests dominated the process.

The track record speaks for itself. Since 1923, the average gap between the date of Irish general elections and the censuses on which the constituencies used were based has been 9.1 years (the record is held by the general election of 1933, 22 years after the 1911 census, whose results were used by the 1923 electoral act). Of nine commissions to date that have recommended new Dáil constituencies, *not one saw its recommendations translated into legally defined constituencies that were used in a general election before the next census intervened* (though there is still hope for the commission that reported in 2012). It is true that in two cases (the commissions that reported in 1980 and in 1998), the first general election under the new boundaries took place before the results of the new censuses were actually published; but in four other cases (the commissions reporting in 1983, 1990, 1995 and 2004) the first general election under the new boundaries took place *after the results of a new census showed that these boundaries were already out of date.* In three of these cases, this was based on preliminary census results (in 1986, these showed very large inequalities); in the fourth (the 2006 census), final results were available, and showed that the modest departure from a uniform deputy–population ratio in the 2005 act (a gap of 15.4% separating the highest from the lowest deputy–population ratio) had already more than doubled, to 31.8% (ranging from Dun Laoghaire, 10.6% below the national average, to Dublin West, 21.2% above it). The results of another commission (1988) were entirely set aside, and it is too early at this point to assess the role of the most recent commission.

In this context, it is hard to resist the alarming conclusion that the obviously serious task of defending the principle of equal representation has been sacrificed to the apparently frivolous pursuit of a constitutional will-o'-the-wisp. The present system clearly seeks only to use a formal, objective historical criterion, not to reflect continuing population change. Since constituency commissions have been introduced, it has taken, on average, almost three years (specifically, 35 months) from the date of the census for a boundary revision act to be passed. This period could be halved if the procedure suggested here were adopted (the final census reports on which the commissions based their findings appeared on average 18 months after the census dates). Furthermore, although the High Court ruled in 2007 that the commission is required to use final rather than preliminary census data, if the latter were used the period of delay could be shortened to three months from the date of the census.[30]

In fact, the preliminary report (compiled from local enumerators' summaries immediately after the census) provides an extremely accurate forecast of the figures in the final report (based on the actual census forms), and was used as the basis for one electoral act (1947). In 2006, the preliminary data on Dáil constituency populations deviated only very slightly from the final figures—the deviations ranged between 0.01% and 0.63%. Because of the pace of recent population movement, it is likely that the population data in the preliminary census reports offer a more accurate indicator of population on the day of their publication than do the data in the final reports. By waiting for final corrected (but essentially historical) data, in other words, the boundary review process works with data that are *less* likely to reflect the contemporary population than the preliminary figures were.

Constituency size

Some would argue that the relatively large constituency size proposed here is incompatible with the single transferable vote system of proportional representation. This is a potentially serious issue: STV indeed implies modest constituency size, in that it is based on voters ranking individual candidates, an exercise that can have meaning only if there is some restriction on the number of candidates, or provision for some kind of 'ticket' voting as in Australia. In the past, though, voters in Galway have been able to cope with a nine-member constituency; large constituencies have been common in local elections and in Northern Ireland Assembly elections; and in 1925 the electorate survived a big event, the election of 19 senators from a list of 76 candidates by STV. If some of the constituencies suggested here appear too large, other solutions are possible. Galway would be entitled to nine seats in 2006, for instance, but it could be disaggregated into its two component administrative counties, Galway County and the new Galway County Borough.

But this objection could be stood on its head. The practice since 1947 of restricting maximum constituency size to five is of questionable compatibility with the constitution. This was written into the terms of reference of the various boundary commissions, where this was initially described as 'traditional'—a misleading epithet for a pattern that in 1980 was still relatively recent, but which in the intervening period has come to be seen as 'normal'. One commission, that of 1988, was even required to confine itself to three- or four-member constituencies, except when five-member constituencies might have been necessary to avoid a breach of county boundaries.

The constitution, however, requires not just use of the single transferable vote, but *proportional representation* (i.e. the representation of political forces in the Dáil in approximately the same proportion as among those voting).[31] This requires moderately large constituencies, since the threshold for representation (which approximates to the Droop quota, as used in Dáil elections) will otherwise be too high: 25% in a three-seat constituency, 20% in a four-seater and 17% in a five-seater, for example. The relationship between proportionality and constituency size is well established, with large constituencies considered important for the representation not just of smaller parties but also of other groups such as women (Shugart, 1994: 32–33).[32] Although it has been acknowledged that in practice the Irish system performs well in delivering relatively proportional results, average constituency size has been described as 'strikingly low' in comparative terms (Gallagher, 2009b: 517).[33] This reduced level of proportionality seems particularly inappropriate at a time when Irish society is becoming more complex and diverse: in this increasingly multicultural state, proportional representation is arguably more important than ever.

Relationship to administrative boundaries

The system proposed here suggests tackling the anomalous Irish position by simply switching to the system that is normal for proportional representation. Ireland's unusual approach to constituency boundary revision is not the only instance where electoral law deviates from the norm in proportional representation systems. Casual vacancies in Dáil membership, for instance, are filled in by-elections where the whole constituency is treated as a single-member district, a clear violation of the fundamental principle of proportional representation.[34] But there is another aspect of Irish institutional exceptionalism that makes the constituency boundary revision process even more difficult: the country's peculiar one-and-a-half-tier system of local government. Half of the lower tier (rural district councils/poor law unions) was abolished in the 1920s, leaving only certain types of large town with their own system of local government, and even they are scheduled for abolition under proposals announced by the Government in 2012 (Department of the Environment, 2012). This made the identification of any recognisable units below the level of the county for purposes of constituency boundary delimitation exceptionally difficult, aggravating the challenge of creating familiar looking electoral units—a position unique to Ireland.[35]

The longevity of Irish counties as administrative units (they have existed as stable territorial units in more or less their present shape since the early seventeenth century) seems to have made them a powerful focus of local loyalty, extending to a range of forms of popular mobilisation from the late eighteenth century onwards. This has been reinforced by their significance as key units for more than a century in popular Gaelic games, and perhaps also by the weakness of local democracy below the level of the county. It has been argued that changes in boundaries can have an alienating effect on the electorate, which may be confused as to the identity of their new constituency, and may even become politically demobilised (the frequently changing boundaries of the South West inner city of Dublin seem to offer evidence of this; Kavanagh, 2003: 95). It has also been argued that 'given the highly localised and clientelistic nature of Irish politics, a county, or area, that lacks a TD runs the risk of becoming politically marginalised and this may lead to increased levels of political disengagement and lower levels of electoral participation in these areas' (Kavanagh, 2003: 94). It is indeed likely that TDs will be tempted to give less attention to slices of neighbouring counties that have been appended to their longer-established home bases, and to second-guess future decisions of constituency commissions by concentrating instead on what they believe will be their steady bailiwicks. This is not to argue that county boundaries should be sacrosanct, or that they should be given the same weight as major units in federal systems, such as US states. But the unrelenting revision of constituencies that has been characteristic of the Irish experience is unnecessary unless a very narrow standard of equal representation is specified, and this risks coming into conflict with other important principles that a democratic constitution should protect.

Constitutional options

The core suggestion of this chapter—that reapportionment between fixed constituencies should replace redistricting as a mechanism for maintaining the principle of equality in the deputy–population ratio—could possibly be implemented without constitutional change. A decision could be made, for example, to introduce a system like the one proposed here on the basis of the 2011 census results. This would produce a very unfamiliar *pattern* of constituencies (two three-member, six four-member, nine five-member, six six-member, three seven-member, one eight-member and two nine-member constituencies); but the *shape* of the constituencies themselves would be very familiar, based on well-recognised administrative areas. Their average size would be large, but they would be more clearly compatible with the constitution than the present pattern. They would have the great merit of predictability: following future censuses, the Central Statistics Office could simply recalculate the apportionment of seats and so report to, say, the clerk of the Dáil. As the constitution currently stands, the Oireachtas would then need to give effect to these and, though complaints would not disappear completely, the chances of more widespread acceptance would be greatly enhanced.

A new system of this kind might be seen as conflicting with a literal interpretation of article 16.2.3° of the constitution, and especially with its authoritative Irish wording; but in this respect it is in the same position as *all boundary revision acts since 1923*. On the other hand, it should be seen as compatible with the principle that the constitution seeks to defend, that of equality of representation, so there is a case for introducing it without constitutional amendment. If the courts were to rule this impossible, then constitutional amendment could be contemplated. In that event, there would be a case for considering an issue that has been ignored in this chapter: whether equality should be measured in respect of the population, or only, as in several other jurisdictions, in respect of the electorate.[36] Whatever the outcome of any such debate, it is hard to argue that Ireland should continue to hold out against an apportionment system that other countries using proportional representation take for granted: it should be acknowledged that in this respect public policy embarked down the wrong route in the 1920s (the one signposted 'British system' rather than 'Proportional representation'), and that it is time to try to get back on a less arduous and more appropriate path.

In fact, this approach has scarcely been considered by the various bodies that investigated the desirability of constitutional change in this area. The possibility of establishing an independent commission that would design constituency boundaries was raised by the Committee on the Constitution (1967: 19–21), which also suggested that insistence on a uniform deputy–population ratio be relaxed, to allow variance of up to 25% between the lowest and highest ratios. The Constitution Review Group (1996: 49) was of similar mind as regards a constituency commission, but did not see embedding this in the constitution as a pressing matter. The seventh progress report of the All-Party Oireachtas Committee on the Constitution (2002: 13–14, 67–8) felt that there was no need to relax the requirement for equality of suffrage, nor did it see any need to give the constituency commission a constitutional basis. The first progress report of the same body (1997a: 75–8) had already suggested the absorption of the constituency commission in a broader electoral commission, and the fourth report of the Joint Committee on the Constitution (2010b: 17, 20–21) endorsed this, while advising that existing natural and administrative boundaries be respected as far as possible. Although the idea of abolishing the constituency commission in favour of a mechanical process was considered by the same committee (Joint Committee on the Constitution, 2010b: 94–5, 140–42, 175–7), this attracted little support from parliamentarians. The Convention on the Constitution (2013b) did not consider this matter directly, but voted overwhelmingly in favour of a change that would facilitate it: introducing constituencies returning larger numbers of members, with five as the minimum (rather than, as at present, the maximum) number of members in any one constituency.

CONCLUSION

This chapter has highlighted the difficulties that have confronted those charged with revising constituency boundaries in Ireland. In the early years of the state, politicians were not particularly preoccupied with this aspect of electoral law. Later, however, classic forms of electoral engineering calculated to maximise party advantage were devised. Three strategies may be identified: biased distribution of seats favouring regions in which one's own party is strong, manipulation of boundaries as in classical gerrymander, and adjustment of seat numbers to favour one's own party, a particularly subtle device (Mair, 1986: 299–307). When the 1959 constituency boundary bill appeared to discriminate against Dublin and in favour of rural areas, opposition anger spilled over into a court challenge. The High Court judgment that the act was unconstitutional and subsequent insistence on a rigid deputy–population ratio ruled out this practice for the future, but it also unintentionally provided a cloak for gerrymandering by encouraging, if not forcing, governments to micromanage constituency boundaries. The introduction of an independent constituency commission in 1980 depoliticised the process, but boundaries have continued to be amended as vigorously as ever. By contrast, in continental European proportional representation systems, the principle of suffrage equality is met by periodic reallocation of seats to stable administrative districts using a simple arithmetical formula.

A sceptic might see the current Irish constituency boundary revision process as a spurious gesture towards equal representation, and it might be excused if it contributed significantly towards achieving this. But it does not. The process of constituency boundary revision in independent Ireland has a sad history. It has distracted and aggravated politicians; it has annoyed and demotivated voters; it has diverted officials from other tasks and wasted their time; it has been responsible for unnecessary costs, delays, uncertainties and inconveniences; and especially from 1961 until the establishment of a boundary commission it has opened the door to gerrymandering (even if efforts in this direction have not necessarily been effective).

The independent constituency commissions have been charged with an exceptionally unappealing task. They have been asked to close a badly designed, flimsy stable door after the horse has bolted—to design, in conformity with arguably inappropriate criteria, constituencies that would have met these criteria had a general election taken place on the same day as the census, but that are unlikely to meet them in any future election. As in other countries using proportional representation, constituency boundaries should be fixed, and equal representation should be procured not by changing areas but by varying the allocation of deputies, in a simpler, more predictable, more consistent and more legitimate system. To achieve this, Ireland needs no more resources than any other country using proportional representation: it does not need a succession of teams of highly qualified boundary architects, but a single moderately numerate apportionment mechanic.

NOTES

1. This chapter is based on Coakley, 2007 and Coakley, 2008a, and draws on Coakley, 1980a and Coakley, 2008b.
2. Letter to the Taoiseach from Riobárd Ó Dálaigh, secretary of the council, 24 March 1969; Taoiseach's Department papers, National Archives, 2000/6/652 (formerly S 18,290).
3. This discussion is based on the constitutions, electoral laws and other official publications of the countries in question; for links to their parliamentary

websites, see www.ipu.org. Further information has been derived from Chryssogonos, 2007.

4. Alongside the Hare quota (in elections, number of votes divided by number of seats), two others are widely used: the Droop quota (number of votes divided by one more than the number of seats) and the Imperiali quota (number of votes divided by two more than the number of seats). When used in elections, these quotas may require more precision; thus, the Droop quota (which typically leaves a fractional remainder) is truncated, if necessary, and 1 is added, to ensure that this is 'the smallest number for which it is impossible that more than k candidates should attain it', where k is the number of seats (Dummett, 1984: 269); see Gallagher, 2009b, and Sinnott, 2010, for discussions of this system in Ireland.

5. The process of seat distribution in the House of Representatives takes place in two stages: a preliminary apportionment of seats to states on the basis of population, and the delimitation of single-member constituencies within states depending on the outcome of this apportionment.

6. The geometric mean is the nth root of n numbers multiplied by each other; the arithmetic mean is the sum of n numbers divided by n. For example, the arithmetic mean of 5 and 6 is $(5 + 6)/2$, or 11/2, or 5.50; the geometric mean of the same two numbers is $\sqrt{(5\times6)}$, or $\sqrt{30}$, or 5.48. For an overview of these systems, see Balinski and Young, 2001; for a comprehensive analysis of their application to the allocation of seats to parties, see Gallagher, 1992.

7. Ireland's allocation was reduced to 12 seats, but on the basis of the 2011 census two systems (the largest remainder and Sainte-Laguë ones) would have allocated these in the same way, as 7–3–1–1, between the four provinces, while the D'Hondt system would not have allocated any seat to Ulster, giving an additional seat instead to Leinster.

8. Up to the end of the nineteenth century, Irish local administration recognised four tiers: 32 counties, more than 300 baronies, more than 2,000 civil parishes and more than 60,000 townlands. The Local Government (Ireland) Act, 1898, reorganised the two intermediate tiers: the baronies were replaced by just over 300 county districts (rural districts, urban districts and municipal boroughs, each now with its own elective council), and civil parishes disappeared for administrative purposes, replaced by more than 3,700 district electoral divisions or, in larger urban areas, wards (Coakley, 1979).

9. *Dáil Debates*, 21 March 1934, vol. 51, col. 1295, for 'Kellymandering'; there were many references to 'mutilation' of boundaries on the same occasion, e.g. cols 1271–2, 1282–3, 1301–3.

10. *Dáil Debates*, 28 October 1959, vol. 177, col. 379.

11. 'John O'Donovan, Plaintiff, v. The Attorney General, Defendant', *Irish Reports* 1961, pp. 114–56.

12. *Dáil Debates*, 27 November 1968, vol. 237, col. 1243, and 4 December 1968, cols 1809, 1829.
13. *Seanad Debates*, 10 April 1974, vol. 77, col. 818, and 30 April 1974, col. 1433.
14. For the respective reports of the commissions, see Ireland, 1980; 1983; 1988; 1990; 1995.
15. The smaller parties were vehemently opposed to the proposals—not surprisingly, in view of the fact that Fianna Fáil sources were quoted as predicting that the minor parties would lose 10 seats, of which six would go to Fine Gael and four to Fianna Fáil (*Irish Times*, 9 November 1988). After some vacillation, Fine Gael also came out against the proposals, sealing their fate, since the minority Fianna Fáil government would have been unwilling to risk a Dáil defeat on the matter (*Irish Times*, 16 November 1988).
16. For the commission reports, see Ireland, 1998, 2004, 2007, 2012a.
17. *Dáil Debates*, 25 September 2008, vol. 661, col. 907.
18. To set this in context, the number of Austrian regional constituencies in 2013 is almost the same as that of current Irish constituencies, 39; but the number of words required to describe these was only 425; calculated from *Bundesgesetz über die Wahl des Nationalrates (Nationalrats-Wahlordnung 1992 – NRWO)*, as revised, Anlage 1 (www.ris.bka.gv.at) [24 June 2007]. This compares with 3,022 words to describe 40 constituencies in the 2013 Irish act.
19. Electoral divisions were created by the Poor Relief (Ireland) Act, 1838, for the election of 'guardians' of the boards of the network of workhouses then established. They were renamed 'district electoral divisions' by the Local Government (Ireland) Act, 1898, when they also became units for the election of rural district councillors (the position in towns was a little more complicated, and in larger towns the corresponding units were known as 'wards'). The last general election of boards of guardians and of rural district councils from these constituencies took place in May 1914. The elections due in 1917 were deferred due to the war, and the Local Government (Ireland) Act, 1919, introduced proportional representation, grouping district electoral divisions into multi-member 'district electoral areas'. It was in these new units that the local elections of 1920 took place. In the Irish Free State, the boards of guardians were abolished in 1923 and the rural district councils in 1925, except in Dublin, where they survived until 1930 (Roche, 1982: 50–2). In 1994, district electoral divisions and wards were renamed 'electoral divisions'. In rural Ireland, most electoral divisions have retained precisely the same boundaries since the reorganisation of poor law administration in 1850.
20. Rapid population growth meant that the 1930 local government extension was long overdue; though radical, it was not as far-reaching as had been recommended by the Report of the Greater Dublin Commission of Inquiry (McManus, 2002: 89–90). Later changes in the government of greater Dublin also tended to lag

behind population growth, an important consideration for this chapter.

21. An alternative 'malapportionment index' that takes account of the deviations of all constituencies from the mean population–deputy ratio showed Ireland in the mid-1990s as having a score of 2.6%, rather lower than Austria, Greece and Spain, but higher than Finland, Portugal and Switzerland, to name some of the countries with which it can most easily be compared (Samuels and Snyder, 2001: 660–1).

22. Work on the Irish text of the constitution proceeded simultaneously with the English version, beginning in October 1936 with translation of an earlier draft, and de Valera claimed that his own work on the constitution rested on this; but he did not deny outright that the Irish version finally presented to the Dáil was a translation (Mac Giolla Choille, 1988). It seems clear from the Dáil debates that all major decisions on the content of the constitution were made through the medium of English.

23. 'John O'Donovan, Plaintiff, v. The Attorney General, Defendant', *Irish Reports* 1961, pp. 114–56, at p. 132.

24. In Baker v. Carr, *United States Reports* 369 (1962): 186–349, the court held that it was appropriate for federal courts to intervene to ensure fair apportionment; in Wesberry v. Sanders, *United States Reports* 376 (1964): 1–51, such intervention took place in Georgia, the court ruling that 'as nearly as is practicable one person's vote in a congressional election is to be worth as much as another's'; and in Karcher v. Daggett, *United States Reports* 462 (1983): 725–790, it ruled against the redistricting arrangement in New Jersey, on the grounds that a deviation of 0.7% between the highest and lowest ratios was excessive, in effect calling for mathematical parity in the population of congressional districts. As an indication of the kind of parameters viewed as acceptable by US experts, the American Political Science Association (1951: 154–5) had earlier recommended much more sensibly that approximate equality between congressional districts could be obtained by ensuring that deviations should remain within a 10% band on either side of the mean within an individual state, and that they should in no case exceed 15%.

25. Calculated from Mills, 2001: 2. This means that while, for example, Colorado was struggling to achieve complete equality in the range of 614,465 to 614,467, adjacent Utah was struggling to ensure that its three congressional districts were similarly equal—to each other, not to Colorado's (and they were, at 744,389 for one district and 744,390 for the other two). In view of the level of inter-state inequality, a US federal district court ruled in 1991 that the whole apportionment system was unconstitutional, but it was overruled by the Supreme Court in Department of Commerce v. Montana, *United States Reports* 503 (1992): 442–466, which held that the goal of equality was 'illusory for the nation as a whole' (p. 463), but not so within states.

26. On the complexity of electoral district delimitation issues—which should be sufficient to scare off even the most determined boundary architect—see essays in Grofman et al, 1982, and Forgette and Winkle, 2006.

27. 'O'Donovan v. Attorney General' (1961): 155. Justice Budd's judgement was widely interpreted subsequently as permitting a 'tolerance' level of 5% above or below the average deputy–population ratio. Mr Justice Clarke has, however, noted that this interpretation (apparently based on expressing 1,000, the average population of a district electoral division, as a percentage of 20,000, the average deputy–population ratio at the time) is misleading: the figure of 1,000 needs to be expressed as a percentage of total population, which ranged at the time from about 100,000 in a five-seat to 60,000 in a three-seat constituency, giving a 'tolerance' level of somewhere between 1.0% and 1.7%; see 'Murphy and another v. Minister for Environment and others', [2007] IEHC 185, ss. 3.12–13; *Irish Reports* 2008: 438–75.

28. See judgment by Chief Justice Maguire, 'In re Art. 26 of the Constitution and the Electoral (Amendment) Bill, 1961', *Irish Reports* 1961, pp. 169–83, at p. 183. This view was echoed by the constituency boundary commission in 1980 (Ireland, 1980: 13). In its 1988 report a more specific conclusion was reached: 'the Commission considered that a departure from the mathematical average of 8% or over would be unacceptable and, in all probability, contrary to the provisions of the Constitution relating to equality of representation' (Ireland, 1988: 28).

29. 'Murphy v. Minister for Environment' (2007).

30. See 'Murphy v. Minister for Environment' (2007); ss. 6.13, 8.3, where Mr Justice Clarke asked 'whether measures can be put in place to minimise the gap between the availability of census figures and the enactment of legislation'.

31. The 2007 High Court judgment fired a warning shot regarding the overriding need to defend proportionality; see 'Murphy v. Minister for Environment' (2007), s. 7.3.

32. This point is also made in respect of Irish elections by Engstrom (1987), but is disputed in the case of the 2002 election by White (2006).

33. Early studies suggested that the system was reasonably proportional (Laver and Mair, 1975; Gallagher, 1975; O'Leary, 1979: 107–10), and concluded that while constituency size was likely to have an impact, this was surprisingly small. Although constituency size clearly has big potential effects, these often cancel each other out (Gallagher, 1986: 258–60). But intention matters too; and it has been noted that 'only in the Republic of Ireland was there a marked and prolonged tendency to reduce the size of constituencies within which PR was sought; and it was only there that an apparently deliberate attempt was made, for a period between 1969 and 1977, to "gerrymander" the size of constituencies in favour of particular parties' (Carstairs, 1980: 217).

34. On the by-election anomaly, see Gallagher, 1996. In list-based proportional

representation systems, when casual vacancies occur the next candidate on the list of the party where the vacancy occurs is given the seat; in Malta, the only other sovereign state to use STV for election of its house of representatives, casual vacancies are filled by a recount of the papers of the candidate causing the vacancy.

35. The normal two-tier continental European system of local government juxtaposes a 'high' level (county, province or *département*), of which there is a small number of large units, with a 'low' level (commune or municipality), of which there is typically a very large number of small units. The populations of the latter normally range widely in size, but on average are low; in 1980, for instance, the mean population per commune was 30,000 in Sweden, 24,000 in Germany, 19,000 in Denmark, 17,000 in the Netherlands and in Belgium, 7,000 in Italy, 3,000 in Luxembourg, 2,000 in Switzerland and 1,500 in France (based on Roche, 1982: 12–13 and United Nations, 2007). Subsequent large-scale mergers of municipalities would have increased these figures. In Ireland, not more than about 15% of the population live in legally defined local authority areas below the level of the county or county borough; the mean population in 2006 of the main units (the 34 administrative counties and county boroughs) was 125,000. For a comparative overview, see Glassner, 1993: 143–9.

36. Consideration of this issue raises important questions in political theory regarding the nature of political representation, and the debate as to whether this should reflect people's interests or the people's will. Although distribution of parliamentary seats in proportion to population is common in continental Europe, there are countries (such as Portugal and Sweden) where it is the electorate that is used, while in Finland it is the citizen population that counts. Whatever the outcome of the theoretical debate, data on the electorate have the merit that they are available annually rather than, as in the case of population, quinquennially. This is not to say that they are unproblematic: although it has been argued that the electoral register can be used as a basis for estimating population in intercensal years (Whelan and Keogh, 1980), there was a known problem of systematic over-inclusion in the 1920s (Sinnott, 1995: 85–87), and a study of more recent data showed that the electoral register contains significant errors arising mainly from changes in address, though measures to correct for these are available (Keogh and Whelan, 1986). There are typically big variations in the ratio of registered electors to population. In 2006, for instance, the extremes were represented by Donegal South-West (where 87% of the population was entitled to vote) and Dublin South-East (where the corresponding figure was only 57%). Variations of this kind are to be explained by such factors as the distribution of immigrants and of the population of third-level colleges, hospitals and prisons.

APPENDIX C: POSSIBLE AUTOMATIC DISTRIBUTION OF DÁIL SEATS TO FIXED CONSTITUENCIES, 1922–2013

The four tables that follow are based on hypothetical constituencies that might have been created on the foundation of the state, and later modified slightly, as discussed in the text. Except as indicated below, constituencies correspond to administrative counties (with Limerick and Waterford county boroughs included in the counties of the same name, and the two ridings of Tipperary merged as a single constituency). Cork East comprises the rural districts of Cork, Fermoy, Mallow, Midleton, Mitchelstown and Youghal, and the urban districts of Cobh, Fermoy, Mallow, Midleton and Youghal; Cork West comprises the rest of the county. The two original divisions of Dublin City comprise the dispensary districts of Dublin North and Dublin South respectively; the two 'inner' constituencies comprised originally six inner-city wards in the North and 10 in the South, and corresponding areas subsequently; the 'outer' constituencies comprise the old outer suburbs, plus the new suburbs added in 1930. The constituencies of Dun Laoghaire, Fingal and Dublin South respectively comprise the territories of the corresponding counties (though these were defined only in 1994). The constituency of Clondalkin consists of 12 electoral districts (seven in Clondalkin, three in Lucan and two in Palmerstown); Tallaght consists of the rest of South Dublin County.

Table (a) reports raw population figures for each constituency, as derived from Census of Ireland, volume 1, for the years in question. Table (b) shows how these would have been converted into a distribution of the total number of deputies (140 initially, rising to 166 in 1979) according to the Sainte-Laguë (Webster) highest average system. Table (c) reports the resulting population–deputy ratios. Table (d) indicates how far each of these ratios deviates, as a percentage, from the overall ratio. In each table, constituency names in italics refer to constituencies that would have disappeared.

Data for certain census years (1951, 1961, 1971, 1981, 1991, 2002 and 2011) have been omitted to save space. Since they are not reported, the following points may be made about the impact that these 'missing' years might have had on the summary data at the bottom of the tables. In Table (b), the mean sizes in the 'missing' years remained within the limits of the years described in the table, except that in 1971 the maximum number of seats in any constituency (second row from the bottom) would have been only seven. In Table (c), the differences between the largest and smallest ratios (bottom row) would have remained within the limits of the years described here, except that they would have been higher than these limits in 1951 (6,090), 1961 (5,388) and 1971 (6,232), and lower in 1981 (4,082) and 1991 (3,591). In Table (d), the deviations would have remained within the limits of the years described here (bottom three rows), except that there would have been a bigger deviation below the average in 1971 (–11.9%), and there would have been bigger deviations above the average in 1951 (17.5%), 1961 (18.3%) and 1971 (17.4%); and bigger overall differences would have occurred in 1951 (28.8%), 1961 (26.8%) and 1971 (29.3%).

(a) Population by hypothetical constituency

Constituency	Population at selected census years									
	1911	*1926*	*1936*	*1946*	*1956*	*1966*	*1979*	*1986*	*1996*	*2006*
	111,214	105,466	103,066	100,793	97,977	94,056	107,824	114,174	116,952	137,907
Cavan–Monaghan	162,628	147,583	137,959	127,570	113,804	99,754	104,096	106,344	104,257	120,000
Clare	104,232	95,064	89,879	85,064	77,176	73,597	84,919	91,344	94,006	110,950
Cork City	76,673	78,490	80,765	75,595	80,011	122,146	138,267	133,271	127,187	119,418
Cork East	118,633	109,939	109,415	112,416	113,280	83,260	115,575	134,231	149,052	195,758
Cork West	196,798	177,318	165,777	155,657	143,372	134,297	142,276	145,233	144,271	166,119
Donegal	168,537	152,508	142,310	136,317	122,059	108,549	121,941	129,664	129,994	147,264
Galway	182,224	169,366	168,198	165,201	155,553	148,340	167,838	178,552	188,854	231,670
Kerry	159,691	149,171	139,834	133,893	122,072	112,785	120,356	124,159	126,130	139,835
Kildare	66,627	58,028	57,892	64,849	65,915	66,404	97,185	116,247	134,992	186,335
Laois–Offaly	111,461	104,132	101,417	103,383	99,057	96,312	107,278	113,119	112,062	137,927
Limerick	143,069	140,343	141,153	142,559	137,881	137,357	157,407	164,569	165,042	184,055
Longford–Westmeath	103,806	96,665	92,553	91,167	87,091	81,889	90,670	94,875	93,480	113,737
Louth	63,665	62,739	64,339	66,194	69,194	69,519	86,135	91,810	92,166	111,267
Mayo	192,177	172,690	161,349	148,120	133,052	115,547	114,019	115,184	111,524	123,839
Meath	65,091	62,969	61,405	66,232	66,762	67,323	90,715	103,881	109,732	162,831
Tipperary	152,433	141,015	137,835	136,014	129,415	122,812	133,741	136,619	133,535	149,244
Waterford	83,966	78,562	77,614	76,108	74,031	73,080	87,278	91,151	94,680	107,961
Wexford	102,273	95,848	94,245	91,855	87,259	83,437	96,421	102,552	104,371	131,749
Wicklow	60,711	57,591	58,569	60,451	59,906	60,428	83,950	94,542	102,683	126,194
Dublin City – North	*161,551*	*172,196*	–	–	–	–	–	–	–	–
Dublin City – North inner			125,734	106,320	191,860	174,470	136,789	115,363	113,509	128,866
Dublin City – North outer			90,926	122,079	57,589	112,406	179,710	192,451	173,707	165,663
Dublin City – South	*143,251*	*144,497*	–	–	–	–	–	–	–	–
Dublin City – South inner			146,278	126,672	174,355	155,335	122,006	106,643	114,523	132,613
Dublin City – South outer			105,165	150,980	115,650	125,591	106,081	88,292	80,115	79,069
Dublin county	*172,394*	*188,961*	*118,822*	*130,142*	*166,327*	*105,628*	–	–	–	–
Dublin – Dun Laoghaire						121,617	169,116	180,675	189,999	194,038
Dublin – Fingal							123,638	138,479	167,683	239,992
Dublin – South							146,343	–	–	–
Dublin – Clondalkin								60,186	74,210	93,252
Dublin – Tallaght								139,360	144,518	153,683
Leitrim–Sligo	*142,627*	*127,295*	*118,355*	*106,966*	*93,906*	*81,835*	–	–	–	–
Roscommon	*93,956*	*83,556*	*77,566*	*72,510*	*63,710*	*56,228*	–	–	–	–
Connacht East							136,643	137,673	132,853	148,612
Total	3,139,688	2,971,992	2,968,420	2,955,107	2,898,264	2,884,002	3,368,217	3,540,643	3,626,087	4,239,848

(b) Seat allocation by hypothetical constituency

Constituency	Seat distribution (Sainte-Laguë)									
	1911	1926	1936	1946	1956	1966	1979	1986	1996	2006
Carlow–Kilkenny	5	5	5	5	5	5	5	5	5	5
Cavan–Monaghan	7	7	6	6	5	5	5	5	5	5
Clare	5	4	4	4	4	4	4	4	4	4
Cork City	3	4	4	4	4	6	7	6	6	5
Cork East	5	5	5	5	5	4	6	6	7	8
Cork West	9	8	8	7	7	6	7	7	7	7
Donegal	7	7	7	7	6	5	6	6	6	6
Galway	8	8	8	8	8	7	8	8	9	9
Kerry	7	7	6	6	6	5	6	6	6	6
Kildare	3	3	3	3	3	3	5	6	6	7
Laois–Offaly	5	5	5	5	5	5	5	5	5	5
Limerick	6	7	7	7	7	7	8	8	7	7
Longford–Westmeath	5	4	4	4	4	4	4	5	4	4
Louth	3	3	3	3	3	3	4	4	4	4
Mayo	9	8	7	7	6	6	6	5	5	5
Meath	3	3	3	3	3	3	5	5	5	6
Tipperary	7	7	6	7	6	6	7	6	6	6
Waterford	4	4	4	4	4	4	4	4	4	4
Wexford	5	4	4	4	4	4	5	5	5	5
Wicklow	3	3	3	3	3	3	4	4	5	5
Dublin City – North	7	8	–	–	–	–	–	–	–	–
Dublin City – North inner		6	5	9	8	7	5	5	5	
Dublin City – North outer		4	6	3	5	9	9	8	7	
Dublin City – South	6	7	–	–	–	–	–	–	–	–
Dublin City – South inner		7	6	8	8	6	5	5	5	
Dublin City – South outer		5	7	6	6	5	4	4	3	
Dublin county	8	9	6	6	8	5	–	–	–	–
Dublin – Dun Laoghaire						6	8	9	9	8
Dublin – Fingal							6	7	8	9
Dublin – South							7	–	–	–
Dublin – Clondalkin								3	3	4
Dublin – Tallaght								7	7	6
Leitrim–Sligo	6	6	6	5	5	4	–	–	–	–
Roscommon	4	4	4	3	3	3	–	–	–	–
Connacht East							7	7	6	6
Total	140	140	140	140	140	140	166	166	166	166
Smallest no. of seats	3	3	3	3	3	3	4	3	3	3
Largest no. of seats	9	9	8	8	9	8	9	9	9	9
Mean constituency size	5.6	5.6	5.2	5.2	5.2	5.0	5.9	5.7	5.7	5.7

(c) Population per deputy by hypothetical constituency

Constituency	Population per deputy									
	1911	1926	1936	1946	1956	1966	1979	1986	1996	2006
Carlow–Kilkenny	22,243	21,093	20,613	20,159	19,595	18,811	21,565	22,835	23,390	27,581
Cavan–Monaghan	23,233	21,083	22,993	21,262	22,761	19,951	20,819	21,269	20,851	24,000
Clare	20,846	23,766	22,470	21,266	19,294	18,399	21,230	22,836	23,502	27,738
Cork City	25,558	19,623	20,191	18,899	20,003	20,358	19,752	22,212	21,198	23,884
Cork East	23,727	21,988	21,883	22,483	22,656	20,815	19,263	22,372	21,293	24,470
Cork West	21,866	22,165	20,722	22,237	20,482	22,383	20,325	20,748	20,610	23,731
Donegal	24,077	21,787	20,330	19,474	20,343	21,710	20,324	21,611	21,666	24,544
Galway	22,778	21,171	21,025	20,650	19,444	21,191	20,980	22,319	20,984	25,741
Kerry	22,813	21,310	23,306	22,316	20,345	22,557	20,059	20,693	21,022	23,306
Kildare	22,209	19,343	19,297	21,616	21,972	22,135	19,437	19,375	22,499	26,619
Laois–Offaly	22,292	20,826	20,283	20,677	19,811	19,262	21,456	22,624	22,412	27,585
Limerick	23,845	20,049	20,165	20,366	19,697	19,622	19,676	20,571	23,577	26,294
Longford– Westmeath	20,761	24,166	23,138	22,792	21,773	20,472	22,668	18,975	23,370	28,434
Louth	21,222	20,913	21,446	22,065	23,065	23,173	21,534	22,953	23,042	27,817
Mayo	21,353	21,586	23,050	21,160	22,175	19,258	19,003	23,037	22,305	24,768
Meath	21,697	20,990	20,468	22,077	22,254	22,441	18,143	20,776	21,946	27,139
Tipperary	21,776	20,145	22,973	19,431	21,569	20,469	19,106	22,770	22,256	24,874
Waterford	20,992	19,641	19,404	19,027	18,508	18,270	21,820	22,788	23,670	26,990
Wexford	20,455	23,962	23,561	22,964	21,815	20,859	19,284	20,510	20,874	26,350
Wicklow	20,237	19,197	19,523	20,150	19,969	20,143	20,988	23,636	20,537	25,239
Dublin City – North	23,079	21,525	–	–	–	–	–	–	–	–
Dublin City – North inner			20,956	21,264	21,318	21,809	19,541	23,073	22,702	25,773
Dublin City – North outer			22,732	20,347	19,196	22,481	19,968	21,383	21,713	23,666
Dublin City – Sorth	23,875	20,642	–	–	–	–	–	–	–	–
Dublin City – South inner			20,897	21,112	21,794	19,417	20,334	21,329	22,905	26,523
Dublin City – South outer			21,033	21,569	19,275	20,932	21,216	22,073	20,029	26,356
Dublin County	21,549	20,996	19,804	21,690	20,791	21,126	–	–	–	–
Dublin – Dun Laoghaire							20,270	21,140	20,075	21,111	24,255
Dublin – Fingal							20,606	19,783	20,960	26,666
Dublin – South							20,906	–	–	–
Dublin – Clondalkin								20,062	24,737	23,313
Dublin – Tallaght								19,909	20,645	25,614
Leitrim–Sligo	23,771	21,216	19,726	21,393	18,781	20,459	–	–	–	–
Roscommon	23,489	20,889	19,392	24,170	21,237	18,743	–	–	–	–
Connacht East							19,520	19,668	22,142	24,769
Overall ratio	22,426	21,229	21,203	21,108	20,702	20,600	20,290	21,329	21,844	25,541
Smallest ratio	20,237	19,197	19,297	18,899	18,508	18,270	18,143	18,975	20,029	23,306
Largest ratio	25,558	24,166	23,561	24,170	23,065	23,173	22,668	23,636	24,737	28,434
Difference										
(largest – smallest)	5,321	4,969	4,264	5,271	4,557	4,903	4,525	4,661	4,708	5,128

(d) Deviations from mean deputy–population ratio, by hypothetical constituency

Constituency	Deviation from average ratio									
	1911	1926	1936	1946	1956	1966	1979	1986	1996	2006
Carlow–Kilkenny	−0.8	−0.6	−2.8	−4.5	−5.3	−8.7	6.3	7.1	7.1	8.0
Cavan–Monaghan	3.6	−0.7	8.4	0.7	9.9	−3.2	2.6	−0.3	−4.5	−6.0
Clare	−7.0	12.0	6.0	0.7	−6.8	−10.7	4.6	7.1	7.6	8.6
Cork City	14.0	−7.6	−4.8	−10.5	−3.4	−1.2	−2.7	4.1	−3.0	−6.5
Cork East	5.8	3.6	3.2	6.5	9.4	1.0	−5.1	4.9	−2.5	−4.2
Cork West	−2.5	4.4	−2.3	5.3	−1.1	8.7	0.2	−2.7	−5.6	−7.1
Donegal	7.4	2.6	−4.1	−7.7	−1.7	5.4	0.2	1.3	−0.8	−3.9
Galway	1.6	−0.3	−0.8	−2.2	−6.1	2.9	3.4	4.6	−3.9	0.8
Kerry	1.7	0.4	9.9	5.7	−1.7	9.5	−1.1	−3.0	−3.8	−8.8
Kildare	−1.0	−8.9	−9.0	2.4	6.1	7.4	−4.2	−9.2	3.0	4.2
Laois–Offaly	−0.6	−1.9	−4.3	−2.0	−4.3	−6.5	5.7	6.1	2.6	8.0
Limerick	6.3	−5.6	−4.9	−3.5	−4.9	−4.7	−3.0	−3.6	7.9	2.9
Longford– Westmeath	−7.4	13.8	9.1	8.0	5.2	−0.6	11.7	−11.0	7.0	11.3
Louth	−5.4	−1.5	1.1	4.5	11.4	12.5	6.1	7.6	5.5	8.9
Mayo	−4.8	1.7	8.7	0.2	7.1	−6.5	−6.3	8.0	2.1	−3.0
Meath	−3.3	−1.1	−3.5	4.6	7.5	8.9	−10.6	−2.6	0.5	6.3
Tipperary	−2.9	−5.1	8.3	−7.9	4.2	−0.6	−5.8	6.8	1.9	−2.6
Waterford	−6.4	−7.5	−8.5	−9.9	−10.6	−11.3	7.5	6.8	8.4	5.7
Wexford	−8.8	12.9	11.1	8.8	5.4	1.3	−5.0	−3.8	−4.4	3.2
Wicklow	−9.8	−9.6	−7.9	−4.5	−3.5	−2.2	3.4	10.8	−6.0	−1.2
Dublin City – North	2.9	1.4	–	–	–	–	–	–	–	–
Dublin City – North inner			−1.2	0.7	3.0	5.9	−3.7	8.2	3.9	0.9
Dublin City – North outer			7.2	−3.6	−7.3	9.1	−1.6	0.3	−0.6	−7.3
Dublin City – South	6.5	−2.8	–	–	–	–	–	–	–	–
Dublin City – South inner			−1.4	0.0	5.3	−5.7	0.2	0.0	4.9	3.8
Dublin City – South outer			−0.8	2.2	−6.9	1.6	4.6	3.5	−8.3	3.2
Dublin county	−3.9	−1.1	−6.6	2.8	0.4	2.6	–	–	–	–
Dublin – Dun Laoghaire						−1.6	4.2	−5.9	−3.4	−5.0
Dublin – Fingal							1.6	−7.3	−4.0	4.4
Dublin – South							3.0	–	–	–
Dublin – Clondalkin								−5.9	13.2	−8.7
Dublin – Tallaght								−6.7	−5.5	0.3
Leitrim–Sligo	6.0	−0.1	−7.0	1.4	−9.3	−0.7	–	–	–	–
Roscommon	4.7	−1.6	−8.5	14.5	2.6	−9.0	–	–	–	–
Connacht East							−3.8	−7.8	1.4	−3.0
Deviations from average										
Biggest below	−9.8	−9.6	−9.0	−10.5	−10.6	−11.3	−10.6	−11.0	−8.3	−8.8
Biggest above	14.0	13.8	11.1	14.5	11.4	12.5	11.7	10.8	13.2	11.3
Difference (largest – smallest)	23.7	23.4	20.1	25.0	22.0	23.8	22.3	21.9	21.6	20.1

7

GOVERNMENT MINISTERS: TECHNOCRATS OR PARLIAMENTARIANS?

Given their crucial role in running the modern state, the manner in which ministers are appointed seems to have attracted surprisingly little attention. Long-running crises in government formation in such countries as Belgium and Italy certainly make the headlines, and draw attention to the role of caretaker governments in managing the state for what are sometimes prolonged periods. The ease with which British prime ministers may appoint whomever they wish to cabinet by nominating them to the House of Lords contrasts with the apparently more restrictive norms that govern this process in Ireland. Those wedded to the notion that ministers must be parliamentarians are sometimes shocked by constitutional provisions in such countries as France, the Netherlands and Norway that permanently *preclude* ministers from sitting in parliament.

The proposals for electoral reform discussed in Chapter 5, often explicitly linked to a stated wish to broaden the channel of recruitment to ministerial office, are unlikely to deliver dramatic results in this respect. First, as indicated in Chapter 5, comparative evidence has shown that constituency workloads under other electoral systems continue to be formidable, and raises questions about the alleged positive impact of electoral reform (Gallagher, 1987, 2009b; Gallagher and Komito, 2010; Farrell, 2010). Second, the focus on elections to the Dáil as the only route to ministerial office is misplaced: the closed systems in the United Kingdom and especially in Ireland are striking deviations from the more open ministerial recruitment system typical of continental Europe.

The eccentric assumption that the only route to government office is through the lower house of parliament places a heavy burden on perceptions of the role of Dáil deputy: TDs are expected to be not just representatives and legislators, but also potential ministers, a load placed on them not by the electoral system but by the ministerial recruitment formula. The object of the present chapter is to explore this peculiar feature of the Irish experience. The first section looks at the comparative position, initially from a constitutional perspective and then from a behavioural one, setting in context the unique system of ministerial recruitment in Ireland. The second section examines Irish provisions for ministerial appointment in this area, first at a constitutional level and then as applied in practice. The final section assesses the prospects for change.[1]

MINISTERIAL RECRUITMENT:
A COMPARATIVE PERSPECTIVE

The constitutions of the world provide abundant evidence about the relationship between parliament and government, and about the principles in accordance with which ministers are selected and retained in office. The first part of this section seeks to generalise about the global pattern. As in other areas, though, examining constitutional provisions will tell us only part of the story. The section continues, therefore, by reviewing the mechanisms of ministerial appointment that are followed in practice.

Constitutions and ministers

At first sight, and in its most central aspects, the process of government formation and the relationship between government and parliament in Ireland follow the same pattern as elsewhere in Europe. With very few exceptions (Switzerland is the most obvious), there is a common model. At its core lies the principle of governmental answerability to parliament: governments can remain in office only for so long as they enjoy the confidence of the lower house (see Gallagher et al., 2011: 48–63). Elsewhere, there may be additional conditions. In some bicameral systems, such as that of Italy, there is a requirement also of answerability to the upper house; and in semi-presidential systems, such as that of France, the President, too, can independently appoint and dismiss governments and ministers. But in all of these cases the lower house of parliament plays a critical role in the appointment of a government. Even if the constitutional provisions are not as explicit as in Ireland (where the Dáil is required to nominate the prime minister and to approve the members of a new government, who are then formally appointed by the President), any new government can survive only if it has the endorsement of the lower house, or at least its passive support (in that a majority will not vote against it).

There are obvious alternatives to this principle. The outstanding one is the presidential system of the United States and of Latin American countries: the cabinet is appointed by the President, but is not answerable to parliament. Thus, 'divided government' or 'cohabitation' of a kind inconceivable in Europe is possible, as discussed in Chapter 3. In the USA, a cabinet appointed by a Republican President can survive even if congress is controlled by the Democrats (as under the latter years of the Bush presidency, 2007–09), and one appointed by a Democratic President can work with a congress controlled by the Republicans (as under the Clinton presidency, 1995–2001). Congress can make the life of such administrations difficult, but cannot bring them to an end. The weapon of impeachment by congress is (at least in theory) an instrument to punish criminal wrongdoing, not a device to check politically objectionable behaviour. There are some formal similarities between this system and the relationship between parliament and the executive in Switzerland once a new government has taken office: there, the seven-member federal government is elected by the lower house (as elsewhere in Europe), but it cannot be dismissed during its fixed four-year term (though this is of theoretical importance only, since Swiss governments since 1959 have always been four-party coalitions enjoying the support of an overwhelming majority of parliamentarians, with some modification of this *Zauberformel* or 'magic formula' after 2003).

The distinction between the presidential and parliamentary systems of government is defined by the separation of powers and functions that lies at its heart, not by the separation of personnel between government and parliament. The presidential system classically precludes dual membership of parliament and government; when Hillary Clinton joined the first Obama cabinet, for instance, she had to resign her Senate seat. But the parliamentary system does not imply the opposite: there is no need for government ministers to be parliamentarians. This system does entail attendance by government ministers in the lower house, and their answerability to it; but it is not a requirement that they be voting members. On the contrary, separation of personnel is more common than the dual minister–deputy mandate that is taken for granted in Ireland.

The unusual Irish position will become clearer if we look at arrangements in other parliamentary democracies. There are three patterns of relationship between membership of parliament and membership of government in Europe. In the first, and most common traditionally, dual membership is permitted but not required. Most European countries still fall into this category, with cabinets made up of a mixture of parliamentarians and non-parliamentarians. In the second group, one of growing importance, dual membership is prohibited: cabinet members may not be members of parliament. France, Luxembourg, the Netherlands and Norway are long-standing members of this group, which was joined in 1976 by newly democratic Portugal; two other countries that originally belonged to the first group eventually also prohibited ministers from holding parliamentary seats— Sweden in 1974 and Belgium in 1995.[2] This leaves two countries isolated in the third, residual category: Ireland and the United Kingdom, each of which requires all cabinet members to be serving parliamentarians, though not necessarily members of the lower house (Bergman et al., 2006: 148–52).

Routes to ministerial office

When we turn to examine the routes to ministerial office that exist in practice, it becomes clear that while the constitutional position is a strong influence and sets parameters that cannot be transgressed, other factors affect the outcome. The most open pattern is represented by the presidential system, where there are few constraints on the president's power of selection. As one study of US practice concluded,

> there is no existing corps of notables or functionaries who stand in the wings, ready to assume the cloaks of office when the new government takes power. Instead, the newly elected president puts together his administrative leadership from the vast reservoir of talent that is found in prominent positions in diverse institutions: business, the academy, the professions, and government itself. Prior political service may be important, particularly if it is service to the successful president himself, but it is certainly not a requirement. (Mann and Smith, 1981: 213)

Congress, it is true, has a role, in that senior executive appointments require approval by the Senate; but this is largely a foregone conclusion, since the Senate has approved 97% of all such appointments (Mann and Smith, 1981: 226). Nevertheless, we should not discount Senate influence, since presidents may tailor their nominations, second-guessing the Senate's position.

In parliamentary systems, party politicians play a major role in government even where the constitution does not require ministers to be members of parliament, or where it altogether bans parliamentarians. In pre-war

Japan, for instance, where there was no requirement of parliamentary membership, almost half of all ministers were drawn from parliament; under the post-war constitution, which requires only that a majority of ministers be parliamentarians, appointments tend to be made overwhelmingly from the House of Representatives, with some from the second chamber, and a handful from outside parliament (Tomita, Baerwald and Nakamura, 1981: 241). In Spain over the period 1976–95, only 19% of ministers had no prior political experience (Bar, 1997: 133–4). In other European countries, though, the trend seems to be rather in the opposite direction, with the importance of parliamentary experience diminishing. Thus, in an early study of Italy, Dogan (1981: 192–3) concluded that 'members of government are recruited from among parliamentarians', with few exceptions; but Verzichelli (2009: 89) points out that, over the period 1996–2006, 39% of ministers were 'outsiders', with no parliamentary experience. In Belgium, similarly, Frognier (1997: 91) showed that 82% of cabinet members were also members of parliament in the post-war decades; but Dumont, Fiers and Dandoy (2009: 132) report a big increase in the number of non-parliamentarians appointed ministers since the beginning of the 1990s.

Overall, there has been a considerable level of variation in the background of ministers in Europe. A survey covering the period 1945–84 showed that three quarters of all ministers had been members of parliament before joining the government, but with big differences from country to country. At one extreme were the 'truly parliamentary' types in respect of composition, Ireland and the United Kingdom; at the opposite were the 'semi-parliamentary' types, represented by the Netherlands, Norway, Sweden, Finland, Austria and France, where the parliamentary route accounted for about two thirds of ministers (in the Netherlands the figure was only 53%). In between were countries such as Germany, Belgium, Luxembourg, Denmark and Iceland, with a smaller but still significant presence of ministers without parliamentary experience (De Winter, 1991: 44–47; for updates, see the various chapters in Dowding and Dumont, 2009a). It is to be emphasised here that it is the prior background experience of ministers that is being discussed; having been appointed, in many cases they choose to resign their parliamentary seats, and in a growing number of states they are required to do so, as we have seen.

The British case is particularly important given its role as a model for so many other states, its political cultural impact on Ireland, and the British government's direct involvement in the drafting of the original Irish constitution of 1922. There, the House of Lords has been very extensively used as a route to cabinet membership. Long gone, it is true, are the days of William Pitt (who was the only member of the House of Commons in the first cabinet he formed, in 1783; the rest were peers). By the early twentieth century it was taken for granted that senior posts such as that of Prime Minister and Foreign Secretary could only be held by members of the Commons, but a sizeable representation of peers in the cabinet continued (Daalder, 1963: 5–10).[3] Surprisingly enough, even as the business of government became more complex, the proportion of ministers brought into the cabinet from non-political backgrounds remained small—about 15% of the total over the period 1916–58 (computed from Willson, 1959). Non-parliamentarians may still be appointed, but on the understanding that they would quickly win seats in parliament. Thus, for example, in October 1964 Harold Wilson appointed two non-parliamentarians, Frank Cousins and Patrick Gordon Walker, to his cabinet; Cousins quickly won a seat at a by-election, but Walker resigned as Foreign Secretary when he failed to secure election to the House of Commons.[4] A recent example was the appointment of Peter Mandelson as Secretary of State for Business, Innovation and Skills in October 2008; he was appointed to the House of Lords at the same time. The clear trend, though, has been for the number of ministers from the House of Lords to be reduced to the point of disappearance (Parry and Maer, 2012).

In other Commonwealth countries, variants of the Westminster practice are the norm. The second chamber is also a channel to ministerial office in Canada, where the government leader in the Senate is always included in the cabinet; any non-parliamentarians appointed to government are expected to find seats 'within a reasonable time' (Dawson and Dawson, 1989: 44–45). In Australia, where, unlike Canada and the UK, the second chamber is elected, appointment through the Senate is not possible in the same way; when outsiders become ministers they must secure election to one or other house of parliament within three months (Hamer, 1996: 74–75). In India, where in practice a non-parliamentary route to cabinet membership is common, ministers must nevertheless secure parliamentary seats within six months (Sisson, 1981: 152). In New Zealand the position is starker: there is no second chamber, and in effect only parliamentarians may become ministers (Mulgan, 2004: 75–80).

STATE BUILDING AND MINISTERIAL APPOINTMENTS IN IRELAND

While there was an important sense in which the United Kingdom bequeathed its own approach to government formation to the new Irish Free State, the leaders of the new Irish government in 1922 were not disposed to follow British models slavishly. In particular, they sought to follow continental European models in seeking to allow the appointment of a set of ministers who would not be parliamentarians. This section looks first at the innovative provisions of the 1922 constitution, and then turns to the process by which these provisions ceased to have any real effect.

Ministerial office and the 1922 constitution

The notion of ministers as a committee of the Dáil has been embedded since that body's first meeting on 21 January 1919, when the new Dáil constitution provided for a prime minister (*Príomh-aireach*, later to become known as President) and four ministers, all of whom were to be members of the Dáil.[5] Later changes in the Dáil constitution (on 1 April 1919, when the maximum size of the cabinet was expanded from five to 10, and 23 August 1921, when it was reduced to seven) left this position unaltered. All members of the Provisional Government which held office from 16 January to 6 December 1922 were also members of the Dáil.[6]

This strictly parliamentary mode of ministerial recruitment was not entirely a matter of choice. Political realities (in particular, the fact that the Dáil had to operate against the authority of the *de jure* state, run by the British administration through Dublin Castle) meant that the parliamentary route was one of the few channels by which an effective and democratically legitimated counter-elite could emerge. But this episode also appears to confirm the strength of commitment of the Irish revolutionary elite to parliamentary government (Farrell, 1969: 135; 1971: 83).

Options were widened while the new constitution was being drafted following the Anglo-Irish Treaty of December 1921. True, the provisions of the constitution would have to be compatible with the terms of the Treaty, and would have to be endorsed by the British Parliament as well as being approved by the Dáil. But the central preoccupation of the British was to protect the position of the crown, and as long as this was secure they were content to tolerate a wide measure of independence as regards the mechanics of political institutions. The constitutional provisions in respect of the composition of government evolved in three stages.

First, a constitutional drafting committee nominally chaired by Michael Collins but otherwise composed of non-parliamentarians was given the task of urgently preparing a new constitutional blueprint in early 1922. Collins, who attended only the first meeting, instructed the committee to produce 'a free democratic constitution' that would break with the past (Kennedy, 1928: 443). The committee cast its net wide in looking for models, and finally presented the government with three drafts. The draft ultimately adopted provided for a mixture of the British and Swiss models of government formation. This draft (labelled B) was produced by James Douglas and others (for background, see Douglas, 1998: 82–5). Another draft (A) was produced by the acting chair of the committee, Darrell Figgis, and others, and a third (C) by two independent minded professors, Alfred O'Rahilly and James Murnaghan. All three drafts made provision for ministers who would not be parliamentarians.[7]

In the draft that was adopted as a basis for further elaboration, four members of the government or 'Executive Council', all Dáil deputies, would be responsible for the most 'political' areas and would be collectively answerable to the Dáil: the Uachtarán (President), Tánaiste, Minister for External Affairs and Minister for Finance. Other domestic policy areas would be quarantined from this: they would be the responsibility of other ministers, to a maximum of eight, elected by the Dáil but not themselves members of it (though the Dáil could allow up to two of these to be TDs). These would be nominated by a committee representative of the Dáil, but could also be nominated by 'functional or vocational councils', should such be established; and they would hold office for a fixed, four-year term, regardless of any dissolution of the Dáil. The Executive Council would function as a single collective authority, except in matters relating to external affairs, which would be managed by the core group of four.

Second, following the government's effective endorsement of this draft, the blueprint was further revised by the committee, which made some small but significant changes (dropping External Affairs and Finance as named core ministries, increasing the number of 'extern ministers' who could be Dáil deputies to three, and providing that all terms of office would end with a dissolution of the Dáil). These provisions survived the intense round of negotiations with the British, where the focus was on the issue of the crown, and the draft constitution was finally published on the morning of the general election, 16 June 1922.[8] Although this innovative document reflected in part the enthusiasm and open-mindedness of those who drew it up, the distinction between two types of minister responded to a particular reality:

the need, if at all possible, to find space for anti-Treaty representatives in the government. The implication was that it would be possible to let pro-Treaty ministers get on with managing the constitutional question, while allowing anti-Treaty deputies to hold ministerial office in clearly delimited policy areas on which the Dáil would make separate decisions. This was the kind of coalition for which provision was made in the Collins–de Valera 'pact' of May 1922, which provided for an uncontested Dáil election and a government comprising five pro-Treaty and four anti-Treaty ministers, with the President and the Minister for Defence as separate office holders (Hopkinson, 1988: 98).[9]

The third stage was the enactment of the new constitution. By the time the draft made its way to the new Dáil for approval in September 1922, political realities had changed. The pact had been abrogated by Collins (who had himself been killed on 22 August) and civil war had broken out. Nevertheless, the thinking behind the original proposal survived: Home Affairs Minister Kevin O'Higgins described the provisions for government composition as representing 'a very real desire to get away from the British Party system' by distinguishing between the political core, who would be vulnerable to defeat in the Dáil, and the more non-political extern ministers.[10] The articles on government composition were, however, referred to a Dáil committee, whose recommendations were incorporated in the revised text. Chaired by Gerald FitzGibbon, QC, the committee included four members of the pro-Treaty Sinn Féin party, three of Labour, one Farmers' Party deputy and two independents from Dublin University, including FitzGibbon himself. The committee produced a unanimous report, and though, strangely, the report was formally rejected by the Dáil, its provisions were incorporated through a series of amendments.[11] These changes, though at first sight innocuous, had far-reaching effects. The most important was the dropping of the requirement that a certain number of ministers be non-parliamentarians; under the new wording, they might, but need not be, TDs. In addition, the Executive Council was now restricted to an inner grouping of not more than seven nor fewer than five ministers (including the President and Vice President of the Council and the Minister for Finance), who would be collectively answerable to the Dáil. Alongside these, a set of extern ministers would be appointed on the recommendation of a committee 'impartially representative' of the Dáil, and would serve for the life of the Dáil. The total number of ministers, including those in the Executive Council, continued to be capped at 12.

The new constitution was hailed for its novelty, for putting unwritten British constitutional provisions into written form, and for experimenting boldly with these. It was described as 'a most exciting political experiment in a most exciting milieu' (Saunders, 1924: 345), and as novel in 'the tendency of its framers to break away from English models' (Kohn, 1932: 271). But in the final version of the constitution the breach with the British model was in reality less dramatic. As Nicholas Mansergh (1934: 166–7) suggested, the original proposals were indeed 'a striking innovation', but by the time they had found their way into the final draft of the constitution 'the vitality of the scheme disappeared'. In the words of Basil Chubb (1970: 181), the original proposal was 'enacted in only an emasculated form'.

Constitutional change

Four later constitutional changes had implications for the position of ministers from outside the Dáil. First, an amendment in 1927 (the fifth amendment) increased the maximum size of the Executive Council from seven to 12. This left the extern minister category theoretically in existence, but made it easier to accommodate all ministers within the Executive Council, reflecting government disquiet with the existing system.[12] The measure was adopted following some resistance in the Seanad and criticism in the Dáil, where Labour leader Thomas Johnson argued, not implausibly, that 'this experiment, confessedly an experiment, has not been tried, and whatever value was in it has not had a chance of finding expression', since ministers seemed to see themselves as answerable to the government rather than to the Dáil.[13]

Second, on 13 June 1928 the Dáil considered a further constitutional amendment to loosen up eligibility for ministerial office (this had emerged from the deliberations of a joint committee of the two houses). The proposal would require three members of the Executive Council (the President, Vice President and Minister for Finance) to be members of the Dáil, while the remaining members could be drawn from either house. The change was opposed by Fianna Fáil on the grounds that, as de Valera argued, 'the Executive Council should be completely composed of members of this House, who have to face their constituents afterwards and would be able to face criticism here'.[14] A government amendment to the effect that no more than one member of the Executive Council could be a senator was accepted, greatly watering down the original proposal (this became the fifteenth amendment, 1929).

Third, the abolition of the Seanad in 1936 altogether removed the possibility of ministerial appointments from this house (the twenty-fourth amendment, 1936). This left one 'external' route to ministerial office still in existence, at least theoretically: non-parliamentarians could still be appointed ministers (though not members of the Executive Council) if the Dáil so wished.

The fourth change was the new constitution of 1937. This altogether dropped the notion of extern ministers, but increased the maximum size of the government from 12 to 15. It reintroduced, in article 28.7.2°, a provision that up to two members of the government might be senators. The Taoiseach, Tánaiste and Minister for Finance were exempted from this: they are required to be Dáil deputies.

THE PRACTICE OF MINISTERIAL SELECTION IN IRELAND

Even cursory examination of the Irish case will illustrate the extent to which practice is even more restrictive than in Britain and other Commonwealth countries; it has been argued that from a comparative perspective Irish heads of government have 'the most limited pool from which to choose their cabinet' (O'Malley, 2006: 319). This tendency asserted itself immediately in 1922, as the whole significance of allowing the appointment of 'extern' ministers became transformed by political practice. Although provision for appointments from outside the Dáil was more restrictive under the 1937 constitution, it was not non-existent; but it was little availed of. These developments are discussed in turn in this section.

Appointments under the 1922 constitution

When the constitution came into effect on 6 December 1922, the appoint-ment of extern ministers immediately arose as a concrete issue, and the great significance of Dáil membership became clear. The political culture from which this perspective emanated had become obvious even before 1922. Brian Farrell (1969: 135) described the 1919 constitution as 'in Bagehot's famous phrase, "a hyphen which joins, a buckle which fastens" the settled framework of the British cabinet system on the uncertain political progress of an incipient independence movement'. He later plausibly argued that political experience during these formative years showed that 'Irish political culture was already developed into an established and sturdy parliamentary mode prior to political independence' (Farrell, 1971: 83).

The strength of this perspective became apparent after the constitution came into effect on 6 December 1922. William Cosgrave, who became first President of the Executive Council, nominated the six leading members of his outgoing administration to be members of the Executive Council (bringing its size to the maximum number of seven). This left the Dáil entitled to appoint a committee to nominate a further five. Its freedom of action was curtailed by a suggestion from Cosgrave that the terms of reference of the committee require it to recommend nominees for three ministries: agriculture, fisheries and the post office. The 15-member committee, elected on 8 December, was dominated by the pro-Treaty Sinn Féin party with nine members, but it also included two Labour, two Farmers' Party and two independent deputies. It reported unanimously on 14 December, and its recommendations were accepted by the Dáil. Perhaps not surprisingly, the three new ministers were Dáil deputies, and all had been members of the outgoing government: Patrick Hogan continued as Minister for Agriculture and J.J. Walsh as Postmaster General; and Fionán Lynch, a minister without portfolio in the outgoing government, was appointed to the new post of Minister for Fisheries.[15] Of the 11 ministers in the outgoing government, only one, Eamonn Duggan, was not appointed to the Executive Council (but he was made a parliamentary secretary in 1924).

On 20 September 1923, following the general election, this process repeated itself: Cosgrave again appointed the same seven ministers to be members of the Executive Council, and he recommended that the local government portfolio be added to the three existing 'extern' ministries, on which a Dáil committee would make a decision. The 15-person committee, elected on 25 September, had an identical political composition to that of 1922. It met and reported on 3 October. When its report reached the Dáil, there was, for the first time, a vigorous debate about the extent to which the spirit of the provisions for extern ministers was violated. Opposition speakers alleged that the decision had been taken in advance by the governing party, with Labour leader Thomas Johnson claiming that 'there was no pretence or no attempt even to consider qualifications'.[16] But as one government deputy bluntly put it, 'What is sauce for the goose is sauce for the gander. To the victors the spoils of war. The Government Party has only done in this case what the high priests who are condemning them ... would do if the same opportunity turned up for them.'[17] Not surprisingly, the three outgoing extern ministers were duly reappointed by the Dáil; a fourth TD, Seamus Bourke, was appointed Minister for Local Government.

When the next round of ministerial appointments fell due on 23 June 1927, the constitutional position had changed; the President had the option of proposing extern ministers, but there was no pressure on him to do so, as the maximum size of the Executive Council had been expanded to 12 by the fifth amendment to the constitution discussed above. Accordingly, three of the four outgoing extern ministers were promoted to Executive Council status (the fourth, Bourke, was made a parliamentary secretary), and no extern minister was appointed subsequently.

Remarkably, despite Fianna Fáil's strong objections to the appointment of senators as ministers, in forming his first Executive Council on 9 March 1932 de Valera included Senator Joseph Connolly, Fianna Fáil leader in the Seanad, as Minister for Posts and Telegraphs, alongside eight Dáil deputies.[18] He repeated this in forming his second government on 8 February 1933, now appointing Senator Connolly to the Department of Lands and Fisheries. But the days of senators in the Irish Free State were numbered. On 29 May 1936 the Seanad disappeared from Ireland's constitutional structure, and with it this particular route to ministerial office. De Valera briefly considered reactivating the appointment of extern ministers to allow Senator Connolly to continue in office, but decided against this course of action. De Valera expressed the implausible view that a representative selection committee of

Table 7.1: Extern ministers and ministerial appointments from Seanad Éireann, 1922–2013

Date	Minister	Portfolio	Comment
Extern ministers			
14 Dec. 1922	Patrick Hogan, TD	Agriculture	Outgoing from same post in Provisional Government
14 Dec. 1922	J.J. Walsh, TD	Postmaster General	Outgoing from same post in Provisional Government
14 Dec. 1922	Fionán Lynch, TD	Fisheries	Outgoing minister without portfolio in Provisional Government
10 Oct. 1923	Patrick Hogan, TD	Agriculture	Reappointment
10 Oct. 1923	J.J. Walsh, TD	Postmaster General	Reappointment
10 Oct. 1923	Fionán Lynch, TD	Fisheries	Reappointment
10 Oct. 1923	Seamus Bourke, TD	Local Government	New appointment
Ministers from Seanad Éireann			
9 Mar. 1932	Sen. Joseph Connolly	Posts and Telegraphs	Fianna Fáil leader in Seanad
8 Feb. 1933	Sen. Joseph Connolly	Lands and Fisheries	Fianna Fáil leader in Seanad
16 May 1957	Sen. Sean Moylan	Agriculture	Taoiseach's nominee to Seanad
20 Oct. 1981	Sen. James Dooge	Foreign Affairs	Taoiseach's nominee to Seanad

Note: 'Extern ministers' were not members of the Executive Council and were not required to be Dáil deputies, though in practice all were indeed TDs.

the kind required by the constitution could no longer be put together, a view not shared by his officials; but the matter was not pursued.[19] With this went Senator Connolly's ministerial post; he left political life to become chairman of the Commissioners of Public Works. This set of appointments is summarised in Table 7.1, which also reports on subsequent ministerial appointments from the Seanad.

Appointments under the 1937 constitution

Since the appointment of Senator Connolly, and under the 1937 constitution, the power to make appointments from the Seanad has been used only twice. The first occasion was in 1957. In forming his new government on 20 March, de Valera announced that he would be appointing a defeated Dáil candidate, Sean Moylan, as Minister for Agriculture by first nominating him to the Seanad; the Minister for External Affairs, Frank Aiken, would hold the portfolio in the meantime. This appointment came in for some criticism in the Dáil on 16 May on grounds that it was undemocratic, as Mr Moylan had just lost his seat in the general election, but the appointment easily went through. Following Senator Moylan's death on 16 November 1957 after six months in office, this arrangement came to an end.

The second occasion was on 30 June 1981, when Garret FitzGerald, following an identical procedure, announced his intention of appointing Professor James Dooge, an academic who had retired from a long Seanad career four years earlier, as Minister for Foreign Affairs. This time, Professor John Kelly, Minister for Industry and Energy, would hold the portfolio until Professor Dooge's nomination to the Seanad took effect. This initiative was opposed by Fianna Fáil on the grounds that it was 'a departure from well settled constitutional practice', as party leader Charles Haughey put it.[20] The appointment took place only following a division at the end of a debate that extended over two days. Dr FitzGerald attributed this cultural resistance to the fact that this provision had only been used once before and 'most people had probably forgotten that it existed' (FitzGerald, 1992: 363).

Cultural resistance to outside appointments extends outside the pool of government ministers; the Irish experience suggests that junior ministerial appointments are also seen as the preserve of parliamentarians. Even before 1922, Dáil deputies tended to monopolise such posts. For example, three such positions were created on 2–4 April 1919 (three 'directors' of new departments), and a fourth was created a little over a year later. Nine non-cabinet ministers were appointed in 1921 and 1922, and 'assistant ministers' also in 1922; all of these were Dáil deputies. The status of junior office holders was regularised in 1924 with the creation of the post of parliamentary secretary, who could be drawn from either the Dáil or the Seanad, and whose numbers were limited to seven. The post was retitled 'minister of state' in 1977, and the maximum number was increased to 10; it was further increased to 15 (1980), 17 (1995) and 20 (2007). Of the many holders of these posts since 1924, though, every one has been a Dáil deputy.

ASSESSING THE MINISTERIAL RECRUITMENT SYSTEM

The Irish experience of drawing on external expertise in making ministerial appointments is, then, a strictly limited one. The originality of the 1922 constitution was succeeded by the more conservative provisions of the 1937 constitution, which were much closer to the British model. Furthermore, the practice of ministerial appointments has virtually confined these to currently practising politicians. Two problems with Ireland's experiment in this area may be identified: a structural one, as regards internal contradictions in the model adopted, and a political cultural one, in respect of elite expectations. This section first discusses this issue before going on to assess the likelihood of constitutional reform in this area.

Constraints on ministerial recruitment

The new Irish state began its life with a bold experiment in constitutional innovation by creating the office of extern minister. Like many of the other constitutional innovations of the time, this reflected an original blueprint that showed the influence of both British and continental European (or specifically Swiss) constitutional traditions, as well as responding to political realities of the time (the need to bridge the gulf between the two wings of Sinn Féin). Rather than pursuing the middle ground between the two models, though, the constitution created a hybrid system that was never likely to work. Instead of simply allowing for non-parliamentary membership of the government (the norm in continental Europe), it created a distinction between an inner cabinet of politically sensitive ministries (to be headed by Dáil deputies who would be collectively answerable to the Dáil) and an outer tier of less sensitive ministries (whose incumbents would be selected by but not otherwise dependent on the Dáil).

In this respect, the analysis of the founding fathers was naïve: they believed that stable government would be impossible in the context of proportional representation, and pursued an inclusive formula for ministerial appointments. The resulting compromise between a potentially unstable inner cabinet and a stable outer tier, designed 'to enlist the abilities and services of men who had no party political attachments or who would not cooperate with the political party in power in the Executive Council' (Kennedy, 1928: 444), was never likely to prove workable.

The defects of the new system were clear at an early stage. Kohn (1932: 271–83) highlighted three. First, the distinction between 'political' and 'non-political', or between 'executive' and 'extern' ministers, was 'devoid of any reality in the conditions of the modern state', as all decisions would ultimately be political, especially since they would typically entail expenditure, on which political agreement would be needed. As Justice Minister Kevin O'Higgins put it in 1926,

> Our experience of the working of the extern Minister idea has led us to think that it is not as valuable a constitutional idea as we once thought it would be ... Where it breaks down is that every Department radiates into the Department of Finance, and that while theoretically one may say this Minister has single responsibility to the Dáil and to the country for his Department ... aloofness of such Ministers from the Executive Council and its works and pomps is largely theoretical. They have to turn to the Finance Department, and there is collective responsibility for that Department.[21]

Second, Kohn argued, the fact that extern ministers would enjoy greater security of tenure than their more powerful colleagues in the Executive Council 'must inevitably produce a tense psychological problem' (Kohn, 1932: 280). Third, the mere fact that such ministers would be appointed by parliament rather than by the head of the government would destroy cabinet cohesion. Mansergh (1934: 156–171) agreed with these criticisms: the main problem was the dual nature of the ministry, making conflict between two types of ministers likely, and resting on an unsustainable distinction between the political and administrative domains. Experience confirms this view: one of the extern ministers, J.J. Walsh, used his constitutional independence to criticise the government on major policy matters (O'Sullivan, 1940: 89). This evokes the image of the Northern Ireland Executive, which includes parties that differ radically on major policy issues, and that engage freely in criticism of each other; but the independence of extern ministers under the 1922 constitution was, at least in theory, considerably greater.

We may identify a further reason for the failure of this system to take root in Ireland. An effort was made to introduce it in circumstances where the notion that ministers must be Dáil deputies was already strongly ingrained. This had already been the practice in the Dáil since 1919, and the steadily increasing predominance of members of the British House of Commons over members of the House of Lords in British cabinets pointed to Commons membership as the primary source of legitimacy for a minister. In addition, given the prestige of ministerial office, it is only to be expected that members of Dáil parties would jealously protect access to that office, restricting it to themselves—and thereby creating an ideological justification to the effect that 'democracy' requires ministers to be 'democratically elected' parliamentarians. A debate featuring this argument took place on each occasion that a senator was appointed minister, and appears to have had considerable impact on public opinion, notwithstanding its flimsy basis, as discussed below.

Constitutional options

Apart from some initial interest in the question in the early 1920s, the process of ministerial selection is an issue that has generated very little public debate in Ireland. The Committee on the Constitution (1967) did not address the issue at all. The Constitution Review Group (1996: 92) considered the possible appointment of non-elected 'executive experts' as ministers, but noted the argument that 'democracy is best served by a situation where the people control the Oireachtas and through the Oireachtas the government', and did not propose any change. The position of the All-Party Oireachtas Committee on the Constitution (2003: 12) was similar. It saw no need for constitutional change, but considered the idea of yet a further tier of executive appointments from the Dáil (parliamentary private secretaries on the British model), concluding that 'this proposal merits further consideration'. Introducing such a tier would not require constitutional reform, but would probably be politically unrealistic in circumstances where the existing set of office holders has come in for criticism because of the financial burden they place on the state. Surprisingly, the Convention on the Constitution (2013b), though not asked to consider the matter, voted 55–42 to allow the appointment of non-parliamentarians as ministers, and it voted 59–40 to require deputies appointed as ministers to resign their Dáil seats.

There are two obvious obstacles to any kind of reform in this area. The first is the self-interest of Dáil deputies. Given the attractions of ministerial office, especially in the context of the increased professionalisation of political roles, it is only to be expected that those who form the tiny pool from which ministers are drawn (the members of the ruling parties in the Dáil) would resent any attempt to broaden this pool to include even senators, not to mention non-members of the Oireachtas (O'Malley, 2009: 182). It is striking that the constitution drafting committee that initially proposed the introduction of non-parliamentary ministers in 1922 did not include any TDs, and that the committee that effectively neutralised this provision later in the same year consisted entirely of TDs. Second, a deeply embedded ideology has emerged to justify the status quo. This rests on the view, articulated by de Valera in 1929 but often repeated by others on all sides of the Dáil, that all ministers should be Dáil deputies answerable to the electorate. This view conflicts with the experience of other democracies, as described above. It also conflicts with first principles of democratic theory: it is far from clear why the minister responsible for the formation and implementation of Irish foreign policy, Eamon Gilmore, should be especially answerable to 11,000 voters in Dún Laoghaire, or why 10,000 voters in Dublin North should have a particular influence over the minister responsible for the state's entire health service, Dr James Reilly. But political cultural values need not have a rational basis, and absence of logic is unlikely to undermine TDs' commitment to the belief that they alone should be entitled to be ministers.

It is not clear that merely *permitting* non-parliamentarians to be appointed to government would have much impact, given the nature of Irish elite political culture. If, however, the constitution were to be changed to *require* ministers to be non-parliamentarians, two important consequences would follow. First, the door would be open to the appointment of political and non-political figures who occupy particular representative positions in civil society or who possess special skills that would be valuable in a cabinet, a particularly important consideration at a time of economic crisis. This would not, of course, prohibit Dáil deputies from assuming ministerial office, and presumably talented politicians who had established their reputations through the political route would continue to dominate the cabinet in Ireland, as they do elsewhere. Second, by forcing TDs appointed to ministerial office to resign their Dáil seats, it would greatly strengthen the position of the Dáil. On the government side, in particular, there would be a much larger set of Dáil deputies free to focus on the legislative process and to develop leadership skills in this area (Van der Hulst, 2000: 48). The government would no longer, as at present, be a committee of the Dáil so powerful as to overshadow all other committees; it would be an external body, answerable to the Dáil, its members commonly present in the chamber, but not having a vote there.

Abolition of the dual mandate would have certain side-effects that would have to be addressed. For example, if a large number of newly elected Dáil deputies were forced to resign their seats to become ministers this would immediately create a set of casual vacancies, which under the current system would have to be filled by a series of by-elections. But there are several alternatives that would eliminate the need for by-elections—which in any event are not compatible with proportional representation, as discussed in Chapter 5.[22] Even without going as far as moving to other electoral formulas such as the list system, provisions could be made for replacement of resigning TDs by substitute candidates nominated at the time of each general election (as in Irish elections to the European Parliament), or by a recount of the further preferences of the candidate vacating the seat (as in Malta).

CONCLUSION

Appointments to the government from outside the Dáil have, then, been of little significance in Ireland, and ministers emerging from the Seanad have not been assisted by the perceived modest prestige of that chamber (Chubb, 1974: 3). There is nevertheless a case for constitutional reform that would extend the pool of potential ministerial talent by aligning the Irish political system more closely with the European model of ministerial selection. This is not to undervalue the contribution of the many distinguished Irish ministers whose management and political skills enable them to perform effectively in a range of different departments, and who would continue to do so under changed ministerial selection rules. But overall ministerial effectiveness would be likely to be enhanced by some reduction in the burden of Dáil work and constituency representation, and by opening the door to ministerial office to a much wider number of potential appointees.

It would be unfair to dismiss the idea of non-parliamentary ministers on the basis of the experience of the 1920s: that early provision was never properly tested, but it was in any case inherently flawed. Aside from its obvious technical defects, it has been rightly criticised as conflicting with democratic theory, since under the original scheme extern ministers would not be answerable to anyone (Mansergh, 1934: 165–6). But that argument should not be confused with the contemporary dismissal of non-parliamentary ministers on the same grounds: they would and should, as elsewhere, be answerable to parliament.

It is true that a more open recruitment system would not necessarily restore faith in under-performing government. Furthermore, 'outside' ministers would be likely to encounter particular problems arising from their parliamentary and political inexperience, given that much of their work would have to be conducted in the Dáil chamber, resulting in further management issues for the head of government (Dowding and Dumont, 2009b: 7). Neither would allegations of ministerial incompetence, arrogance and corruption be brought to a magical end. An observation about the character of European cabinets will have a familiar ring for Irish readers:

> It is widely known from the scandal sheets and anecdotal evidence (though not extensively documented in the academic literature) that cabinet members often gratify themselves with fancy cars and living quarters, use government airplanes for private trips, host unnecessarily lavish receptions, or make other inappropriate uses of government money. (Bergman et al., 2006: 146)

It would, then, be a mistake to assume that an institutional reform of the kind discussed in this chapter would act as a panacea for Ireland's political ills, much less its economic problems. But, in the long term, there is a case for going back to the broad-minded perspective of the founders of the state and for lifting the restrictive and damaging barriers that lie in the way of recruitment to ministerial careers in government.

NOTES

1. This chapter is a revised version of Coakley, 2010.
2. In Belgium, this has been described as a 'sleeping mandate': as in Bulgaria, Estonia and Slovakia, ministers must relinquish their parliamentary roles on assuming office, but may resume them on leaving government (Dowding and Dumont, 2009b: 6).
3. A remarkable feature of the British cabinet system has been the survival of the aristocracy in positions of power long after parliamentary reform had undermined its capacity to influence the House of Commons through control of 'closed' boroughs. Using a demanding definition of aristocracy, Laski (1928) showed how the proportion of sons of members of the titled nobility holding cabinet office declined only slowly, from 73% under the '*ancien régime*' (1801–31) through 64% (1832–66), 60% (1867–84), 58% (1885–1905) and 49% (1906–16) to 27% (1917–24). This was achieved in part through the practice of sons of peers taking seats in the House of Commons.
4. Cousins was elected to the safe Labour seat of Nuneaton on 21 January 1965, but Gordon Walker narrowly lost the by-election in Leyton on the same day in a surprise result (*Irish Times*, 22 January 1965).

5. For the official Irish text of the constitution, see *Dáil Debates*, F, 21 January 1919, 13; for an English translation, Farrell, 1969: 135–6 and 1971: 86–7.

6. The Provisional Government was established under article 17 of the Anglo-Irish Treaty, which did not define the manner in which it was to be constituted. The official listing of Irish governments identifies the following: (1) First Cabinet, 21 January 1919; (2) Second Cabinet; 1 April 1919; (3) Dáil Cabinet (Pre-Treaty), 21 August 1921; (4) Dáil Cabinet (Post-Treaty), 10 January 1922; (5) First Provisional Government, 16 January 1922; (6) Second Provisional Government, 16 June 1922; (7) First Executive Council, 6 December 1922, and so on, up to the Eighth Executive Council, 21 July 1937; (15) First Government, 29 December 1937, and so on, up to the present (the 29th Government was formed on 9 March 2011); see National Archives, Taoiseach's Department, Ministerial appointments: summary, 1919–, S 14175 A 1. The post-Treaty Dáil cabinet, headed by Arthur Griffith (10 January–12 August 1922) and then by William Cosgrave (12 August–6 December 1922), overlapped with the provisional government headed first by Michael Collins (16 January–22 August 1922) and then by William Cosgrave (25 August–6 December 1922). Griffith's government was answerable to the Dáil; Collins's notionally owed its authority to the members of parliament of Southern Ireland, who had met once to approve the Provisional Government. The potential for conflict between the two governments was reduced to a minimum by the close working relationship between Griffith and Collins (who, in any case, served in Griffith's government) and by the almost complete overlap of personnel between the two. Since Cosgrave succeeded Griffith as Chairman of the Provisional Government, and succeeded Collins as President of the Dáil government, the two offices were in effect merged.

7. For the texts of drafts A and B, see Akenson and Fallin, 1970: II: 57–74 and 74–93; for draft C, Farrell, 1970–71: III: 124–35; and for the text finally forwarded to London, Akenson and Fallin, 1970: III: 41–53.

8. Rialtas Sealadach na hÉireann, 1922; United Kingdom, 1922; *Irish Times*, 16 June 1922.

9. For the text of the pact, see *Dáil Debates*, 20 May 1922, vol. S2, 479; on the 'pact' election of 1922, see Gallagher, 1981.

10. *Dáil Debates*, 20 September 1922, vol. 1, cols 487–8.

11. See Committee on Executive Articles (1922) and *Dáil Debates*, 12 October 1922, vol. 1, cols 1535–75.

12. *Dáil Debates*, 1 December 1926, vol. 17, cols 418–20.

13. *Dáil Debates*, 1 December 1926, vol. 17, cols 420–22.

14. *Dáil Debates*, 13 March 1929, vol. 28, col. 1293.

15. In making the formal appointments, constitutional niceties of a kind that were less obvious at the political level were strictly observed. Five official notices appeared: of the appointment of the President, the Executive Council, and, individually, of each of the three extern ministers; National Archives, Taoiseach's Department, Appointment of First Executive Council, S 8901; and *Iris Oifigiúil* 6 and 14 December 1922.

16. *Dáil Debates*, 10 October 1923, vol. 5, col. 194.

17. Cork East Cumann na nGaedheal Deputy Thomas O'Mahony, *Dáil Debates*, 10 October 1923, vol. 5, col. 197.

18. Ironically, this appointment, and de Valera's decision to hold the position of Minister for External Affairs himself (1932–48), brought the Irish Free State back into alignment with practice in other Commonwealth countries (where the norm was that the prime minister held the external affairs portfolio, and the second chamber was represented in the cabinet).

19. See Extern ministers: procedure file (1935), National Archives, Taoiseach's Department, S 8242. Connolly (1996: 388) states that he turned down an offer from a colleague to resign from the Dáil to create a 'safe' seat for him.

20. *Dáil Debates*, 20 October 1981, vol. 330, col. 113.

21. *Dáil Debates*, 1 December 1926, vol. 17, cols 418–19.

22. For a discussion, see Gallagher, 1996.

8
CONCLUSION: A CASE FOR INSTITUTIONAL REFORM?

In launching a 'decade of centenaries' that began in 2012, the Irish government announced its commitment to commemorating a sequence of early twentieth-century events that left their mark on modern Ireland. These ranged from the Ulster Covenant and the Home Rule Bill of 1912 to the Easter Rising and the Battle of the Somme in 1916; and the terminal date implied that commemoration would extend ultimately to the creation of an independent Irish state in 1922.[1] In 2022, then, 'official Ireland' will look back at 1922, the year of Ireland's first constitution, of the creation of a new British dominion, the Irish Free State, and, indeed, of the start of a bitter civil war. From the vantage point of the early 2010s it is tempting to ask what 'official Ireland' itself will look like in 2022. This is not simply because such forecasting is interesting, but because it is centrally relevant to the theme of this book: the issue of constitutional and institutional reform in the mid-2010s.

Some may argue that undertaking institutional reform at this point amounts to closing the stable door after the horse has bolted. It is true that reform of the kind that has been discussed so vigorously in Ireland since 2008 will not reverse the consequences of the flawed decisions that caused grievous economic, social and political problems in the first place, though it may help to mitigate their effects. But if the challenge is to deliver wise, effective and far-seeing government to meet future challenges, it is important to try to foresee what these challenges might be, and to ask what kind of political system might best respond to them.

This chapter therefore engages in some crystal-ball gazing, speculating on the nature of Irish politics and society in the state's centenary year of 2022. The first broad question relates to the patterns of demographic, social and economic change that are already under way, and the kind of society that is likely to be their outcome. But important developments in the international standing of the state (specifically, its position within the EU) are also to be expected—developments whose full implications are not yet clear, but which are likely to have a bearing on the options that will be open to decision makers in the years to come. These changes have implications for any agenda of constitutional and institutional reform, an agenda whose content is assessed from a normative and from an analytical perspective in the concluding section of this chapter.

IRISH SOCIETY IN 2022

While projection and forecasting—driven by the need to anticipate future societal needs—form an integral part of the work of economists, demographers and other social analysts, it is notoriously difficult to go further than broad projections based on risky assumptions about underlying determinants. Not only do these assumptions become less reliable the more distant the future point that is being targeted, but it is unlikely that appropriate account will be taken of all causal factors. Subject to this, however, and to the possibility of entirely unpredictable developments that will throw projections utterly off course, it is possible to speculate about the future shape of Irish society: about population size and structure, about social and cultural life, and about developments in the area of the economy.

Challenging though it is to forecast patterns of demographic change, conditional projections of population growth are regularly undertaken. The periodic post-census projections of the Central Statistics Office are an important example. Using data from the 2011 census and other sources, the most recent of these suggested that overall population will increase from 4.6 million in 2011 to somewhere between 4.9 and 5.3 million by 2026, and to the 5.0–6.7 million range by 2046 (Ireland, 2013: 27, 32). But this big expansion will be unevenly distributed across age groups: it is predicted that the current relatively sustainable dependency ratio of 49 (the number of children aged under 15, plus the number of adults aged 65 or more, as a percentage of the population aged 15–64) will increase to at least 56 by 2026 and to at least 68 by 2046 (but it may increase to as much as 61 by 2026 and to 82 by 2046). Even the lower of these scenarios will place a big strain on the working population, which will be required to support a huge expansion in school places, with the primary school population set to increase by at least 88,000 (and possibly as much as 100,000) by 2021, and a big increase in the population of secondary school age, peaking in the years 2021–26 (Ireland, 2013: 28). On top of this, though, there will be a growing problem of retirement welfare and elder care, as the population aged 65 or more is projected to increase from half a million in 2011 to more than 850,000 in 2026, and to 1.4 million by 2046.

There is a positive side to this dynamic population movement, which so strongly reverses the pattern that was to develop during and after the Irish famine of 1845–49: it is associated with advances in living conditions and in medical care that have seen life expectancy increase from 57.4 for males in 1926 to 77.9 in 2010, projected to increase to 85.1 by 2046; the corresponding figures for women are 57.0 (1926), 82.7 (2010) and 88.5 (2046) (Ireland, 2013: 13–15). But, while it will impose a huge additional burden on the state, changing population structure will also present an important challenge for social integration, and require thoughtful policy making. Allowing for continuing immigration, the large foreign-born population and their immediate descendants are likely to expand more rapidly in Ireland than in most other EU states, to comprise 25–30% of the population by 2021, 33–38% by 2041 and 36–45% of the population by 2061, depending on the model used as basis for the projection (Lanzieri, 2011).

Chapter 2 discussed two further changes that were characteristic of the twentieth century, each of which had implications for traditional conceptions of Irish identity: decline in church-going rates among Catholics, and the further erosion of the Irish language. The data on the age profile of those attending church discussed in Chapter 2 suggest that this decline is set to continue. This appears to be associated with a drop-off in other religious practices, in traditional Catholic religious beliefs, and in the authority of the Catholic church. Thus, a survey of religious attitudes and behaviour in 2007–08, as well as recording a drop in weekly church attendance to 42%, from 79% 19 years earlier (in 1988–89, when a comparable survey was undertaken), noted a smaller but still significant decline in personal prayer (down from 90% praying at least weekly in 1988–89, to 72%) and in perceived 'closeness to God' (down from 93 to 86%), but a critical drop from 80 to 27% in those going to the sacrament of confession several times a year or more often (Mac Gréil and Rhatigan, 2009). These changes suggest a qualitative adjustment in the character of religious belief and commitment, and this has been associated with a dramatic decline in the number of clergy, with a steep fall especially after 1990 (Conway, 2011). The dwindling numbers preparing for the priesthood and the progressive ageing of serving priests mean that, unless current trends change, the 1,965 priests working in Irish parishes in 2012 will have dropped to 450 by 2042 (Kelly, 2012). This will leave the church with no choice other than combining parishes and increasingly involving nuns (whose numbers are also diminishing rapidly) and the laity, though the parishioners who seek to avail of church services have also been declining in numbers. As it has been put, 'presbyteries are not as full as before but neither are churches' (Conway, 2010), suggesting a vicious circle of decline. The crisis is vividly summarised in the statistical picture of diocesan administration:

> By 2020, the number of priests in Dublin will drop by about 36%, from 456 to about 294 … Meanwhile priests' income in Dublin has fallen 15% in the past two years to an average of €24,079 per annum, as weekly Mass attendance hovers at 14%. What has been happening in Dublin is reflected in each of the 26 Catholic dioceses on the island. In each, too, as the priests get older and their income drops, their workload increases. This is due to parish clustering, whereby priests who would normally serve in just one parish must now also take care of the needs of the faithful in nearby parishes as well. (McGarry, 2012)

Chapter 2 also discussed the steady decline in everyday use of Irish. What does the future have in store here? Formally, the state remains committed to promoting more extensive colloquial use of the Irish language, and to providing services through its medium (Ireland, 2010: 3). But the position of Irish as a living language continues to deteriorate. An official commission of enquiry noted in 2002 that, while nominally 74% of residents in Gaeltacht areas had some knowledge of Irish, only 26% of families with school children in those areas were receiving a state grant that recognised their fluent use of Irish. The report went on:

> Irish in the Gaeltacht is facing a crisis, due to both internal and external factors. The external threat to the Gaeltacht community comes from State and private sector organisations which give no linguistic recognition to this distinct community. Irish is also threatened from within, as its own community loses confidence in its status as a distinct language community, a community under pressure from a major world language. (Coimisiún na Gaeltachta, 2002: 9)

The commission attributed the decline of the language in part to 'hypocrisy and insincerity at State level', reflected in the continued provision of state services to Irish speakers in English only, resulting in cynicism in the

Gaeltacht (Coimisiún na Gaeltachta, 2002: 19). A more recent comprehensive report on the sociolinguistic status of Irish (using census, survey and other data) described the critical erosion of the language as a consequence of suburbanisation and speculative building that reinforced the process of Anglicisation. As the authors described the process:

> Language shift away from Irish is being driven by social dynamics. Gaeltacht communities are linked into regional, national and inter-national networks which gradually influence the linguistic composition of the Gaeltacht community. Additionally, the linguistic composition of some Gaeltacht areas has been transformed due to their location: their physical proximity to developing urban centres makes them attractive for suburban settlement. Other Gaeltacht areas are coming under pressure from demographic factors of a similar type due to their attractiveness as tourist destinations, with non-Irish language speakers taking up temporary or permanent residence in these areas of great natural beauty. (Ó Giollagáin et al., 2007: 10)

The education system, ironically, has assisted the Anglicisation process: 46% of school-going children in the Gaeltacht are from English-speaking backgrounds, and their school experience does not succeed in converting them into active speakers of Irish. On the contrary, 'participation of English speakers in the education system in Gaeltacht schools is reinforcing the use of English among young native speakers of Irish' (Ó Giollagáin et al., 2007: 11). The research team found that only 24% of the current Gaeltacht population live in districts where the language is not under immediate threat of extinction as a communal language.[2] These comprise a cluster in Connemara, with almost 11,000 Irish speakers; a small area in Donegal, with almost 4,000; the tip of the Dingle peninsula, with a little more than 1,000; and a tiny pocket in northwest Mayo, with 250 Irish speakers (computed from Ó Giollagáin et al., 2007: 18–23).

Like the demise of other national shibboleths, such as the attainment of Irish unity, it is unlikely that the prospective disappearance of Irish as a communal language in the Gaeltacht will rock citizens' complacency to the core. For some, these issues are a matter of indifference. For those who regard them as 'core values', the option of denial is available: after all, Ireland might still some day be united, and it is still possible to argue that the Irish language will survive. But for a state that has invested so much of its self-defined identity in the Irish language—giving it superior constitutional and legal status to English, securing recognition for it at EU level and investing heavily for almost a century in teaching it in English-speaking Ireland—the critical state of the Gaeltacht means that a decision point has been reached, requiring a rethink of policy in the educational and other sectors.

It is likely that Ireland will have more material problems to contend with. Like other western societies, it will have to cope with the effects, so far unpredictable, of global warming. The question of waste disposal and management of the environment will require a degree of long-term planning that has not so far been evident. The state's enthusiastic but belated embrace of motorway construction and *de facto* promotion of road transport have come at a time when oil costs seem set to rise in the medium term, with an OECD report suggesting that the price of crude oil might more than double by 2020 (Fournier et al., 2013). Longer-term security of access to oil is uncertain, and the viability of alternative energy sources is as yet unclear; and careful planning regarding the interdependent areas of food and energy security will be necessary. It is impossible to predict how developments in these areas will evolve, but there can be little doubt that 'worst case' scenarios will make heavy demands on political leaders.

There is one area where we can be sure that big challenges lie ahead, though their precise dimensions and form remain uncertain. The state has incurred a formidable debt as a consequence of the banking collapse, and is struggling with a big structural general government deficit. While growth prospects for 2013 and 2014 are currently reasonable, they depend on the general health of the European economy, whose future is by no means certain (Economic and Social Research Institute, 2013). But the state will face a difficult task in the future in meeting its targets under the EU fiscal compact, which will require it to produce a substantially balanced budget by 2019; on current trends, it is likely to be able to meet its budgetary deficit targets up to 2015, but projection after that is difficult because of a range of longer-term uncertainties (Weymes and Bermingham, 2012). In the light of global economic uncertainties, the unpredictability of future developments at EU level, the unresolved challenge of the Irish government's structural deficit, the unknown implications of the crisis in personal and mortgage debt for Irish banks, and potential losses from the programme of the National Assets Management Agency, the state faces a difficult future.

'So what?', it might be asked—what is the significance of these changes for political institutional planning? There appear to be implications in three areas: community, identity and economy. The decline in traditional religious belief and practice, the erosion of the moral leadership role of Catholic bishops and priests and the marginalisation of parochial clergy as local community leaders (due to their declining numbers and growing ecclesiastical burdens) will leave an important gap precisely as the need for moral leadership and for agencies to assist in social integration is increasing due to the growing diversity of the population and other social challenges. The falling numbers of nuns and priests have left a gap in service provision in healthcare and education, presenting not just a challenge for the state but also an opportunity for private sector providers whose ultimate goals focus on profit rather than public service. The very dominance of the Catholic church in the past, and its role for so many as the sole source of moral teaching, have left a costly legacy, with big implications for public attitudes and behaviour in a context where past clerical hegemony did nothing to promote the emergence of a secular moral system. God may have been replaced by Caesar in Irish public life, but Caesar has not had time to develop an ethical position.

Related to this, the public sense of Irish identity is likely to come under challenge. Defined in the past by memory of a once widely used ancestral language and by reference to a tradition of historical distinctiveness (with rejection of English political, economic and cultural influence at its core), it will be necessary to redefine this to take account of the decline of the Irish language, of growing diversity and of renewed emphasis on the English or British heritage. The 'decade of centenaries' referred to above represents an important strand in this redefinition, as it tries to strike a delicate balance between events that mark milestones in the establishment of the state and episodes that conflict with the nationalist narrative. But the most obvious challenge of all will be in the economic area: how to discharge the enormous debts so far incurred by the state, and how to cope with those yet to come. In all of this, the need for a far-seeing political leadership in obvious, though it may well be the case that the political leaders dealing with many of these problems will be drawn from an unexpected source.

THE IRISH POLITY IN 2022

Political projections are scarcely easier than social or economic ones.[3] It would have been extremely difficult, on 6 December 1922, the date on which the constitution of the Irish Free State came into force, to have predicted what the same state would look like 10 years later. With de Valera and his anti-Treaty republicans marginalised electorally and on the pathway towards military defeat, the Lord Lieutenant replaced by a Governor-General appointed by the King, and new state institutions defining Ireland as a component of the British Commonwealth, it looked as if the struggle for Irish independence had finally ended in a stable compromise. By December 1932, however, de Valera was head of government, the Governor-General had abandoned the Viceregal Lodge and disappeared from public life, and the Commonwealth itself had become a looser alliance of near-independent states. Had this been predictable in 1922, the civil war might never have taken place.

One of the most central determining factors in the Irish political future is the relationship with the EU. The steady absorption of core member states in a quasi-federal political entity has been one of the more remarkable aspects of western Europe's geopolitical development, as pointed out in Chapter 2. Even more remarkably, this development has traditionally been projected as *unremarkable*, natural, inevitable and positive—as something to be so taken for granted that the ultimate goal of the 'European project' needs neither to be defined nor to be discussed, and it is opposition to this process, rather than support for it, that needs to be explained. Yet, given the link between nationalism and state building, and the powerful nationalist tradition in certain EU member states, not least Ireland, it would not be at all surprising to find a tension between the pursuit of European integration and the survival of traditional loyalties to the nation-state. Signs of any such tensions are, however, not very obvious, and efforts to construct a federal-type European entity seem capable of coexisting with deeply embedded, sub-federal nationalist values—though the ultimate success of these efforts is by no means certain. The rest of this section considers first the profile of Irish attitudes to the EU, and then the changing character of the EU itself.

What conclusions may we draw about the nature of Irish attitudes to the European integration process? Brian Girvin (2010), having considered a range of opinion poll and other evidence, concluded that there was little evidence that Irish national identity was being seriously challenged by any kind of emerging European identity. Indeed, it continues to be the case that most people in Ireland regard themselves as exclusively or primarily 'Irish' rather than 'European', a pattern that is replicated in other west European states. Opinion poll data show that when asked to place themselves in four categories describing their sense of identity 'in the near future' (Irish only, Irish and European, European and Irish, European only), big majorities opt for the first two categories, outnumbering the two 'European' categories by at least 10 to one over the period 1992–2010, with a similar outcome in the three other countries with which Ireland was compared in Chapter 2—the UK, Denmark and Portugal.[4]

Table 8.1: Perceptions of EU and support for policy areas, Ireland and selected European countries, 2012

Issue area	Ireland	UK	Denmark	Portugal	EU
General attitude					
Trust in EU	−24	−59	3	−32	−29
Feel attached to EU	−9	−45	−13	−15	−6
Positive image of EU	10	−29	15	−11	3
Agree unification should be speeded up	41	16	36	63	44
Support for:					
EU as monetary union	66	−64	−41	25	12
Common EU foreign policy	38	−12	−7	36	33
Common EU defence and security policy	9	15	36	46	51
EU as 'federation of nation-states'	−3	−30	−58	15	9

Note: The questions were: 'For each of the following institutions, please tell me if you tend to trust it or tend not to trust it: the European Union' (the table reports the proportion trusting minus the proportion not trusting); 'Please tell me how attached you feel to the European Union' (the table reports the proportions very attached plus fairly attached, minus the proportions not very attached plus not attached at all); 'In general, does the European Union conjure up for you a very positive, fairly positive, neutral, fairly negative or very negative image?' (the table reports all positive minus all negative responses); 'Which [of these cards] corresponds best to what you would like?', with seven cards referring to the pace of European unification, ranging from 1 ('standing still') to 7 ('running as fast as possible') (the table reports the difference between the sum of the three 'fastest' positions and the sum of the three 'slowest' positions); 'What is your opinion on each of the following statements? Please tell me for each statement, whether you are for it or against it', with the following issue areas: 'A European economic and monetary union with one single currency, the euro', 'A common foreign policy of the 27 Member States of the EU', and 'A common defence and security policy among EU Member States' (the table reports positive responses minus negative ones); and 'Please tell me to what extent you agree or disagree with each of the following statements: the EU should develop further into a federation of Nation-States' (the table reports those agreeing minus those disagreeing). The last column refers to the weighted average for all EU member states. *Source: Eurobarometer* no. 77, May 2012 for the first seven areas; no. 78, November 2012 for the last.

Public perceptions of the EU itself, in Ireland and in other member states, tend to be rather mixed. Table 8.1 compares the position in this respect in 2012 with the three comparator countries, and also with the EU overall. General levels of trust in the EU are low—indeed, negative, in that more people mistrust the EU than trust it on average throughout the member states. The position is similar as regards feelings of attachment towards the EU. Nevertheless, the overall image of the EU is positive, and the Irish are reportedly enthusiastic about speeding up the unification process (according to the 'Eurodynamometer' which seeks to measure this). When it comes to specific institutional changes within the EU, however, an uneven picture emerges. Notwithstanding recent economic problems, Ireland, like other eurozone countries, remains strongly committed to the euro, in sharp contrast, unsurprisingly, to the UK and Denmark. Irish public opinion is in general favourable towards a common EU foreign policy. On common defence policy, Denmark and Portugal are keen for an EU role, while the UK is reserved, and Irish popular reservations are greatest of all (though in 2012 more people favoured an EU defence role than were opposed to it). The most important question, however, concerns the possible establishment of a federal Europe. Here, once again, the UK and Denmark stand out as sceptical, but even in Ireland more respondents were opposed to this idea than were in its favour.

Figure 8.1: Perceptions that EU membership is a good thing, Ireland, UK and EU, 1973–2011

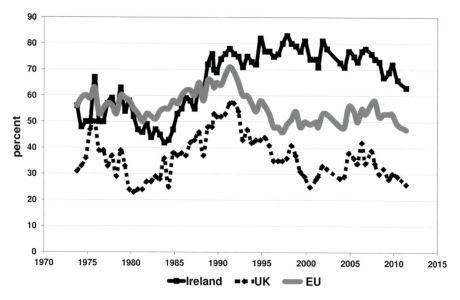

Note: The lines report those responding 'a good thing' to the following question: 'Generally speaking, do you think that Ireland's membership of the EU is a good thing, a bad thing, or neither good nor bad?', and corresponding questions in the UK and in other EU member states. *Source: Eurobarometer* reports 1–75, 1974–2011 (including results of European Commission poll, September 1973).

These data are not altogether consistent with each other, or with qualitative assessments of public opinion. It is known, for example, that a strong strand of public opinion in the UK favours withdrawal from the EU, and that this strand appeared stronger than that supporting EU membership in 2011–12; this seems incompatible with the apparently strong support in the UK in 2012 for speeding up the process of European unification.[5] Similarly, there has been a long-standing public attachment in Ireland to neutrality. Thus, in 1991, when asked 'should Ireland drop its neutrality, to take part in a common defence policy in the EC (European Community)?', 25% were in favour and 64% against.[6] A survey in 2008, shortly after the Irish electorate voted against the Lisbon treaty, showed strong levels of support for Irish neutrality, a feature associated with opposition to the treaty (Sinnott et al., 2009: 17–18). Yet levels of Irish acceptance of a common EU defence and security policy appear to be at variance with this, suggesting problems of measurement and, perhaps, conflicts of definition.

With a view to illustrating the position over time, Figure 8.1 takes a single, straightforward, clear question that has been asked since the early 1970s— perception that Irish membership of the EU is a good thing—and reports responses from 1973 to 2011, comparing the Irish responses with those in the UK, and in the EU overall. Until the mid-1980s, the Irish position was close to the EU average in the region of 50–60%, with the UK well below this. Between then and the end of the century Irish support rose, while that in the EU overall fell; a belated Irish decline began around the turn of the century, with a drop from about 80% to a little more than 60%. This figure is still comfortably above the EU average, but appears to point to a drop in support at the same time as the pace of EU integration is quickening.

Rather than simply relying on survey data, though, some of the dilemmas facing Irish policy makers are illustrated in Table 8.2. This reports the results of referenda on EU-related matters over the period 1972–2012. The Irish votes against the Nice Treaty (2001) and against the Lisbon Treaty (2008) may have shocked the Irish political establishment, which strongly endorsed the pro-integration position at each referendum, but, given the fact that Ireland is one of the EU's more enthusiastic members, they also suggest that many more countries would have rejected these two treaties had they been given a chance to vote on them (just as French and Dutch voters had rejected the European constitutional treaty in 2005). What is remarkable about the referenda that were carried is not the size of the victory margin, but the reality that so substantial a portion of the electorate was prepared to disregard the advice of the country's political, business and trade union leadership.

Table 8.2: Results of referenda on EU-related matters, Ireland, 1972–2012

Date	Issue	Yes	No	Turnout
10 May 1972	Membership of EC	83.1	16.9	70.9
26 May 1987	Single European Act	69.9	30.1	43.9
18 June 1992	Maastricht Treaty	69.1	30.9	57.3
22 May 1998	Amsterdam Treaty	61.7	38.3	56.2
7 June 2001	Nice Treaty	46.1	53.9	34.8
20 October 2002	Nice Treaty	62.9	37.1	48.5
12 June 2008	Lisbon Treaty	46.6	53.4	53.1
2 October 2009	Lisbon Treaty	67.1	32.9	59.0
31 May 2012	EU Fiscal Compact	60.3	39.7	50.6

Source: Ireland, 2012c.

Irish voters, then, have endorsed successive treaties that have deepened the level of European integration, even if on each occasion they were encouraged to believe that they had little choice. But the implications of these decisions have not always been clear. The EU fiscal compact, for instance, may be seen as an integral component in a plan to restore Ireland to economic health, but the extent to which it will restrict the options available to Irish policy makers in the future has been subject to little debate, notwithstanding the enormous implications of this instrument for autonomous Irish policy making in future. The government may have inserted a commitment in the constitution to remain outside a common EU defence structure (as part of the amendment approved by the second referendum on the Lisbon Treaty in 2009), but even before this the Irish defence forces had contributed contingents to EU- or NATO-led operations in Bosnia and Herzegovina (1997), Kosovo (1999) and Afghanistan (2001). While an assessment of the Irish military contribution to the EU before the adoption of the Lisbon Treaty suggested that this was 'likely to remain limited' (Laffan and O'Mahony, 2008: 195–6), subsequent developments implied a much higher level of Irish government commitment. Ben Tonra (2012: 232) concluded in 2012 that Ireland's engagement with the European Security and Defence Policy was 'wholehearted and wideranging', and that, in relation to the size and extent of its resources, Ireland was 'a well above-average contributor to EU military operations'.

The tension between elite willingness to engage in close military cooperation under the umbrella of the EU and continuing public attachment to the notion of military neutrality has been obscured by the difficulty in defining the word itself. Rather than seeking to meet the comprehensive criteria of the Hague Convention (1907), successive Irish governments reduced 'neutrality' to the single criterion of non-membership of a military alliance, a condition sufficiently undemanding to make it difficult for critics to argue that Ireland was in breach of the neutrality principle (Tonra, 2012: 224). In any event, there are real difficulties in defining the term 'neutrality' (Agius and Devine, 2011; Devine, 2011), and these have been used by critics to undermine Ireland's record (Devine, 2006), implying that since neutrality has already been lost, or never existed, there is little to debate.

More broadly, assessments of Ireland's role in the EU have increasingly emphasised the extent to which it is hard-headed and instrumental rather than rosy-eyed and principle-based. It is true that official discourse appears to rest on a self-image as a 'model member-state', whose sovereignty and national identity were not threatened by EU membership (Hayward, 2009: 123–39; 2010: 114). Indeed, the outcome of the second Lisbon referendum in 2009 has been interpreted as indicating that Ireland had returned to the point from which it had set out 50 years earlier, when it first sought membership of the European Communities: 'the simple calculation that it is better to be part of Europe than risk being cast adrift from it' (Hayward, 2012: 150).

Pragmatic public attitudes of this kind sit uneasily alongside ambitious elite efforts at the construction of a European federal entity (though these ambitions are not necessarily shared by all who participate in and contribute to these efforts). Even if political leaders vary in their vision of the end-point in the integration process, it makes sense for them to refer to a 'pooling' of sovereignty by member-states rather than a 'transfer' of sovereignty to Brussels, if sovereignty is seen as a matter of degree rather than having a binary quality; these are just different perspectives on the same process, but the former term sounds more reassuring and less threatening than the latter. It also makes sense for the same political leaders to dismiss the Westphalian model of the state as obsolete, since, in the first place, this has for long been true from the standpoint of *Realpolitik* if not from that of international law, and in any case the EU project may be seen in one important respect precisely as an attempt to reverse the Westphalian settlement: to replace a network of sovereign states by an overarching multinational structure resembling a modern, more integrated and democratised version of the Holy Roman Empire.[7]

The description of the emerging EU in public opinion surveys as a 'federation of nation-states' is paradoxical and contradictory. Such a possible future structure could more accurately be described as a simple federation: an entity where many aspects of public policy are conducted at the level of the EU's current 28 member-states, but where responsibility for foreign affairs and defence (areas in which all federations exercise control) lies in Brussels. The notion of a federal Europe implies, at a minimum, a single diplomatic service (with existing 'national' diplomatic services being in part absorbed by this, but mainly converted into networks of trade and cultural missions) and a unified military force (perhaps initially represented by a single command structure overlaying notionally separate 'national' military forces). These inevitable implications of the most plausible interpretation of the 'European project' tend not to arise in Irish political debate, perhaps because, as elsewhere in the EU, some political leaders are conscious of the absence of public support for this, while others are reluctant to accept the implications of the federal scenario. One of the rare exceptions is former European Parliament President Pat Cox, who acknowledged that the issue would ultimately have to be tackled, but that this would be difficult: 'the F-word, as they call it in Britain, probably is a sensitive one here in Ireland. I think that will be a difficult debate because the recent episodes—the difficulties about debt, about who pays what—have woken people up: they are a lot more attuned and sensitive to what is or is not happening in the EU, to who makes and who takes policy' (Cox, 2013: 54).

The evolution of Ireland's relationship with the EU has already had an enormous impact on the character of the Irish state, and on its policy process (Laffan and Tonra, 2010). Quite apart from its effects in such visible domains as foreign policy, it has transformed agricultural policy and imposed limits on the Irish government's freedom of action in such areas as environmental protection, not a traditional priority of Irish policy makers. It has had far-reaching and decisive influence on economic policy, pushing Ireland, and other member-states, in the direction of dismantling the state sector and opening areas of public service provision to competition from private, profit-seeking enterprises (Storey, 2013).

The EU's future evolution is likely to raise fundamental issues for the Irish political elite over the coming decade. It is of course possible that the experiment in European integration will falter or even fail, placing fundamental responsibilities back on the shoulders of Irish politicians. But if the integration process continues in the direction of federal union, there may come a point where political leaders in Ireland, as elsewhere, will be forced to acknowledge to their people the extent to which political power in key areas has passed out of their hands—or they may choose not to acknowledge the extent of change that has been taking place. This is likely to be associated with difficult tensions and issues of management of expectations; but in a federal Europe the stakes at 'national' level would also be much lower.

TOWARDS 2022: THE PROSPECTS FOR INSTITUTIONAL REFORM

It may seem strange that, in looking at the prospective shape of the Irish polity in 2022 in the previous section, little reference was made to the singular problems of the Irish state and to its domestic politics. This was designed to highlight the reality that the context within which the Irish political elite will be called on to make decisions for the future of their country is likely to be fundamentally different from what it was in the 1970s—and, indeed, from what it is still imagined to be today. The stakes, in other words, are likely to be lower than if Irish politicians had fuller control over the future of the state (though Ireland's formal constitutional sovereignty, like that of other small states, was never reflected in the real political world). Nevertheless, it is important to explore what measures might best help to enhance decision-making processes, since it will continue to be the case that decisions made in Dublin will have a huge impact on people's everyday lives, and, in any case, we cannot be at all certain of the shape that the EU may take in the future.

What structures might best serve the state, in other words, in relation to the long-term challenges presented in Chapter 2 and discussed further in this chapter? The challenges include many arising from Ireland's economic difficulties: dealing with the multi-faceted after-effects of a catastrophic boom–bust cycle and preventing the recurrence of anything comparable to this; rectifying the related problems of unemployment, emigration and inequality; and restructuring the health, welfare and educational systems. But they also extend to the social and political areas: integrating or accommodating minorities of various kinds in an increasingly diverse society, coping with the legacy of the erosion of traditional institutions such as the Catholic church and the marginalisation of such symbolically important communities as native speakers of Irish, managing Ireland's relationship with the EU, and responding to increased citizen alienation from the political process.

This book has discussed five representative areas in which reform might be considered—areas selected not because they are outstanding examples of the potential for reform, but because they illustrate different aspects of the reform process and highlight its limitations. The areas considered in Chapters 3–7, and the broad conclusions drawn in respect of each, were as follows.

- **The office of President**. Before Mary Robinson asserted a more independent role for the President in 1990, the Irish presidency was widely considered to be politically irrelevant. Since then, incumbents have demonstrated the extent to which the President can play a significant public role, by exercising vigilance in those areas in which an independent function is given by the constitution, by making public statements and gestures on issues of broad concern, and by acting as a unifying and representative symbol. These changes have undermined earlier calls for the office to be abolished, and the debate on reform of the presidency has confined itself to minor matters, such as qualifying age, term of office, and system of nomination.

- **The composition of the Seanad**. While the notion of a vocational second chamber had its defenders in the past, there appears now to be a consensus that if a second chamber is to survive at all, its composition needs to be amended. As in other bicameral systems in unitary states, though, it is not easy to devise a legitimate system of representation that stops short of rivalling the moral authority of the Dáil. If it is not elected in the same democratic way as the Dáil, how should it be composed? No alternative system of representation proposed so far has drawn wide support. Any arrangement designed to be 'non-political' will be unrealistic, unless the Seanad is altogether shorn of power. Perhaps in part because of these dilemmas, the option of simply abolishing the second chamber has commended itself to the Government.

- **The Dáil electoral system**. Early critics of proportional represen-tation argued, as in 1959 and 1966, that it should be replaced by the plurality system, as it is too representative: it allows smaller parties a more or less proportional presence in the Dáil, and deprives larger parties of the 'bonus' seats needed to form a single-party government. More recent critics have also argued that it is too representative, but now because the single transferable vote form makes deputies too dependent on their voters, leaving them with heavy constituency workloads that distract them from the business of government; list systems would, it is argued, prevent this, though many critics prefer a hybrid system that combines the list system with deputies elected from single-member districts. The comparative literature on the impact of the electoral system on constituency workloads is, however, inconclusive, and alternative electoral systems would have certain unexpected political consequences in Ireland, suggesting a need for caution in reform plans.

- **Constituency boundaries for Dáil elections.** As in the case of the electoral formula, the manner in which constituency boundaries are drawn has a big impact on the fortunes of individual deputies. The unintended consequences of a High Court case in 1961—designed to proof the boundary revision system against political abuse— ironically opened the system up to alleged gerrymandering on a large scale. The introduction of an independent boundary commission in 1980 ended this, but micro-management of boundaries to a degree that is foreign to proportional representation systems continued. There is, however, limited support for the most obvious solution: to leave constituency boundaries fixed and substantially coinciding with those of administrative areas, while periodically reallocating seats to them on the basis of an automatic formula after each census.
- **The selection of government ministers.** The idea of allowing the appointment as ministers of outside 'experts' who are not themselves parliamentarians has been discussed in recent inquiries into the constitution, but has attracted little support. The constitution currently allows for the appointment of up to two ministers from the Seanad, but this has rarely been availed of. A shift to the normal European system (which allows non-parliamentarians to be appointed, and in some cases prohibits dual membership of parliament and government) would greatly increase the size of the pool of those eligible for ministerial posts and would relieve a great deal of the burden on the Dáil, allowing it to function more effectively; but it would be unlikely to attract political support from those who would see themselves as potential victims of any experiment of this kind—serving Dáil deputies.

It is possible to forecast, with some certainty, what some key features of the Irish constitution would look like if a constitution were to be drawn up afresh in the early years of the twenty-first century, based on other European constitutions but removed from local political cultural bias. Such a constitution would provide for a President as head of state; the President would be elected by the two-ballot system, from among candidates nominated by parliamentarians, registered parties, or a certain minimum number of voters; and he or she would have limited powers, in general subject to government veto, though with a role in the prime ministerial selection process, and with the right to speak and travel freely. As a unitary state (though with a much larger number of local councils than at present),

Ireland would not have a senate or second chamber. Dáil deputies would be elected by means of the list system of proportional representation, with provision for personal voting within lists; but personal votes would have little impact by comparison with rank on the party list. Constituency boundaries would be fixed, and would in general coincide with those of counties; after each census, the director of the Central Statistics Office would inform a senior state officer (such as the clerk of the Dáil, or even the President) of the new allocation of deputies to constituencies on the basis of whatever formula was provided for in legislation, and this would be rubber-stamped. Ministers would be collectively answerable to the Dáil, but the Taoiseach would not be required to appoint Dáil deputies (and there would be pressure to abolish the dual mandate, so that any TD appointed a minister would have to resign his or her Dáil seat, at least for the duration of term of ministerial office).

But we are not starting from a blank sheet, and the impact of political culture is profound. Recommendations to date on constitutional reform have been very modest, with the Committee on the Constitution (1967), the Constitution Review Group (1996) and the subsequent Oireachtas joint committees indicating broad support for existing provisions. The Convention on the Constitution was given a restricted agenda, and the Government's plan to abolish the Seanad has been by far the most radical proposal to date. Indeed, the implications of the considerations presented in this book for constitutional reform are rather conservative, and not far from the thrust of the several reviews mentioned above. There appears to be little need to redefine the office of President; the electoral system is not in crying need of overhaul; and the system for constituency boundary revision could be amended, arguably, without constitutional change. This leaves the Seanad and the ministerial recruitment process as areas where constitutional amendment is important. Indeed, these two areas might be linked. It could be argued that if the Seanad is to be abolished, then the constitution should also be amended to allow for the appointment of ministers who are not TDs—or even to prohibit the dual mandate, thus freeing up Dáil deputies to concentrate on matters of legislation and policy. Indeed, if the services of 60 senators are abruptly terminated, the Dáil will need all available resources, and prohibiting a dual ministerial–deputy mandate would make sense. Alternatively, if the Seanad were to be reformed rather than abolished, there would still be a case for ending the *de facto* requirement that all ministers be TDs.

There is certainly a strong argument for amending the constitution to remove glaring conflicts between the Irish and English versions—conflicts whose significance has been substantially overlooked. Article 25.4.4 of the constitution provides that in cases of conflict between the English and Irish versions of the constitution, the Irish version shall take precedence. This is of central importance because of the extent to which, as is normal in the relationship between languages, exact translation from one to the other is not possible. Thus, for example, in the two articles of the constitution dealing with the office of President alone (articles 12 and 13), no fewer than 149 discrepancies between the two versions of the constitution have been identified, and two of these are substantial.[8] First, the English version identifies 34 as the age at which citizens become eligible to stand as candidates, whereas the correct (Irish) version specifies 35 as the age. The English version of the constitution also allows an outgoing President to nominate himself or herself as a *candidate* for re-election; but the correct (Irish) version makes it clear that any such nomination is to the *presidency*, not to candidacy for the presidency, ruling out the prospect of an election should a President decide to self-nominate (though this causes other complications).[9] As mentioned in Chapter 6, furthermore, the English text of the constitution requires conformity with a uniform deputy–population ratio from constituency to constituency 'so far as it is practicable', whereas the Irish version specifies the much more demanding condition that this hold true 'so far as it is possible'— a point apparently overlooked by the courts.

Even if the constitution is not amended, though, the shape of Irish political institutions could be altered by law. For example, there is explicit provision for granting the President additional powers by means of ordinary legislation (though powers so granted can only be exercised on the advice of the Government, as the constitution currently stands). The constitution was amended in 1979 to allow university representation in the Seanad to be provided for by ordinary legislation, but no such legislation was ever introduced; and the election of members to the five panels is entirely governed by legislation (though the designation of the panels is fixed by the constitution). While the single transferable vote system is stipulated in the constitution for Dáil elections, existing provisions (relating, for example, to ballot design and structure) may be amended by law. A more conventional system of apportionment of seats to constituencies could be brought about by law, provided it did not, to the satisfaction of the courts, breach the principle of a uniform deputy–population ratio from constituency to constituency.

In most constitutions, however, and especially in older ones, there is an important 'unwritten' component. Custom and usage shapes the way in which the constitutional text is interpreted. Prolonged non-use of a power given to a particular institution may cause it to wither; but opportunistic use of a power *not* given to a particular institution may in the long term cause such use to be seen as legitimate. Thus, the Government traditionally vetted presidential speeches, but this practice was brought to an end by Mary Robinson without any constitutional or legal change. There is nothing to stop the Taoiseach from using his 11 Seanad nominees to represent specific sectors of Irish society, but certain traditions in this area (such as the appointment of at least one senator from Northern Ireland) have lapsed. The Taoiseach might also, as a matter of principle, appoint one minister from the Seanad (a tradition initiated by de Valera in 1932), but this failed to become a feature of political life under the 1937 constitution. While it is possible to make some adjustments to Irish political institutions without formal constitutional change, then, such adjustments tend to be marginal and not necessarily enduring.

CONCLUSION

This book has presented what can only be described as a lukewarm case for constitutional reform. Part of this caution arises from the difficulty that is encountered in predicting future needs, the future status of the state, and the future shape of the EU. It is difficult to predict Ireland's future economic performance, to be certain that the euro will survive, and to be confident that Ireland will continue to form part of the eurozone. This will be determined mainly by developments within the eurozone itself, but the UK's relationship with Europe will continue to be a major influence in this respect. The future of the euro will of course also have big implications for the European federal process. In important respects, European monetary union resembled an each-way bet. If the euro scheme had worked with minor or even with major wrinkles, it would create favourable conditions for further political union; but if the euro scheme were to run into such serious trouble that only radical integration could save it, then political union would be presented as necessary. Ironically, then, the divisions and difficulties provoked by the euro have become the main drivers of further economic and political integration. These processes have, in turn, lifted much of the decision-making burden off the Irish state, lowering the stakes in domestic politics.

But there is a second reason for caution in advocating constitutional reform. It is very tempting to blame 'the system', or underlying structures, for defects that are more properly attributable to individuals, or to human agency. Campaigns for constitutional reform may end up not only in failing to tackle real issues, but in distracting attention from them. In large measure,

Ireland's problems may be laid at the door of short-sighted policy makers, whether in government or in the civil service. Reforming political structures will have at most a limited impact on underlying political cultural values, the transformation of which constitutes a much bigger challenge. However, the argument that far-reaching constitutional and institutional reform is unnecessary, and unlikely in any event to resolve problems that are primarily cultural, not institutional, is not an argument for constitutional stasis. Instead, a case can be made for reform in certain sectors that is likely to have a positive impact.

The effect of such reform will probably be minimal unless the more profound challenge of Ireland's unusual mass and elite political culture is recognised. Changing this culture is a much more difficult and longer-term political project, with bigger implications for educational policy (including the university curriculum) than for constitutional–legal experimentation, and is not the subject of this book; but it is important to acknowledge its underlying importance. As Robert Putnam (1993: 17) put it, citing the historical French and Italian experience, 'two centuries of constitution-writing around the world warn us ... that designers of new institutions are often writing on water. Institutional reform does not always alter fundamental patterns of politics.' While noting the importance of political institutions, then, in the management of crisis and change, we need to be aware of its limits: however wisely designed the structure, it will still be operated by humans.

NOTES

1. See the official website, www.decadeofcentenaries.com, which lists the early events being marked and offers further details.
2. The research group divided the Gaeltacht into three categories. Category A districts were defined as those where more than 67% of the total population are daily speakers of Irish, and 'exhibit stable levels of Irish language use except in the language behaviour patterns of the younger age groups'. In category B are districts where 44–66% of the total population are daily speakers of Irish, but 'the use of Irish has declined as a communal language in the area and its use among young people occurs predominantly in an educational context'. In category C are districts where less than 44% of the total population are daily speakers of Irish, with weak communal use of the language (Ó Giollagáin et al., 2007: 13). As well as the 24% of the Gaeltacht population in category A districts, 9% were in category B and 67% in category C districts.

3. But, for an example, see the recent engaging discussion of an article by Patrick Pearse, written in 1906 but imagining an independent, Irish-speaking Ireland in 2006 (Fanning, 2013).

4. In the 1990s, the mean lead of 'primarily Irish' over 'primarily European' identifiers was 84%, rising to 85% in the early 2000s (2000–05) and to 86% in 2010. The corresponding figures for these three periods in the UK were 77%, 85% and 90%; in Denmark 87%, 85% and 90%; in Portugal 86%, 89% and 81%; and in the EU overall 73%, 78% and 77%; computed from *Eurobarometer* 37–73, 1993–2010; see Eurobarometer Interactive Search System, ec.europa.eu/ public_opinion/ cf/index_en.cfm

5. A series of Ipsos-MORI polls over the period 1977–2012 shows supporters of British withdrawal strongly outnumbering supporters of EU membership in the late 1970s and early 1980s, a reversal of this position in the late 1980s and early 1990s, and a smaller lead for the pro-EU group from 1996 to 2007; in 2011 and 2012, however, supporters of withdrawal were once again in the lead (computed from Ipsos-MORI, 2012).

6. MRBI survey for *Irish Times*, January 1991; data available from Michael Marsh's Irish Opinion Poll Archive; see www.tcd.ie/Political_Science/ IOPA

7. Never a systematically organised entity, the Holy Roman Empire was fatally weakened by the Thirty Years War (1618–48) and the Westphalian settlement that brought it to an end, but survived as an alliance of effectively independent states until 1806.

8. See Ó Cearúil, 1999, which deals with the topics covered in this book: the office of President (pp. 115–208), the Seanad (pp. 295–377), the electoral system (pp. 280–2), constituency boundary revision (pp. 271–80) and ministerial appointment (pp. 423–4).

9. The Irish version of the constitution would apparently allow two or more current or former presidents to be nominated to the office (not as candidates for the office) simultaneously. Thus, in 2004, when Mary McAleese nominated herself for a second term, Mary Robinson could also have done so. The constitution (Irish version) provides no mechanism for resolving such a clash. In practice, though, Mary McAleese nominated herself as a *candidate*, and, in the absence of any other candidate, she was declared elected on 1 October 2004 (*Iris Oifigiúil*, 5 October 2004, No. 80: 1035). On the Irish version, see Ó Cearúil, 1999: 138–40.

REFERENCES

Agius, Christine, and Karen Devine (2011) '"Neutrality: a really dead concept?": a reprise', *Cooperation and Conflict* 46 (3): 265–84

Aisin-Gioro, Pu Yi (1989) *From Emperor to Citizen: The Autobiography of Aisin-Gioro Pu Yi.* Beijing: Foreign Languages Press

Akenson, D.H., and J.F. Fallin (1970) 'The Irish civil war and the drafting of the Free State constitution', *Eire–Ireland* (I) 5 (1) pp. 10–26; (II) 5 (2): 42–93; (III) 5 (4): 28–70

Allen, Kieran (2009) *Ireland's Economic Crash: A Radical Agenda for Change.* Dublin: Liffey Press

All-Party Oireachtas Committee on the Constitution (1997a) *First Progress Report.* Pn 3795. Dublin: Stationery Office

All-Party Oireachtas Committee on the Constitution (1997b) *Second Progress Report: Seanad Éireann.* Pn. 3835. Dublin: Stationery Office

All-Party Oireachtas Committee on the Constitution (1998) *Third Progress Report: The President.* Pn. 6250. Dublin: Stationery Office

All-Party Oireachtas Committee on the Constitution (2002) *Seventh Progress Report: Parliament.* Pn. 11281. Dublin: Stationery Office

All-Party Oireachtas Committee on the Constitution (2003) *Eighth Progress Report: Government.* Pn. 12839. Dublin: Stationery Office

Almond, Gabriel A., G. Bingham Powell and Robert J. Mundt (1996) *Comparative Politics: A Theoretical Framework*, 2nd ed. New York: HarperCollins

Ameller, Michel (1966) *Parliaments: A Comparative Study on the Structure and Functioning of Representative Institutions in Fifty-Five Countries*, new ed. London: Cassell, for the Inter-Parliamentary Union

American Political Science Association (1951) 'The reapportionment of congress', *American Political Science Review* 45 (1): 153–7

Archer, Jeffrey, and Graham Maddox (1976) 'The 1975 constitutional crisis in Australia', *Journal of Commonwealth and Comparative Politics* 14 (2): 141–57

Bagehot, Walter (1928 [1872]) *The English Constitution*, 2nd ed. London: Oxford University Press

Baldwin, Nicholas D.J. (2001) 'Concluding observations', *Journal of Legislative Studies* 7 (1): 171–80

Balinksi, Michel L., and H. Peyton Young (2001) *Fair Representation: Meeting the Ideal of One Man, One Vote*. 2nd ed. Washington, DC: Brookings Institution Press

Bar, Antonio (1997) 'Spain', in Jean Blondel and Ferdinand Müller-Rommel, eds, *Cabinets in Western Europe*, 2nd ed. Basingstoke: Macmillan, pp. 116–35

Barry, Frank, ed. (1999) *Understanding Ireland's Economic Growth*. Basingstoke: Macmillan

Barry, Frank (2013) 'Politicians, the bureaucracy and economic policymaking over two crises: the 1950s and today', *Journal of the Statistical and Social Inquiry Society of Ireland* 42, forthcoming

Bendix, Reinhard (1978) *Kings or People: Power and the Mandate to Rule*. Berkeley: University of California Press

Bergman, Torbjörn, Wolfgang C. Müller, Kaare Strøm and Magnus Blomgren (2006) 'Democratic delegation and accountability: cross-national patterns', in Kaare Strøm, Wolfgang C. Müller and Torbjörn Bergman, eds, *Delegation and Accountability in Parliamentary Democracies*. Oxford: Oxford University Press, pp. 109–220

Binchy, Daniel A. (1936) 'Proposals for a new Senate', *Studies* 25 (97): 20–32

Blackburn, Robert (1995) *The Electoral System in Britain*. Basingstoke: Macmillan

Blais, André, Louis Massicotte and Agnieszka Dobrzynska (1997) 'Direct presidential elections: a world summary', *Electoral Studies* 16 (4): 441–55

Bloch, Marc (1973) *The Royal Touch: Sacred Monarchy and Scrofula in England and France*, translated by J.E. Anderson. London: Routledge and Kegan Paul

Blondel, Jean (1973) *Comparative Legislatures*. Englewood Cliffs, NJ: Prentice Hall

Bochel, Hugh, and Andrew Defty (2012) '"A more representative chamber": representation and the House of Lords', *Journal of Legislative Studies* 18 (1): 82–97

Bogdanor, Vernon (1984) *What is Proportional Representation? A Guide to the Issues*. Oxford: Martin Robertson

Borthwick, R.L. (2001) 'Methods of composition of second chambers', *Journal of Legislative Studies* 7 (1): 19–26

Boyle, Richard, and Muiris MacCarthaigh (2011) *Fit for Purpose? Challenges for Irish Public Administration and Priorities for Public Service Reform* (Research Paper no. 4). Dublin: Institute of Public Administration

Bradshaw, Brendan (1973) 'The beginnings of modern Ireland', in Brian Farrell, ed., *The Irish Parliamentary Tradition*. Dublin: Gill and Macmillan, pp. 70–87

Bromage, Arthur W., and Mary C. Bromage (1940) 'The vocational senate in Ireland', *American Political Science Review* 34 (3): 519–38

Bryce, James (1921) *Modern Democracies*, Vol. 2. London: Macmillan

Brynn, Edward (1978) *Crown and Castle: British Rule in Ireland 1800–1830*. Dublin: O'Brien Press

Buckland, Patrick (1972) *Irish Unionism: One: The Anglo-Irish and the New Ireland 1885–1922*. Dublin: Gill and Macmillan

Byrne, Elaine A. (2012) *Political Corruption in Ireland, 1922–2010: A Crooked Harp?* Manchester: Manchester University Press

Cain, Bruce E. (1984) *The Reapportionment Puzzle*. Berkeley: University of California Press

Carstairs, Andrew McLaren (1980) *A Short History of Electoral Systems in Western Europe*. London: George Allen and Unwin

Carty, R.K. (1981) *Party and Parish Pump: Electoral Politics in Ireland*. Waterloo, Canada: Wilfrid Laurier Press

Casey, James (1992) *Constitutional Law in Ireland*, 2nd ed. London: Sweet and Maxwell

Casey, James (2000) *Constitutional Law in Ireland*, 3rd ed. Dublin: Round Hall Sweet and Maxwell

Central Statistics Office (2012) *Residential Property Price Index October 2012*. Dublin: Central Statistics Office

Charlier, Paul (1991) 'La monarchie constitutionnelle de Belgique, la crise d'Avril 1990', *Revue juridique et politique* 45 (1): 34–42

Chryssogonos, Kostas (2007) An introduction to Greek electoral law; available at www.cecl.gr/rigasnetwork/databank/reports/r8/gr_8_chryssogonos.html (18 July 2007)

Chubb, Basil (1954) 'Vocational representation and the Irish Senate', *Political Studies* 2 (2): 97–111

Chubb, Basil (1970) *The Government and Politics of Ireland*. Stanford, CA: Stanford University Press

Chubb, Basil (1974) *Cabinet Government in Ireland*. Dublin: Institute of Public Adminstration

Chubb, Basil (1978) *The Constitution and Constitutional Change in Ireland*, new ed. Dublin: Institute of Public Administration

Chubb, Basil (1991) *The Politics of the Irish Constitution*, new ed. Dublin: Institute of Public Administration

Clinch, J. Peter, Frank Convery and Brendan Walsh (2002) *After the Celtic Tiger: Challenges Ahead*. Dublin: O'Brien Press

Coakley, John (1979) 'Spatial units and the reporting of Irish statistical data: an examination of the evolution of regional divisions', *Administration* 27 (1): 31–55

Coakley, John (1980a) 'Constituency boundary revision and seat redistribution in the Irish parliamentary tradition', *Administration* 28 (3): 291–328

Coakley, John (1980b) 'The Irish Senate election of 1977: voting in a small electorate', *Parliamentary Affairs* 33 (3): 322–31

Coakley, John (1982) 'An election damaging to the presidency', *Irish Times*, 16 November

Coakley, John (1987) 'The Senate elections', in Howard R. Penniman and Brian Farrell, eds, *Ireland at the Polls 1981, 1982, and 1987: A Study of Four General Elections*. Durham, NC: Duke University Press, for the American Enterprise Institute, pp. 195–205

Coakley, John (1990) 'The Senate election', in Michael Gallagher and Richard Sinnott, eds, *How Ireland Voted 1989*. Galway: Centre for the Study of Irish Elections, pp. 148–61

Coakley, John (1993) 'The Senate elections', in Michael Gallagher and Michael Laver, eds, *How Ireland Voted 3: The General Election of 1992*. Dublin: Folens; Limerick: PSAI Press, pp. 135–45

Coakley, John (1997) 'Dvukhpalatnost' i razdelenie vlastei v sovremennykh gosudarstvakh' [Bicameralism and the division of powers in contemporary states], *Polis* 3 (39): 148–168

Coakley, John (1998) 'Úloha hlavy státu v soucasné politice' [The role of the head of state in contemporary politics], *Politologická revue* 4 (1): 26–42

Coakley, John (2005) 'Ireland's unique electoral experiment: the Senate election of 1925', *Irish Political Studies* 20 (3): 231–69

Coakley, John (2007) 'Revising Dáil constituency boundaries: Ireland in comparative perspective', *Administration* 55 (3): 1–29

Coakley, John (2008a) 'Does Ireland need a constituency commission?', *Administration* 55 (4): 77–114

Coakley, John (2008b) 'Electoral district delimitation in Ireland', in Bernard Grofman and Lisa Handley, eds, *Redistricting in Comparative Perspective*. Oxford: Oxford University Press, pp. 155–72

Coakley, John (2010) 'Selecting Irish government ministers: an alternative pathway?', *Administration* 58 (3): 1–26

Coakley, John (2011) 'The last senate election?', in Michael Gallagher and Michael Marsh, eds, *How Ireland Voted, 2011*. Basingstoke: Palgrave Macmillan, pp. 240–63

Coakley, John (2012a) 'An ambiguous office? The position of head of state in the Irish constitution', *Irish Jurist* 48: 43–70

Coakley, John (2012b) 'The prehistory of the Irish presidency', *Irish Political Studies* 27 (4): 539–58

Coakley, John (2012c) *Nationalism, Ethnicity and the State: Making and Breaking Nations*. London: Sage

Coakley, John, and Michael Laver (1997) 'Options for the future of Seanad Éireann', in All-Party Oireachtas Committee on the Constitution, *Second Progress Report*. Dublin: Stationery Office, pp. 32–107; also available at http://archive.constitution.ie/reports/2nd-Report-Seanad.pdf

Coakley, John, and Maurice Manning (1999) 'The Senate elections', in Michael Marsh and Paul Mitchell, eds, *How Ireland Voted, 1997*. Boulder, CO: Westview Press, pp. 195–214

Coakley, John, and Gerald O'Neill (1984) 'Chance in preferential voting systems: an unnaceptable element in Irish electoral law?' *Economic and Social Review* 16 (1): 1–18

Cohan, A.S., R.D. McKinlay and Anthony Mughan (1975) 'The used vote and electoral outcomes: the Irish general election of 1973', *British Journal of Political Science* 5 (3): 363–83

Coimisiún na Gaeltachta (2002) *Report: Tuarascáil*. Dublin: Coimisiún na Gaeltachta

Coleman, Marc (2009) *Back from the Brink: Ireland's Road to Recovery*. Dublin: Transworld Ireland

Collins, Stephen (2005) *Breaking the Mould: How the Progressive Democrats Changed Irish Politics*. Dublin: Gill and Macmillan

Commission on Vocational Organisation (1943) *Report*. P. 6743. Dublin: Stationery Office

Committee on Executive Articles (1922) *Report of Committee on Executive Articles of Constitution of Saorstát Éireann Bill* (Reports of Committees, vol. 1, T5). Dublin: Provisional Parliament

Committee on the Constitution (1967) *Report of the Committee on the Constitution* (Pr. 9817.) Dublin: Stationery Office

Conefrey, Thomas (2011) *Unemployment and Labour Force Participation during the Recession* (Economic Letter Series, 2011 (4)). Dublin: Central Bank of Ireland

Conley, John J., SJ (2004) 'Remembering King Baudouin, witness to life', *Life and Learning* 14: 113–19

Connolly, Joseph (1996) *Memoirs of Senator Joseph Connolly (1885–1961): A Founder of Modern Ireland*, ed. J. Anthony Gaughan. Dublin: Irish Academic Press

Constitution Review Group (1996) *Report of the Constitution Review Group.* (Pn 2632). Dublin: Stationery Office

Convention on the Constitution (2013a) *First Report of the Convention on the Constitution: (i) Reducing the Voting Age to 17; and (ii) Reducing the Presidential Term of Office to Five Years and Aligning It with the Local and European Elections.* Dublin: Convention on the Constitution

Convention on the Constitution (2013b) *Convention on the Constitution—Press Release 9 June.* Dublin: Convention on the Constitution

Conway, Brian (2010) 'Trends in demand and supply factors in the Irish Catholic Church', *Irish Catholic*, 12 August

Conway, Brian (2011) 'The vanishing Catholic priest', *Contexts* 10: 64–5

Cox, Pat (2013) 'Interview with Pat Cox', in Aziliz Gouez, ed., *Forty Years A-Growing: An Overview of Irish–EU Relations.* Paris: Notre Europe–Jacques Delors Institute, pp. 36–54

Curran, Joseph M. (1980) *The Birth of the Irish Free State, 1921–1923.* Tuscaloosa: University of Alabama Press

Daalder, Hans (1963) *Cabinet Reform in Britain, 1914–1963.* Oxford: Oxford University Press

Dabbs, Jack Autrey (1971) *Dei Gratia in Royal Titles.* The Hague: Mouton

Dáil Éireann (1937) *Special Report of the Special Committee on the Seanad Electoral (Panel Members) Bill, 1937.* Dublin: Stationery Office

Dawson, R. MacGregor and W.F. Dawson (1989) *Democratic Government in Canada*, 5th ed., rev. Norman Ward. Toronto: University of Toronto Press

Dellepiane Avellaneda, Sebastian, and Niamh Hardiman (2010) 'The European context of Ireland's economic crisis', *Economic and Social Review* 41 (4): 473–500

Dempsey, Noel (2010) 'Speech by Minister Dempsey at the McGill summer school', 19 July; available at www.noeldempsey.ie/index.php/national-speech/speech-by-minister-dempsey-at-the-macgill-summer-school

Department of the Environment (1996) *Representation of Emigrants in Seanad Eireann: A Consultation Paper Issued by the Minister for the Environment.* Dublin: Department of the Environment

Department of the Environment (2012) *Putting People First: Action Programme for Effective Local Government.* Dublin: Stationery Office

Department of the Taoiseach (2011) *Statement of Common Purpose* [Programme for Government]; available at http://per.gov.ie/wp-content/uploads/ProgrammeforGovernmentFinal.pdf

Derbyshire, J. Denis, and Ian Derbyshire (1996) *Political Systems of the World*, 2nd ed. Oxford: Helicon

Devine, Karen M. (2006) 'The myth of "the myth of Irish neutrality": deconstructing concepts of Irish neutrality using international relations theories', *Irish Studies in International Affairs* 17: 115–39

Devine, Karen M. (2011) 'Neutrality and the development of the European Union's common security and defence policy: compatible or competing?', *Cooperation and Conflict* 46 (3): 334–69

De Winter, Lieven (1991) 'Parliamentary and party pathways to the cabinet', in Jean Blondel and Jean-Louis Thiébault, eds, *The Profession of Government Minister in Western Europe.* Basingstoke: Macmillan, pp. 44–69

DiClerico, Robert E. (1995) *The American President*, 4th ed. Englewood Cliffs, NJ: Prentice Hall

Dogan, Mattei (1981) 'La sélection des ministres en Italie: dix règles non-écrites', *International Political Science Review* 2 (2): 189–209

Dooge, James (1987) 'The role of the Seanad', in Patrick Lynch and James Meenan, eds, *Essays in Memory of Alexis FitzGerald*, pp. 133–59. Dublin: Incorporated Law Society of Ireland

Doolan, Brian (1984) *Constitutional Law and Constitutional Rights in Ireland.* Dublin: Gill and Macmillan

Douglas, James G. (1998) *Memoirs of Senator James G. Douglas (1887–1954): Concerned Citizen*, ed. J. Anthony Gaughan. Dublin: University College Dublin Press

Dowding, Keith, and Patrick Dumont, eds (2009a) *The Selection of Ministers in Europe: Hiring and Firing.* London: Routledge

Dowding, Keith, and Patrick Dumont (2009b) 'Structural and strategic factors affecting the hiring and firing of ministers', in Dowding and Dumont, 2009a, pp. 1–20

Duffy, Jim (1990) 'The presidency' (parts 1–4), *Irish Times*, 24, 25, 26 and 27 September

Duffy, Jim (1993) 'Ireland', in Republic Advisory Committee, *An Australian Republic: The Options, Vol. 2, Appendices.* Canberra: Australian Government Publishing Service, pp. 111–85

Dummett, Michael (1984) *Voting Procedures.* Oxford: Clarendon Press

Dummett, Michael (1997) *Principles of Electoral Reform.* Oxford: Oxford University Press

Dumont, Patrick, Stefaan Fiers and Régis Dandoy (2009) 'Belgium: ups and downs of ministerial careers in a partitocratic state', in Dowding and Dumont, 2009a, pp. 125–46

Dunleavy, Janet Egleson, and Gareth W. Dunleavy (1991) *Douglas Hyde: A Maker of Modern Ireland.* Berkeley: University of California Press

Dunleavy, Patrick, Helen Margetts and Stuart Weir (1992) 'How Britain would have voted under alternative electoral systems in 1992', *Parliamentary Affairs* 45 (4): 640–55

Durkan, Joe (2012) 'Governance issues and the financial crisis in Ireland', paper presented at the Workshop on European Governance and the Problems of Peripheral Countries, Vienna, 12–13 July; available at www.foreurope.eu

Duverger, Maurice (1978) *Echec au roi.* Paris: Albin Michel

Duverger, Maurice (1980) 'A new political system model: semi-presidential government', *European Journal of Political Research* 8 (2): 168–83

Duverger, Maurice, ed. (1986) *Les régimes semi-présidentiels.* Paris: Presses Universitaires de France

Economic and Social Research Institute (2012) *Quarterly Economic Commentary, December.* Dublin: Economic and Social Research Institute

Economic and Social Institute (2013) *Quarterly Economic Commentary, Spring.* Dublin: Economic and Social Research Institute

Elgie, Robert (1999) 'The politics of semi-presidentialism', in Robert Elgie, ed., *Semi-Presidentialism in Europe.* Oxford: Oxford University Press, pp. 1–21

Elgie, Robert (2011) *Semi-Presidentialism: Sub-types and Democratic Performance.* Oxford: Oxford University Press

Elgie, Robert (2012) 'The President of Ireland in comparative perspective', *Irish Political Studies* 27 (4): 502–21

Engstrom, Richard L. (1987) 'District magnitudes and the election of women to the Irish Dáil', *Electoral Studies* 6 (2): 123–32

Engstrom, Richard L. (2002) 'The post-2000 round of redistricting: an entangled thicket within the federal system', *Publius: The Journal of Federalism* 32 (4): 51–70

Eurostat (2012a) *Tables by Theme, Gini Coefficient*; available at epp.eurostat.ec.europa.eu

Eurostat (2012b) *Tables by Theme, People at Risk of Poverty or Social Exclusion*; available at epp.eurostat.ec.europa

Eurostat (2012c) *Tables by Theme, Overcrowding Rate*; available at epp.eurostat.ec.europa

Fanning, Bryan (2009) *New Guests of the Irish Nation*. Dublin: Irish Academic Press

Fanning, Bryan (2011) *Immigration and Social Cohesion in the Republic of Ireland*. Manchester: Manchester University Press

Fanning, Bryan (2013) 'Patrick Pearse predicts the future', *Dublin Review of Books*, issue 35, 20 May; available at www.drb.ie/essays/patrick-pearse-predicts-the-future

Fanning, Bryan, and Neil O'Boyle (2010) 'Immigrants in Irish politics: African and East European candidates in the 2009 local government elections', *Irish Political Studies* 25 (3): 417–35

Farrell, Brian (1969) 'A note on the Dáil constitution of 1919', *Irish Jurist* 4 (1): 127–38

Farrell, Brian (1970–71) 'The drafting of the Irish Free State constitution', parts I–IV, *Irish Jurist* (I) 5 (1): 115–40; (II) 5 (2): 343–56; (III) 6 (1): 111–35; (IV) 6 (2): 345–59

Farrell, Brian (1971) *The Founding of Dáil Éireann: Parliament and Nation Building* (Studies in Irish political culture, 2). Dublin: Gill and Macmillan

Farrell, Brian (1985) 'Ireland: from friends and neighbours to clients and partisans: some dimensions of parliamentary representation under PR-STV', in Vernon Bogdanor, ed., *Representatives of the People? Parliamentarians and Constituents in Western Democracies*. Aldershot: Gower, pp. 237–64

Farrell, Brian, ed. (1988) *De Valera's Constitution and Ours*. Dublin: Gill and Macmillan.

Farrell, David M. (2010) 'Irish electoral reform: three myths and a proposal', paper presented to MacGill Summer School, Glenties, Co Donegal, 19 July; available at politicalreformireland.files.wordpress.com/2010/07/irish_electoral_reform-2.pdf

Farrell, David (2011) *Electoral Systems: A Comparative Introduction*, 2nd ed. Basingstoke: Palgrave Macmillan

Farrell, David, and Ian McAllister (2006) *The Australian Electoral System: Origins, Variations and Consequences*. Sydney: UNSW Press

Fine Gael (2011) *Fine Gael Manifesto: Let's Get Ireland Working.* Dublin: Fine Gael.

Finer, Herman (1946) *The Theory and Practice of Modern Government,* Vol. 1. London: Methuen

Finland (1894) *Finlands folkmängd den 31 december 1890. Population de la Finlande au 31 decembre 1890* (Official Statistics of Finland VI.22). Helsingfors: Kejserliga Senatens Tryckeri

Fiseha, Assefa (2007) *Federalism and the Accommodation of Ethnic Diversity in Ethiopia: A Comparative Study,* rev. ed. Nijmegen: Wolf Legal

Fish, Steven M., and Matthew Kroenig (2009) *The Handbook of National Legislatures: A Global Survey.* Cambridge: Cambridge University Press

FitzGerald, Garret (1992) *All in a Life: An Autobiography.* Dublin: Gill and Macmillan

FitzGerald, Garret (2008) 'Why a reformed PR system deserves our vote', *Irish Times,* 16 February

Flood, Christopher G. (2002) *Political Myth.* London: Routledge

Forde, Michael (1987) *Constitutional Law of Ireland.* Cork: Mercier

Forgette, Richard, and John W. Winkle III (2006) 'Partisan gerrymandering and the Voting Rights Act', *Social Science Quarterly* 87 (1): 155–173

Forum of Federations (2012) *Federalism by country;* available at www.forumfed.org/en/federalism/by_country

Foster, R.F. (2007) *Luck and the Irish: A Brief History of Change 1970–2000.* London: Allen Lane

Fournier, Jean-Marc, Isabell Koske, Isabelle Wanner and Vera Zipperer (2013) *The Price of Oil: Will It Start Rising Again?* (OECD Economics Department Working Paper no. 1031) Paris: OECD

Frognier, André-Paul (1997) 'Belgium', in Jean Blondel and Ferdinand Müller-Rommel, eds, *Cabinets in Western Europe,* 2nd ed. Basingstoke: Macmillan, pp. 75–97

Gallagher, Michael (1975) 'Disproportionality in a proportional electoral system: the Irish experience', *Political Studies* 23 (4): 501–13

Gallagher, Michael (1977) 'The presidency of the Republic of Ireland: implications of the "Donegan Affair"', *Parliamentary Affairs* 30 (4): 373–84

Gallagher, Michael (1980) 'Candidate selection in Ireland: the impact of localism and the electoral system', *British Journal of Political Science* 10 (4): 489–503

Gallagher, Michael (1981) 'The pact general election of 1922', *Irish Historical Studies* 21 (84): 404–21

Gallagher, Michael (1986) 'The political consequences of the electoral system in the Republic of Ireland', *Electoral Studies* 5 (3): 253–75

Gallagher, Michael (1987) 'Does Ireland need a new electoral system?' *Irish Political Studies* 2: 27–48

Gallagher, Michael (1988) 'The President, the people and the constitution', in Brian Farrell, ed., *De Valera's Constitution and Ours*. Dublin: Gill and Macmillan for Raidió Telefís Éireann, pp. 75–92

Gallagher, Michael (1991) 'Proportionality, disproportionality and electoral systems', *Electoral Studies* 10 (1): 33–51

Gallagher, Michael (1992) 'Comparing proportional representation electoral systems: quotas, thresholds, paradoxes and majorities', *British Journal of Political Science* 22 (4): 469–96

Gallagher, Michael (1996) 'By-elections to Dáil Éireann 1923–96: the anomaly that conforms', *Irish Political Studies* 11: 33–60

Gallagher, Michael (1999) 'Republic of Ireland', in Robert Elgie, ed., *Semi-Presidentialism in Europe*. Oxford: Oxford University Press, pp. 104–23

Gallagher, Michael (2009a) 'Conclusion', in Gallagher and Mitchell, 2009, pp. 535–78

Gallagher, Michael (2009b) 'Ireland: the discreet charm of STV', in Gallagher and Mitchell, 2009, pp. 511–32

Gallagher, Michael (2012) 'The political role of the President of Ireland', *Irish Political Studies*, 27 (4): 522–38

Gallagher, Michael, and Lee Komito (2010) 'The constituency role of Dáil deputies', pp. 230–62 in John Coakley and Michael Gallagher, eds, *Politics in the Republic of Ireland*. London: Routledge

Gallagher, Michael, Michael Laver and Peter Mair (2011) *Representative Government in Modern Europe*, 5th ed. New York: McGraw-Hill

Gallagher, Michael, and Michael Marsh, eds (2011) *How Ireland Voted 2011*. Basingstoke: Palgrave Macmillan

Gallagher, Michael, and Paul Mitchell, eds (2009) *The Politics of Electoral Systems*, rev ed. Oxford: Oxford University Press

Gallagher, Michael, and A.R. Unwin (1986) 'Electoral distortion under STV random sampling procedures', *British Journal of Political Science* 16 (2): 243–53

Gallagher, Michael, and Liam Weeks (2003) 'The subterranean election of the Seanad', in Michael Gallagher, Michael Marsh and Paul Mitchell, eds, *How Ireland Voted 2002*. Basingstoke: Palgrave Macmillan, pp. 197–213

Galligan, B.J. (1980) 'The Kerr–Whitlam debate and the principles of the Australian constitution', *Journal of Commonwealth and Comparative Politics* 18 (3): 247–71

Galligan, Yvonne (2012) 'Transforming the Irish presidency: activist presidents and gender politics, 1990–2011', *Irish Political Studies*, 27 (4): 596–614

Garvin, Thomas (1969) *The Irish Senate*. Dublin: Institute of Public Administration

Gélard, Patrice (2006) *Second Chambers in Europe: Parliamentary Complexity or Democratic Necessity?* (Study no. 335/2005). Strasbourg: Council of Europe

Gilmartin, Mary (2012) *The Changing Landscape of Irish Migration, 2000–2012* (Working Paper no. 69, October). Maynooth: National Institute for Regional and Spatial Analysis

Ging, Debbie, Michael Cronin and Peadar Kirby, eds (2009) *Transforming Ireland: Challenges, Critiques, Resources*. Manchester: Manchester University Press

Girvin, Brian (2010) 'Becoming European: national identity, sovereignty and Europeanization in Irish political culture', in McCall and Wilson, 2010: 59–93

Glassner, Martin Ira (1993) *Political Geography*. New York: Wiley

Goodare, Julian (1996) 'The estates in the Scottish Parliament, 1286–1707', *Parliamentary History* 15 (1): 11–32

Grangé, Jean (1987) 'Irlande: le Sénat (Seanad Éireann)', in Mastias and Grangé, 1987, pp. 291–316

Gray, Peter, and Olwen Purdue, eds (2012) *The Irish Lord Lieutenancy, c.1541–1922*. Dublin: UCD Press

Grofman, Bernard, Arend Lijphart, Robert B. McKay and Howard A. Scarrow, eds (1982) *Representation and Redistricting Issues*. Lexington, MA: Lexington Books

Gudgin, G., and P.J. Taylor (1979) *Seats, Votes and the Spatial Organisation of Elections*. London: Pion

Hacker, Andrew (1963) *Congressional Districting: The Issue of Equal Representation*. Washington, DC: The Brookings Institution

Hague, Rod, and Martin Harrop (2008) *Comparative Government and Politics*, 8th ed. Basingstoke: Palgrave

Hamer, David (1996) 'Parliament and government: striking the balance', in Julian Disney and J.R. Nethercote, eds, *The House on Capital Hill: Parliament, Politics and Power in the National Capital*. Leichhart: Federation Press, pp. 63–80

Hamilton, Alexander, James Madison and John Jay (1970 [1787–8]) *The Federalist: Or, the New Constitution*. London: Dent

Hardiman, Niamh (2010) 'Institutional design and Irish political reform', *Journal of the Statistical and Social Inquiry Society of Ireland* 39: 53–69

Hardiman, Niamh (2012) 'Conclusion: changing Irish governance', in Niamh Hardiman, ed., *Irish Governance in Crisis*. Manchester: Manchester University Press, pp. 212–29

Hare, Thomas (1859) *A Treatise on the Election of Representatives, Parliamentary and Municipal*. London: Longman, Brown, Green, Longman and Roberts

Harris, B.V. (2009) 'The Irish President, the New Zealand Governor-General and the head of state in a future New Zealand republic', *New Zealand Law Review* 2009 (4): 605–57

Harris, Clodagh, ed. (2005) *The Report of the Democracy Commission: Engaging Citizens: The Case for Democratic Renewal in Ireland*. Dublin: New Ireland Press, for TASC

Hayward, Katy (2009) *Irish Nationalism and European Integration: The Official Redefinition of the Island of Ireland*. Manchester: Manchester University Press

Hayward, Katy (2010) '"For mutual benefit": Irish official discourse on Europeanization and Hibernicization', in McCall and Wilson, 2010: 95–118

Hayward, Katy (2012) 'The European Union: national and supranational dimensions to foreign policy', in Tonra et al., 2012: 131–51

Healy, Sean J., Brigid Reynolds and Micheál Collins (2011) *A New and Fairer Ireland: Securing Economic Development, Social Equity and Sustainability*. Dublin: Social Justice Ireland

Herman, Valentine, with Françoise Mendel (1976) *Parliaments of the World: A Reference Compendium*. London: Macmillan

Hermens, F.A. (1972 [1941]) *Democracy or Anarchy? A Study of Proportional Representation*. New York: Johnson Reprint Corporation

Hogan, Gerard (1989) 'Legal and constitutional issues arising from the 1989 general election', *Irish Jurist* 24 (2): 157–81

Hogan, Gerard (2012a) The 1937 Constitution. Dublin: Convention on the Constitution [Address to the Constitutional Convention, Dublin Castle, 1 December 2012]; available at www.constitution.ie

Hogan, Gerard (2012b) *The Origins of the Irish Constitution 1928–1941*. Dublin: Royal Irish Academy

Honohan, Patrick (2010) *The Irish Banking Crisis: Regulatory and Financial*

Stability Policy 2003–2008/A Report to the Minister for Finance by the Governor of the Central Bank. Dublin: Central Bank; available at www.bankinginquiry.gov.ie

Hood, Susan (2002) *Royal Roots—Republican Inheritance: The Survival of the Office of Arms.* Dublin: Woodfield Press

Hopkinson, Michael (1988) *Green against Green: The Irish Civil War.* Dublin: Gill and Macmillan

Horgan, John (1997) *Mary Robinson: An Independent Voice.* Dublin: O'Brien Press

Huckabee, David C. (2001) *The House of Representatives Apportionment Formula: An Analysis of Proposals for Change and their Impact on States.* Washington, DC: Congressional Research Service, Library of Congress

Hughes, Ian, Paula Clancy, Clodagh Harris and David Beetham (2007) *Power to the People? Assessing Democracy in Ireland.* Dublin: TASC

Hussey, Gemma (2009) 'Our political system is no longer fit for purpose', *Irish Times*, 4 May

Hutcheson, Derek S. (2011) 'The seismology of psephology: "earthquake elections" from the *Folketing* to the *Dáil*', *Representation* 47 (4): 473–90

International Idea (2010) *Table of electoral systems worldwide*; available at www.idea.int/esd/world.cfm

Inter-Parliamentary Union (1962) *Parliaments: A Comparative Study on the Structure and Functioning of Representative Institutions in Forty-One Countries.* London: Cassell

Inter-Parliamentary Union (1986) *Parliaments of the World: A Comparative Reference Compendium*, 2 vols. Aldershot: Gower

Inter-Parliamentary Union (2012) *Parline database*; available at www.ipu.org

Ipsos-MORI (2012) European Union membership: trends [30 November 2012]; available at www.ipsos-mori.com/researchpublications/researcharchive/2435/European-Union-membership-trends.aspx?view=wide

Ireland (1980) *Dail Éireann Constituency Commission: Report* (Prl. 8878). Dublin: Stationery Office

Ireland (1983) *Dail Constituency Commission: Report* (Pl. 1774). Dublin: Stationery Office

Ireland (1988) *Dail Constituency Commission: Report* (Pl. 5984). Dublin: Stationery Office

Ireland (1990) *Dail Constituency Commission: Report* (Pl. 7520). Dublin: Stationery Office

Ireland (1995) *Dail Constituency Commission: Report* (Pn. 1619). Dublin: Stationery Office

Ireland (1998) *Constituency Commission Report 1998* (Pn. 5074). Dublin: Stationery Office

Ireland (2004) *Constituency Commission: Report on Dáil Constituencies 2004* (Prn. 1554). Dublin: Stationery Office

Ireland (2007) *Constituency Commission: Report on Dáil and European Parliament Constituencies 2007* (Prn. A7/1347). Dublin: Stationery Office

Ireland (2010) *20-Year Strategy for the Irish Language 2010–2030*. Dublin: Stationery Office

Ireland (2012a) *Constituency Commission Report 2012: Dáil and European Parliament Constituencies 2012* (Prn. A12/0834). Dublin: Stationery Office

Ireland (2012b) *Ireland: Highlights from Census 2011, part 1*. Dublin: Stationery Office

Ireland (2012c) *Referendum Results 1937–2012*. Dublin: Department of the Environment, Community and Local Government

Ireland (2013) *Population and Labour Force Projections 2016–2046*. Dublin: Stationery Office

Johnston, Edith M. (1963) *Great Britain and Ireland 1760–1800: A Study in Political Administration*. Edinburgh: Oliver and Boyd

Johnston-Liik, Edith Mary (2002) *History of the Irish Parliament 1692–1800: Commons, Constituencies and Statutes*, 6 vols. Belfast: Ulster Historical Foundation

Joint Committee on the Constitution (2010a) *Third Report: Results of Survey of Members of Both Houses of the Oireachtas: The Electoral System, Representative Role of TDs and Proposals for Change*. Dublin: Stationery Office

Joint Committee on the Constitution (2010b) *Fourth Report: Article 16 of the Constitution: Review of the Electoral System for the Election of Members to Dáil Éireann*. Dublin: Stationery Office

Katz, Richard S. (1981) 'But how many candidates should we have in Donegal? Numbers of nominees and electoral efficiency in Ireland', *British Journal of Political Science* 11 (1): 117–22

Kavanagh, Adrian (2003) 'The constituency commission', *Irish Political Studies* 18 (2): 89–99

Kavanagh, Adrian, and Noel Whelan (2013) *Potential outcomes for the 2007 and 2011 Irish elections under a different electoral system: a submission for the Convention on the Constitution.* Dublin: Convention on the Constitution; available at constitution.ie

Kavanagh, Aileen (2012) 'The Irish Constitution at 75 years: natural law, Christian values and the ideal of justice', *Irish Jurist* 48: 71–101

Kelly, John M., Gerard Hogan and Gerry Whyte (2003) *The Irish Constitution*, 4th ed. Dublin: LexisNexis Butterworths.

Kelly, Michael (2012) '75pc less priests in 30 years', *Irish Catholic*, 5 September

Kelly, Morgan (2007) 'On the likely extent of falls in Irish house prices', *Economic and Social Research Institute Quarterly Economic Commentary: Special Articles*, 2: 42–54

Kennedy, Hugh (1928) 'Character and sources of the constitution of the Irish Free State', *American Bar Association Journal* 14 (8): 437–45

Keogh, Dermot, and Andrew J. McCarthy (2007) *The Making of the Irish Constitution 1937: Bunreacht na hÉireann.* Cork: Mercier

Keogh, Gary, and Brendan J. Whelan (1986) *A Statistical Analysis of the Irish Electoral Register and Its Use of Population Estimation and Sample Surveys.* Dublin: Economic and Social Research Institute

Kirby, Peadar (2009) 'Contesting the politics of inequality', in Ging, Cronin and Kirby, 2009, pp. 190–204

Kirby, Peadar (2010) *The Celtic Tiger in Collapse: Explaining the Weaknesses of the Irish Model*, 2nd ed. Basingstoke: Palgrave Macmillan

Kitchin, Rob, Justin Gleeson, Karen Keaveney and Cian O'Callaghan (2010) *A Haunted Landscape: Housing and Ghost Estates in Post-Celtic Tiger Ireland* (NIRSA Working Paper 59). Maynooth: National Institute for Regional and Spatial Analysis, NUIM; available at www.nuim.ie/nirsa/research/documents/WP59-A-Haunted-Landscape.pdf

Kohn, Leo (1932) *The Constitution of the Irish Free State.* London: George Allen and Unwin

Labour Party (2011) *Towards Recovery: Programme for a National Government 2011–2016.* Dublin: Labour Party

Laffan, Brigid (2010) 'Accountability and performance: challenges to Ireland', paper presented at the 30th MacGill Summer School, Glenties, Co. Donegal, 20 July

Laffan, Brigid, and Jane O'Mahony (2008) *Ireland and the European Union.* Basingstoke: Palgrave Macmillan

Laffan, Brigid, and Ben Tonra (2010) 'Europe and the international dimension', in John Coakley and Michael Gallagher, eds, *Politics in the Republic of Ireland*, 5th ed. London: Routledge, pp. 407–33

Lakeman, Enid (1982) *Power to Elect: The Case for Proportional Representation.* London: Heinemann

Lane, Jan-Erik, and Svante Ersson (1994) *Comparative Politics: An Introduction and New Approach.* Cambridge: Polity Press

Lanzieri, Giampaolo (2011) *Fewer, Older and Multicultural? Projections of the EU Populations by Foreign/National Background* (Eurostat Methodologies and Working Papers Cat. No KS-RA-11-019-EN-N). Luxembourg: Publications Office of the European Union

Laski, Harold J. (1928) 'The personnel of the English Cabinet, 1801–1924', *American Political Science Review* 22 (1): 12–31

Laundy, Philip (1989) *Parliaments in the Modern World.* Aldershot: Dartmouth

Laver, Michael (1998) *A New Electoral System for Ireland?* Dublin: Public Policy Institute, Trinity College Dublin

Laver, Michael (2002) 'The role and future of the upper house in Ireland', *Journal of Legislative Studies* 8 (3): 49–66

Laver, Michael, and Peter Mair (1975) 'Proportionality, PR and STV in Ireland', *Political Studies* 23 (4): 491–500

Le Goff, Jacques (1993) 'Le roi dans l'occident médiéval: caractères originaux', in Anne J. Duggan, ed., *Kings and Kingship in Medieval Europe*, pp. 1–40. London: Centre for Late Antique and Medieval Studies, King's College London

Leahy, Pat (2010) 'Standards in public life and accountability', paper presented at the 30th MacGill Summer School, Glenties, Co. Donegal, 20 July

Leahy, Pat (2011) 'The need to change our political culture is paramount', Paper presented at the Dublin Economic Workshop, Kenmare, Co. Kerry, 14–16 October

Lijphart, Arend (1984) *Democracies: Patterns of Majoritarian and Consensus Government in Twenty-One Countries.* New Haven, CT: Yale University Press

Lijphart, Arend (1992) 'Introduction' in Arend Lijphart, ed., *Parliamentary versus Presidential Government.* Oxford: Oxford University Press, pp. 1–27

Lijphart, Arend (1994) *Electoral Systems and Party Systems: A Study of Twenty-Seven Democracies 1945–1990.* Oxford: Oxford University Press

Lijphart, Arend (2009) 'Foreword', in Gallagher and Mitchell, 2009, pp. vii–x

Lijphart, Arend, and Galen A. Irwin (1979) 'Nomination strategies in the Irish STV system: the Dáil elections of 1969, 1973 and 1977', *British Journal of Political Science* 9 (3): 362–70

Little, Conor (2011) 'The general election of 2011 in the Republic of Ireland: all changed utterly?', *West European Politics* 34 (6): 1304–13

Litton, Frank, ed. (1988) *The Constitution of Ireland 1937–1987*. Dublin: Institute of Public Administration

Llanos, Mariana, and Detlef Nolte (2003) 'Bicameralism in the Americas: around the extremes of symmetry and incongruence', *Journal of Legislative Studies* 9 (3): 54–86

Lynch, David (2010) *When the Luck of the Irish Ran Out: The World's Most Resilient Country and Its Struggle to Rise Again*. Basingstoke: Palgrave Macmillan

MacCarthaigh, Muiris (2005) *Accountability in Irish Parliamentary Politics*. Dublin: Institute of Public Administration

MacCarthaigh, Muiris, and Maurice Manning, eds (2010) *The Houses of the Oireachtas: Parliament in Ireland*. Dublin: Institute of Public Administration

MacDonagh, Oliver (1977) *Ireland: The Union and its Aftermath*. London: George Allen and Unwin

Mac Giolla Choille, Breandán (1988) 'I dtaobh an tsaothair sin na Gaeilge ar an mBunreacht' [On the project of the Irish version of the constitution], *Feasta* 41 (1): 63–8

Mac Gréil, Micheál, and Fergal Rhatigan (2009) *The Challenge of Indifference: A Need for Religious Revival in Ireland*. Maynooth: Department of Sociology

Magee, Harry (2011) 'Government to consider referendum on abolition of Seanad', *Irish Times*, 3 January

Mair, Peter (1986) 'Districting choices under the single transferable vote', in Bernard Grofman and Arend Lijphart, eds, *Electoral Laws and their Political Consequences*. New York: Agathon Press, pp. 289–307

Mair, Peter (2010) 'Paradoxes and problems of modern Irish politics', paper presented at the 30th MacGill Summer School, Glenties, Co. Donegal, 20 July

Mann, Dean E., and Zachary A. Smith (1981) 'The selection of U.S. cabinet officers and other political executives', *International Political Science Review* 2 (2): 211–34

Manning, Maurice (2010) 'The Senate', in MacCarthaigh and Manning, 2010, pp. 153–66

Mansergh, Nicholas (1934) *The Irish Free State: Its Government and Politics*. London: George Allen and Unwin

Marongiu, Antonio (1968) *Medieval Parliaments: A Comparative Study*, translated by S.J. Woolf. London: Eyre & Spottiswoode

Marriott, J.A.R. (1910) *Second Chambers: An Inductive Study in Political Science*. Oxford: Clarendon Press

Marsh, James G., and Johan P. Olsen (2006) 'Elaborating the "new institutionalism"', in R.A.W. Rhodes, Sarah A. Binder and Bert A. Rockman, eds, *The Oxford Handbook of Political Institutions*. Oxford: Oxford University Press, pp. 3–20

Marsh, Michael (1981) 'Localism, candidate selection and electoral preferences in Ireland: the general election of 1977', *Economic and Social Review* 12 (4): 267–86

Martin, Shane (2010) 'The committee system', in MacCarthaigh and Manning, 2010, pp. 285–302

Massicotte, Louis (2001) 'Legislative unicameralism: a global survey and a few case studies', *Journal of Legislative Studies* 7 (1): 151–70

Mastias, Jean, and Jean Grangé, eds (1987) *Les secondes chambres du parlement en Europe occidentale*. Paris: Economica

Matthijs, Herman (2012) 'De kostprijs van de monarchie in Europa' [The cost of the monarchy in Europe], unpublished paper; available at www.dutchnews.nl/news/img/Cost of royalty.pdf

McCall, Cathal, and Thomas M. Wilson, eds (2010) *Europeanisation and Hibernicisation: Ireland and Europe* (European Studies, vol. 28). Amsterdam: Rodopi

McCarthy, Colm (2011) 'Don't reform the Seanad, scrap it', *Sunday Independent*, 9 January

McDowell, R.B. (1964) *The Irish Administration 1801–1914*. London: Routledge and Kegan Paul

McDowell, R.B. (1979) *Ireland in the Age of Imperialism and Revolution, 1760–1801*. Oxford: Clarendon Press

McDunphy, Michael (1945) *The President of Ireland: His Powers, Functions and Duties*. Dublin: Browne and Nolan, The Richview Press

McGarry, Patsy (2008) *First Citizen: Mary McAleese and the Irish Presidency*. Dublin: O'Brien Press

McGarry, Patsy (2012) 'New thinking vital to meet crisis of vocations and faith', *Irish Times*, 8 June

McGowan-Smyth, Jack (2000) 'The Irish Senate: the case for Seanad Éireann', *Representation* 37 (2): 147–53

McManus, Ruth (2002) *Dublin, 1910–1940: Shaping the City and Suburbs*. Dublin: Four Courts Press

McWilliams, David (2007a) 'A country in denial', *Sunday Business Post*, 15 July

McWilliams, David (2007b) 'Crashing property market begins to reveal its casualties', *Sunday Business Post*, 21 October

Mee, Michael (1996a) 'The changing nature of the presidency: the President and the Government should be friends. Part I', *Irish Law Times* 14: 2–7

Mee, Michael (1996b) 'The changing nature of the presidency: should the office be expanded? Part II', *Irish Law Times* 14: 30–33

Meehan, Ciara (2012) 'Constructing the Irish presidency: the early incumbents, 1938–73', *Irish Political Studies* 27 (4): 559–75

Meisel, Joseph S. (2011) *Knowledge and Power: The Parliamentary Representation of Universities in Britain and the Empire*. Oxford: Wiley-Blackwell

Meredith, David, and Chris van Egeraat (2013) 'Revisiting the National Spatial Strategy ten years on', *Administration* 60 (3): 3–9

Meredith, J. C. (1913) *Proportional Representation in Ireland*. Dublin: Edward Ponsonby

Mill, John Stuart (1912 [1861]) 'Considerations on representative government', in *On Liberty. Representative Government. The Subjection of Women. Three Essays*. London: Oxford University Press, pp. 145–423

Mills, Karen M. (2001) *Congressional Apportionment: Census 2001 Brief*. Washington, DC: US Census Bureau; available at www.census.gov/prod/2001pubs/c2kbr01-7.pdf

Money, Jeanette, and George Tsebelis (1992) 'Cicero's puzzle: upper house power in comparative perspective', *International Political Science Review* 13 (1): 25–43

Monmonier, Mark (2001) *Bushmanders and Bullwinkles: How Politicians Manipulate Electronic Maps and Census Data to Win Elections*. Chicago: University of Chicago Press

Morgan, David Gwynn (1985) *Constitutional Law of Ireland: The Law of the Executive, Legislature and Judicature*. Dublin: Round Hall Press in Association with Irish Academic Press

Morgan, David Gwynn (1999) 'Mary Robinson's presidency: relations with the government', *Irish Jurist* 34 (1): 256–75

Morison, John (1997) '"A disposition to preserve and an ability to improve": the report of the Constitution Review Group in the Republic of Ireland', *Public Law* 1997 (1): 55–65

Mulgan, Richard, ed. (2004) *Politics in New Zealand*, 3rd ed., updated by Peter Aimer. Auckland: Auckland University Press

Mulreany, Michael, ed. (2009) *Economic Development 50 years on, 1958–2008*. Dublin: Institute of Public Administration

Murphy, David, and Martina Devlin (2009) *Banksters: How a Powerful Elite Squandered Ireland's Wealth*. Dublin: Hachette Books Ireland

Murphy, Gary, and Theresa Reidy (2012) 'Presidential elections in Ireland: from partisan predictability to the end of loyalty', *Irish Political Studies*, 27 (4): 615–34

Murphy, Mary (2009) 'The politics of redirecting social policy: towards a double movement', in Ging, Cronin and Kirby, 2009, pp. 174–89

Myers, A.R. (1975) *Parliaments and Estates in Europe to 1789*. London: Thames and Hudson

National Democratic Institute (1996) *A Comparative Study of Second Chambers of Parliament in Selected Countries*. Washington, DC: National Democratic Institute; available at www.ndi.org/files/032_ww_comparative.pdf

Needham, Catherine (2009) 'Legislative–executive relations', in Judith Bara and Mark Pennington, eds, *Comparative Politics: Explaining Democratic Systems*. London: Sage, pp. 120–44

New Zealand (2012) *Department of the Prime Minister and Cabinet: Annual Report for the Year Ended 2012*. Wellington: Department of the Prime Minister and Cabinet

Nohlen, Dieter (1969) 'Begriffliche Einführung in die Wahlsystematik', in Dolf Sternberger and Bernhard Vogel, eds, *Die Wahl der Parlamente und anderer Staatsorgane. Band I: Europa*. Berlin: Walter de Gruyter, pp. 1–54

Nolan, Brian, Philip J. O'Connell and Christopher T. Whelan, eds (2000) *Bust to Boom? The Irish Experience of Growth and Inequality*. Dublin: Institute of Public Administration

Norton, Philip (2004) 'How many bicameral legislatures are there?', *Journal of Legislative Studies* 10 (4): 1–9

Norton, Philip (2007) 'Adding value? The role of second chambers', *Asia Pacific Law Review* 15 (1): 3–18

Notten, Geranda, and Chris de Neubourg (2007) *The Policy Relevance of Absolute and Relative Poverty Headcounts: What's in a Number?* (Working Paper MGSoG/2007/WP006). Maastricht: Maastricht Graduate School of Governance, Maastricht University

Nurmi, Hannu (1983) 'Voting procedures: a summary analysis', *British Journal of Political Science* 13 (2): 181–208

Nyberg, Peter (2011) *Misjudging Risk: Causes of the Systemic Banking Crisis in Ireland. Report of the Commission of Investigation into the Banking*

Sector in Ireland. Dublin: Stationery Office; available at www.bankinginquiry.gov.ie

O'Brien, Dan (2013) 'Reports show frustration at glacial pace of reform', *Irish Times*, 4 April

Ó Cearúil, Micheál (1999) *Bunreacht na hÉireann: A Study of the Irish Text*. Dublin: Government Publications, for the All-Party Oireachtas Committee on the Constitution

Ó Cinnéide, Colm (2012) '"The people are the masters": the paradox of constitutionalism and the uncertain status of popular sovereignty within the Irish constitutional order', *Irish Jurist* 48: 249–74

O'Connell, Declan (1981) 'Proportional representation and intraparty competition in Tasmania and the Republic of Ireland', *Journal of Commonwealth and Comparative Politics* 21 (1): 45–70

O'Connor, Paul (2012) 'Editor's note', *Irish Jurist* 48: vii–x

Ó Giollagáin, Conchúr, Seosamh Mac Donnacha, Fiona Ní Chualáin, Aoife Ní Shéaghdha and Mary O'Brien (2007) *Comprehensive Linguistic Study of the Use of Irish in the Gaeltacht: Principal Findings and Recommendations*. Dublin: Department of Community, Rural and Gaeltacht Affairs

Ó Glaisne, Risteárd (1993) *Dúbhglas de hÍde (1860–1949): Náisiúnach Neamh-spleách 1910–1949* [Douglas Hyde (1860–1949): An Independent Nationalist 1910–1949]. Dublin: Conradh na Gaeilge

O'Hearn, Denis (1998) *Inside the Celtic Tiger: The Irish Economy and the Asian Model*. London: Pluto

Oireachtas Éireann (1928) *Report: Committee on the Constitution and Powers of, and Methods of Election to, Seanad Éireann*. Dublin: Stationery Office

Oireachtas Éireann (1947) *Report of the Joint Committee on Seanad Panel Elections 1947*. Dublin: Stationery Office

O'Keefe, Denis (1936) 'The problem of the Senate', *Studies* 25 (98): 204–14

O'Leary, Cornelius (1975) 'Ireland: the North and the South', in S. E. Finer, ed., *Adversary Politics and Electoral Reform*. London: Anthony Wigram, pp. 153–83

O'Leary, Cornelius (1979) *Irish Elections 1918–1977: Parties, Voters and Proportional Representation*. Dublin: Gill and Macmillan

O'Leary, Don (2000) *Vocationalism and Social Catholicism in Twentieth-Century Ireland: The Search for a Christian Social Order*. Dublin: Irish Academic Press

O'Leary, Olivia, and Helen Burke (1998) *Mary Robinson: The Authorised Biography*. London: Hodder and Stoughton

O'Malley, Eoin (2006) 'Ministerial selection in Ireland: limited choice in a global village', *Irish Political Studies* 21 (3): 319–36

O'Malley, Eoin (2009) 'Constructing and maintaining Irish governments', in Dowding and Dumont, 2009a, pp. 179–93

O'Malley, Eoin (2011) *Contemporary Ireland*. Basingstoke: Palgrave Macmillan

O'Malley, Eoin, and Muiris MacCarthaigh (2012) 'Introduction: the context for governing Ireland', in Eoin O'Malley and Muiris MacCarthaigh, eds, *Governing Ireland: from Cabinet Government to Delegated Governance*. Dublin: Institute of Public Administration, pp. 1–14

O'Malley, Tom (2012) 'A fitting anniversary tribute', Ex Tempore (website), 9 May; available at www.extempore.ie/2012/05/09/a-fitting-anniversary-tribute

O'Rahilly, Alfred (1936) 'The constitution and the Senate', *Studies* 25 (97): 1–19

Orshansky, Mary (1969) 'How poverty is measured', *Monthly Labor Review* 92 (2): 37–41

O'Sullivan, Donal (1940) *The Irish Free State and its Senate: A Study in Contemporary Politics*. London: Faber and Faber

O'Toole, Fintan (2010) *Ship of Fools: How Stupidity and Corruption Sank the Celtic Tiger*, updated ed. London: Faber and Faber

Parker, A.J. (1982) 'The "friends and neighbours" voting efect in the Galway West constituency', *Political Geography Quarterly* 1 (3): 243–62

Parry, Keith, and Lucinda Maer (2012) *Ministers in the House of Lords* (Standard Note: SN/PC/05226). London: House of Commons Library

Patterson, Samuel C., and Anthony Mughan (2001) 'Fundamentals of institutional design: the functions and powers of parliamentary second chambers', *Journal of Legislative Studies* 7 (1): 39–60

Piesse, E.L. (1913) 'Bibliography of proportional representation in Tasmania', *Papers and Proceedings of the Royal Society of Tasmania*: 39–75

Pitkin, Hanna Fenichel (1972) *The Concept of Representation*, new ed. Berkeley: University of California Press

Preece, Alun A. (2000) 'Bicameralism at the end of the second millennium', *University of Queensland Law Journal* 21 (1): 67–84

Pulzer, Peter G.J. (1975) *Political Representation and Elections in Britain*, 3rd ed. London: George Allen and Unwin

Purvis, Matthew (2011) *House of Lords: Party and Group Strengths and*

Voting (House of Lords Library Note 2011/022). London: House of Lords Library; available at www.parliament.uk/briefing-papers/LLN-2012-026

Puttnam, Robert D., with Robert Leonardi and Rafaella Y. Nanetti (1993) *Making Democracy Work: Civic Traditions in Modern Italy*. Princeton, NJ: Princeton University Press

Rafter, Kevin (2012) 'Redefining the Irish presidency: the politics of a "non-political" office, 1973–90', *Irish Political Studies* 27 (4): 576–95

Reeve, Andrew, and Alan Ware (1992) *Electoral Systems: A Comparative and Theoretical Introduction*. London: Routledge

Regling, Klaus, and Max Watson (2010) *A Preliminary Report on the Sources of Ireland's Banking Crisis*. Dublin: Government Publications. Available at www.bankinginquiry.gov.ie

Reidy, Theresa (2008) 'The Seanad election', in Michael Gallagher and Michael Marsh, eds, *How Ireland Voted 2007: The Full Story of Ireland's General Election*. Basingstoke: Palgrave Macmillan, pp. 187–204

Reynolds, Albert, with Jill Arlon (2009) *My Autobiography*. London: Transworld Ireland

Reynolds, Andrew, Ben Reilly and Andrew Ellis (2005) *Electoral System Design: The New International IDEA Handbook*. Stockholm: International Institute for Democracy and Electoral Assistance

Rialtas Sealadach na hÉireann [Provisional Government of Ireland] (1922) *Draft Constitution of the Irish Free State to be submitted to the Provisional Parliament*. Dublin: Eason

Richardson, H.C., and G.O. Sayles (1964) *The Irish Parliament in the Middle Ages*, new ed. Philadelphia: University of Pennsylvania Press

Riker, William H. (1992) 'The justification of bicameralism', *International Political Science Review* 13 (1): 101–116.

Roberts-Wray, Sir Kenneth Owen (1966) *Commonwealth and Colonial Law*. London: Stevens

Robins, Joseph (2001) *Champagne and Silver Buckles: The Viceregal Court at Dublin Castle 1700–1922*. Dublin: Lilliput

Robson, Christopher, and Brendan Walsh (1973) *Alphabetical Voting: A Study of the 1973 General Election in the Republic of Ireland*. Dublin: Economic and Social Research Institute

Roche, Desmond (1982) *Local Government in Ireland*. Dublin: Institute of Public Administration

Rockow, Lewis (1928) 'Bentham on the theory of second chambers', *American Political Science Review* 22 (3): 576–90

Russell, Meg (1999) 'Second chambers overseas', *Political Quarterly* 70 (4): 411–17

Russell, Meg (2000) *Reforming the House of Lords: Lessons from Overseas.* Oxford: Oxford University Press

Russell, Meg (2001) 'The territorial role of second chambers', *Journal of Legislative Studies* 7 (1): 105–18

Russell, Meg (2012) 'Elected second chambers and their powers: an international survey', *Political Quarterly* 83 (1): 117–29

Ryan, Fergus (2008) *Constitutional Law*, 2nd ed. Dublin: Thomson Round Hall

Sacks, Paul (1976) *The Donegal Mafia: An Irish Political Machine.* New Haven, CT: Yale University Press

Samuels, David, and Richard Snyder (2001) 'The value of a vote: malapportionment in comparative perspective', *British Journal of Political Science* 31 (4): 651–671

Saunders, Allan F. (1924) 'The Irish constitution', *American Political Science Review* 18 (2): 340–5

Saunders, Cheryl (1993) 'Heads of state: a comparative perspective', in *Heads of State: A Comparative Perspective.* Carlton, Australia: Constitutional Centenary Foundation, pp. 4–10

Scully, Roger (2001) 'Dealing with big brother: relations with the first chamber', *Journal of Legislative Studies* 7 (1): 93–104

Seanad Éireann (1952) *Report of the Select Committee on the Seanad Electoral (Panel Members) Bill, 1952.* Dublin: Stationery Office

Seanad Éireann (2004) *Committee on Procedure and Privileges: Sub-Committee on Seanad Reform, Report on Seanad Reform.* Dublin: Stationery Office

Seanad Electoral Law Commission (1959) *Report.* Dublin: Stationery Office

Second House of the Oireachtas Commission (1936) *Report.* Dublin: Stationery Office

Sénat (2012) *Sénats du Monde*; available at www.senat.fr/senatsdumonde/pays.html

Sexton, Brendan (1989) *Ireland and the Crown, 1922–1936: The Governor-Generalship of the Irish Free State.* Dublin: Irish Academic Press

Shell, Donald (2001a) 'Introduction', *Journal of Legislative Studies* 7 (1): 1–3

Shell, Donald (2001b) 'The history of bicameralism', *Journal of Legislative Studies* 7 (1): 5–18

Shugart, Matthew S. (1994) 'Minorities represented and unrepresented', in Wilma Rule and Joseph F. Zimmerman, eds, *Electoral Systems in Comparative Perspective: Their Impact on Women and Minorities*. Westport, CT: Greenwood Press, pp. 31–41

Shugart, Matthew Soberg, and Martin P. Wattenberg (2001) 'Conclusion: are mixed-member systems the best of both worlds?', in Matthew Soberg Shugart and Martin P. Wattenberg, eds, *Mixed-Member Electoral Systems: The Best of Both Worlds?* Oxford: Oxford University Press, pp. 571–96

Siaroff, Alan (2003) 'Comparative presidencies: the inadequacy of the presidential, semi-presidential and parliamentary distinction', *Europe Journal of Political Research* 42 (3): 287–312

Siggins, Lorna (1997) *Mary Robinson: The Woman Who Took Power in the Park*. Edinburgh: Mainstream

Sinnott, Richard (1995) *Irish Voters Decide: Voting Behaviour in Elections and Referendums since 1918*. Manchester: Manchester University Press

Sinnott, Richard (2010) 'The electoral system', in John Coakley and Michael Gallagher, eds, *Politics in the Republic of Ireland*, 5th ed. London: Routledge, pp. 111–36

Sinnott, Richard, Johan A. Elkink, Kevin O'Rourke and James McBride (2009) *Attitudes and Behaviour in the Referendum on the Treaty of Lisbon: Report Prepared for the Department of Foreign Affairs*. Dublin: Geary Institute, University College Dublin

Sisson, Richard (1981) 'Prime ministerial power and the selection of ministers in India: three decades of change', *International Political Science Review* 2 (2): 137–57

Smyth, John M. (1972) *The Theory and Practice of the Irish Senate*. Dublin: Institute of Public Administration

Steed, Michael (1987) 'Indirect election' in Vernon Bogdanor, ed., *The Blackwell Encyclopaedia of Political Institutions*. Oxford: Blackwell, p. 285

Sterne, Simon (1871) *On Representative Government and Personal Representation*. Philadelphia: J.B. Lippincott and Co.

Storey, Andy (2013) *Chronicle of a crisis foretold: the political economy of the European Project*. Paper prepared for presentation at the New Left Perspectives Seminar Series, Sofia, 6 June

Suiter, Jane (2008) 'The Irish Dáil election 2007', *Irish Political Studies* 23 (1): 99–110

Sutton, Ralph (1958) 'A real Seanad', *Studies* 47 (186): 169–76

Sweeney, Anthony (2009) *Banana Republic: The Failure of the Irish State and How To Fix It*. Dublin: Gill & Macmillan

Sweeney, Paul (2008) *Ireland's Economic Success: Reasons and Prospects.*
Dublin: New Island

Swenden, Wilfried (2004) *Federalism and Second Chambers: Regional
Representation in Parliamentary Federations: The Australian Senate and
German Bundesrat Compared.* Brussels: Presses Interuniversitaires
Européennes–Peter Lang

Temperley, Harold W.V. (1910) *Senates and Upper Chambers: Their Use and
Function in the Modern State, with a Chapter on the Reform of the House
of Lords.* London: Chapman and Hall

Tomita, Nobuo, Hans Baerwald and Akira Nakamura (1981) 'Prerequisites
to ministerial careers in Japan 1885–1980', *International Political Science
Review* 2 (2): 235–56

Tonra, Ben (2012) 'Security, defence and neutrality: the Irish dilemma', in
Tonra et al., 2012, pp. 221–41

Tonra, Ben, Michael Kennedy, John Doyle and Noel Dorr, eds (2012) *Irish
Foreign Policy.* Dublin: Gill and Macmillan

Tsebelis, George, and Jeanette Money (1997) *Bicameralism.* Cambridge:
Cambridge University Press

Uluots, J., and J. Klesment, eds (1937) *Die Verfassung der Republik Estland.*
Tallinn: Estländische Druckerei

United Kingdom (1910) *Report of the Royal Commission on Electoral
Reform* (Cmnd 5163). London: HMSO

United Kingdom (1916) *Government of Ireland: Proposals Presented to
Parliament.* London: HMSO

United Kingdom (1922) *Draft Constitution of the Irish Free State.* Cmd.
1688. London: HMSO

United Nations (2007) Population Division of the Department of Economic
and Social Affairs of the United Nations Secretariat, *World Population
Prospects: The 2006 Revision and World Urbanization Prospects: The 2005
Revision.* New York: United Nations; available at www.un.org

United Nations (2012) *Demographic Yearbook 2011.* New York: United
Nations

van der Eijk, Cees, and Mark N. Franklin (2009) *Elections and Voters.*
Basingstoke: Palgrave Macmillan

Van der Hulst, Marc (2000) *The Parliamentary Mandate: A Global
Comparative Study.* Geneva: Inter-Parliamentary Union

Verzichelli, Luca (2009) 'Italy: the difficult road towards a more effective
process of ministerial selection', in Dowding and Dumont, 2009a, pp.
79–100

Walsh, Brendan (2006) 'When unemployment disappears: Ireland in the 1990s', in Martin Werding, ed., *Structural Unemployment in Western Europe: Reasons and Remedies*. Cambridge, MA: MIT Press, pp. 187–208

Walsh, Ed (2010) 'Our system of governance assures a deficit of talent', *Irish Times*, 6 July

Walsh, John (2008) *Patrick Hillery: The Official Biography*. Dublin: New Island

Watts, Ronald L. (2008) *Federal Second Chambers Compared* (Working Paper 2008-02). Kingston: Institute of Intergovernmental Relations, Queen's University; available at www.queensu.ca/iigr/WorkingPapers/papers/2008-02.pdf

Weeks, Liam (2010) 'Membership of the houses', in MacCarthaigh and Manning, 2010, pp. 106–28

Weymes, Laura, and Colin Bermingham (2012) *Fiscal Compact: Implications for Ireland*. Dublin: Central Bank of Ireland (Economic Letter Series Vol. 2012, No. 9)

Wheare, K.C. (1953) *Federal Government*, 3rd ed. London: Oxford University Press

Wheare, K.C. (1968) *Legislatures*, 2nd ed. London: Oxford University Press

Whelan, Brendan J., and Gary Keogh (1980) 'The use of the Irish electoral register for population estimation', *Economic and Social Review* 11 (4): 301–18

Whelan, Karl (2009) 'Policy lessons from Ireland's latest depression', in Joe Mulholland and Finbarr Bradley, eds, *Ireland's Economic Crisis—Time to Act*. Dublin: Carysfort Press, pp. 26–32

Whelan, Karl (2010) 'Policy lessons from Ireland's latest depression', *Economic and Social Review* 41 (2): 25–54

Whelan, Noel (2011) *Fianna Fáil: A Biography of the Party*. Dublin: Gill and Macmillan

White, Timothy J. (2006) 'Why so few women in Dáil Éireann? The effects of the single transferable vote election system', *New Hibernia Review* 10 (4): 71–83

Williams, J. Fischer (1914) *Proportional Representation and British Politics*, London: John Murray

Willson, F.M.G. (1959) 'The routes of entry of new members of the British cabinet, 1868–1958', *Political Studies* 7 (3): 222–32

Wood, Herbert (1935) 'The titles of the chief governors of Ireland', *Bulletin of the Institute of Historical Research* 13 (37): 1–8

Young, John N. (1985) *Erskine H. Childers, President of Ireland: a biography.* Gerrards Cross: Smythe

INDEX